Action Learning and its Applications

Action Learning and its Applications

Edited by

Robert L. Dilworth
Associate Professor Emeritus, Virginia Commonwealth University

and

Yury Boshyk
*Chairman, Global Executive Learning Network,
and the Annual Global Forum on Executive Development
and Business Driven Action Learning*

palgrave
macmillan

First published 2010 by
PALGRAVE MACMILLAN

Palgrave Macmillan in the UK is an imprint of Macmillan Publishers Limited,
registered in England, company number 785998, of Houndmills, Basingstoke,
Hampshire RG21 6XS.

Palgrave Macmillan in the US is a division of St Martin's Press LLC,
175 Fifth Avenue, New York, NY 10010.

Palgrave Macmillan is the global academic imprint of the above companies
and has companies and representatives throughout the world.

Palgrave® and Macmillan® are registered trademarks in the United States,
the United Kingdom, Europe and other countries.

ISBN: 978-0-230-57641-4

This book is printed on paper suitable for recycling and made from fully
managed and sustained forest sources. Logging, pulping and manufacturing
processes are expected to conform to the environmental regulations of the
country of origin.

A catalogue record for this book is available from the British Library.

A catalog record for this book is available from the Library of Congress.

10 9 8 7 6 5 4 3 2 1
19 18 17 16 15 14 13 12 11 10

Printed and bound in Great Britain by
CPI Antony Rowe, Chippenham and Eastbourne

Dedicated to Robert L. Dilworth (1936–2009), Brigadier General, scholar, friend of Reg Revans and mentor to many – one of traditional action learning's greatest practitioners.

Contents

Part II   Themes

Part III   Perspectives

Tables, Figures, Boxes and Illustrations

Tables

Figures

Boxes

Illustrations

Preface

Robert L. Dilworth and Yury Boshyk

This book, as is true of its companion volume, *Action Learning: History and Evolution*, sets out to provide an in-depth address of action learning – something that has largely been absent from the recent literature on the subject. There has been a skewing effect toward techniques, when that is secondary to what constitutes action learning. When the philosophical underpinnings of action learning are absent, the subject becomes hollow, and its distinctive personality can be lost. That is unfortunate, since much of the power of action learning is found in the philosophy that drives it, centered on the simple precepts of Revans. Both of these volumes on action learning set out to expose fully, once again, the essence of action learning, while also making clear that action learning can take a variety of forms within the framework that the precepts provide.

There are several ways to gauge the value of a book. One of them is its comprehensiveness and the degree of authenticity in what is expressed; another, what specific perspectives do the authors bring to the table? Is it diverse, or does it flow entirely out of one basic methodological mold?

In terms of comprehensiveness, this book provides wide-ranging perspectives, and proves that action learning comes in a variety of shapes and sizes – even though many of the basic precepts of action learning's principal pioneer, Reg Revans, are usually in evidence. This book covers some topics for the first time, Chapter 12 dealing with Future Search in Action Learning, a model developed by Marvin Weisbord and Sandra Janoff that has gained a wide following. There is also an appreciation that organization development (OD) has some important interplay with action learning, but this is not strongly evident in the literature. In Chapter 9, Warner Burke, one of the founders of the OD school, and a leading authority on OD, writing with Debra Noumair, outlines the relationship between action learning and OD.

The importance of questioning inquiry in action learning, drawing from Revans' Learning Equation ($L = P + Q$) – Learning = Programmed Instruction + Questioning Inquiry – receives a penetrating examination by Marilee Adams in Chapter 7. Verna Willis looks at the relationship between action learning and action research, a topic that has often been awkwardly addressed in the past. While there is an understanding that teams and team process are important to action learning, this is almost never singled out for specific attention. Chapter 8 by Michael Huge of ITAP International and John Bing corrects this.

To bring special relevance to practitioners, various sectors are addressed in order to show how action learning can be applied and adapted in a variety of contexts, including health care, education, government, the military, the business world, and community and civil society. This makes it possible to make cross-comparison between the degree of development and penetration of action learning in these sectors.

In terms of authors, those who appear in this book are well-recognized authorities in their respective fields. A number of them have broad international exposure. They also include a number who have a background in either psychology, OD or change management programs. A rich blend of perspectives is represented.

Because the learner perspective needs to be represented, in Chapter 13 we include a series of short informal essays by learners about their experiences. Some of these individuals have also developed into designers and promoters of action learning. One author started in her business as a dishwasher and, by demonstrated ability, went on to become the Chief Learning Officer and director of a major corporate university that is based on action learning.

One aspect of action learning that tends to be problematic and neglected is critical reflection. Revans made clear that you need both action and reflection. Reflection can be hard to come by in Western societies and the results oriented business culture. Any activity, such as reflection, that is perceived as an interruption of workflow is viewed as a distraction. The irony is that the reflective component is what can deliver the strategic advantage and help build the capacity of the organization. Geert Egger from Denmark tackles this "conundrum" and paradox head-on in Chapter 16. He shows how "platforms for reflection" can be built into the process that not only promote reflection, but also can prove valuable to business leaders.

Stephen Mercer, in Chapter 14, shows the roller coaster ride that can be action learning. When practiced in a robust manner – and GE management systems are known for their dynamism, vitality and adaptive qualities – action learning can be an important agent of change.

Much has been written about the learning organization, popularized by Peter Senge's work – what a learning organization is and is not, and what distinguishes it. The debate involved is similar to the debate over what constitutes a "high-performing organization," a label that can be too loosely and undeservedly assigned. Whether you are talking about learning organizations or high-performing organizations, the subject can be illusive and filled with contradictions. Even though the definitions are not always clear or congruent, there seems to be some agreement around the proposition that organizations that make a practice of consciously learning and raising the bar in terms of knowledge acquisition (and wisdom) are still in the minority. There is a great deal of "lip service" about this organization or that organization being a learning organization, but it can turn out to be unjustified bragging rights.

And those who really are learning organizations do not need to say it. They simply are.

Chapter 10, by Judy O'Neil, Karen Watkins and Victoria Marsick, does a good job of identifying the driving forces in a learning organization. Action learning can be an important tool for creating, and then sustaining, learning organizations; namely, a learning culture. Reg Revans was a forerunner, ahead of Senge and others, in understanding that there was such a thing as a learning organization, and that action learning could be primary highway for getting there.

When you bring all the topics together in this book, you end up with a deeper survey of action learning and its applications than you are likely to find elsewhere. Most books about action learning focus on one sector, such as the business sector, or on one approach to action learning. This book is more eclectic, containing different perspectives and approaches, allowing the reader to draw his or her own conclusions on what can work best for them in practice. Some of the paradigms covered are even in conflict with one another, but there is no better way to arrive at your own judgments than by comparing disparate points of view.

Revans did not want action learning directed along narrow passageways. He wanted the value of action learning to be demonstrated by its ready adaptation to different contexts and cultures, while believing that certain ingredients should be present – A **REAL** PROBLEM, empowerment of the learners; making questioning inquiry the start point and central to the process; operating in teams (which he called "sets") of five or six, all team members to be equal, no designated team leader; an emphasis on balancing action with reflection; ideally placing learners outside their expertise and comfort zones in order to trigger "fresh questions"; a preference for teams where all team members share a common problem; a minimum of external facilitation by experts; and simply trusting the process.

At the end of the book, we focus in on the future of action learning, looking ten years ahead. We argue that there are some precepts that have fallen by the wayside and need to be brought back into view. We do not recommend that on the basis of completeness – with every pronouncement by Revans to be considered sacred and slavishly followed. Revans understood that action learning would evolve and had to be in step with the times. But some of Revans' precepts, that can be considered highly relevant to the times in which we live and the challenges we face, are being consciously jettisoned or ignored. We believe that a return to a more authentic brand of action learning could bring significant improvements in the results being realized.

When we look ten years ahead in Chapter 18, we do not see a more elaborate assembly of action learning techniques. Rather, we see a return to relative "purity," getting rid of techniques and practices that work against action learning and constrain results. That may seem like a simple charge, but it is not. Action learning practices have drifted so far away from the central principles of action learning in some cases as to be almost unrecognizable to those who have studied and practiced action learning in depth. Further, some practitioners have built "safe" and lucrative practices by concentrating more on technique and facilitator skills, suggesting that the facilitator is the centerpiece and end all, and that, without a prescribed learning coach certificate, you are not "cleared" to practice action learning. That is sheer baloney.

If you read through both our volumes carefully, you will have the authentic principles of action learning in clear view. Compare them with what you have been told previously, and examine the logic behind them. We think you will agree with us that action learning has some very powerful properties, and it does not take a rocket scientist or six-figure consultant to "inoculate" you with action learning.

In terms of modifying Revans precepts, we believe that his rejection of the use of simulations as unreal and fabricated needs to be revisited. We contend that some of the sophisticated simulations available today that address very real possibilities, if not probabilities, such as a terrorist attack and dealing with natural disasters like Hurricane Katrina, deserve a place at the action learning table. We address some of the applications in Chapter 4.

We hope that the reader/practitioner finds this book provocative, honest, and of value. This book is best viewed in juxtaposition with the companion text *Action Learning: History and Evolution*.

Postscript

Shortly before the final submission of the manuscripts for both volumes my co-editor, Robert L. Dilworth passed away on June 6, 2009. My sense of loss is still beyond adequate expression. We made a wonderful and deeply intellectually enriching journey together, even though we knew that there was much still to do to trace and understand the history, evolution and applications of action learning worldwide, and the story of its principal pioneer, Reg Revans. We both started our examination from different perspectives: he from having worked with Reg Revans and I from a non-traditional (Organizational Development influenced) approach, learned from over 20 years of practice in the business world. Nevertheless, in our mutual exploration of the history and evolution of action learning he found a renewed respect for Reg Revans and traditional action learning, and I, a new-found respect for the theory and practice of traditional action learning and its founder.

Lex was an inspirational partner and mentor. He was always ready to help, to share his knowledge and experience: a true "partner in adversity." Many people around the world feel the same and are very grateful for his generosity, unstinting assistance and encouragement. One manifestation of this respect was a Special Tribute paid to Lex at the 14th annual Global Forum on Executive Development and Business Driven Action Learning – a community of practice – of which he was a valued member. A special award was launched in his honor – the Robert L. Dilworth Award for Outstanding Achievement in the Field of Executive Development and Action Learning. In this way, we shall maintain his memory, his contributions, and his values and commitment. This volume is dedicated to Lex. His long-time collaborator, Professor Verna J. Willis, coauthor with Lex of a seminal book on action learning, has written a memorial and biography for which we would like to thank her. To Doris, we express our deeply felt sympathy for her loss, and we hope she realizes that she will always be a special and warmly welcomed member of the Global Forum community.

YURY BOSHYK

Acknowledgements

Robert L. Dilworth and Yury Boshyk

This book would have been impossible without Reg Revans. There would simply be no action learning along the lines he expressed without him. He was an important force in Lex's professional life, and while Yury Boshyk never met him, he spent a great deal of time studying his life and body of work. It helped identify the nature of Revans' Quaker background and how the "Clearness Committee," an approach designed to bring discernment to difficult issues confronting a church member, was driven by questioning inquiry, a central building block of action learning. We feel that Reg would be very pleased with what is contained in this book and its sister volume because of its clear linkage to his precepts. For all those reasons and more, our most significant acknowledgement goes to Reg Revans, who might as well have been a third editor. We followed his azimuths throughout. He was always there.

Networking plays an important role in life and how our views come to be shaped. Both Yury and I have a broad network of professional associates, and this was an invaluable resource in developing the two volumes on action learning. We thank all of them for their suggestions and support. There are many people we could acknowledge by name, but we will focus in on a few that were especially important to us. David Botham of England, the founding director of the Revans Institute for Action Learning and Research at the University of Salford, now the Revans Academy at the University of Manchester, provided a continuous stream of useful information, including insights on Revans' thinking. Albert Barker, one of Revans' closest friends and associates, was able to fill in the most intimate details of Revans' life, allowing us to vividly show how Revans viewed a variety of theories and philosophies.

Lex often indexed to the work of Jack Mezirow, a preeminent voice in the area of adult learning and education. He also has been highly influential in terms of transformative learning theory. It became evident that basic principles of adult learning, such as learner centeredness and empowerment (or emancipation) of learners, can be directly related to action learning. Further, action learning, when practiced in a robust way, can be transformative. When you significantly advance yourself through learning, you cannot help but be transformed in some way. You become a changed person.

Yury has seen his principles of business driven action learning take root around the world, an approach that reinforces traditional action learning and Revans' precepts. This became ever more evident as work on the two books proceeded. Yury acknowledges all the clients and attendees of the annual Global Forums on Executive Development and Business Driven Action Learning for the variety of management approaches and forms of action learning that they exposed him to over the years. Many of those perspectives found their way in to the two volumes.

To the wonderful authors who contributed to this volume and the first, we owe a deep debt of gratitude for their dedication and subject matter mastery. A number of them knew Revans and have many years of experience with action learning to draw on. It could not have been a better field of authors.

Each of us acknowledges the other. The collaboration between Yury and Lex on this book project had good chemistry from the outset, and we complemented each other's knowledge in important ways.

Finally, we express love and warm appreciation to our wives, Nadia Boshyk and Doris Dilworth for putting up with our bursts of energy and immersion in the book project to the occasional exclusion of almost everything else.

Notes on Contributors

Marilee G. Adams (Marilee@InquiryInstitute.com) is an executive coach and coach educator, organizational consultant and facilitator, and professional speaker. She is the president and founder of the Inquiry Institute, a consulting, coaching, and educational organization and the originator of the Question Thinking methodologies. Marilee is the author of *Change Your Questions, Change Your Life: 7 Powerful Tools for Life and Work*. She also wrote *The Art of the Question: A Guide to Short-Term Question-Centered Therapy*. With Dr. David Cooperrider and Dr. Marge Schiller, she coauthored a chapter for *Advances in Appreciative Inquiry*. She has a chapter in *Positively M.A.D.: Making a Difference in Your Organizations, Communities, & The World*, and has also written articles on expert questioning in coaching and organizational transformation. Marilee's Question Thinking work forms the core of her presentations, keynotes, and workshops in Fortune 500 companies, government agencies, nonprofit organizations, and communities. She is a member of the Core Faculty, Certificates in Leadership Coaching, cosponsored by Adler International Learning and the Ontario Institute for Studies in Education of the University of Toronto. She is affiliated with Columbia University's Learning and Leadership Group at Teachers College.

John W. Bing (jbing@itapintl.com) is founder and Chairman, ITAP International, a consulting firm with global operations. His consulting experience spans the Americas, Europe and Africa, covering the pharmaceutical, consumer product, information technologies industries and United Nations' Agencies. He designed the original version of ITAP International's Team Process Questionnaire and developed a new version of the Culture in the Workplace Questionnaire, originally created by Geert Hofstede. After serving in the Peace Corps in Afghanistan, Dr. Bing coordinated international training as a Regional Training Officer for the Peace Corps.

His consulting took him to Morocco, Tunisia, Ghana, Thailand, Ecuador, Kenya, Lesotho and Swaziland. During that time, he coauthored the manual that later became the Peace Corps' first cross-cultural training guide. Bing has published papers and provided presentations at numerous professional conferences, including those of the Academy of Human Resource Development; he has coedited a volume entitled *Shaping the Future of HRD* in the journal *Advances in Developing Human Resources*, and is a member of the board of that journal. He is a recipient of ASTD's International Practitioner of the Year Award. A graduate of Harvard College, Dr. Bing received his Ed.D. from the Center for International Education, University of Massachusetts.

Yury Boshyk (yury@gel-net.com) is Chairman of the Global Executive Learning Network, a worldwide association of professionals involved for many years in assisting multinationals and organizations in the design and implementation of executive and management programs especially involving business driven action learning. The Network also researches, analyzes and publishes on global trends that affect companies and countries. Since 1996, Yury organizes an annual Global Forum on Executive Development and Business Driven Action Learning, a worldwide community of practice. He lectures widely and works in cooperation with a number of institutions. His most recent article was on "Developing Global Executives: Today and Tomorrow" in *The 2009 Pfeiffer Annual: Leadership Development*. He is the editor of several books on action learning: *Business Driven Action Learning: Global Best Practices* (2000) and *Action Learning Worldwide: Experiences of Leadership and Organizational Development* (2002), both published by Palgrave Macmillan and St. Martin's Press. In 2010, two books on action learning which he coedited with Robert L. Dilworth will be released by Palgrave Macmillan: *Action Learning: History and Evolution* and *Action Learning and its Applications*. Formerly, he was Professor of Strategy, Geopolitics and the International Business Environment at IMD in Lausanne, Switzerland and the Theseus Institute in France. He completed his doctorate at the University of Oxford, and his Master's Degree at the London School of Economics.

Cheryl Brook (Cheryl.brook@ntworld.com) graduated from the University of Salford in 1982 with a degree in arts and social sciences. Following graduation, she worked in London for the national charity Age Concern England as a training officer, and then at the South Manchester University Hospitals NHS Trust for 20 years, becoming head of the training and development department. She earned a Master's Degree in human resource management and became a chartered member of the institute of personnel and development. She met Reg Revans and Lex Dilworth in 1996 at an action learning event held at the hospitals for which she worked. In 2002, she worked as a research assistant to Professors John Burgoyne and Mike Pedler on a major action learning research project based on what was then the Revans Institute at the University of Salford. She is currently completing a PhD at the University of Lancaster on the subject of action learning in the UK health service.

W. Warner Burke (burke1@exchange.tc.columbia.edu) is the E. L. Thorndike Professor of Psychology and Education, coordinator for the graduate programs in social-psychology, and Chair of the Department of Organizational Leadership at Teachers College, Columbia University. His publications include 20 books and over 150 articles and book chapters. His consulting experience has been with a variety of organizations. He is a Diplomate in Business and Consulting Psychology, American Board of Professional

Psychology; a Fellow of the Academy of Management, the Association for Psychological Science, and the Society of Industrial and Organizational Psychology; and past editor of both *Organizational Dynamics* and the *Academy of Management Executive*. Among his awards are the Public Service Medal from NASA, the Distinguished Scholar-Practitioner Award from the Academy of Management, and the Distinguished Professional Contributions Award from the Society of Industrial and Organizational Psychology. His latest book is *Organizational Change: Theory and Practice* (2nd edition, 2008).

Robert L. Dilworth at the time of coauthoring this volume, was a retired U.S. Army brigadier general, with more than 31 years of active service. He served as the 54th Adjutant General of the United States Army, a position dating back to 1775. He was also an Associate Professor Emeritus at Virginia Commonwealth University, Richmond, Virginia, U.S. Earlier, he had taught graduate courses in Management Policy, Marketing and Organizational Behavior for the Overseas Program of Boston University, as well as the John J. College of Criminal Justice in New York City. Since 1991, when he became a collaborator and friend of Reg Revans, the "father" of action learning, Lex spent much of his time writing, researching and lecturing on the subject of action learning. His book, with Verna Willis of Georgia State University, on *Action Learning: Images and Pathways* was published in 2003. In 2008, his book, with Shlomo Maital of the Technion Institute of Management in Haifa, Israel, *Fogs of War and Peace: A Midstream Analysis of World War II*, was published by Praeger Security International. In 2010, his two coedited books with Yury Boshyk on *Action Learning: History and Evolution*, and *Action Learning and Its Applications*, will be released by Palgrave Macmillan. Dilworth held a Bachelors Degree in Advertising and Public Relations from the University of Florida, a Masters Degree in Public Administration from the University of Oklahoma, a Masters Degree in Military Art and Science from the U.S. Army's Command and General Staff College, and a Masters Degree and Doctorate from Teachers College, Columbia University in Adult and Continuing Education. He was also a graduate of the Industrial College of the Armed Forces (ICAF), the Professional Military Comptroller School (PMCS) of the Air University and attended advanced programs at Northwestern University, Harvard University and the University of Michigan. He was president and founder of his own consulting firm, Strategic Learning Scenarios.

Geert R. Egger (geg@people.dk) is Managing Director of Action Lab, Inc., a company specialized in serving clients with action learning flows. He holds a PhD in anthropology and organization, and regularly serves as lecturer and examiner at the Copenhagen Business School as well as at the University of Copenhagen. Apart from that, Geert has published various books and articles (mostly in Danish) on societal trends. However, his interest in organizational interaction made him publish some of his experiences with high-level management layers in the chapter "Development of Boards of Directors" in *The Future of Executive Development* (edited by James Bolt, 2005 Executive Development Associates). Before starting Action Lab, Inc., Geert, among other assignments, worked for ten years at corporate level in Novo Nordisk, the worldwide market leader within Diabetes Care. His areas of responsibility included Management Development, HR Architecture, and Business Facilitation.

Mariana Garban (medlink57@yahoo.co.uk) is a Medical Doctor and a Fellow of Chicago Chest Physicians USA. From 1997–2000, she was Medical Director of Strategy at County Hospitals Vasului, Romania. Her contact with Reg Revans began in 1990. When the funding support for health care in Romania collapsed during a period of political instability, she formed her TB patients into action learning teams, and they helped to maintain and run the hospital. She was a catalyst for the TB Patients Association, called "The Right and Hope for Living." As an MD Pneumologyst of Lung Diseases, she also guided the Emergency Department of Vaslui County, Romania. Mariana attended the First Action Learning and Mutual Collaboration Congress at Heathrow, England, in 1995, with delegates from 18 other nations. That created added opportunities for collaboration with Revans and his close associates, Janet Craig, Albert Barker and David Botham. Mariana has a passion for action learning, having seen it put to good use in practical ways in dealing with the very real challenges facing the health care system in her country.

Michael Huge (mhuge@itapintl.com) is the Director of Research for ITAP International, a consulting firm with global operations. After obtaining his Master's Degree in Communication from Ohio State University, Michael worked in Ohio's government as a legislative staffer and as a research associate at Ohio State University. Huge's peer-reviewed work has appeared in journals such as *Communications Research*, *Political Behavior*, and the *International Journal of Public Opinion Research*. He is a member of the International Testing Commission, and his current research focuses on statistical analysis of differences between cultures, as well as assessing team effectiveness in the workplace. He has contributed to ITAP's improvement and revision of the Culture in the Workplace Questionnaire, as well as ITAP's Team Process Questionnaire.

Sandra Janoff (sjanoff@futuresearch.net) is a psychologist and consultant, and has worked with corporations, government agencies, and communities worldwide on issues of globalization, sustainability and human practices. She was a staff member in Tavistock conferences sponsored by Temple University in Philadelphia and the Tavistock Institute of Human Relations in Oxford, England. She also has run training workshops in system-oriented group dynamics. Sandra taught mathematics and chemistry from 1974–84 in an experimental high school, and ran workshops in Pennsylvania schools on alternative practices in education. She is coauthor with Yvonne Agazarian of "Systems Thinking in Small Groups" for the *Comprehensive Textbook on Group Psychotherapy*. Her research on the relationship between moral reasoning and legal education was a lead article in the *University of Minnesota Law Review*. She is coauthor, with Marvin Weisbord, of *FutureSearch: An Action Guide to Finding Common Ground in Organizations and Communities* (2nd edition, 2000).

James L. Kelly (jkelly11@cox.net) serves in the Pentagon as the Chief of Logistics Integration, Office of the Deputy Chief of Staff, Army G4. He is a retired Army Aviator and a veteran of the first Gulf War and Bosnia. He holds an Airline Transport Certificate for both airplanes and helicopters. Jim earned a Master of Science Degree in National Resource Strategy from the Industrial College of the Armed Forces, a Master Degree of Public Administration from American University and Undergraduate Degrees in Maintenance Management, Business Administration, and Aviation Maintenance Technology from Embry-Riddle Aeronautical University.

Robert Kramer (Kramer@american.edu) has taught action learning at American University in Washington, DC; at the European Commission in Brussels; at the European Environmental Agency in Copenhagen; and at the state Chancellery (Office of the Prime Minister) in Tallinn, Estonia. From 2002–4, he was an elected member of the board of directors of the Organizational Behavior Teaching Society, a group of 650 management and leadership educators worldwide. Kramer's most recent publication is "Learning How to Learn: Action Learning for Leadership Development," in I. R. Morse (ed.), *Innovations in Public Leadership Development* Washington, DC: M.E. Sharpe/National Academy of Public Administration (2008).

Victoria J. Marsick (marsick@exchange.tc.columbia.edu) is a Professor of Adult and Organizational Learning at Columbia University and Co-Director of the J. M. Huber Institute for Learning Organizations, Department of Organization and Leadership, Teachers College. She holds a PhD from the University of California, Berkeley, in adult education and a Masters Degree in International Public Administration from Syracuse University. Before joining Columbia University, she directed training and development at UNICEF, worked as a development education consultant, and represented World Education in Southeast Asia. Victoria has designed and coached action learning programs for many years. She conducts research with Martha Gephart through the Huber Institute, which partners with organizations to conduct organizational learning assessments, evaluations and action research. Victoria has published widely on informal learning, team learning, action learning, and the learning organization. She is currently working on a book with Martha Gephart entitled *Strategic Organizational Learning* (Butterworth-Heinemann/Elsevier) and recently coauthored *Understanding Action Learning* with Judy O'Neil (AMACOM, 2007). With Karen Watkins, she has coauthored many books and articles on organizational learning; for example, *Sculpting the Learning Organization* (Jossey-Bass, 1993) and *Facilitating the Learning Organization: Making Learning Count* (Gower, 1999).

Stephen R. Mercer (mashang@earthlink.net) consults in the areas of leadership development, business driven action learning, operation of a Corporate University, and the use of free play business simulations. As Vice President, Learning and Leadership at Boeing, he led the creation of the Boeing Learning Center, including construction of a 120-room educational campus and development of an integrated leadership curriculum. Mercer came to Boeing from General Electric (GE), where he managed Executive Education at GE's Leadership Center (Crotonville). He led business driven action learning programs in over 50 countries, as well as customer Executive Programs in China, Southeast Asia and Russia. He had extensive business experience at GE as a systems engineer, as Manager – Transit Equipment Marketing; and as an external marketing consultant. Mercer has an Engineering Degree from City College of New York, and an MBA from Xavier University. He served in the U.S. Army in Germany and Vietnam. He is an advisory board member of the Institute for International Business at St. Louis University, and for the Japan-American Student Conference. He also served on the Board of Visitors of the Defense Acquisition University and the CIA University, and served on the Conference Board's Council on Development, Education and Training.

Debra A. Noumair (Noumair@exchange.tc.columbia.edu) is an Associate Professor of Psychology and Education in the Social-Organizational Psychology Program in the Department of Organization and Leadership at Teachers College, Columbia University. In addition, Dr. Noumair is Director of Executive Education Programs in Organization Development sponsored by Teachers College, Columbia University. A licensed psychologist in the State of New York, she maintains a private practice of organization consultation and executive coaching. At Teachers College, Doctor Noumair focuses on the arena of group and organizational dynamics and the application of systems thinking to individual, team and organizational performance. She teaches courses on organization change and consultation, executive coaching and group dynamics. Dr. Noumair is the author of articles and book chapters on group relations and the analysis of diversity issues in groups, organizations and social systems. She recently edited *Group Dynamics, Organizational Irrationality, and Social Complexity: Group Relations Reader 3*, which brings the theoretical and practical application of group relations concepts to life in teams, organizations, communities and society. Dr. Noumair received her Bachelor's Degree from Boston University, and holds Masters and Doctoral Degrees from Teachers College, Columbia University. She is a member of the American Psychological Association, the Academy of Management, and the Organizational Development Network.

Judy O'Neil (jaoniel@aol.com) is President of the consulting firm Partners for Learning and Leadership, Inc., which specializes in action technologies, including action learning. She holds an Ed.D and M.A in Adult Education from Teachers College, Columbia University, New York, and is on the adjunct faculty at Teachers College. She spent 30 years in the corporate world specializing in human resource development and organizational change. Her publications include *Understanding Action Learning*, coauthored with Victoria Marsick (AMACOM, 2007), *Action Learning: Using Reflection for Learning, Development, and Performance Improvement*, coauthored with Holly O'Grady and Robert Ward, forthcoming in *OD Practitioner; Action Learning: Successful Strategies for Individual, Team, and Organizational Development*, coedited, with Lyle Yorks and Victoria Marsick, *ASTD What Works Online: Action Learning: Real Work, Real Learning* and *A Review of Action Learning Literature 1994–2000 – Parts 1 & 2*, both coauthored with Peter Smith.

Alasdair Philip (hurdies@verizon.net) is a father of two, a global nomad and a manager with DHL Global Forwarding. Having grown up and worked in Asia, Europe, the Middle East and North America, connecting people across continents and cultures is a passion he finds supported by his international logistics career. Alasdair started his logistics career working with the Dutch-based TNT in his native Scotland, before transferring to the United Arab Emirates and Jordan. After the birth of his daughter, he moved to the United States and worked with a private company focused on Internet-based supply chain solutions. In 1998, he started working with Air Express International (AEI) before their 2000 acquisition by Deutsche Post DHL. He has since held business development and general management roles for the world's largest logistics provider, learning something new each and every day. If he had to do something else for a living, it would be a ski instructor.

Isabel Rimanoczy (irimanoc@aol.com) is a Legacy Coach, and a partner with Leadership in International Management (LIM). She is founding member of LIM Argentina and has led the set up of LIM's network in Brazil, Columbia, Peru and Mexico. She has worked in North America, Latin America, Europe and Asia with multinational corporations in the area of change and transition management, coaching and executive development. In 1994, she discovered Action Reflection Learning (ARL) in Sweden and has, since then, researched experiences and further developed the conceptual framework of ARL. She coauthored *Action Reflection Learning: Solving Real Business Problems by Connecting Learning with Earning* (Davies-Black Publishing, 2008), the *LIM Learning Coach Handbook* and the *Leader Coach Handbook*. She is the editor of the electronic newsletter *LIMNews*. She received the Author Scholarship Sven Ake Nilsson for her contribution to knowledge development and scientific innovation, in Klippan, Sweden, in 2005. She is a former Professor of Human Resources for the Master's program at the University of Belgrano, Buenos Aires. Isabel is a Doctoral Candidate at Columbia University and has an MA in Psychology from the University of Buenos Aires, as well as an MBA from the University of Palermo. Her dissertation is on corporate leaders championing sustainability initiatives. She is the Director of IFAL-USA, the International Foundation for Action Learning.

Lillie Graham Sapp (Parousia@aol.com) is a Senior Instructional System Specialist with the Army Management Staff College, Fort Belvoir, Virginia. She has served as a Curriculum Designer, Educational Specialist, Human Resources and Development advisor and facilitator for various agencies, including the Department of Defense, Department of Justice, Department of Mental Health and Retardation, Department of Education in the U.S., and in the UK. Ms. Sapp served in the Army National Guard as a Tactical Wire Specialist. She published an article entitled "A Retrospective on the Psychology of Leadership" for *Perspective in Leadership, Volume II*. Ms. Sapp was recognized by "Manchester's Cambridge Who's' Who of Executives, Professional and Entrepreneur," for her professionalism and contribution to the "Adult Literacy Program of Virginia," and nominated for "Woman of the Year" in 2007. Ms. Sapp holds a BA in Psychology, MIS in Adult Education and Substance Abuse Counseling, and a Post Graduate Certificate in Human Resource Development from Virginia Commonwealth University.

Fran Szabo (fran.szabo@gmail.com) began working with Marriott and Sodexho in 1980. She held positions as dishwasher, cook, food service manager, Human Resources Manager, Training Director and Chief Learning Officer. Up until 2006, she directed Sodexho University activities through curriculum and course design for every level of management and front-line employee. Additionally, Fran served as adjunct faculty for the University of Maryland Masters in General Administration and the University of Delaware Hotel Restaurant and Institutional Management Programs. She currently owns a human resources development company, AdvantEdge, specializing in business and sales workshop facilitation, curriculum design, learning systems implementation, offering blended learning solutions to help employees reach their full potential. She also serves as the North American accrediting advisor for action learning at Revans University. Fran has a Doctorate in Management from Revans University, a Masters Degree in Human Resources and Organizational Development from the University of San Francisco, and holds a Bachelors Degree in neuropsychology from the University of California at Davis. She constantly applies her education in organizational behavior to help organizations design world-class learning systems based on core competencies that employ distance learning technologies to meet the development challenge of hundreds of thousands of geographically dispersed employees.

Karen M. Videtic (kmvidetic@vcu.edu) has taught retail entrepreneurship, management, and fashion design promotions at Virginia Commonwealth

University's (VCU) Department of Fashion Design and Merchandising since 1984. She is the coauthor of *Perry's Department Store: A Retail Buying Simulation* (3rd edition, 2009), and *Perry's Department Store: A Product Development Simulation* (2006). Both textbooks are published by Fairchild Books. In 1997, Professor Videtic spent five months at the University of Ballarat outside Melbourne, Australia, as lecturer for the School of Business. She taught Buyer Behavior, Contemporary Issues in Management and Human Resource Development at graduate and undergraduate levels. Graduate classes used action learning as an integral part of the developmental experience. Professor Videtic's academic experience includes the use of simulation and action learning in courses such as Buyer Behavior, Buying, Retail Store Development, and Line Development. She became involved with action learning while completing coursework toward a PhD, including two courses at the University of Salford, Manchester, England in the summer of 1996, where she met Reg Revans. Dr. Videtic's research interests include the expatriation and repatriation of faculty, and action learning in the fashion/business classroom. She has developed and conducted seminars for VCU faculty prior to her tenure at VCU's School of Design and Arts in Doha, Qatar, as well as the Virginia Port Authority, on cross-cultural topics.

Karen E. Watkins (kwatkins@uga.edu) is Associate Dean for Research and External Affairs, and Professor in Adult Education and Human Resource Development in the College of Education at the University of Georgia. Karen is also a principal of Partners for Learning and Leadership. Dr. Watkins was an Associate Professor of Educational Administration at the University of Texas at Austin, where she directed the graduate program in Adult and Human Resource Development Leadership. Research foci have been the areas of human resource and organizational development. Karen is the author or coauthor of 70 articles and book chapters, and six books. Karen, together with her colleague Victoria Marsick, developed and validated the organizational survey "Dimensions of the Learning Organization," which was the focus of a recent issue of *Advances in Developing Human Resources* entitled *Making Learning Count: Demonstrating the Value of a Learning Culture*. With Victoria Marsick, she coauthored many books and articles on organizational learning; for example, *Facilitating the Learning Organization: Making Learning Count*, (Gower, 1999) and *Sculpting the Learning Organization* (Jossey-Bass, 1993). She has consulted with numerous businesses and industries in the area of action learning, action science and organizational learning cultures. She was voted Scholar of the Year by the Academy of Human Resource Development; served as president of the Academy of Human Resource Development from 1994–6; was named a distinguished graduate by The University of Texas at Austin, Community College Leadership Program; and was inducted into the International Adult and Continuing Education Hall of Fame in 2003.

Marvin R. Weisbord (mweisbord@furturesearch.net) and his colleague Sandra Janoff have, for decades, led meetings in the business, community, education, health care, and science and technology sectors. They codirect the international Future Search Network and are coauthors of *Future Search: An Action Guide* (2nd edition, 2000), and *Don't Just Do Something, Stand There!* (2007). They have managed meetings in Africa, Asia, Europe, India, and North and South America, and trained more than 3500 people in using their learning principles. They are members of the European Institute for Transnational Studies and the Organization Development Network. Marvin consulted with business firms, medical schools and hospitals from 1969–92. He was a partner in Block Petrella Weisbord Inc., a member of the NTL Institute for 20 years, and is a Fellow of the World Academy of Productivity Science. He has written dozens of articles on the theory and practice of organizational change. He received a Lifetime Achievement Award in 2004 from the Organization Development Network, which voted his book *Productive Workplaces* (1987) among the five most influential books of the past 40 years. He is also author of *Organizational Diagnosis* (1978), *Discovering Common Ground* (1992) and *Productive Workplaces Revisited* (2004).

Verna J. Willis (vwillis@gsu.edu) is an Associate Professor Emeritus of Georgia State University in Atlanta, Georgia, U.S., where she designed graduate degrees in Human Resource Development. The Academy of Human Resource Development, of which she is a founding member, gave her an annual award for having the top academic program in human resource development. She holds B.A. and M.A. Degrees in English; a Ph.D. in Educational Research; and has had residential teaching experience in the Middle East and Indonesia, along with Higher Education consultancies in Europe and Africa. Earlier, seven years in corporate training management convinced her that organizations can best adapt and grow if they engage Chief Learning Officers (CLOs) with full authority to make systemic changes in learning processes. The first corporate officer in the U.S. with the title and duties of a CLO emerged from her classes. Hundreds of organizations have subsequently added CLOs to their corporate teams, making them accountable for reaping strategic value from learning. Attracted by Revans and his work, she spent a two-month sabbatical at the Revans Centre at the University of Salford in the UK, where archival learning materials, Revans himself and knowledgeable others were within easy reach. Publications owing much to that study period include "Inspecting Cases Against Revans' 'Gold Standard' of Action Learning" in the journal *Action Learning Research and Practice* (2004), and "Spontaneity and Self-Organizing" in *Genuine Action Learning* (2005). She is coauthor with Robert L. Dilworth of *Action learning: Images and Pathways* (2003), and continues to promote action learning in word and deed, closely following the patterns Revans set.

Part I
Sector Overviews

1
Action Learning in Health care
Cheryl Brook

Introduction

Over the last few years, there appears to be growing evidence of action learning being used in the health service for a whole variety of purposes. These include clinical service development and patient involvement (Chivers, 2005; Attwood, 2007), role clarification and role development (Richardson et al., 2008), partnership working (Willis, 1986), service improvement (Pedler and Abbott, 2008a; 2008b) and leadership development (Blackler and Kennedy, 2006). This chapter focuses upon action learning in the particular context of the U.K. National Health Service (NHS) for the simple reason that, at the time of writing, it appears to be at its most developed and widespread there.

What, then, is the practice of action learning in the U.K. health care sector? The aim of this chapter is to examine the nature of that practice by exploring the kinds of problems being addressed, some of the features of action learning as practised by staff in the service, and whether or not practitioners intend to go on making use of it in the future. In support of this, I will draw upon a case example of action learning practice in the service taken from my own experience, together with findings established from a recent piece of research in the NHS.

There is a sense in which Revans' action learning has grown up and come of age in the U.K. NHS. Revans had an almost lifelong interest in the service and its problems. As long ago as 1938 (predating the birth of the NHS, which occurred in 1948), Revans produced a memorandum concerned with the training of student nurses in which was contained the germ of the action learning idea.[1] He conducted key operational research in the health service of the 1950s, producing important data on such diverse factors as student nurse wastage rates, average length of service of categories of nursing staff, and sickness absence rates; and he initiated attitude surveys amongst staff anticipating the annual NHS attitude surveys of staff which have now become accepted national policy. He led the Hospital Internal

Communications Project in the mid 1960s, a very significant action learning program, which involved ten hospitals across London and no less than 38 projects. And, at a time of great and continuing public scandals in the 1960s and 1970s in what were then termed "mental handicap" hospitals, he led action learning projects which were directed towards improving the delivery of services to that very vulnerable constituency – which, unusually for the times, included not only clinical staff but relatives and patients themselves.[2]

The research discussed here shows that action learning in the health service is widespread, that it is directing itself at a wide range of problems, and appears to be on an upward trend. This chapter will draw upon some of those research findings (which largely relate to what is being done in the name of action learning in the NHS) and also the author's own experience of facilitating action learning in the health care sector. It deals with a number of issues of action learning practice, including the kinds of problems respondents have been working on in their action learning, whether or not real action takes place in the workplace, and the use participants make of questioning and facilitation. Before proceeding, however, it may be useful to give a brief background note on the context for this chapter: the U.K. NHS.

Background: The U.K. National Health Service

The NHS employs over 1.3 million people, which, it has often been pointed out, makes it one of the largest employers in the world, along with the Chinese Liberation Army, the Indian Railways and the Walmart Supermarket chain. The health care services it provides are universal, comprehensive, and, for the most part, free at the point of use. It is funded through general taxation and, in consequence, central government controls much of the strategic direction of the service. In recent times, this has increasingly led to the setting of very detailed performance targets (in areas such as, for example, inpatient and outpatient waiting times for treatment) and the close governmental monitoring and scrutiny of performance against such targets. In such an atmosphere of close political scrutiny, Pettigrew et al. have alluded to the "panics" and "crises" which frequently afflict the service and which are not helped by its "segmentation" and "incoherence," as it is "divided on every conceivable axis: political and managerial; professional and managerial; professional and professional ... and of course geography and care group" (1992, p. 291). Moreover, according to Pettigrew et al.:

> It is a management system which features endemic short termism and over reaction ... One of the most obvious pathologies (*associated with such a culture*) is that managers and professionals in the NHS find it very difficult to disentangle the urgent from the important. (1992, p. 288)

Lewis and Gillam have argued that – even to those who champion the health service – it is "an organisation beset with problems." In support of this statement, they point to an almost bewildering range of difficulties including, *inter alia*, "insufficient capacity to deliver required levels of care, weak incentives leading to weak performance, limited patient choice, lack of co-operation between public and private providers and top down centralism which seeks to command and control local NHS organisations" (2003, p. 78). If this were not enough, one could add in, amongst other things, escalating costs, demographic shifts (such as the increasingly ageing population), advances in medical technologies, policy changes and ever-increasing public expectations and demands.

It may be that action learning has found its place in the NHS because it can help to turn the panics and problems of the service into necessary sustainable action, and learning from that action. A central tenet of action learning is to treat problems which are real, risky, urgent and messy. Moreover, it can provide the reflective space needed to assist in distinguishing importance from urgency.

Action learning practice in the NHS

Between 2004 and 2005, I conducted a survey of action learning practice in the NHS, and interviewed practitioners about their work in action learning. The research grew out of a previous research project which had attempted to gauge the extent, growth and variety of action learning across all sectors in the U.K.[3] I was interested in knowing what kind of action learning practice was going on in the health service, and what uses were being made of it. The approach I took was to make use of the questionnaire instrument which we had designed for the earlier project. This questionnaire yielded 95 respondents from across the U.K. I followed this up with further more in-depth interviews with a subset of that total. Respondents came from different types of health service organization (acute care, mental health, strategic health authority, etc.) and different professional backgrounds (nurses, doctors, psychologists, therapists, professional managers, etc.).

The results showed that action learning was being used by a wide range of health service staff to deal with an equally wide range of problems. These ranged from significant organizational development problems (such as, for example, redesigning an entire dental service or ensuring equity of access to mental health services) through to what might be termed "deep" personal development issues (such as how to deal with "confrontational and manipulative behaviour from work colleagues," managing "toxic" emotions in the workplace, and looking at how the individual manager impacts upon others). In this respect, an interesting finding from this piece of research (which confirms a finding from the earlier research project) is the increasing

---

Box 1.1   Some examples of organizational development problems

1. Achieving agreement to a new uniform;
2. Establishing integrated care pathways;
3. Implementing changes in practice (i.e., shift patterns);
4. Managing the human dimensions of change that have occurred as a result of service changes;
5. The organizational impact of large scale computer system implementation;
6. Organizational implementation of shared governance for nurses and midwives;
7. Creation of new roles in the service (e.g., stroke rehabilitation nurse);
8. Creation of an inter-agency improvement plan (NHS, local government, police and so on) working in a two ward "patch" of a local authority area;
9. Developing the patient advocacy and liaison role;
10. Developing a care pathway strategy;
11. Reducing dietetic waiting lists;
12. Setting up support groups for carers of older people.

---

emphasis upon individually determined problems as distinct from collectively determined ones.

Boxes 1.1 and 1.2 give the reader some examples of some of the action learning problems which practitioners described working on in their responses.

The research also looked at what action learners in the NHS saw as the most important features of action learning for them. An interesting finding from this was that 84 per cent associated action learning with bringing about personal change and development as against 64 per cent who associated it with achieving organizational change. This indicates a possible shift in the NHS toward personal development and away from organizational development, and mirrors the earlier finding from the general action learning survey of practice.

The data did throw up some interesting contradictions. For example, only 14 per cent of the total saw facilitation by a team (set) adviser as important to them in their view as to what action learning is about, yet 81 per cent said they actively used a facilitator in their practice of action learning. Having said this, some respondents spoke about their involvement in wholly self-managed action learning with only minimal use of an external facilitator to get the process started. Revans himself saw the facilitator as an *accoucheur* (literally, "male midwife"), there to "speed the integration of the set" but not to create dependency (Revans, 1998).

Another contradiction in the data concerned the issue of questioning. In terms of what was regarded as important to their view of action learning,

---

Box 1.2 Some examples of personal development and "own job" problems

1. Dealing with confrontational and manipulative behavior from colleagues;
2. Dealing with a role change;
3. Adjusting to normal work after a secondment;
4. Recognition of "what makes me tick" and how that affects the people with whom I work;
5. Personal career development;
6. Managing my transition from staff nurse to ward sister;
7. Personal development/career development issues;
8. Conflict management;
9. Coping with role developments;
10. Managing difficult people at work;
11. Clarification of my role as an NHS trust training and development manager;
12. Coaching/mentoring the staff members I line manage in order to develop their interpersonal skills.

---

only 22 per cent of respondents selected questioning, yet, later on, when asked to identify those practices which usually feature in their own practice of action learning, 91 per cent opted for "being helped through questioning." This is a noteworthy outcome, given that the idea of QI (Questioning Insight) is absolutely central to Revans' action learning.

In terms of how effective action learning is for these practitioners, most respondents gave largely anecdotal examples, and relatively few were able to offer examples of systematic evaluation. Some found the question quite difficult to answer and felt conscious of giving what they themselves felt to be "woolly answers." For example, respondents spoke of "getting things done" in the workplace as a consequence of their action learning, or they described increased levels of confidence or that they felt they dealt with issues differently as a result of their involvement. Some were able to point to what they felt were clear achievements – changes to nursing assessments, for example, and the introduction of nurse prescribing. One answered that action learning was effective because it was practical and that, in their experience, much medical research was remote from clinical experience. Yet another said she that knew it was effective because she could point to "compelling evidence of changes in her own – and others' – behaviour."

Some limitations and difficulties

What, then, are the limitations or difficulties of action learning in the NHS? Some found beginning with action learning one of the most difficult parts of the whole process. One respondent said that the question "What is action learning?" hung over everything unanswered at the beginning, and that "especially at the start it felt like I was trying to grasp fog." Respondents pointed to issues such as the difficulty of admitting vulnerabilities which one respondent – herself a doctor – said that the medical profession had particular difficulty in doing, and that such a lack of readiness or preparedness to share issues had caused the failure of some teams. This, however, is not a uniquely health service-based problem. Boshyk has written about the difficulties involved in getting some senior executives in business and industry to admit to the need to embrace learning and self-development (2002, p. 31).

Some respondents alluded to the feeling that it was often the "individual against the system" and that, because teams are quite small (usually no more than six people), the impact can feel rather limited and participants may feel they are missing out on "the big picture." The development and experience of "network" action learning, which allows for interconnectivity and interaction between different teams, may assist with this problem (Donnenberg, 1997). The question of the time it can take to build up trust is also seen by respondents to be an issue. By far the most common limitation for respondents lay in the fact that the NHS is a frenetically busy environment and participants' commitment is all too easily corroded by lack of time.

Despite these constraints and limitations, 64 per cent of respondents said they would be using more action learning in the future – which suggests a healthy interest in its future use.

In order to give a flavor of the work and impact of an action learning team in an acute hospital setting, I next draw upon a published example from the author's own experience as a team facilitator with one such team in an acute hospital setting.

Action learning in an NHS Trust: A case example[4]

The program came about as the result of a collaboration with the Revans Institute at the University of Salford, with team members working toward the completion of a Masters degree by action learning.[5] One aim was to root the program as far as possible in the work environment, and so team meetings invariably took place on the hospital site. Team members were clear at the outset that they wanted to work on real problems in the workplace.

Participants included a respiratory nurse practitioner, an accident and emergency (trauma) senior nurse manager, a medical administration manager, and a general divisional manager with responsibility for the division of medicine. All those involved (including the facilitator) worked for a large NHS trust in the North of England, which, at the time, had an annual budget of £181 million, and around 3,500 staff.

Team members met every two weeks for approximately two to three hours for just over two years. It has to be said that time constraints proved to be a serious issue throughout the program, and sometimes, of necessity, team meetings took place in antisocial hours. This is how team members themselves described the general format of team meetings:

- "We usually started with a 'gossip' session, and an opportunity to talk about what was uppermost in our minds, but actually this was useful in learning about how the Trust operated politically, and in learning to trust each other as team members. We heard from others about what they were 'up to', what they'd done since last time, what worked and what hadn't worked."
- "Questions were a vital part of the process. These questions were about what individuals were trying to do and why, what was stopping them from doing what they had wanted to do, and what they'd learned from the attempts they'd made."
- "Team members then usually talked about what they were going to do next." In this case, team members brought individual (rather than collectively determined) problems for consideration.

The areas of work – he problems upon which the team members concentrated – were as follows:

- Rationalizing children's services
- Implementing medical consultant appraisal
- Implementing annualized hours for nursing staff
- Seeking ways to use the rapid response (hospital at home) to best effect for accident and emergency patients
- Developing a nurse-led asthma clinic.

These problems met Revans' criterion of being genuine problems and not "puzzles" and, for some of the team members in particular, their "problem" was something they lived and breathed as part of their daily working lives, and so, to paraphrase Revans, it carried, for them, a significant risk of penalty in the event of failure. Following completion of written dissertations, team members were asked to respond to the following question: Do you feel what you've done in your research work has had any real impact on a) the area in which you work; and (b) the trust as a whole?

The answers given were as follows:

Children's services manager

I feel the change, the impact, has actually been on me rather than on the trust at large. I am a lot more focused and clearer in my vision (than before). I am more politically aware, and the political dynamics within the trust are much more evident to me. (Without the set) I don't think that agreement with regard to children's services in accident and emergency would have happened. It may have had a different outcome – a less favourable one as far as I was concerned.

Medical administration manager

This was a large undertaking that had the potential to change working conditions for all (medical) consultants... We now have a trained consultant body (comprising) over 160 individuals, which is (now) largely committed to the system... The introduction of the system in the face of some hostility and many constraints taught me a great deal that can be applied in the future.

Divisional manager

Introducing annualized hours has been positive. Staff on the surgical wards where we first introduced it do feel valued, we are using agency staff less and it has created continuity of care. Now we've proved it can work, its starting to happen in accident and emergency, in urology and on acute wards.

Senior nurse manager, accident and emergency

From my perspective, the impact of my learning has extended beyond the trust through to Manchester Health Authority and the Health Action Zone. The set has allowed me to learn from my action 'in the real world'. I think its questionable whether a traditional academic course would have promoted the positive benefits of my research so readily.

Respiratory nurse specialist

Trying to develop a new nurse-led asthma service... initially appeared to be a straightforward process... The service has improved care given to patients with asthma. But it has not yet made any significant change to the numbers of patients attending accident and emergency... As for myself, I feel I have undergone a metamorphosis and become much more politically aware of how issues related to a small project like mine can impact upon the strategic development of the trust.

Whilst the program proved to be beneficial for team members, questions remained about engaging the wider organization, and ensuring that the benefits of action learning were more widely felt and understood. The experience of facilitating this team also made the present writer aware of the powerful emotional and political fallout that action learning can sometimes generate, especially in a large and complex organization. Participants sometimes needed time in the team in order to let off steam about some of the issues they were facing which were not necessarily to do with the identified problem. Additionally, the experience points to a particular difficulty with team members bringing individual problems for consideration. Some participants may not necessarily have a vested interest in others' success with a problem, and there is always an issue in making sure everyone has sufficient "air time." In this case, because everyone came from the same organization, there were areas of overlap in terms of the problems under consideration – for example, the children's services issue and the work being done in accident and emergency impacted upon each other, and particular agreements could be reached on a way forward.

Discussion

Blackler and Kennedy have written of their experiences in delivering an action learning program for NHS chief executives, and have observed that what they had not anticipated was the strength of feeling and the emotional impact that the process would sometimes engender (2006, p. 89). The team members from the case example more than once observed to me that action learning helped them to deal with what could often prove to be a highly politicized, tense and difficult work environment. Revans himself had observed that hospitals were "institutions cradled in anxiety"(1982, p. 263) not only because professionals and others are dealing on a daily basis with patients and relatives who may be *in extremis*, but also because they are working in an environment which is open to constant public and political scrutiny. Moreover, despite expressing the hope that more teams would emerge enabled to ask these much needed fresh questions, the health service's more usual preference is for experts to lead the way, rather than the potentially risky and time consuming strategy of learning from and with each other.

The work of people like Vince and Martin (1993) has focused attention on the contribution action learning can make to managing emotions and politics at work. They proposed a working model to look "inside" action learning, comprising not only the "rational" cycle of behavior expressed in Revans' original conception (such as observation, audit and review), but also an "emotional cycle" (anxiety, risk taking, struggle, etc.). Such an approach can yield considerable benefits in an environment such as the health service but, as indicated, the emotional fallout from engaging in the process of action learning demands attention as well.

In the earlier research project, we argued that our assessment of current action learning practice had revealed some radical variations on Revans' classical principles, one of which included critical action learning (Pedler et al., 2005, p. 59). In this approach, managers and professionals are encouraged to develop the skills of critical thinking and critical questioning, and to apply these skills to the problems they encounter with a view not only to understanding institutional and interpersonal practices, but also to changing them (Rigg and Trehan, 2004). It seems to me there is considerable scope for the use of critical action learning in the health service, as this criticality can potentially be brought to bear on the power dynamics, emotions, stresses, anxieties and risks inherent in the work managers and professionals do in the service.

It would also appear that respondents aim to increase their use of action learning into the future and are convinced of its value. Though it must be borne in mind that this finding is based on a relatively small sample, taken together with accounts from the literature it may be suggested that action learning has, indeed, spread in the service, and the indications are that it will continue to do so. But its impact on some of the bigger, riskier organizational development issues faced by the service, of the kind indicated in the long list of almost intractable problems given at the start of this chapter, is arguably more marginal than advocates of action learning would perhaps wish to see. This remains a considerable challenge for action learners in the health service.

Conclusion

The case example demonstrates the impact an action learning team can have in the health service, albeit on a relatively modest scale. Participants elected to work upon problems in their areas which were fraught with some risk and difficulty, and were in no sense "easy options". Team members wanted the Hospital Trust to make genuine use of the research and change work undertaken by the team, and the opportunity for more teams to emerge enabled to ask the "fresh questions" to which Revans often alluded.

Despite the lack of an agreed definition for action learning (Revans himself never formally defined it, preferring to say what action learning is not), the research outlined here indicates that its principal features appear to be well understood by NHS respondents, despite those apparent contradictions in the data. This is especially the case in terms of some of those well-known features of practice such as having small teams of approximately six or so people, using questioning, and having action as a key driving force. Revans was very wary of action learning teams growing "dependent" upon the facilitator, yet the evidence here suggests that the facilitator has become something of a fixture. An interesting debate stems from this finding. Some action learning practitioners and academics, such as Rigg, argue that facilitation, far from being something which should be limited to a "process only" and "minimalist" focus, should actively draw upon, for example, "facilitators' organizational and wider public service knowledge" (Rigg and Richards, 2006, p. 200). In this way, argues Rigg, facilitators become not only developers and supporters of team members, but also creators of knowledge.

The findings also indicate that the *philosophy* of action learning appears to have spread, as well as the method. The research found examples of Revans' action learning principles being used in mentoring, coaching and aspects of day-to-day managerial practice in the health service.

It appears that action learning in the NHS is generally more focused on personal development and change than on achieving organizational change. This replicates a finding from the earlier general action learning research project. The findings indicate many "own job" projects and, notable among these, are references to work on dealing with conflict, confrontation, managing "toxic" emotions in the workplace and dealing with the effects of bullying in the workplace.

Returning to the question of why action learning has apparently found its place in the health care service, it may be suggested that one reason is that learning and engaging with real problems in such complex, dynamic and anxiety-ridden organizations demands much more of individuals working in it than reliance alone upon a stock of previously undertaken training, education and development. Undoubtedly vital though such a knowledge and skill base is, messy, urgent problems require insightful questions. This is what action learning promises.

Acknowledgements

The section entitled "Action Learning in the Health Service: A case example" is reproduced by kind permission of the *Training Journal* and is based on an article by the author published in the *Training Journal* in August 2002.

The author would like to acknowledge with gratitude the advice given by Professor Mike Pedler in the writing of this chapter.

Notes

1. The memorandum is *The Entry of Girls into the Nursing Profession*, which Revans himself maintained was "[t]he first responsible proposal to practice action learning." One source for this assertion is Revans (1995).
2. See, for example, Revans (1982).
3. See Pedler et al. (2005). This article came about as a result of an action learning research project led by Professors Mike Pedler and John Burgoyne in 2002–3, on which the author was engaged as research assistant.
4. Taken from Brook (2002).
5. The Revans Institute at Salford University no longer exists. A Revans Academy opened in 2008 at the University of Manchester, U.K.

14   *Cheryl Brook*

References

Attwood, M. (2007) "Challenging from the Margins into the Mainstream – Improving renal services in a collaborative and entrepreneurial spirit", *Action Learning: Research and Practice*, 4(2), pp. 191–8.

Blackler, F. and Kennedy, A. (2006) "The Design and Evaluation of a Leadership Programme for Experienced Chief Executives from the Health Sector", in C. Rigg and S. Richards (eds.), *Action Learning, Leadership and Organisational Development in Public Services* (Ozon: Routledge).

Boshyk, Y. (ed.) (2002) *Action Learning Worldwide: Experiences of leadership and organizational development* (Basingstoke: Palgrave MacMillan).

Brook, C. (2002) "Action Learning in South Manchester", *Training Journal*, August, pp. 28–30.

Chivers, M. (2005) "Ordinary Magic: Developing Services for Children with Severe Communication Difficulties by Engaging Multiple Voices", *Action Learning: Research and Practice*, 2(1), pp. 7–26.

Donnenberg, O. (1997) "Network Learning in an Austrian Hospital", in M. Pedler (ed.), *Action Learning in Practice* (Aldershot, U.K./Brookfield, VT: Gower Press).

Lewis, R. and Gillam, S. (2003) "Back to the Market: Yet more reform in the National Health Service", *International Journal of Health Services*, 33(1), pp. 77–84.

Pedler, M. and Abbott, C. (2008a) "Lean and Learning: Action Learning for Service Improvement", *Leadership in Health Service,* 21(2), pp. 87–98.

Pedler, M. and Abbott, C. (2008b) "'Am I Doing It Right?' Facilitating Action Learning for Service Improvement", *Leadership in Health Service,* 21(3), pp. 185–99.

Pedler, M., Burgoyne, J. and Brook, C. (2005) "What has Action Learning Learned to Become?", *Action Learning: Research and Practice*, 2(1), pp. 49–68.

Pettigrew, A., Ferlie, E. and McKee, L. (1992) *Shaping Strategic Change in Large Organisations: The Case of the National Health Service* (London: Sage).

Revans, R. W. (1982) "Helping Each Other to Help the Helpless", in R. W. Revans (ed.), *The Origins and Growth of Action Learning* (Bromley, Kent: Chartwell-Bratt).

Revans, R. W. (1995) "Disclosing Doubts", a report of the First International Action Learning Mutual Collaboration Congress, April 17–25, 1995 (Appendix 1 Health Services).

Revans, R. W. (1998) *ABC of Action Learning* (Lemos & Crane: London).

Richardson, J., Ainsworth, R., Allison, R., Billyard, J., Corley, R. and Viner, J. (2008) "Using an Action Learning Set (ALS) to Support the Nurse and Allied Health Professional Consultant Role", *Action Learning: Research and Practice*, 5(1), pp. 65–77.

Rigg, C. and Richards, S. (eds.) (2006) *Action Learning, Leadership and Organisational Development in Public Services* (Oxon: Routledge).

Rigg, C. and Trehan, K. (2004) "Reflections on Working with Critical Action Learning", *Action Learning: Research and Practice*, 1(2), pp. 149–65.

Vince, R. and Martin, L. (1983) "Inside Action Learning: An Exploration of the Psychology and Politics of the Action Learning Model," *Management Education and Development*, 24(3), pp. 206–15.

Willis, M. (1986) "Partnership Action Learning", in C. Rigg and S. Richards (eds.), (2006) *Action Learning, Leadership and Organisational Development in Public Services* (Oxon: Routledge).

2
Action Learning in Education

Robert L. Dilworth

Introduction

This chapter will examine the application of action learning programs in the field of education internationally, beginning with a look at the societal context in the United States, including receptivity of educational institutions to action learning related concepts. The focus then turns to secondary school systems and their ripeness for action learning interventions.

I next cover 13 institutions of higher learning: eight of them in the United States, the remainder in the United Kingdom, Continental Europe, or at multiple international sites. Three criteria drove my selection of these institutions:

1. Examination of some programs with which I have a deep familiarity. Several fall in this category (e.g., Virginia Commonwealth University, Georgia State University and the University of Salford). This allows me to explain some of the fine points of these programs;
2. Arrival at a mix of programs that provides a variety of approaches;
3. Selection of some programs that were highly successful and yet ended up being cancelled. What can we learn from these examples to avoid similar pitfalls?

This selective sampling of universities serves to demonstrate that action learning is not a "cookie cutter" type formulation. The recipe for achieving action learning can vary widely, while at the same time still delivering significant results.

Virginia Commonwealth University (VCU) will receive the most concentrated address for two reasons. First, this program closely follows the Revans' model. Second, covering some of the details of the program can provide an initial template for those considering establishment of an action learning program in higher education. The author was a close associate of Revans, and will show how the VCU program closely aligns with Revans' precepts.

The chapter concludes with a summary analysis and examination of how these thirteen university-based programs compare. How are they alike and how are they different? What are some of the common threads running through all or most of the programs?

The context within which action learning occurs in the United States

Action learning is by its very nature, when practiced in the way Revans intended it to be applied, contradictory to many of the traditional educational methods used by our schools. Historically, the emphasis has been on the centrality of the teacher and a didactic approach to instruction, with the learners viewed as vessels into which you "pour" knowledge. Paulo Freire, the Brazilian educator and philosopher, called this "banking education," teaching by formula and, in a way, detached from life (Freire, 1987, pp. 39–41).

There can be an absence of interaction, between teacher and students, and between the students themselves. There can also be little opportunity for the students to engage in discussion of issues of the day or to grapple with real problems. The material used can therefore be seen as lacking in relevancy by the learners, and therefore fail to motivate learning. Action learning is nearly the complete opposite of this description. Action learning proceeds from the supposition that the learner is central and ought to be empowered, taking personal responsibility for their own learning. It also suggests that learners need some freedom to exercise their curiosity and demonstrate spontaneity. Learning is paramount, not memorizing facts or slavishly following set routines.

The restrictiveness of what happens in the classroom has become even more pronounced in recent years. Under the "No Child Left Behind" legislation in the United States, Standards of Excellence (SOE) testing has often come to dominate what occurs in the classroom. The teacher teaches to the test. Whether the school stays accredited, the teacher retains his or her job, bonuses are paid, or the school system receives a significant infusion of state and federal funds, can be dependent on the student test scores. Therefore, rote recall and moving down narrow pathways to achieve favorable test results can be the order of the day. True learning opportunities can be driven off the table. The programs of instruction (POEs), which can govern almost every minute of the teacher's time, further block interaction. This is, of course, not true of every school – but it is clearly the norm in many of them.

If the existing secondary education systems produced uniformly good results, that would be another thing, but there are clear signs that, overall, they do not produce the required results. The National Adult Literacy Survey (NALS) Report, released by the Educational Testing Service (ETS) at Princeton University and the newly created National Institute for Literacy in 1992 – a direct result of the National Literacy Act of 1991 – was a "wake-up call." This was the first comprehensive examination of adult literacy and basic skills in the nation's history. It was a scientific sampling, and it included both young people and older U.S. residents. Even the prison population was surveyed. The survey used interviews that were roughly 45 minutes in length, where the interviewee was asked practical questions – like reading a subway map, determining the size of a tip in a restaurant, balancing a checkbook, and understanding the content of a simple newspaper article.

The survey found that 23 percent of U.S. adults (totaling 40 to 44 million people) were at the lowest level of educational ability (level 5). People in this category are, at most, able to perform tasks involving brief uncomplicated text, totaling the amount on a bank deposit slip, or locating information in a short news article, but many with difficulty. Another 25 to 28 percent of U.S. adults (about fifty million) were at the next lowest level of functional literacy and basic skills. Skills at this level were more varied, but still quite limited. A follow-on survey, the International Adult Literacy Survey (IALS), was conducted during the period 1994–8. This involved 22 countries, the United States being one of them. The United States showed no real gain from the first survey, and periodic surveys since point to a continuation of rather abysmal results. With a national literacy and basic skills shortfall of this magnitude, it seems clear that our secondary school systems are not delivering the goods.

Action learning in secondary school systems

Problems in our secondary education systems roll over into adulthood when young people seek employment. The problems relating to acquiring well-educated people in the workplace is not new. They became particularly acute as technology advanced. Jobs at the bottom end of the skill ladder are diminishing in number, and when businesses cannot identify qualified people in the United States, they find it necessary to search for them elsewhere. A senior Motorola human resources executive told me that they were having to tap into the labor pool of young people in Eastern Europe, where they could readily find people with solid mathematics and science skills.

The Office of Technology Assessment in the U.S. government noted that:

> Many American firms have found training employees for new technology more difficult than anticipated. Many workers need to upgrade their skills before they can handle other training (1990, p. 7).

Said another way, also drawing from the Office of Technology Assessment Report – and directly relevant to the technological environment we face today:

> American manufacturing and service workers have the skills for yesterday's routine jobs. But these workers will need new skills to function well in the more demanding work environments that increasingly characterize competitive industries able to provide high-wage jobs (1990, p. 1).

While written in 1990, nineteen years ago, this quote could have been written yesterday. Companies find themselves unable to obtain the highly qualified workers they need, especially those who have been well educated in mathematics and science. It is true, even in an economic downturn such as that being experienced in 2009.

We make the point in Chapter 18, "Looking to the Future of Action Learning," that action learning does not necessarily come with the brand name embroidered on it. You can be involved with action learning without identifying or recognizing it as such. I will provide two examples from secondary schools that prove this point and, in each instance, I will point out how they succeed or fail to match with action learning precepts. A third example is, patently, action learning – in name as well as in substance.

Revans had a special understanding of schools, having even set up an entire school district in England at one time. He also had a very special feeling for children and their natural spontaneity. Revans observed that children could naturally engage in trusting dialogue, and they felt free to go where their natural curiosity might lead them, unfettered by bureaucratic constraints and traditional thought. He worked with children and education systems in Australia and in the inner city of Manchester, England. He also had a keen interest in higher education, and was frustrated throughout his life by encounters with teaching methods that he believed stifled learning rather than promoted it. He did work with Southern Methodist University in the United States and, as a professor at the University of Manchester, he endeavored to bring experiential learning methods to the classroom, but ended up being rebuffed by his academic colleagues, who preferred to maintain the *status quo*. Revans' work with action learning is an important backdrop to this chapter.

A middle school in Pomona, California

My first example occurred during the week beginning March 15, 2009. A middle-school teacher in Pomona, California challenged his students to write essays about the economic downturn and how it was affecting their lives. He could sense the stress in the classroom resulting from financial pressures on their families, and he felt this would be a way of encouraging them to give voice to their concerns. He was both astounded and thrilled by the work he received. The students reported that their lives were heavily impacted. The family finances were so tight in one case that the student held back on the food he consumed at dinnertime so there would be more food for his brothers.

Many of the students were in a state of anguish, and having to shoulder worries and responsibilities beyond their years. Family homes had been lost as a result of foreclosure and, in some cases, their temporary lodgings were now also in jeopardy. All but one of the students indicated that they were either working in casual employment, or looking for such work to help support their families.

The teacher challenged his students to share their story beyond the school, suggesting that they create a blog. They acted on his recommendation. The message they provided was a telling one, and it ended up attracting attention nationwide. It even found its way to the White House. During a visit to California, President Barack Obama visited the school to talk to the students (Lehrer 2009). However, the story does not end there. The students themselves then set about establishing a student association where they could help each other out – whether it was lunch money, phone cards, or some other necessity. It is this kind of opportunity – provided, in this instance, by a very shrewd and intuitive teacher, sensitive to the plight of his students – that can open up avenues for students to learn life skills and problem-solving. This was not "banking education": it was dealing with real life issues – which stands at the very centre of action learning.

This example fits with action learning for several reasons. First and foremost, the teacher empowered his students to do what they considered appropriate. The blog was theirs, not his. All students were equal in the process. The problems that they were dealing with were real, not fabricated, or from a textbook. They also had ample opportunity to reflect on their personal state of affairs, and reflection is a key component of action learning. Finally, it was a case of questioning insight. Questions drove the process and the critical reflection that occurred.

The second example, like the first, does not carry the action learning label *per se*. It is also important for some different reasons. One criticism of our secondary school systems is that they do not challenge the students. They can assign low expectations to them, rather than causing them to stretch and grow. This can be especially true in inner city schools with many minority children from poor families. That is what makes this story so poignant. A teacher bucked the system and proved that minority children from poor families can defy the odds and achieve test scores in line with America's finest college preparatory schools, and some action learning precepts were involved. They simply needed the opportunity and challenge.

He set his expectations high, rather than low, and his students met and exceeded them. However, in the process he ended up in almost continuous conflict with educators who preferred the *status quo*. In the end, he found it necessary to leave. He was even receiving death threats. The linkage here to action learning is that you try to set the expectations high by asking the learners to confront highly complex problems and learn from them. It places the bar higher than is customary in traditional education and training programs.

The story of Jaime Escalante, mathematics teacher

Jaime Escalante immigrated to the United States in 1964 from Bolivia, where he had taught physics and mathematics. To prepare for a teaching job in America, he studied science and mathematics at the University of Puerto Rico. He also earned a degree in biology from the University of Pasadena in California, as well as a degree in mathematics from California State University, studying calculus.

He was hired by Garfield High School in East Los Angeles to teach mathematics. He was initially disheartened by the lack of preparation of his students, and almost left. But, as he came to know his students, he experienced an epiphany. He ended up committing to teach his students, treating them not as poor minority students, but as young people who were simply looking for a chance in life. He was constantly attacked as he elevated standards in his classroom. But a new principal supported Escalante's efforts. He started a calculus class for his students, a course that had never been offered before. It had been considered impossible for such students to grasp higher mathematics.

Escalante came into the national spotlight in 1981, when 18 of his students passed the Advanced Placement Exam in calculus. The ETS at Princeton would not trust the results. How could minority students in the inner city of Los Angeles possibly achieve such test scores? Further, they found some similar errors in their answers on the exam (determined later to be simply reflective of a technique Escalante had used to teach them) that suggested to them that cheating had occurred. ETS disallowed the scores. Escalante, after talking to his disheartened students, convinced them to study for the exam again. He then successfully petitioned ETS for a retest. A team from ETS came to Garfield High School and closely monitored that test. Twelve of the 14 who took the retest of the Advanced Placement Exam passed it.

By 1987, 73 students had passed the Advanced Placement Exam in calculus, an incredible record. By 1990, the calculus program had grown to over 400 students, causing class sizes to go to 50 students in some instances, since the school would not hire added teachers. He was attacked by a new principal for excessive class size, a violation of union rules. At that point, Escalante left, and some of the assistants that had worked with him left as well. The program then headed downhill and, in effect, evaporated (Wikipedia 2009).

What can be taken away from this in terms of action learning? Escalante empowered his students to learn, and he set high expectations for them. It was a classic case of the "Pygmalion effect." He used real problems to spark interest and engagement. If you set expectations high, people will strive to meet them. If you set expectations low – which had been the case for these minority students throughout their school experience – then they will tend to limit their performance to meet the lower expectations.

He used examples from life to drive home his points in teaching mathematics. Facing one unruly class early in his time at Garfield High, he pulled out a knife, threw an apple up in the air, splitting it cleanly into two halves as it came down. He held up the two pieces of the apple and explained that they were halves. He then said, "Now let's settle down and learn about fractions." He was nurturing and disciplined, but not intrusive. He taught the students that it was their responsibility to learn, not his. As in action learning, the learner was central, the asking of questions was encouraged and led to new approaches and solutions, and he asked them to reflect on what they wanted to make out of their lives. His classroom was a comfortable and trusting climate in which to learn.

Letter from a Head Girl

In Dilworth (2010), we provide some examples of how Reg Revans was able to mobilize action learning initiatives. We include the example of Willetton Senior High School, the largest high school in Western Australia. So enthusiastic about action learning did the students become, that they petitioned the government of Western Australia to allocate funds for the construction of a building, which the students referred to as a "Q" Factory – borrowing from Revans' Learning Equation, where Learning equals Programmed Instruction, plus Questioning Insight (L = P + Q).

The Q Factory was built, at a cost of over 100,000 Australian dollars. It was used by the students to meet and discuss issues in the world and in their lives. The school became self-governing by students, parent participation climbed, and academic performance increased. There was a long waiting list to be accepted into the school because of its reputation and action learning component. On June 1, 1991, the Principal of the school, Brendon Davies, wrote a letter to Revans. One paragraph in that letter says it all:

> Everyone believes Willetton to be a marvelous school and raves about the wonderful intangible spirit. They are amazed that the kids like going there and that they have no rules nor any vandalism. Why is it they ask, that so many staff members are involved far beyond their job descriptions and work for long hours without remuneration? Of course the answer is not some guru Principal but action learning. I think the "upward communication of doubt" in our administrative style would now match that of any corporation you have dealt with. The rewards have been immeasurable for our school and I feel that this facet of change has been one of our most successful.

What did it look like through the eyes of a student? Revans received this letter from the Head Girl at Willetton School at about the same time. Here is her assessment:

Dear Professor Revans,

My name is Natalie Limpus and I am the Head Girl of Willetton Senior High School. You may recall me in the photograph wearing the $L = P + Q$ teeshirt [Note: Referring to Revans' Learning Equation].
I recently had a conference with Mr. Davies [the school principal] and he allowed me to read your inspiring letter.

I became very anxious and excited about the prospect of maybe being able to discuss our ideals and methods of schooling, which do indeed create a more harmonious and educationally beneficial environment, with fellow students in Florida or Washington.

I am very proud of our school and I believe that every school in the world has the potential to reach the same high standards as Willetton.

In order for our school to run efficiently and effectively, like Willetton Senior High School, there needs to be a lot of teamwork, not just between students themselves, but between students and teachers. There needs to be mutual respect and cooperation.

Since we the student representatives, have been involved in the better schooling program, and since we have recognized and experienced the changes made to Willetton, I feel we are capable of discussing our knowledge and worthwhile methods with other schools around the world. I am therefore extremely serious to contact students in Washington and meet with them in order to discuss our schools, and how such a worthwhile education system like Willetton is possible to achieve.

If possible, could you please enable me to contact these keen students in Washington, as I want to help them achieve as highly as we have at Willetton, and create a better world. I would be most appreciative if you could supply the name and address of a contact person in Washington. The method of education at Willetton may be the first step to saving humanity.

I appreciate and thank you for your time and only hope that Willetton can help the rest of the world realize that a major part of humanity can be saved, through a better education system.

Yours sincerely,

Natalie Limpus
Head Girl, Willetton Senior High School (Limpus 1991).

Summing up the application of Action Learning in secondary school systems

As the Willetton School example demonstrates so clearly, action learning can make important inroads. In the United States, there are emerging signs of empowerment of students similar to those that occurred at Willetton, such as students participating in Parent–Teacher Association (PTA) meetings. There have even been cases of students at middle-school level developing the agenda for PTA meetings and playing a role in leading them. *Action Learning in Schools* (Aubisson *et al.* 2009) addresses how to reframe teachers' professional learning and development. It includes 100 case studies of action learning by teams of teachers in schools. It also provides advice for initiating and sustaining action learning, and illustrates how action learning can link with classroom practise so closely that it becomes part of what teachers do, rather than an add-on.

Young people have important points of view that need to be heard, rather than suppressed by rigid approaches to education. Action learning can be an important vehicle for allowing the voices of young people to be heard. In fact, young people can teach the adults in some cases. A first-cousin of mine purchased a desktop computer for her five-year-old grandson to use to entertain himself when he visited. The first time he was to use it, she sat down to instruct him on how to use various features. He brushed her hands away and said, "Grandma, let me show you a short cut!"

If we want young people to be responsible adults, able to make their own decisions, earn a living, and enjoy a rich life, they need to have a chance to test their wings as they grow up. Action learning can provide this opportunity.

Action learning programs in higher education

Action learning is beginning to find its way into higher education. In some respects, it can be an uncomfortable fit. As mentioned earlier in this chapter, professors can find action learning too starkly different from established practises that place the lecture at the epicenter of the teaching experience. Action learning can be more demanding, and can require the students to reach beyond the bounds of fixed curricula. For example, it is common practise in action learning for the students to work on a real project outside the university. This is a way of integrating their knowledge and challenging their intellect.

A vignette from my own experience underscores the degree to which action learning can seem a radical departure from long-established ways of presenting a college-level class. My example relates to my graduate students. I had three action learning teams of students in my classroom hard at work on their individual joint projects one evening. They were empowered, intensively engaged, and the problems they were dealing with were real, complex, and extremely challenging. I was sitting in the front of the classroom in order to be available to them on matters of process, or to identify resources they could call upon.

One of the longtime tenured full professors kept "cruising" by my classroom and looking in the door. He had a troubled look on his face. Finally he stopped, caught my eye, and motioned for me to come out in the hall-way. He said, "I have been watching your class for the last two hours (it was a three-hour class), and you have been sitting in the classroom the entire time, looking relaxed, and disengaged from what's happening. I even heard students laughing from time to time. Have you given up teaching?" It was fortunate that he had stepped forward to question what was happening, because it gave me a chance to explain what was taking place. I started by telling him that I had not given up teaching, but I had taken up learning. I also told him I knew of no rule forbidding laughter in a classroom.

He was quite amazed at the responsibility the students had been given, and that they had been entrusted with such weighty problems to deal with. He realized that there was a great deal going on in that classroom, and that the students were learning by having to grapple with some very thorny issues – issues that were not fabricated or out of a case study. They were bread and butter issues that the companies they were dealing with were facing and urgently needed to resolve. As far as the students were concerned, most would have told this professor, had he asked, that they were engaged in one of the most important learning opportunities they had experienced in their lives.

There are now clear signs that action learning is creating some important "bridgeheads" in higher education. This is not all that surprising, because the world of business is increasingly adopting action learning as a key approach for staying competitive and developing executive talent. That trend is now finding its way into the universities. Thirteen examples of action learning being practiced in higher education establishments now follow. Several of them demonstrate this bridge between business-related programs in univer-sities and the corporate world.

Jesse H. Jones Graduate School of Management, Rice University (USA)

The program summary/advertisement, as outlined on the World Wide Web, reads as follows:

> Building upon knowledge of traditional management concepts acquired in your first year of the Rice MBA program, you'll gain practical experi-ence in consulting and implementing change within a dynamic host company in the Action Learning Project. Over an intensive eight-week period, your team will examine a selected company's processes, and make detailed recommendations for improvements needed, then present your findings to senior management, with guidance from faculty and a corporate liaison (Jesse H. Jones Graduate School of Management 2009).

They make clear that the multidisciplinary faculty team that supports the process does not serve as part of the consulting team. They merely facili-tate the educational process, provide insight and perspective, and assure rigorous analyses. While the students are supported by faculty, the work is entirely done by the students.

Fremont College (USA)

Here is the way the basic essence of the program is explained:

> Classroom learning is far different than actually working in a given field. With the help of our CEO Business Advisory Board we researched how to bridge the gap between the classroom and the workplace... More importantly, how to prepare students for their first day at work... The answer – based on years of business research – is to employ a highly advanced intensive learning model you'll find only at Fremont College. We call it PAL – Professional Action Learning Embedded with Industry.
>
> ...
>
> Our courses immerse you in the subject matter. You will see and experience what you are learning. This dynamic approach makes it easier – and much faster – because you are learning by doing (Fremont College 2009).

Hult International Business School's MBA Program (London, Boston, Dubai, Shanghai)

This program focuses on an action learning approach that melds theory to practise. Here is their statement on essence of the program:

> We believe that you cannot learn everything in a classroom. Our action learning approach ensures that you have the opportunity to test the theories that you learn from your professors in real business situations. During our fourth module, you will participate in an Action Learning Project. Joining a small team coached by a faculty member or outside professional, you will conduct a project with a real company. You will use your research, analysis and management skills to tackle your client's business need... Theoretical concepts will come to life during your Action Learning Project and simulation exercises (Hult International Business School 2009).

It is interesting to note here that simulations are a part of the process. We make the point in Chapter 18, "Looking to the Future of Action Learning," that, properly done, simulations deserve a seat at the table of action learning. This runs counter to Revans' beliefs, but the world has moved on, and simulations can be extraordinarily real and compelling.

Frederick A. and Barbara M. Erb Institute, University of Michigan (USA)

A description of the program follows:

> Erb students apply their interdisciplinary education in two real-world consulting projects. Through the School of Natural Resources and Environment

(SNRE) Master's Project and the Ross Multidisciplinary Action Project (MAP) students have added value to myriad corporations and nonprofit organizations. Examples include the development of sustainable business strategy, streamlining processes to reduce operational waste, and developing models to measure organizational effectiveness in the pursuit of sustainability... It allows students to further hone their integrated problem-solving skills and communication skills, and is one of the salient features of the MBA/MS Program.

Many Erb Institute MBA/MS students utilize action learning projects and summer internships to pursue international opportunities. Erb students have conducted work in more than 35 countries and six different continents during their time in the program (Erb Institute 2009).

This action learning program is international and interdisciplinary in character, with much emphasis in such areas as social entrepreneurship, green development, ethics of corporate management, and cultural norms in global business.

Gaia University

As is true of the Erb Institute at the University of Michigan, Gaia University has a very strong orientation toward sustainability, ecology, and ethical behavior. However, the strong emphasis on the business sector is absent. In fact, the social dimension is so much in evidence, that it can be construed as a movement to transform societies, as much as an institution of higher learning.

Gaia is a university that is, essentially, without walls, with much of what the student does being accomplished wherever they reside and work, including organizations that affiliate with Gaia. The connection with the students is largely via the Internet and email.

Here is how they portray their action learning program:

> Widescale human learning and unlearning are the keys to making the transition from our current eco-destructive culture to a fresh, designed culture that is eco-constructive and socially just... Using self-directed learning as our prime learning/unlearning strategy we put students (Associates) in charge of their own transitions, free to follow routes which open up before them, guided by their tutors and mentors... We notice the vital signs of an awakening of transitional energy amongst the world's peoples and so, we have launched Gaia University to provide the support we can to these bold world changers and future generations of earth caretakers (Gaia University 2009).

The action learning projects involved are specific to each student and determined by the student. The university defines what comprises an acceptable project in the broadest terms.

Project experience can include elective workshops, internships, apprenticeships, immersions, "gap year" activities, volunteering and working for projects, part-time vacation and livelihood work experience. An Associate chooses their work experiences and projects deliberately to meet their learning needs and suit their circumstances. Associates spend the bulk of their time on-project and/or "in-work" and, during this time, typically 11 months a year, are not "at college" although they are "in-program" (Gaia University 2009).

One can translate this approach as "anything goes." It is difficult to see how this program can be rigorous. Students are apparently invited to record what they would have been doing to begin with in their lives and in their jobs.

Department of Public Administration and Policy, American University (USA)

This program, inaugurated by Professor Bob Kramer, provides a rich action learning experience. Most of the graduate students involved occupy leadership positions in government, some at the most senior levels. Roughly 20 percent of each cohort comes from the U.S. Department of Defense. Students determine projects to work on in their various agencies and can assemble action learning teams to deal with the effort. They must orient their agency associates on the action learning process.

The program at American University is a sophisticated one, and draws on the basic underpinnings of action learning as articulated by Revans. In 2008, I had a chance to audit 13 end-of-course reports by students on their action learning projects and their action learning experience. The projects, selected in discussion with Professor Kramer, were complex and extremely challenging. They had to be thoroughly mapped in proposal format beforehand and, when fully developed, they became a contract between the student, his agency sponsor and Professor Kramer. What impressed me most were the rigorous analysis and the deep self-reflection that occurred. It was obvious that some of the students had been through an experience that had changed them as leaders and managers. Further, the projects that they had undertaken had made a significant difference to the agencies they served (Kramer 2007, 2007/08). (See Chapter 3 in this volume, "Transformative Action Learning in the U.S. Government," by Robert Kramer and James L. Kelly.)

Department of Educational Leadership, School of Education, Florida Atlantic University (USA)

The author helped to seed this program in the late 1990s; it took hold and has flourished. It involves a capstone course that is provided to the higher education students and kindergarten through the twelfth grade (K–12) doctoral students in the summer semester. Action learning teams of students work on joint problems that are affecting schools and school districts in that part of Florida. Many of the students fill administrative roles in the various school districts.

The problems/projects are real, and deal with issues that are substantive and important. A recent action learning team had a school superintendent as its client. The project concerned a major knowledge management initiative and the better sharing of information between the schools. The school superintendent attached great importance to the project and considered it part of his legacy. The students did some thorough analysis and tested various aspects of the system.

The nature of the facilitation provided to the teams is evolving, but has been on the side of close involvement with what the students are doing, rather than guiding the path they should take in fulfilling their project responsibilities. On completion of their projects, the student teams present their results to the senior school officials who are their clients.

This particular action learning program provides important services to the communities within geographical proximity to FAU (i.e., the Boca Raton area of Florida).

The two professors who have been involved with the action learning program at FAU make the point that action learning programs demand more of the professor than a traditional course. They are more challenging and require skilful orchestration, but the two professors also indicate that action learning programs are extremely rewarding in terms of the degree of learning and growth that occurs (Acker-Hocevar and Maslin-Ostrowski 2009).

The Technion Institute of Management (TIM), Haifa, Israel

The Technical Institute of Management (TIM) is the executive education arm of Technion, Israel's university of science and technology, which was founded in 1924. TIM was launched in 1998, and is Israel's leading executive development institute and a pioneer in action learning methods. Technion has a strong organization of supporters in the United States, known as the American Technion Society (ATS). A group of ATS supporters in Boston initiated the idea of establishing TIM and provided funding for it. Lester Thurow, former MIT Sloan School of Management dean, who became famous for propelling MIT's Sloan Business School to the top ranking among business schools, has served as TIM's Chairman since TIM's inception

In 1998, the TIM began an action learning program. The centerpiece of the program is the team project, "whose objective is to serve as an action framework for learning...The program includes an intensive international management trip to a knowledge-based business centre abroad, where participants meet CEOs and government leaders" (Maital *et al.*, 2002, p. 212).

As conceived, and striving to follow an Action Reflection Learning (ARL) model, TIM used "learning facilitators" as well as "business coaches." The plan was to have the learning facilitators (who would have expertise in organization development (OD) and training) monitor the process and alert the business coaches to specific business issues that arose. That did not always happen, so TIM, in effect, swapped the two roles. The business coaches were given the lead, and the learning facilitators were put on the "back burner." This created a new set of problems when the business coaches tended to treat the action learning teams as typical task teams and issue instructions (pp. 221–2).

Critical reflection, a key component of action learning, was not occurring. They concluded that this was due, in part, to cultural reasons: "It appears that the reflective part of the learning process may not be culturally viable in Israel" (p. 221). This is an interesting observation, and this lack of inclination to reflect can also be considered a problem in the United States, as well as in a number of other Western cultures.

As indicated, the ARL model was what TIM set out to follow. That model gives great attention to the reflective component, and it is induced by frequent interventions in the action learning process. When they removed the learning facilitator from the monitoring role, that trigger went away.

Those who closely adhere to Revans' teachings do not believe in the highly interventionist role characterized by the ARL model, believing that learners are their own best facilitators and that a learning coach can help bring about reflection by means other than frequent interruptions of the process. In contrast, TIM's experience, as they report it, reflects the hard realities of the high-pressure high-tech environment. It was found that cross-functional teams composed of senior leaders from diverse company businesses needed frequent intervention in order to maintain momentum, schedule meetings and, especially, to reflect on the team's shortcomings in its teamwork processes. TIM claims that the self-managed team approach crumbled in the face of exigencies hard-pressed managers had to deal with.

The Human Resource Development Program, George Washington (GW) University (USA)

The Human Resource Development program at George Washington University was started in 1965 under the direction of Professor Len Nadler. It has many distinguished graduates. The action learning component of the program was developed by Professor Michael Marquardt after he had been exposed to action learning at an international conference on action learning in London in 1995 (Marquardt and Carter, 1998, p. 59).

The action learning part of the program is linked to their Executive Leadership Program (ELP) doctoral program. Comprising twelve courses, one of them is specific to action learning. It is customarily taken somewhere between the fourth and twelfth course in the program. The course lasts four weeks if taken during a regular semester and six weeks if taken during the summer. There is also an ELP program in Singapore offered by GW. It is organized as a cohort, whereas the on-campus program in Washington is not.

The first class session in the action learning course begins with a 30-minute overview of action learning, followed by a demonstration by the professor, and then discussions related to what happened and the theory and practise of action learning. Students are ultimately formed into action learning teams, and they undergo a proposal submission process in arriving at an action learning project that is suitable. Marquardt reports that these individual action learning projects, taken from the student's work environment, are meant to be urgent and important. They must also be something that they are empowered to act on and not someone else's problem.

The students are obviously very familiar with the projects they are working on, but are unfamiliar with those of the other students in their action learning team. Class sessions are scheduled twice a week, and are taken up with discussions within the team about individual projects and progress being made. Facilitation within the team rotates among the team members. Marquardt "floats around" during the sessions as an overall facilitator. The grade in the course is determined by the professor on the basis of a learning journal students submit at the end of the course, as well as the professor's observations of individual student performance during the semester (Marquardt, 2009).

Unlike some other programs, where the problem or project being dealt with is a joint problem that all team members work on, the GW program has each student working on their own problem. This tends to create less of a bonding effect in the team than having to work on a joint problem. In this respect, the GW program is similar to the program at American University and the way the program had been organized at the Revans Institute for Action Learning and Research at the University of Salford in England. Some other programs have made action learning the centerpiece of their program, rather than a one-course offering (e.g., Rice University, Fremont College, University of Salford). Another distinguishing feature is that the students in the GW program do not present their results to senior management as part of the course, as is the case at Virginia Commonwealth University, Fremont College, Rice University and some other schools. Further, the number of contact hours in the course (30) is significantly fewer than some of the other university programs because of the way their semester system is set up.

Human Resource Development Program at Georgia State University (USA)

The action learning component of the Human Resource Development (HRD) Program at Georgia State University was created by Professor Verna Willis in 1996. From the outset, it closely aligned with Revans' precepts. The action learning course was the capstone of her Master's Degree program in HRD. Her overall HRD program came to be designated as the top HRD program in the United States by the Academy of Human Resource Development (AHRD) in 1997.

Each of her action learning courses had up to five action learning teams, primarily Master's Degree students, but also with a sprinkling of doctoral students. A major real problem or project was assigned to each team to work with and arrive at possible solutions for the client. These projects resulted from advance contacts by Professor Willis with the companies. The projects were significant and diverse. One project involved working with the company that produces the phone book *Yellow Pages*. The company suspected that they were overproducing the number needed, thus incurring what was believed to be a large unnecessary cost. The action learning team performed a thorough analysis that proved the company's suspicions to be true. The action learning team pinpointed a critical gap in numerical information, not originating in the client's own business but in the phone company it supplied. The fix had to occur in the company's order-taking system, and was accomplished by adding a field to the computer screens used by their employees whenever customers added new services. Tightening the numbers on the actual volume of book production needed was projected to yield future annual cost savings of over US$1 million.

In another project, a large church wanted to know how to deal with a recently donated property. The action learning team studied their situation and presented them with definitive alternatives. Another team worked with the Georgia Department of Labor Vocational Rehabilitation Program. The effort focused sharply on properly supporting minority populations and the disadvantaged. As can often be true with action learning projects, the action learning team became extremely wrapped up in the Rehabilitation Project, to the extent that they dealt with it as if it were their own problem. These projects were often a service to the community.

Students were required to write a final report for the client and give a formal PowerPoint presentation to them, with all team members participating. The client representatives were always senior managers for the organizations, whether they were public or private (Willis 1998, 2009).

The reflective component was dealt with by the maintenance of learning journals and submission of reflective essays on the experience. During the course, external facilitation of the action learning teams was held to a minimum. This is in keeping with Revans' philosophy regarding facilitation – namely, that the action learning team members themselves are their own best facilitators. Professor Willis started the action learning course by orienting the class on action learning. She then ran them through some action learning discussions around a hypothetical problem to guide them through effective ways of asking questions.

The program was highly successful from a couple of standpoints. First, the enrollments were good; second, the student evaluations of the course and the experience were outstanding. Two other professors gave her program tacit support, but never contributed to her action learning program. When

Professor Willis retired in 2005, neither of the other professors wanted to assume responsibility for the program. Therefore, it was discontinued.

Collaboration between the School of Education and the School of Business at the University of Texas, Austin (USA)

As was true of the program at Georgia State University, this University of Texas Program no longer exists. However, it was a very successful program and its legacy is worth remembering. It was a very robust program, and contributed a number of lessons in design of action learning programs in higher education.

The School of Education and the School of Business had entered into a collaboration based on an agreement between the two deans. They believed that a program formed on the basis of synergy between the two schools could benefit the schools and the university. The action learning program became the basis for this collaboration, organized by Professor Annie Brooks of the School of Education, with the assistance of the School of Business, including funding support. The Management Department of the School of Business and the Human Resource Development Leadership component of the School of Education worked as partners in this effort.

Called the "MHRDL Program," the action learning component extended over a two-year period.

> The three credit hour action learning course was "taught" by a permanent faculty member responsible for the course's organization, effectiveness and the learners' grades. It was supplemented by a course in gathering and analyzing organizational data to support the need for action learning participants to gather, analyze and interpret data (Brooks, 1998, p. 51).

At the center of the program were individual projects that were to be worked on by the graduate students. The projects came from the organization in which the graduate student worked. The projects had to be within the graduate students' authority to act on, and not someone else's problem. Professor Brooks worked with each student to determine the project. A distinguishing feature of this program – and in keeping with Revans' precept that problems/projects must be real, highly challenging, and even daunting – was the degree to which this program lived up to that standard. When Brooks had finished working with the student to identify and describe the project, it met these tests very well.

Doctoral students were used as team advisors/learning coaches to help the students grasp the nature of critically reflective questions. However, they would not usually interrupt the activities of the team. As a capstone to the two-year action learning experience, the students went to the University of Ballarat in Australia, where they worked with Australian enterprises in Ballarat and Melbourne on issues of concern to the companies. They dealt with the very top people in each enterprise. The end products of this two-year excursion in action learning were a Master's Degree report on the experience and what they had each learned, as well as a report to the primary enterprise in which they had done their project work (Brooks, 2009). The depth of this program can be seen in excerpts from a journal article by Brooks (1998, pp. 54–5):

> The breakthrough point for everybody, students and faculty alike, was the point at which we began to share our own "bloody ignorance". ...
> A challenge for many students was to understand that *no one* had a solution to the problem on which they were working, and that if a solution had existed, someone probably would have already implemented it.
> ...
> I didn't get what action learning was about for the longest time. I kept collecting articles about my problem off the internet and from other places so that I had a whole notebook full of what Annie [Professor Brooks] called "secondary data." Then, finally one day it hit me when she was talking about learning. She didn't tell me to do this or anything, it was just something she said that triggered me. I went back to the company and started interviewing people closest to the problem. From them, I learned that I had the problem all wrong.
> ...
> The breakthrough came when she [the student] saw that the answers to her questions were within her own company and not with experts.
> ...
> Frequently, students found that the problem they began with was not the problem that needed a solution.
> ...
> As an indication of their increased leadership ability, several of the students were promoted while working on these projects.

Why did a program with such an outstanding track record have to discontinue operations? The dean of the Business School left, and his successor immediately undertook a program to cut costs. Because the action learning program had a rather low enrollment on his yardstick, he decided it was more cost effective to have larger classes and use a lecture hall. On that basis, the program was killed.

The Revans' Institute for Action Learning and Research, University of Salford (UK)

This is yet another case of a program that no longer exists, even though all the signs seemed to point to its continuation over time. Dedicated in 1995 at the University of Salford, Revans himself had a direct hand in its creation, including selection of its first director, David Botham. He was a longtime colleague of Revans. All of Revans' personal papers went to the University of Salford as part of the arrangement.

Several faculty members were hired, including John Morris, someone with a long history with action learning. Donna Vick, who had been a Master's Degree student of the author, became the first Revans' Scholar and was given a full scholarship to receive her Doctoral Degree there. On graduation, she joined the faculty at the Revans Institute. The Institute (originally called a "Centre") offered degrees in action learning at Associate Degree level, as well a Bachelor's Degree, Master's Degree and Doctoral level qualification. The entire curriculum was action learning based. Over the course of the first few years of its existence, it earned a reputation for its research, receiving a five-star rating, the highest academic rating for research in the UK.

Students operated in action learning sets of five or six, and each student had their own project to pursue. They had to be real problems. The project came from within the student's own place of employment. This would be the basis of their research in meeting program requirements. A number of the projects were related to the National Health Service (NHS). However, there was a variety of other client organizations as well and, as time went on, companies began sending in teams of students (Botham and Vick, 1998, pp. 5–16).

It is not surprising that the Revans Institute oriented on Revans' precepts, but there were variations. Revans' emphasis on the unfamiliar – having people work outside their comfort zone – was not followed. Since the students always worked on projects that were from their organizations, of which they were fully cognizant, they were within their normal comfort zone. It is instructive to note that the unfamiliarity component, as important as it was to Revans, is absent from action learning programs in many cases.

The facilitator role was handled on the basis of "invitation only." Once the action learning process was proceeding – such as action learning team meetings – the facilitator would only intervene if invited to do so by the team. However, the facilitator was almost always in the room when the team met. Therefore, there had to be a feeling of being watched, and that can constrain the openness of communication.

What caused the program to decline? There are probably several reasons for the program's demise, but the university's interest in the program seemed to fade, despite high enrollments. It had become a popular degree program. By 2009, the program had closed its doors. The University of Manchester has now created a Revans Academy of Action Learning and Research to take the place of the Institute at the University of Salford but, while it has been dedicated, it is still in the developmental stage (Botham and Vick, 1998).

School of Education, Virginia Commonwealth University

The author created this program in 1994, and it continues to be in place. When the author retired in 2004, another professor, Terry Carter, carried the program forward, continuing the basic course design.

When the author arrived at VCU in 1993, the capstone course of the program was an Adult Education Seminar, which culminated with a comprehensive exam. The purpose of the course seemed ill defined, and students would puzzle over the need for a comprehensive exam that seemed tangential to the objectives of the program. The author, who had met Reg Revans in 1991 and had been in frequent contact with him, persuaded his faculty associates to discontinue the comprehensive exam and begin using an action learning course as the capstone (Dilworth, 1998).

The course, from the beginning, was straight out of Revans' playbook, perhaps more so than any other course in existence. The students operated in action learning teams of four to six. Careful attention was given to team composition. Each team was designed to be as diverse as possible in terms of gender, ethnicity, background and learning styles (determined by administering the Honey–Mumford Learning Style Questionnaire). They were purposely matched with problems and projects that were as far removed from their expertise and prior experience as possible. The author was able to work with organizations in the immediate locale of the university: Washington DC, Roanoke, Virginia and, in one case, Kansas City. Each team project was extremely difficult, even daunting – Revans suggested that the more daunting the problem, the more learning occurs – and usually quite urgent to the organization involved. The problems came from the top of the organization. Here, you see several of Revans' precepts being honored: the problems were as real as you can get, and the students found themselves working on an unfamiliar problem and in an unfamiliar setting.

What is a daunting problem, and what does it mean to put the learner on entirely unfamiliar ground? One semester, one of the teams in my action learning course comprised five women and one man. None had any military experience and most had very little familiarity with human resource development. This team was matched with the largest U.S. naval weapons systems laboratory in the State of Virginia at Dahlgren. The laboratory was the single-largest employer of scientists and engineers in Virginia.

The problem/project this team was given was to advise the laboratory on their HRD programs, and how they could be better geared to help elevate the fighting capabilities of the U.S. navy on the high seas in times of war. Most would agree that this project meets every definition of what can be termed "daunting." The students were in a state of shock after they received their project. They struggled with this challenge but, 14 weeks later, they went into the laboratory and briefed its senior leadership on what they had found and what they recommended. Was it a worthy report? I watched a senior scientist taking notes as quickly as he could write as they presented their findings. The students had struck chords that no one had thought of at the laboratory – which is, of course, Revans' reason for sending people into unfamiliar territory. They do not ask the expert type questions. They ask "fresh questions," which aligns with Revans' Learning Equation and the need to start with questioning inquiry, not an examination of what happened before. It can lead to breakthroughs.

I watched over 30 teams go through this process over a period of 12 years. Many of the problems were at least as challenging as the one I have already described. They involved, for example, design of a worldwide employee recognition program for Time-Life–The Music People, with the students providing 28 "turn key" programs to them, as well as building in the need for cross-cultural sensitivity in dealing with employees in non-U.S. cultures. Another team helped design the first Human Resource Development Handbook for the federal government, working with the Federal Interagency Council on Human Resource Development. Distributed worldwide, 10,000 copies were published, and the Handbook received the Vice-President's Hammer Award for innovations in government.

One team helped the National Academy of Public Administration (NAPA) in Washington develop a national Communications Strategy. Another team worked with one of the major telecommunications companies in reviewing the curriculum of their large corporate university. Another team worked with a US$2 billion computer chip company on shortening the order-to-cash cycle. That company, almost overnight, found that it had lost many of its orders to China and had to close down operations abruptly. One student said: "It does not get any more realistic than this!" Other graduate students went to England to work on complex action learning projects related to the NHS. One team even worked with a major scrap metal firm in Roanoke, Virginia in helping them set up a new company to disassemble 1300 obsolete locomotives for shipment to developing countries.

Not one of the teams failed to deliver. This has continued with Terry Carter at the helm. She has students working on projects with a small radio station (ways to develop more committed and involved listeners); an adult literacy project (gaining greater commitment from learners to stay in the program); and a large stone company, dealing in architectural stone, that has had to downsize because of the economy (how to maintain a committed and engaged workforce as the downsizing takes place).

Other features of the program are maintaining a learning log based on critical incidents to spark reflection: When were you were most engaged, distanced, puzzled or affirmed? The students also set up portfolios to consider and display their best work. Terry Carter has now taken the reflective practise piece and has the students enter it in blogs. The students exchange thoughts about their individual reflections electronically (Carter, 2009).

Here, you see Revans' critical reflection precept being covered. He argued that, ultimately, the largest learning yield comes from the reflective component. The problem, on the other hand, is the "engine of learning."
Facilitation was nonintrusive – another Revans precept. When teams were meeting, I was not there. I would enter the team area and dialogue only by invitation. I wanted their process to go forward uninterrupted. I scheduled meetings with each team (e.g., to talk about the reflective component) so as in no way to interrupt their normal activities. At the start of the course, I "jump-started" their understanding of action learning, including an explanation and demonstration of the process. After that, I monitored what was happening and served, initially, as an intermediary with the client (that role belonged to the team as we moved forward). Every member of the teams was equal. There were no designated leaders –another Revans precept.

At the end of the course, the students turned in a reflective essay covering the dynamics of what had happened in the process and within their team. This was 20 to 25 pages in length. They also turned in a seven-page report on their personal learning, tied to critical incidents during the experience.

In Week 12 of the 15-week semester, they gave me a dress rehearsal of what they proposed to present to the senior managers of the organization. On this one occasion, I "took my gloves off." At all other times, I had assiduously stayed out of the team process and had in no way guided their effort. What they presented had to be their own and a product of their collective effort, not mine. In this one instance, I was critiquing them as the professor, as an experienced business consultant, and someone who has given many presentations to senior leaders. I had them present without interruption. The rule was that every member of the team had to participate in the final 45-minute presentation to top management. Only after they had finished, did I provide my feedback. It was "no holds barred," covering the good, the bad, and the not so good.

I told them that I was not *requiring* them to change anything. *They* needed to decide, and I did not need to see the presentation again until they presented it to the corporate leaders in the 14th week. I did not want to see their final report, which was to be passed to the client at the time of the final oral presentation, ahead of time. They were to pass it to me at the same time that they provided it to the client. I did not advise them on the format of their final report or recommend a format. That was their decision to make. *What I was communicating to them was that I trusted them, and I trusted the process.* There were four dynamics that I counted on:

1. They did not want to disappoint me;
2. They did not want to let the team down;
3. They did not want to disappoint themselves; and
4. They wanted to uphold the reputation of their university.

38   *Robert L. Dilworth*

Table 2.1   Summary of 15-week course

Week 1	Course introduced and action learning explained.
Week 2	Course organization continues.
Week 3	Action learning teams are formed, and their projects announced and explained.
Week 4	Teams meet with the client and discuss mutual expectations.
Week 5	On-site with client to further discuss the nature of the project and to sign a Memorandum of Understanding (MOU) with the client. This covers what students will deliver and what the client is expected to deliver in terms of support.
Weeks 6 and 7	Teams are engaged in working on their problems.
Week 8	Teams go on-site and provide an in-process review to the client.
Weeks 9 to 11	Teams work on projects. Time is set aside for "Hybrid" teams to meet (composed of team members from all teams) to discuss the learning taking place, and to reflect collectively on what is happening.
Week 12	Each team provides a dress rehearsal to the professor, privately.
Week 13	Teams make final refinements to their oral presentations, and finalize their written reports to the client.
Week 14	Final presentation to the client at their place of business.
Week 15	Celebrate success and discuss what happened. Hybrid teams meet for the last time to reflect critically on learning that has occurred. Final essays are turned in.

Collectively, the way the action learning program is organized and orchestrated upholds Revans' most fundamental precept: *Learners are to be empowered.*

Table 2.1 is a summary look at the way the course unfolded, based on my design and the way it was managed, week-by-week.

Conclusion

The examples provided show that action learning can occur in different forms in the educational sector, whether it is in a secondary school system or in higher education. The obstacles that are encountered are quite similar to those that can be encountered in the business sector. When practiced in a robust way, with the problems or projects to be addressed being of true consequence, action learning constitutes an OD change strategy. It tends to jostle the *status quo* and, in some cases, might create significant groundswells. Victoria Marsick, of Columbia University, tells the story of an action learning program being introduced at a major corporation. The leadership set their employees free to challenge established ways of doing business in the process, and they also told the employees they would give them strong sponsorship and support. What the employees came up with frightened the leadership and they quietly quashed the program.

When you set people loose to tackle problems that have defied solution, the people in the organization that could not bring the problem to heel are not likely to be ecstatic when an action learning team solves the problem, especially if the team members have no expertise in the area being examined.

In the educational domain, the reasons for rejecting an action learning program can take a different form. In the case of the three programs I have covered that were terminated, each stemmed, in part, from the fact that they looked different from traditional educational systems and approaches. As in biology, the human organism (call it an "organization") will be inclined to reject any foreign body. We see that in human heart transplants and we see it in organizations, where what seems different can be rejected. For those reasons, and Revans well understood the phenomena – they frustrated him no end, there can be a tendency to practice "safe" action learning. It looks trendy, but does not cause any conflict with existing systems. There are quite a few action learning programs around that conform to this pattern.

The 13 university programs outlined are, for the most part, on the side of robustness. This can be seen in the case of the following examples: Rice University, Hult International Business School, Fremont College, the Erb Institute, Georgia State University (GSU), the University of Texas and the Virginia Commonwealth University. Of the 13 university programs, 10 used joint problem action learning teams, as opposed to individual team member problems from the workplace; the University of Texas, George Washington University, and the University of Salford followed the individual project approach. While the individual project approach can be effective, the learning yield would seem to be somewhat lower. The bonding effect among the learners can be significantly less than is usually true of a joint action learning project, where success depends on cooperative team effort. Revans would refer to this phenomenon as "partner in adversity." On the other hand, the American University Program seems to be quite robust, in that some of the individual problems seem to be extremely substantive.

As pointed out earlier, essentially the unfamiliarity dimension is missing. Also missing, in the case of a number of the programs, is any mention of Revans whatsoever. In some cases, he is not even given a passing reference. The fact that Revans' work has largely been out of print for 20 years contributes to fuzzy awareness about his precepts. None of the universities appears to use teams that have designated leaders. Facilitation of team activity can range widely, from somewhat intensive interventions in the process to limited interventions. However, there seems to be a trend to go with more facilitation, rather than less. I attribute this to three reasons:

- To make certain that critical reflection occurs from a learning perspective;
- A (probable) perceived need to maintain control and avoid unpredictable outcomes, which can be inherent in some Human Resource Management/ Development programs; and
- Consultancy: if you give the learners broad latitude, the client might start to question why he needs the consultant(s), and what constitutes "value added." Therefore, it is played through with abundant interventions by a facilitator to maintain the mystique that you need an expert in order to navigate the action learning process – which is simply not true.

As has been pointed out elsewhere, a facilitator has an important role, but it is not in the area of constant interventions that unnecessarily provide a "crutch" to the learner, and can even constrain their spontaneity and creativity.

Whereas there has been clear movement to bring action learning to higher education, it appears much less pronounced and more tentative in the case of secondary school systems, where teaching methods can be precisely proscribed, with only limited opportunity for experimentation with experiential forms of learning.

If action learning is allowed to take root in educational programs and is nurtured, it can be a key force in improving the quality of education and building the economic competitiveness of the country.

What lessons can we take away from the review of the three failed action learning programs in higher education?

1. You need broad top level support. If the dean/headmaster of the school or the department head involved really do not understand action learning, or oppose it, the program is in jeopardy from the very beginning. This was the "kiss of death" for the University of Texas program. A new dean summarily swept it out of the door in the name of cost effectiveness. Economy of scale was his gauge: lecture hall configurations were cheaper to deal with than classes of 15 students. Learning does not appear to have entered the equation;
2. When action learning is viewed as a novelty or token program, rather than part of the mainstream curriculum, it is probably going to end up being marginalized. What you hope for is that it will become an integral part of the main academic program;
3. You need more than one professor practicing action learning. Someone has to be ready to step forward. This saved the Virginia Commonwealth University and Florida Atlantic University programs, when the original

professor who conceptualized the program and brought it to life retired or transferred to another university. This is what killed the Georgia State University program, plus there was no leader in the school willing to support and sustain the action learning program, or take any steps to keep it viable.

Survival of an action learning program is not the ultimate goal. If the precepts of action learning become so deeply compromised that they are no longer readily identifiable as action learning – in order to avoid conflict and create a state of near absolute harmony with traditional teaching methods – it can be chalked up as a questionable victory.

References

Acker-Hocevar, M. (Washington State University) and Maslin-Ostrowski, P. (Florida Atlantic University) (2009) Teleconference with Robert L. Dilworth on 8 April.

Aubisson, P., Ewing, R. and Hoban, G. (2009) *Action Learning in Schools: Reframing Teachers' Professional Learning and Development* (London: Routledge Education, Taylor & Francis Group.

Botham, D. and Vick, D. (1998) "Action Learning at The Revans Centre", *Performance Improvement Quarterly*, 11(2), pp. 5–16.

Boshyk, Y. and Dilworth, R. L. (forthcoming) *Action Learning: History and Evolution* (Basingstoke: Palgrave Macmillan).

Brooks, Annie (Texas State University) (2009) Interviewed by Robert L. Dilworth on April 14.

Brooks, A. (1998) "Educating Human Resource Development Leaders at the University of Texas, Austin: The Use of Action Learning to Facilitate University–Workforce Collaboration", *Performance Improvement Quarterly*, 11(2), pp. 48–58.

Carter, Terry (School of Education, Virginia Commonwealth University) (2009) Interviewed by Robert L. Dilworth on 14 April.

Davies, B. (Principal of Willetton Senior High School in Western Australia) (1991) Letter to Reg Revans, June 1, on the subject of action learning.

Dilworth, R. and Willis, V. (2003) *Action Learning: Images and Pathways* (Malabar, FL: Krieger).

Dilworth, R. (1998) "Action Learning at Virginia Commonwealth University: Blending Action, Reflection, Critical Incident Methodologies and Portfolio Assessment", *Performance Improvement Quarterly*, 11(2), pp. 17–33.

Dilworth, R. (1998) "Action Learning in a Nutshell", *Performance Improvement Quarterly*, 11(1), pp. 28–43.

Dilworth, R. L. (2010) "Explaining Traditional Action Learning: Concepts and Beliefs," in Y. Boshyk and R. L. Dilworth (eds), *Action Learning: History and Evolution* (Basingstoke, U.K. / Newyork: Palgrave Macmillan), p. 3.

Erb Institute (2009) Available at www.erb.umich.edu (accessed March 5, 2009).

Fremont College. "Action Learning Program". Available at www.fremont.edu/admissions/professional-action-learning (accessed March 5, 2009).

Freire, P. (1987) *A Pedagogy for Liberation* (Massachusetts: Bergen & Garvey).

Gaia University (2009) Action Learning Program. Available at www.gaiauniversity.org (accessed March 5, 2009).

Hult International Business School (2009) "Commentary on its Action Learning Program". Available at www.hult.edu (accessed April 5, 2009).

Kramer, R. (2007/08) "Leading Change through Action Learning", *Public Manager*, 36(3), winter, pp. 38–44.

Kramer, R. (2007) "How Might Action Learning Be Used to Develop the Emotional Intelligence and Leadership Capacity of Public Administrators", *Journal of Public Affairs Education*, 13(2), pp. 205–30.

Lehrer, J. (2009) "Commentary on a Middle School in Pomona, California", *Jim Lehrer News Hour*, PBS, March 20.

Limpus, N. (1991) Letter from "Head Girl" at Willetton Senior High School in Western Australia to Reg Revans, June.

Maital, S., Cizin, S. and Ramon, T. (2002) "Action Learning and National Competitiveness Strategy: A Case Study on the Technion Institute of Management", in Yury Boshyk (ed.), *Action Learning Worldwide* (Basingstoke: Palgrave Macmillan).

Marquardt, M. (George Washington University) (2009) Interviewed by Robert L. Dilworth on April 13.

Marquardt, M. and Carter, T. (1998) "Action Learning and Research at George Washington University", *Performance Improvement Quarterly*, 11(2), pp. 59–71.

National Literacy Act of 1991 (1991) Public Law 102–73) (Washington, DC: s Congress).

Maslin-Ostrowski, P. (FAU) (2009) Teleconference with Robert L. Dilworth on 8 April.

Office of Technology Assessment, US Congress (1991) "Worker Training: Competing in the New International Economy", OTA-ITA-457 (Washington, DC: US Government Printing Office).

Revans, R. (1983) *The ABC of Action Learning* (Bromley, Kent: Chartwell-Bratt).

Rice University (2009) Action Learning Program in the School of Business. Available at www.rice.edu (accessed April 5, 2009).

Jesse H. Jones Graduate School of Management School of Management (2009) Available at www.giving.rice.edu (accessed April 5, 2009).

Willis, V. (Associate Professor Emerita, Georgia State University) (2009) Interviewed by Robert L. Dilworth on April 14.

Willis, V. (1998) "Action Learning: Design Features and Outcomes at Georgia State University", *Performance Improvement Quarterly*, 11(2), pp. 34–47.

Wikipedia (2009) "Jaime Escalante" (former mathematics teacher at Garfield High School in Los Angeles). Available at http://en.wikipedia.org/wiki/Jaime_Escalante (accessed April 12, 2009).

3
Transformative Action Learning in the U.S. Government

Robert Kramer and James L. Kelly

Introduction

From 2002 until 2005, Robert Kramer served as director of the executive leadership Master of Public Administration (MPA) program at American University (AU) in Washington, DC. An executive cohort at AU consisted of about 20 participants, most of whom were senior officials in the US government or military. On taking over as director, Kramer's first challenge was to address the problem of transfer of learning from the classroom to the workplace, a problem that had languished at AU – and at every other university teaching public administration – for decades.

Traditionally, after 20 months of intensive weekend courses, the executive leadership MPA program at AU culminated with a "comprehensive" exam, which required participants to prepare detailed answers in academic writing style, over a 48-hour period, to a set of questions concerning a case study. No matter how hard they tried, however, the faculty who graded the exams could rarely reach consensus on the "right answers" to these questions. Since the case study was always too brief to explore the full context of the problem, and none of the actors identified in the case could be interviewed, faculty always saw the "right answers" through the lens of their functional discipline in public administration – bureaucracy; budgeting; ethics; administrative law; research and evaluation; etc. – leading to interminable disagreements in grading and to not a few near-nervous breakdowns by executive participants.

Kramer decided to abandon this comprehensive exam, the main result of which seemed to be to infantilize adults who were being forced to answer questions about problems they cared nothing about and, in any event, could take no action to resolve. But what should take its place? After much reflection, he chose to replace the exam with business-driven action learning (Boshyk, 2002). He would require each of his participants to negotiate a "learning contract" with him and an executive sponsor for the conduct of a real-time work-related project involving real risk and real results.

The purpose of the executive MPA, as Kramer reframed it, was not merely to "master" the intellectual knowledge contained in the academic silos of public administration: administrative law, human resource management, statistics, policy evaluation, budgeting, etc. He would continue to invite executive participants to study public administration through the traditional lenses and vocabularies of each of these functional courses. According to Robert Kegan (2000), functional courses such as these are valuable since they represent "learning aimed at increasing our fund of knowledge, at increasing our repertoire of skills, at extending already established cognitive capacities"(p. 48). This is what Kegan calls "informational learning" – learning that deepens our knowledge about an *existing* frame of reference. "Such learning is literally in-*form*-ative because it seeks to bring valuable new contents *into* the existing *form* of our way of knowing" (*ibid.*, p. 49).

However, learning of this kind, no matter how useful, does not encourage an epistemological transformation in learners. It is not "transformational learning," which, according to Kegan (2000), radically shifts the frame of knowing itself by questioning the taken-for-granted assumptions of the existing epistemology. This is "trans-*form*-ative" learning, where the frame of reference itself – the "form" of knowing – undergoes a radical and discontinuous shift. Informational learning, although valuable because it can stimulate "a change in behavioral repertoire or an increase in the quantity or fund of knowledge" (*ibid.*, p. 48), cannot stimulate a shift in mindset. In essence, informational learning is closely correlated with the received wisdom, accepted beliefs, standard models or prevailing ideologies held by public administration academics.

By adopting action learning, Kramer revisioned his purpose as an executive educator to grow *learning leaders in public service*. What, exactly, are the characteristics of a learning leader?

- A learning leader is a person who models inquiry and critical reflection while grappling, under conditions of high anxiety, with wicked public problems when no one knows what to do but immediate action must be taken.
- A learning leader is a person who learns all the time, not merely for the purpose of applying one of the functional tools of public administration to get a job done.
- A learning leader is a person who is willing to challenge conventional wisdom and unlearn assumptions and beliefs that have outlived their value.
- A learning leader is a person who demonstrates a high level of sensitivity to the anxiety others (especially subordinates) may experience in learning, and who possesses the emotional intelligence (i.e., self-awareness, courage, creative will and empathy) to enable others to learn and unlearn.

These characteristics of a learning leader led Kramer to formulate a second, equally vital outcome for executive education: in addition to learning leaders, he was going to develop *teaching leaders in public service*. What does a teaching leader teach? Not programmed knowledge or the conventional wisdom found in public administration texts or learned through pre-packaged experiential exercises or role plays. By definition, programmed knowledge deals only with past solutions to past problems, and it is insufficient for those who need to learn continually under conditions of "permanent white water" (Vaill, 1996), when fresh problems arise that have never been considered by anyone and, therefore, cannot possibly have programmed answers (Heifetz, 1994).

So, what does a teaching leader teach? A teaching leader teaches – in day-to-day, face-to-face relationships with subordinates, peers and superiors in the workplace – *"learning as a way of being"* (Vaill, 1996). Learning leaders, in short, model the way for others to learn and unlearn continually. Therefore, Kramer required each executive participant to *teach the action learning model to others inside their organization*. As they taught action learning to other organizational stakeholders, they were stretching their capacity to lead. Not surprisingly, as they got better at teaching, they would find that they were *learning how to lead*. Learning how to teach would constitute, in part, learning how to lead. And learning how to lead would merge, finally, into learning how to learn and unlearn.

The US$4 billion comprehensive exam

In the US Department of Army, the Assistant Secretary for Acquisition, Logistics and Technology (AS) develops, acquires, fields and sustains most of the Army's war fighting capabilities. These capabilities include everything from basic soldier support to space-based intelligence systems.

To perform this mission, AS manages the Army's capabilities programs throughout each phase of their entire lifecycle. Key phases of the lifecycle include:

- Concept and technology development
- System development and demonstration
- Production and fielding
- Operations, support and disposal.

Despite its total lifecycle responsibilities, AS strives almost exclusively towards achieving early lifecycle outcomes such as development and production costs, technical performance, and schedule.

However, this over-emphasis on achieving early lifecycle outcomes often has detrimental impacts on later outcomes such as availability, reliability, and affordability. These impacts are the result of the organizational history, processes, and culture of AS, which values the rapid development and production of new capabilities over sustainment of fielded capabilities. This unequal emphasis has three negative ramifications for the fielded capabilities of the U.S. Army:

- Failure to meet availability requirements
- Failure to meet reliability requirements
- Failure to meet operating and support budgets.

James Kelly was a senior acquisition logistician working in AS and a participant in the executive leadership MPA program at American University. Kelly sensed the Army's growing frustration with the performance of AS. Wanting to take action, Kelly persuaded the Deputy Assistant Secretary of the Army for Acquisition, Logistics and Technology (DAS) to sponsor a business-driven action learning project. Kelly believed that by applying action learning, DAS could be transformed to reframe the acquisition logistics mission of AS to unlearn bad habits and improve the organization's overall performance.

The problem

AS is a relatively new organization within the U.S. Department of the Army. AS did not exist before 1988 because the former staff structure separated the research, development, and acquisition responsibilities for the Army's new capabilities programs from the sustainment responsibilities for its fielded capabilities programs. Under this structure, the Secretary of the Army for Research, Development and Acquisition was only responsible for achieving the early lifecycle outcomes. Not surprisingly, a separate staff organization, the Deputy Chief of Staff for Logistics, was responsible for achieving the later lifecycle outcomes. This separation of the staff responsibilities caused the two organizations to work in near isolation. At times, the two groups worked against each other. Recognizing this deficiency, defense acquisition reformers of the 1990s worked with both the Secretary of Defense and the U.S. Congress to restructure Army Headquarters. The aim of this restructuring effort was to create a new staff organization chartered with total lifecycle responsibilities.

In 1998, this new organization formally became AS and, in 2002, the Army enhanced the organization by adding acquisition logistics to DAS. However, when Kelly began his action learning initiative the restructuring efforts had not fully achieved their desired results. Although the Army had an organization chartered with total lifecycle responsibilities, AS was slow to unlearn old beliefs and behaviors, and embrace its new mission. Despite some six years of trying, the Army was still experiencing the same problems with its fielded capabilities. These problems challenged the

Army's ability to meet the relentless demands of the ongoing global war on terror.

Enter Chinook

As a top official in DAS, Kelly wanted to address these problems, especially in the aviation programs for which he was responsible. He also wanted to improve the acquisition logistics processes of AS so that they would not result in the same problems as other fielded capabilities programs. Moreover, he wanted to improve the organizational and cultural deficiencies that were at the root of these problems. However, he knew that addressing all the problems within AS – structural, political and cultural – would be an overwhelming task. He also knew that because AS manages hundreds of capabilities programs across all phases of the lifecycle, it would be difficult to address so many programs within the time constraints of his American University graduation deadline in May 2004.

He decided, therefore, to address the typical problems associated with a single capabilities program. By focusing on one problem, he hoped to find actionable solutions that would be useful for other programs, as well as the entire AS organization. In addition, he sought a project requiring action during the calendar year, adding urgency and risk elements, and enabling the possibility of achieving tangible near-term results.

After researching many candidate programs, Kelly chose the US$4 billion modernization program for the Army's CH-47F Chinook Cargo Helicopter. ("Chinook" refers to the Chinook people of the Pacific Northwest of the

Illustration 3.1   CH-47D Chinook helicopter

United States.) The primary mission of the Chinook helicopter is to move troops, artillery, ammunition, fuel, water, barrier materials, supplies and equipment on the battlefield. Its secondary mission is medical evacuation, disaster relief, search and rescue, aircraft recovery, fire fighting, parachute drops, heavy construction and civil development. The CH-47F can fly at speeds of over 175 mph with a payload of 21,000 lbs (9,530 kg). In 2008, Chinook helicopters logged over 90,000 flight hours in the war zones of Iraq and Afghanistan, fought forest fires across California, provided food and shelter relief to victims of flood and earthquake disasters around the world, and rescued climbers stranded in a snowstorm above 10,000 feet on Mount Ranier in the western U.S.

Modernization would provide future Army and Joint Force Commanders with an improved heavy lift helicopter capability by upgrading 529 of the Army's 40-year-old CH-47D Chinook helicopters. Upgrades include adding a new digital cockpit, flight controls and avionics, more powerful turbine engines, a reduced vibration fuselage, and several other enhancements. Together, these upgrades result in a better-than-new CH-47F helicopter with an expected 20-year service-life extension. These upgrades also improve the helicopter's high altitude hot temperature performance margins (critical for flight in Afghanistan and Iraq), enhance its joint interoperability, and reduce its operating and support costs compared with the CH-47D helicopter. In addition, 72 Special Operations Forces (SOF) variants of the helicopter provide a long range capability to insert or extract SOF troops anywhere in the world.

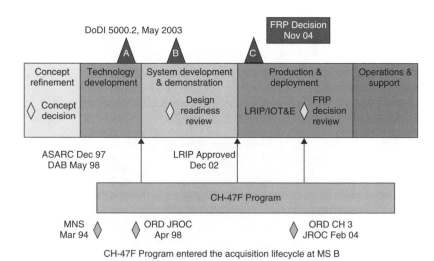

Figure 3.1   Reframing acquistion logistics – a generic overview

Examining the CH-47F program schedule in detail, Kelly discovered that AS had already made most of the milestone decisions for the early phases of the lifecycle. In addition, the U.S. Army and the Boeing Company had already completed the helicopter's development and flight-testing. Because of the successful milestones and tests, the Army awarded Boeing an initial production contract for the first lot of seven helicopters in December 2002. To date, the initial production had been proceeding quite well.

Accordingly, the only major milestone remaining was the full-rate production (FRP) decision scheduled for November 2004. Kelly also discovered that, in typical fashion, AS had focused its CH-47F program objectives on achieving early lifecycle outcomes (production costs, schedule, and technical performance) rather than later lifecycle objectives: availability, reliability, and operating and support costs. Based on past experiences, Kelly believed that this focus would likely result in the CH-47F helicopter experiencing similar problems found in the Army's other fielded capabilities. "How can I help transform the mindset of Army acquisition logistics?" Kelly wondered. "How can I help my colleagues unlearn what is no longer useful?"

Considering the CH-47F program's history, objectives and schedule, Kelly certainly could have chosen something easier for his action learning project. However, he would be playing an important role in meeting the FRP decision milestone. He wanted to do a better job with his part of the milestone so that the CH-47F would not experience the typical problems after fielding. With this in mind, he decided the program's tight schedule and flawed objectives presented an opportunity to test action learning and improve his overall contribution to the milestone. He also wanted to transform the acquisition process for future aviation capabilities programs, while enhancing the overall AS organization.

Results

In mid-December 2003, Kelly's first step was to meet with the DAS to introduce him to action learning and to secure sponsorship for the project. His next step was to meet with various Army staff and CH-47F program officials to gain their support and to solicit from them ideas about the problems. With sponsorship and support in hand, his final step was to select members of the action learning team, listening closely to their ideas and verifying their commitment to the project. In doing so, he picked a team of four all-stars, who would bring key experiences to the table:

• The DAS Policy Division Logistician was an expert at formulating and applying Army and Defense Department acquisition policy and procedures
• The DAS Combat Systems Logistician was proficient at establishing and conducting capabilities program testing and evaluation

- The Acting DAS Combat Support Systems Division Chief was skilled in the requirements-generation process; and, finally
- The DAS Resources, Oversight and Analysis Division Chief was a skilled practitioner of the Defense budget process.

As a result of these meetings and initial feedback, Kelly set near-, mid- and long-term objectives. First, he would use the action learning process to help improve his contribution to the CH-47F FRP decision so that the Army could unlearn its standard operating procedures and minimize the typical post-fielding problems with the helicopter (near-term). Second, he would build on the near-term learning results in order to improve the acquisition process for future aviation capabilities programs (mid-term). Finally, he would build on these transformative learning results in order to reframe the overall acquisition logistics mission of AS (long-term).

In order to demonstrate his capacity as a learning leader, Kelly began to teach action learning to the team before formally starting the project. He spent a significant amount of time helping one member of the team to become a learning coach. Kelly and the coach worked through several days of one-on-one sessions, practicing open-ended questioning techniques, facilitator skills, and problem-solving drills. All told, the team's training and preparation took about 30 days, from mid-January to mid-February 2004.

With the training and preparation complete, the action learning team met for the first time on February 26, 2004. To start the meeting, Kelly acted as the learning coach and another member of the team presented a simple, but real problem for the team to unpack. The problem involved the team member's dilemma over how to use a "free" airline ticket that was due to expire in just a few days. Within 20 minutes of open-ended questioning and dialogue, Kelly knew the team's training and preparation had paid-off. Members quickly determined that the real problem was not deciding how the team member should use the airline ticket, but rather how his family should determine its travel priorities. This was a powerful experience of group unlearning, learning and relearning in action. After a few more minutes of questioning, the team suggested several solutions and the team member was able to act on both the free airline ticket and his family's travel priorities. Following the practice session, Kelly became the problem owner and another team member served as learning coach.

Kelly presented the problems and challenges related to the CH-47F program, explaining that his overall desire was to allow the Chinook to enter FRP, but not experience the typical problems after fielding. After about two hours of questioning, the team agreed that Kelly's immediate problem was deciding how to do a better job at a routine task – making a better logistics contribution to the CH-47F FRP milestone. Upon agreeing on the problem, the team mapped out an initial problem-solving strategy. This included developing, scheduling and conducting a comprehensive integrated logistics support (ILS) review before the milestone. The team felt that the ILS review should cover all of the program's logistics elements, as well as its operating and support cost budgets and its post-fielding evaluation plan (none existed).

With significant learning accomplished, the learning coach closed the meeting by posing several questions, which the team agreed to answer via email after a couple of days of individual reflection. The answers to these questions and the time for reflection allowed Kelly to develop a draft ILS review framework, addressing all of the team's recommendations.

With the draft ILS review framework completed, Kelly met with the CH-47F Army Systems Acquisition Review Council Integrated Product Team (IPT) on March 3, 2004. The IPT is a team of senior Army staff officials who would prepare the CH-47F program for the formal FRP decision milestone in November. During this meeting, Kelly informed the members that he wanted to improve his logistics contribution to the milestone. He also presented his draft ILS review framework, which by now included both aircraft system elements (safety, suitability and supportability), and key logistics support elements (supportability strategy, business case, support cost budget, and post-fielding evaluation plan). He explained to the IPT that he would use this framework to conduct his assessment of the CH-47F program and to formulate his position for the FRP decision.

After Kelly presented his plan, some of the IPT members, especially the CH-47F program logisticians, were clearly uncomfortable with what he was proposing. They explained that, with so much of the program's effort focused on early outcomes, they had little influence on the program's later outcomes. They also made it clear the program would likely face similar post-fielding problems as previous programs had, and that there was little that they could do to change the situation.

However, after further conversation, the IPT agreed that conducting a formal ILS review (using the ILS framework) before the FRP decision would assess the post-fielding potential of the program. If the assessment were negative, the IPT could take steps to improve the program before fielding. Having the IPT validate the ILS review strategy gave Kelly a tremendous boost of confidence. He related his confidence to the rest of the action learning team at its next meeting on March 15, 2004. The positive feedback energized the team, and they began to develop the ILS review for the CH-47F program.

After some powerful questioning, everyone felt that the ILS review should establish measurable goals and objectives for the operations and support phases of the lifecycle, along with a meaningful evaluation plan. All felt the evaluation plan should consider both helicopter system elements and support system elements. They also felt the ILS framework should include an analysis of the financial resources required for this phase of the lifecycle – from budget submission, through execution, and audit. As the project owner,

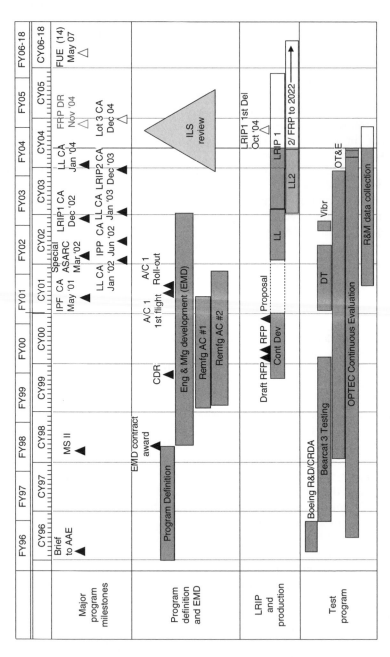

Figure 3.2 Reframing acquisition logistics – specific to the CH-47D

Kelly felt this framework could support all three phases of the project: near-, mid-, and long-term.

By late March 2004, Kelly's action learning team and the IPT settled into a biweekly meeting schedule. The two teams continued to support each other until the CH-47F FRP decision milestone was made in November 2004.

The action learning team's results were impressive. First, they helped Kelly verify the problem and establish a realistic problem-solving strategy. Second, they helped Kelly develop the ILS review framework, which established new policies and procedures for guiding Army capabilities programs throughout the acquisition lifecycle. Third, they helped Kelly apply the ILS review framework to the CH-47F program and improved his contribution to reducing the typical post-fielding problems. Finally, the team helped Kelly prepare to accomplish the other project objectives, for which the ILS review framework would drive changes that reframe the acquisition logistics mindset of AS (long-term).

In August 2008, the Boeing Company was awarded a five-year U.S. Army contract valued at US$4.3 billion for 191 CH-47F Chinooks, plus options for an additional 24 aircraft over the course of the contract.

Transformative learning

Kelly unlearned, learned and relearned a great deal about himself and his organization. While he had always been an effective leader in the very structured hierarchical environment typical of the U.S. Department of Defense, action learning forced him to lead in situations where he had no formal authority and where he had to rely on others for both resources and action. Experiencing a huge shift in bureaucratic mindset, he was forced to unlearn his already successful leadership approach and develop and use new leadership skills – especially brokering, coaching, and facilitating. He dealt with unforeseen challenges ranging from facilitating meetings for senior executives (surprisingly difficult) to leading and coaching peers so that they could meet the FRP decision milestone (surprisingly easy). Over the course of the project, Kelly's leadership style evolved from being "in charge" to working himself "out of a job." He took great pleasure in helping his work teams become self-led groups.

Kelly also learned much about the structure, people, politics and culture of AS, an organization that was still too inflexible and resistant to change, despite the many compelling reasons to transform itself – the end of the cold war, expanding roles and missions, smaller defense budgets, and the often poor performance of the Army's fielded capabilities. As a relatively new senior official on the acquisition logistics team, Kelly had a mindset that largely reflected that of a 20-year Army aviator and test pilot in the field. While he was used to seeing the results of acquisitions decisions for various Army aviation capabilities, he was not used to questioning the activities, policies and processes that led up to those decisions. The power of action learning was in the questions, which promoted learning, unlearning and relearning.

Why did business-driven action learning work so well? All the members of the team had a stake in improving the outcomes for the project and all fully shared in the risk of failing. Kelly discovered that it was relatively easy to employ action learning throughout the U.S. Department of Defense, formally and informally. The ILS review ensured that any logistics support contracts for the Chinook would be performance-based. Applying action learning to other aviation programs has produced meaningful results outside the Chinook initiative. For example, following the Army's termination of the RAH-66 Comanche Helicopter, Kelly has now successfully applied action learning and ILS review to three of the Army's Comanche replacement programs – light armored reconnaissance, a light utility helicopter, and the future cargo aircraft.

References

Boshyk, Y. (ed.) (2002) *Action Learning Worldwide: Experiences of Leadership and Organizational Development* (New York: Palgrave Macmillan).

Heifetz, R. (1994) *Leadership Without Easy Answers* (Cambridge: Belknap Press of Harvard University Press).

Kegan, R. (2000) "What 'Form' Transforms? A Constructive-Developmental Approach to Transformative Learning", in J. Mezirow and Associates (eds.), *Learning as Transformation: Critical Perspectives on a Theory in Progress* (San Francisco: Jossey-Bass), pp. 35–69.

Vaill, P. B. (1996) *Learning as a Way of Being: Strategies for Survival in a World of Permanent White Water* (San Francisco: Jossey-Bass).

4
Action Learning in the Military

Robert L. Dilworth

Introduction

I travel out of two streams of thought in writing this chapter. The first relates to over 31 years of active military experience in the United States Army, including service as a general officer. The second is an 18-year association with action learning, including a close friendship with Reg Revans, the principal pioneer of action learning. These two streams interplay throughout, and I ended up being surprised by how much they mirror one another.

There are several core ingredients you look for in a full expression of action learning. They include a real problem that is difficult to deal with; a team of no more than four to eight people; equality within the team; empowerment of the team to solve the problem; starting with questioning insight rather than past solutions; where possible, placing people outside their comfort zone (unfamiliar setting, unfamiliar problem, unfamiliar associates); and having the learners critically reflect on the experience.

Having worked with many action learning teams that met these tests, I can attest to just how powerful a tonic this can be. Problems that had previously resisted resolution can tumble, and individuals can acquire a much greater sense of self-confidence, having helped overcome a difficult challenge. It is a highly effective way of developing leaders, and the learning that occurs as a result of critical reflection can increase the capacity of both individuals and organizations to deal with future challenges.

One major takeaway from my experience in the military and with action learning is that it does not need to be labeled action learning to be action learning. Some would disagree with this premise, but it is results you are after, and if the results are there and cover most of the bases that are ascribed to action learning, that would seem to meet the tests. From a phenomenological point of view, we learn that a simple question can bring clarity to an issue – "What's happening?" To put it in the vernacular, "If it looks like a duck, walks like a duck and quacks like a duck, it is probably a duck." Revans understood that action learning can occur naturally, and would point to small children at play as an example of action learning. He also realized that this freedom of thought was often altered later by a formalistic and didactic educational experience that could dull the senses in terms of curiosity and spontaneity. Label was much less important to Revans than results. He also understood that action learning can take many different forms and is influenced by the cultural context. He did insist though that it be authentic in terms of being truly empowering, and that it include most of the general dimensions just outlined.

There is probably no institution in the world where action learning is more evident than the U.S. military. It is hard-wired into its genes. It is also pervasive. Much of what happens is centered on small teams and, while they usually have an assigned leader, it is a case of team members helping each other solve very difficult problems, especially exigencies of the moment. In the combat forces of the Army and Marines, you are dealing at the lower rank levels with fire teams and squads that are typically action learning team size. It can also involve a pull-together of small groups to grapple with major problems, something that occurs frequently. In the Air Force, it can be the crew of a B-52 Bomber. In the Navy, it can be small teams of Navy SEALS (Sea, Air, Land), a Special Forces Organization.

Some case examples

Let me now turn to some actual case examples, and you can judge each against the core ingredients in action learning that I have outlined.

Navy SEAL Team 10 (Afghanistan)

A Navy SEAL Team of four was inserted by helicopter in eastern Afghanistan and the Hindu-Kush Mountains, very steep and treacherous terrain. Their mission was to kill a high ranking Taliban leader. Even though well-camouflaged, a small group of sheepherders, boys in their teens, stumbled into their position. They were from a Taliban-controlled village. The decision the team had to immediately make was what to do with the sheepherders. One option was to kill them to avoid compromising an important mission. By simple majority vote, each as an equal, they decided to let them go if they promised to remain silent about what they had observed. The sheepherders gave them their word, even though the SEAL Team believed they would rush to tell the other members of their village. It was a matter of human decency. You did not kill innocent noncombatants.

Within an hour, the Navy SEAL Team was surrounded by the Taliban, even though they had changed their location since release of the sheepherders and re-concealed themselves. A fierce firefight ensued in which the Navy SEALs, although badly outnumbered, killed many of the Taliban attackers. One of the Navy SEAL's, already wounded multiple times, purposely exposed himself to enemy fire in order to call in air support and was killed. Only one of member of the SEAL Team, Marcus Luttrell, was able to escape and evade capture, and was ultimately rescued by Army Rangers.

When you read the account of what happened, it is a study in a small team doing everything in its power to solve a pressing problem by working together (Luttrell, 2007). The SEAL teams are regularly thrust into unfamiliar environments in discharging extremely challenging missions. They are often operating independently, as was the case with Navy SEAL Team 10, and are fully empowered. It is a case of shared decision-making within the team, as in the case of the sheepherders.

One of the SEALs in this example received the Congressional Medal of Honor posthumously and the other three members of the team received the Navy Cross, the second highest decoration for bravery. The President of the United States presented the medal to the lone survivor, Petty Officer First Class Lutrell.

What you find in this example meets a number of the basic tenets of action learning, and the account provided by Marcus Luttrell in *Lone Survivor* (2007) certainly covers the area of critical reflection.

A truck problem (South Korea)

This example is from my personal experience. I was traveling in a jeep with another officer on a remote road in South Korea. We came upon a two-and-a-half ton truck that had broken down. The fuel line had severed and the three junior ranking U.S. Army enlisted men had only a few simple tools and no replacement parts. We offered to squeeze them into the jeep and take them to their base camp. In response, they said "We haven't figured out what to do yet, but we must get this truck running and back to base by sundown!" We stayed with them to make sure that they didn't end up stranded. They made it clear that we should stay out of their way. They were going to solve the problem themselves!

I remember what happened vividly. They engaged in a highly animated and intense dialogue, asking questions of each other, and throwing out ideas. Suddenly, several of their ideas came together and crystallized into a plan. One emptied a large can of peaches and cut out both ends. That became the connection piece for the broken line. With a pair of pliers, they crimped the can around the line so it fitted snugly. They then wrapped bailing wire around it and duct tape to further secure it. When they started the engine, they found that their fix had held and was working. They thanked us for staying with them, and then with a last wave, they roared down the dusty road towards their base camp.

Some will undoubtedly argue that this is simply not action learning. It did not last long enough – just a matter of a few hours. Second, there is no reflection evident. They would be right on both counts. But there are some other ingredients that are strongly in evidence. They felt empowered to fix the problem. In their view, they had to get the truck running. They operated as equals, and they began with questioning insight. There was no template for how to deal with this kind of problem. It was also an unfamiliar problem. There were some important threads of action learning present.

Computer response problem (Fort Monroe, Virginia)

This is the personal example that, more than any other, demonstrated to me the power of action learning. It was a daunting problem that defied the odds. I was serving as the Deputy Chief of Staff for Base Operations Support for the Army's Training and Doctrine command, a major command with worldwide responsibilities, based at Fort Monroe, Virginia. There were about 400 people on my staff, a mix of uniformed military and Army civilian employees. Everyone had a desktop computer and performed much of their work online.

One day I noticed that my screen image was turning over very slowly. It was irritating, and I realized that, when considered in relation to the many transactions I was involved with daily, it represented a drag weight on my productivity. My next move was to check various workstations in my organization. They were experiencing the same problem, but had accepted it as an unavoidable problem. I saw it differently. When you added up the level of inefficiency across the organization caused by this computer-related glitch, it represented hundreds of hours lost in terms of productivity every day.

I called in my computer experts, who felt that they could readily fix the problem. As it turned out, they could not run the problem to earth. Therefore, I called in representatives from the regional office of the large international computer services company that had our account. After a half-day of examining our computer systems, they told me there was both good news and bad news. The good news was that the problem could be fixed. That was obviously no surprise. The bad news was that it would cost US$6 million to fix the problem. In delivering their report to me they were arrogant, matter of fact, and were saying in effect, "Take it or leave it. There are no other options."

The next day I wrote a letter to the Chief Executive Officer of the corporation in New York, told him I was extremely disappointed in the way his company was servicing its accounts, would think twice about renewing our contract with them, and just might suggest to other large organizations at the headquarters that they also look elsewhere for their computer services. Three days later, when I arrived at my office at 7:00 am, there were three gentlemen in business suits waiting for me from the company. They had been flown in from New York to meet with me. They apparently had been told to adopt the "best bedside manner" and they were extremely polite. They spent the better part of a day checking the computer systems. At the end of the day, they said the problem could be fixed but, as their Regional office had already told me, it would cost US$6 million.

After the corporate representatives had left, I weighed my options. There were two obvious ones. I could either live with the problem or come up with US$6 million to get it fixed, money that I did not have and could not justify because of other pressing funding priorities. Living with the mediocrity was not an option I wished to consider. I decided on a third alternative, and when I look back on it, it seems darn right crazy. Having had some success mentoring and working with management interns in earlier assignments, and remembering what they had been able to do when set loose to explore and test their abilities, I called in my 22 management interns from across 14 directorates. Some only knew each other casually, others had never met, and none had worked together before. None had been involved with any major troubleshooting, and only two of the interns were being trained as computer specialists, and they were not that far along in their development track. None of them had any deep computer expertise. They did have two things in common. They were very smart and eager to learn. That is why we had hired them.

I told them I had an interesting learning opportunity for them, if they were interested in accepting it. If they did not agree to pursue it, there would be no hard feelings – after all, what I was inviting them to do had been deemed undoable by the experts – three teams of them in succession – without a considerable outlay of funds. I explained the problem to them in detail and then told them I was willing to turn it over to them to solve. I also told them that while I was not a computer systems expert, I had a hunch that the problem could be fixed for a great deal less than US$6 million. They were very quiet after I finished. "Stunned" is probably the operative word.

After giving them an hour to deliberate, I returned to my office to receive their decision. While all were equal, without any leader designated, and it stayed that way, they had decided on a spokesperson. They had considered the offer carefully, and decided the problem could not get worse, and therefore they would take it on and see what they could do. They were also excited about taking it on.

I told them the rules of engagement as they moved forward:

1. They were fully empowered. I trusted their judgment.
2. If anyone tried to place obstacles in their path, they were to tell me and I would remove them.
3. They did not need to provide me with any updates.
4. If they needed any form of support, I would try to provide it, short of any large sum of money.
5. I would not be hovering over their shoulder.
6. They should try to resolve it as soon as possible, but should not feel rushed.

When the word traveled through the organization of the assignment I had given the interns, some considered it extremely irregular, even "cruel and unusual." However, they should have taken note that the management interns, while certainly challenged, were not intimidated by the problem. They were highly energized by it, and they mustered all of their intellectual gifts and experience in working together in harmony to solve it.

Their first action was to call a meeting of the team to get organized and break down their effort into sub-teams (equivalent to action learning teams). As they were about to begin the first meeting several of our computer experts showed up at the meeting place. The team said, "Why are you here?" The computer experts said that they were there to help in any way possible. The team asked them if they had been able to solve the problem. They, of course, responded that they had not been able to solve it. The team then told them, "Please leave. If we need your assistance, we will ask for it!"

A month later, the computer problem had been fixed, and it had not cost a single penny beyond the time spent by the interns in working on the problem. The team set up a briefing for me. They wanted to explain what they had learned and how they arrived at the solution. The organizational grapevine quickly picked up on the event. We had to use a large conference room, and even at that it was standing room only. The regional representatives from the computer servicing company were there, as were their corporate team from New York. There was great curiosity about how this team of novices had seemingly accomplished what seemed impossible.

It seemed apparent in listening to the management interns brief their solution that they had explored avenues that had not been covered by others. In fact, at one point in their presentation, they turned to the computer experts and said, "You were looking for solutions in the wrong places." They had found an array of causal factors, rather than any single problem driver. It was a series of small adjustments that had brought the responsiveness of the computers up to standard. As Edward Deming, the guru of quality management would say, "It is a matter of controlling the variations." That is what they had done.

Since other major organizations at Fort Monroe might be prone to the same type of problem, the management intern team visited the organizations. They found that the exact same problem was occurring across the board. I had not assigned them that task, but the interns considered it as an implied mission, and they were right. As the interns stated, the overall computer system is only as fast as the slowest horse. If our organizational computers were blazing fast, and the other systems were significantly slower, it would hold us back. Therefore, they fixed the entire computer system.

They next amortized the time it would take to recover the cost of their time to work on the problem, and were able to show that the system would be "in the black" within six months. The team also gave careful consideration to what they had learned, and several classed it as the best learning experience of their lives.

What can you take away from this problem-solving in terms of action learning:

1. Because the interns did not know a great deal about computers, they were induced to ask fresh questions.
2. The problem was real, even daunting, and once they accepted responsibility for the project, they were expected to solve it.
3. They did not know enough to start with customary troubleshooting techniques. They invented their own process.
4. They drew heavily on the intellectual resources of the intern team itself.
5. They were absolutely certain of top management support and backing.
6. They were fully empowered to act, just like the Navy SEAL Team had been.
7. Throughout they operated as equals. There was no leader. They were all leaders at something as the project unfolded.
8. They never seemed to doubt that they would solve the problem.

All the fundamental action learning precepts were followed in this problem-solving.

The Army as a learning organization

The case examples provided present a picture of how action learning can be related to the U.S. military, including some personal examples from my own military career. I now turn to more institutionalized examples of action learning, with a spotlight on the Army.

What will be presented also relates to one aspect that we identify in Chapter 18, on the future of action learning. We believe that technology has now advanced to the point that there is a case for a reinterpretation of Revans' iron clad rule that the problem to be solved in action learning must be real in every sense of the word. For that reason, he believed that any use of simulations violated that basic principle of action learning.

The question now becomes, "How do you define what is real?" That can remind us of the Greek philosopher Socrates' classic question, "What is truth?" What I will be outlining, including the highly sophisticated use of computer technology, is very real to those who are engaged in the learning experience, and every bit as motivating as something that is entirely real and must be dealt with in real time. In fact, the simulations and approaches to be outlined are the very essence of reality – what can be expected on the modern battlefield against a determined and well-trained enemy, and how you overcome the most severe challenges. They are also done in real time.

The National Training Center (NTC) at Fort Irwin California

This vast training landscape for the Army is located in the Mojave Desert. It is one of the Army training centers where the combat units of the U.S. Army train for war. No combat battalion was cleared for deployment during the first Gulf War without first undergoing a baptism of fire at NTC, and not all were found ready for deployment. Systems were used that employed infrared technology in order that both friendly and enemy personnel casualties and equipment losses could be recorded. Infrared devices were mounted on weapons, and troops and equipment had associated devices so that "hits" could be recorded. When a soldier was hit by enemy fire, the device on his uniform would alert him, and he was then out of the fight (although he could be recycled back in later as a replacement).

The one-week, night-and-day operation, with little opportunity for sleep, pitted U.S Army battalions and brigade sized task forces against opposing forces (OPFOR). The opposing forces significantly outnumbered the U.S. and allied forces in the engagement by a wide margin, and were well-trained and equipped to Russian standards (the Iraqi Army was using Russian doctrine and equipment). They were also totally familiar with the terrain, while friendly forces in the exercise had never been on the ground there before.

General Gordon Sullivan (Sullivan and Harper, 1996) refers to OPFOR in this instance as "world class opposing forces." OPFOR personnel wear distinctive uniforms similar to those worn by our potential opponents on a real battlefield. This one-week exercise was unscripted and entirely free-flowing, with highly unpredictable outcomes. It was a true test of stamina, will and combat-related skills. Army personnel returning from the first Iraq War could be heard to say, "The battles in Iraq [some of the largest tank battles since World War II] were 'a piece of cake' next to the experience at NTC. What we did at NTC was really challenging!" One soldier said, "When the going got really tough, my NTC training experience kicked in and carried me through." The training and realism have only improved over the years, and it is reflected in the peak readiness of U.S. Army units that are now deploying to Iraq, Afghanistan and elsewhere.

I can recall a personal anecdote about NTC. In 1989, I was chosen to address the class of the Hungarian Command and General Staff College in Budapest Hungary as part of the first senior officer exchange program between the two countries since the Iron Curtain had been put in place. Hungary was still a member of the Warsaw Pact, and the Berlin Wall was just beginning to come down. Minutes before I was to address the class, the Commandant of the college informed me that there had been a "slight change" in the program. He said, "There will be a number of Russian officers in the audience." During the question and answer period following the lecture, a Russian Officer stood up and said "Tell me about your National Training Center. I understand that you have forces dressed like us that you do battle with as part of the exercise. Why is that?" I told him that was true, because in the event of a war we planned to overcome their tactics and beat them handily!

You might say at this point, "How can this be considered action learning, when you had entire battalions involved, with hundreds of troops?" You have to remember that there were many small teams, including at squad level, that were in the fight and living this very realistic experience. But there is a bigger point. When use of action learning is prevalent in the texture of what is occurring throughout, where do you draw the line at what is and what is not action learning? Do you say that only the smaller formations, like squads, are practicing action learning, or do you concede that the entire organization is working out of an action learning playbook? Can't an entire organization be a learning organization? When I think of a company like GE, I say "Yes." The same holds true for the U.S. Army.

There were many anecdotes that can be gleaned from the NTC experience. In one instance, the battalion leadership was decimated in a battle. As some generals watched the engagement through binoculars, they could sense what was happening. They watched a corporal step forward and take command of the battalion. One of the general's commented, "Damn. Are they good!" That certainly seems like action learning.

NTC is only one of the Army training centers using such realistic scenarios. There is also a Joint Readiness Training Center at Fort Polk, Louisiana. This type of realistic training and learning has become embedded at all levels.

After action reviews (AAR's)

One way learning is harvested is through the after action reviews that follow every exercise at the NTC. They are also used after actual battlefield engagements anywhere in the world. It is a sophisticated process and has clear connections with action learning. Table 4.1 presents the three questions that lead the process (Sullivan and Harper, 1996, p. 195) and, for comparison purposes, the right-hand column presents the three questions that Revans would have us begin with in starting the questioning insight inherent in the action learning process.

Admittedly, the AAR questions follow the action and Revans questions occur at the outset, but the thought processes are much the same. Furthermore, if you compare both sets of questions, you see how they can

Table 4.1 A comparison between after action review questions and Revans' basic questions

After action review questions	Revans' basic questions
What happened?	What is happening?
Why did it happen?	What should be happening?
What should we do about it?	How do we make it happen?

drive the process from beginning to end. A commander in an NTC exercise does not wait until after the exercise is over to ask what happened? He is doing that after every "battlefield" event. The same applies to the other two questions in the after action review set.

The elements of the after action review are (*ibid.*, p. 197):

1 Identifiable event, with associated standards.
2 Identifiable players.
3 Knowledge of what happened (ground truth).
4 Non-threatening environment.
5 Willingness to take personal risks in order for the team to learn and grow.

The dynamics foster openness and mutual interest in arriving at the truth. There is no CYA and no "got ya." The goal is to get better.

> The participants sit down with a facilitator called an observer-controller who has been with them throughout the event, and they discuss what happened ... electronic data collection enables high fidelity recording and playback of events. It is like looking at football games on Monday morning. (*ibid.*, p. 191)

This is a much different Army than I entered and, in the end, an even better one than when I served. There is an ease of communication between officers and noncommissioned officers, and a shared desire for professionalism. Both officers and noncommissioned officers spend extensive time in Army schools and civilian institutions of higher learning, and they are encouraged to read designated literature to deepen their knowledge of their profession and better understand world events. In over 30 years in the military, I spent 10% of my time in school. That is typical for a career officer.

What occurs in the AAR process can be considered the reflective component of a strongly action learning oriented environment. Like any form of action learning, generating the critical reflection that is so key to the learning process is not necessarily easy, but the after action review process gives this some structure and encourages broadest discussion. Sullivan (*ibid.*, p. 54) comments that:

> It is easy to say that leaders must reflect; it is also hard to do. There seem to be two ingredients: time and context. Both are difficult to find, although time may be the easier of the two.

Dialogue is central to the process. Here are some excerpts from the actual dialogue from an AAR (Sullivan and Harper, 1996). General Sullivan, by the way, is a former Chief of Staff of the U.S. Army, and is currently the President of the Association of the U.S. Army.

Commander: I expected the attack would be in the northern part of our sector, against Team Bravo. The terrain seemed to indicate that, and so did our intelligence. So that is where we put our main effort – the strongest minefield, the heaviest artillery fires, the greatest preparation. That's where I was prepared to commit the reserve. But I knew that he (the enemy) might come south (toward Team Charlie) or even do something unexpected, so it was important that I not move too quickly – we were prepared to go either way.

Observer-Controller: How were you going to decide?

Commander: When he came through the mountains to our east (pointing to the map) he would have to commit north or south. At that point he was still nearly twenty kilometers out, but he would be beginning to move fast. Once he committed, I would begin to take him out with long range fires at the same time that we were adjusting back here. The scouts were out there to tell me which way he turned. (p. 198)

As this process suggests, it is a matter of peeling the experience back layer by layer, one question at a time. What you end up with is a very precise picture of what happened, what was learned, and how the new knowledge can be applied in the future. The after action reviews become the basis for refinement of doctrine. While the dialogue covered above is between the Commander and the Observer-Controller, other members of the unit engage in the dialogue as well, so it becomes a very broad learning experience for all.

Field Marshall Erwin Rommel, the famous German General of World War II, developed his own after action review process as a lieutenant in World War I. He would sit down on a tree stump, river bank, or any other suitable place and deeply reflect on what had just occurred and the lessons that could be drawn from it. What happened? Why did the enemy do what they did? How was our response effective? Where did we fall short? How can we better respond to such a challenge in the future? Here is an excerpt from Field Marshall Rommel's reflections after a World War I battle.

Observations: It is difficult to maintain contact in a fog. During the battle in fog at Bleid, contact was lost soon after meeting the enemy, and it was not possible to reestablish it. Advances through fog by means of a compass must be practiced, since smoke will frequently be employed. In a meeting engagement in the fog, the side capable of developing a maximum firepower on contact will get the upper hand. Therefore, keep the machine guns ready for action at all times during the advance. (Rommel, 1979, p. 16)

This after action note-taking led to his book *Infantry Attacks* in 1937, which recorded his reflections after each battle he had fought in during World War I (most recently republished in 2009 by zenith Press). General George S. Patton, Jr, when commanding the Third United States Army in World War II in Europe, kept Rommel's book on his bedside table, so that he could tap into the way Rommel thought, as well as his insights. As indicated, Rommel's reflections were driven by questions, and they were the type of questions that you encounter in action learning.

Other vehicles for capturing learning that have a nexus to action learning

There are a number of ways that the Army captures learning, perhaps more assiduously than any other major organization, military or civilian. Increasingly, it focuses on using virtual means of learning. One example is a network of company commanders that can exchange lessons learned in real time that can be put to immediate use. For example, it can take the form of alerting all in the network to a new insurgent tactic or an improvised explosive device (IED), and how to detect it and neutralize it. Many such networks exist. A company commander in Iraq can share information with his peers in South Korea, Bosnia, or elsewhere.

The Army even has a Center for Lessons Learned, and teams from the Center (called CALL teams) that can travel with units as they deploy in order to capture key lessons learned.

Conclusion

You can have action learning related experiences without having to fly an action learning banner. This revelation can be received coolly or rejected by consultants, who make their money by proving that it is their expertise that makes "true" action learning possible. No one denies the value of a good learning coach or adviser in helping to create, design and orchestrate an action learning program. However, as the U.S military proves, action learning can occur naturally and become embedded in the business processes without coming from a consultant's playbook. In the U.S. military, the corporate culture undoubtedly influences this – a culture that fosters cohesion, harmony, individual initiative, and a constant parade of challenges that are unfamiliar. That is fertile ground for action learning.

For some of the reasons outlined, the basics of action learning have become a part of the military psyche and ethos. It is oriented on improving war fighting capabilities and enhancing leadership development. It produces individual learning, team learning, and organizational learning.

The Navy's "Top Gun" program, for example, is analogous to the NTC experience in that their best fighter pilots compete with the best OPFOR pilots flying the type of aircraft and using the maneuver patterns that Top

Gun program personnel can expect to encounter in combat. Once again, there is a careful critiquing process after each exercise engagement. Time is set aside for reflection.

The Army, in particular, has concentrated much attention in areas that can lead to forms of action learning. The AAR process in the Army can be a model for how you instigate critical reflection and capture the learning that has occurred. As has been outlined, the basic questions that drive it are almost a carbon copy of those used by Reg Revans for arriving at critical issues. The AAR goes far beyond most debriefing processes in the business sector, and it far exceeds what you find in many action learning programs. Getting it right can be a matter of life or death later.

The simulation processes and use of technology by the Army are also extremely sophisticated and, as I have suggested, from an action learning perspective they could not be much more real. They closely approximate the battlefield experience, without the actual casualties of war. Wide-ranging and diversified virtual means of communication are also very much in vogue in exchanging knowledge and lessons learned. It allows the doctrine in the Army to evolve very rapidly in order to meet battlefield conditions, as well as anticipate the doctrine that will be necessary in dealing with future threats.

In many respects, the U.S. Army can be considered a true learning organization, an institution that practices action learning in many different ways. But the same can be said for the entire U.S. military – which is, beyond question, the most capable and most battle-tested military in the world.

References

Luttrell, M. (2007) *Lone Survivor: The Eyewitness Account of Operation Redwing and the Lost Heroes of SEAL Team 10* (Boston, MA: Little Brown).
Revans, R. (1983) *ABC of Action Learning* (Bromley, Kent: Chartwell-Bratt).
Rommel, E. (1979) *Infantry Attacks* (Vienna, VA: Athena Press).
Sullivan, G. and Harper, M. (1996) *Hope is Not A Method* (New York: Broadway Books).

5
Action Learning in the Business World: Past, Present, and Future

Yury Boshyk

Action learning has deep roots and has been practiced in the business world for 55 years, ever since Reg Revans (1907–2003), action learning's founder, organized his first program for coal mine managers in 1954. It has an extensive following among enterprises of all shapes and sizes, and throughout the business world. For two decades now, companies have listed "action learning" as one of the most effective approaches to their executive and management education and development.[1] And some prominent professors of management and leadership – Warren Bennis, for example – tell us that action learning is the wave of the future.[2]

What kind of action learning? And what does the term mean?

But what kind of action learning is the question? And for whom? Reg Revans first used the term "action learning" in published form in 1972. By the mid-1980s, several groups in the business world – particularly in Sweden and the U.S. – began to use this and other variations of the term in different ways from that intended and used by Revans (1983, p. 2). And, over time, a host of new terms and meanings – and, of course, applications –were developed. Today "action learning," can refer to everything from outdoor exercises to just plain old "learning by doing." This is why we have often mentioned that the "house of action learning has many doors." Some reference to these different doors (some have called them "schools" of action learning – which is overly conceptualized and factually incorrect in our view) is required, because how action learning is used by the business community worldwide depends on what one means by the term. For this reason, the first and second parts of this chapter will briefly trace action learning in enterprises as it was directly introduced and implemented by Reg Revans and his colleagues. The chapter will then go on to discuss action learning as it was used by others with a different understanding of the term "action learning." The third part of the chapter will briefly consider the future of action learning in business.

Reg Revans and "traditional" action learning in the business world

What should be made clear is what is meant by "action learning" – both to companies and commentators – because it shapes practice.

Revans was very much involved with the business community – that is, with management issues in business – as a reformist educator (1933–45), professor of management (1955–65), and as a consultant and independent researcher until his passing in 2003, at the age of 95. Most of his writing and work was based on his experiences throughout the world but, especially, in the U.K. and in several other countries, mostly Belgium, Sweden, Egypt, India, Australia, and less so in the U.S. He also had a wide body of experience in other European and Middle Eastern countries both for the private and public sectors.[3]

Revans left behind a rich source of published materials on these experiences but it was only in 1972 that he began to use the term "action learning" to describe his theory and practice. He spent the years 1972–83 clarifying his approach in various publications,[4] suggesting some working but not definitive explanations, including this one: "Learning-by-doing is an insufficient description [of action learning] ... It is rather learning to learn by doing with and from others who are also learning-to-learn by doing" (Revans, 1980, p. 288). It was also his understanding that there can be "no action without learning and no learning without action"; and, that "experience is the best curriculum and colleagues the best teachers" (Revans, 1982, p. 349; Dilworth, 2010). Revans, who was, above all else, a theorist of learning and management, came late to what he called the "logistics" of action learning; that is, the practical details such as obtaining commitment from senior executives and the selection of action learning projects (Revans, 1982, pp. 349–59, 613). According to him:

> Until the GEC [General Electric Company, U.K.] action learning programme was run in 1974, no particular attention had been given to detailed logistics; earlier experiments (collieries, 1952; hospitals, 1964; Inter-University Programme [for Advanced Management], 1968) had assumed homogeneous project design, with all participants working on comparable problems in comparable settings and on comparable terms. The variety of attacks suggested within GEC made it desirable to identify more clearly the relations between all parties involved, and to discriminate between familiar and unfamiliar problems in familiar and unfamiliar settings. (Revans, 1982, p. 613)[5]

But once he had committed himself to the use of this term, he began to document his experiences with the energy common to younger men and not to those in their late 60s and 70s. By 1985, over a 14-year period, nine books on action learning (three in translation) and over 60 articles and reports by Revans appeared, mostly about his work with the business community and management. These centered on his experience with coal mining managers (1954–6); his interaction with the business community as a professor of industrial administration (1955–65), as President of the European Association of Management Training Centres during this period; as head of the Belgian Inter-University Program for Advanced Management (1968–71), consulting for the Organization for Economic Cooperation and Development (OECD) and the International Labour Office (ILO); and also his work in Egypt with companies, the public sector and a university on what was called the "Nile Project" (1969–71). The other seminal experience with the business community and action learning was the General Electric Company's management program from 1974. He would often refer to these experiences with the business community.

These action learning programs were between nine to 12 months in duration, not including the design, and were usually a combination of academic or specialist input and "set" learning, with participants working on one (or more) important business issue(s) given to them by senior executives. They often, but not always, involved a phase in which participants implemented what they thought were solutions to these issues. The most complex program was the Belgian Inter-University Advanced Management Program, discussed in detail elsewhere. (Revans, 1971; Dilworth et al., 2010).

In 1977, a significant article on Revans and action learning was published in the *Harvard Business Review* (Foy, 1977). It was very comprehensive and even described how to "do your own" action learning program. By 1983, a first edition of collected experiences by Revans' colleagues and others based on Revans' inspiration, thinking and practice appeared (Pedler, 1983). In 1985, Revans wrote up a dozen of his experiences in *Confirming Cases*. Despite these developments, it was already clear to some observers that action learning in the U.K. would not be in scale and content like the "massive projects" undertaken by Revans previously (Clutterbuck, 1976).

Revans had a significant following among business leaders in the U.K. Among these were Peter Parker, from the British Institute of Management; Don Newbold, the head of Foster Wheeler; Arnold Weinstock, from the GEC; Adrian Cadbury of Cadbury's, and others. In the U.S., one of his most influential supporters was C. Jackson Grayson, dean of Southern Methodist University Business School and then later head of the American Productivity Center established by President Richard Nixon. George Lombard from the Harvard Business School and Arthur Wellesley Foshay from Columbia University's Teachers' College were also among this group. He had a wide circle of colleagues in the U.S. ever since his days at the University of Michigan (1930–2) as a graduate student on a Commonwealth Fund. But, for a variety of reasons, action learning as he described it, both in theory and practice, never established deep roots in the U.S. corporate world. And in the U.K., action learning was not, it seems, as extensively developed in the business world as it was in U.K. health care system and the not-for-profit sector.

As we mentioned before, he publicly coined the term "action learning" only in 1972, after organization development (OD) and "action research" and "action science" had made major inroads with enterprises in the U.S. and also the U.K. However, business schools in the U.S. and the U.K. did not seem, in general, to be favorably disposed to action learning, and it is interesting to note that there was even much opposition to Revans' action learning in the U.K. One company practitioner at the time, for example, recalls that this opposition came both from academics, who found it easier to grasp OD due to the established research in the area, and from Human Resource personnel organized in the Institute of Personnel Development in the U.K., who did not like the fact that there seemed to be no established procedures for Revans' action learning. Simplistic training was more the norm at this time in a profession that was still "not very strong," Pearce recalled.[6] Revans also advocated worker participation as a form of action learning, for they liked to work and knew best how to make efficiency improvements if allowed to do so, something that some business people may have not appreciated in the socially and politically polarized U.K. (Revans, 1983, pp. 546–65).

Nevertheless, action learning in the business community did continue to develop and expand in the U.K. through a variety of private institutions, like the International Management Centre from Buckingham (IMCB), and through the efforts of individuals who were either directly or indirectly associated with Revans.[7] But the scale was not as great as that compared with other approaches to management education and development in that country.

The "Americanization" of action learning in the business community

In the U.S., the corporate world was involved, along with that of the U.S. Navy and military, with "action research" as developed by Kurt Lewin and others in the 1940s (with the T-(Training) Groups or sensitivity training, and the National Training Laboratory). Action research was one of the important foundations of what later became known as "organization development." By the 1950s, among the companies involved in these pioneering approaches to management education and development were Standard Oil (today, Exxon), Union Carbide, the Detroit Edison Company, Western Electric, and Emery Air Freight, to name but a few (Greiner, 1977; Burke, 1987; 2006). In the 1970s, "action science" with Chris Argyris and Donald Schön (and later Argyris' student, Peter Senge) significantly influenced management education and development in the 1990s. There was a "British" connection for these groups and individuals; however, it was not Revans but, rather, the Tavistock Institute in London – as this institution was also in the Lewin-inspired action research "school" founded in 1946.

72 *Yury Boshyk*

But perhaps even more unfortunate for Revans was the fact that, in the U.S., "action learning" in the business community came to be associated not with him or his practice but, instead, with the use of this term in an admired company called General Electric.

It was in 1985 that Noel Tichy, a professor from the University of Michigan, joined General Electric's management institute in Crotonville, New York (now called the John F. Welch Leadership Center) for a two-year period. Tichy states that he introduced "action learning" to GE during this period.[8] It should, however, be noted that, while his use of the term "action learning" was a dynamic expression that appealed to management, it was used out of the context Revans had defined. Tichy later outlined his understanding of action learning as: "The process of developing employees on hard (e.g., marketing, financing) and soft (e.g., vision, leadership, values) skills by having them work with others on real organizational challenges and reflecting on their decision-making and experiences throughout." It is, however, significant to appreciate that his role at such an influential company and his use of the term "action learning" led to considerable confusion about what the term "action learning" actually meant. He also used phrases such as "compressed action learning" in his writing that further clouded the issue. His followers, such as Dotlich and Noel (1998) (the latter being a former GE colleague) have continued this approach with acknowledgement to Tichy's consulting work. In their context, therefore, action learning is another dimension of OD.[9]

One U.S. academic, Nancy Dixon, has called this approach to action learning the "modified or perhaps Americanized version of action learning." While a considerable "improvement over more traditional lecture-based programmes," she maintains that this form of action learning is really a more sophisticated version of a task force and lacks the depth that one sees in Revans' action learning approach. In particular, the "Americanized version" does not usually involve the *implementation* of team recommendations and, at the same time, does not maximize individual development and behavioral change – both important to Revans, she states. Other differences are that, in Revans' approach, participation is voluntary and not required, and action learning tends to be extended over a period of nine to 12 months and not three weeks to three months, as in the U.S. experiences.

Dixon also asserts that "it is important to acknowledge that, even in its Americanized form, team members *do* learn and teams *do* assist organizations in addressing difficult problems – it is just that they fall short of their potential. It is as if many U.S. companies have grasped the outward form of action learning – that is, teams working on problems – without, however, attending to its essence."[10] This "essence" has been defined by several authors recently (Dilworth and Willis, 2003; Barker 2004; Pedler et al., 2005; Dilworth, 2010).

Action learning's story or use of the term "action learning" in the U.S. underscores a common trend, in that the influence of U.S.-based experiences and theory are grounded in internal cultural and societal realities, and that they are both propagated and seen as having universal appeal and relevance. In reality, this is hardly the case – and even more so, in our multipolar world. The predominance of the U.S.-centric focus is still with us today and is common to many disciplines and endeavors; for example, in the field of OD. An astute observation by one U.S. academic as to the similarities and differences with the U.K. orientation helps us also to appreciate how action learning came to mean one thing to U.S.-based practitioners and another to those from the U.K. and elsewhere:

Though seldom acknowledged by American specialists in organizational behavior, Great Britain has been a rich source of thinking that has greatly influenced our own theoretical developments. We tend to cite names like Joan Woodward, Tom Burns and G. M. Stalker, W. R. Bion, A. K. Rice, Melanie Klein, Fred Emery, Eric Trist, Elliott Jacques, Cyril Sofer, and others as if they are 'one of our own'. Or even more unfortunately, there are many Americans involved in the OD movement who have not even been exposed to the provocative concepts and experiments of these outstanding scholars. NTL [National Training Laboratory] at Bethel, Maine is a household word but a not uncommon question is, 'What and where is the [U.K.] Tavistock Institute?'

There are obvious similarities between [American and British OD approaches]... We see the same underlying cornerstone features – an intense focus on behavioral processes and relationships, a concern for improving behavioral capacities to cope with the future, and a value orientation toward participative methods. In addition, a close parallel exists in terms of developmental stages... for Tavistock from 'group relations training' (similar to T[raining] Group) in the 1950s through a broadened organizational focus in the 1960s to a variety of problem-solving arrangements in the 1970s.

But distinct cultural differences also appear and give... a decidedly British flavor to their orientation ... [O]ne can observe a strong penchant for intellectualizing, an appreciation and patience for the historical flow of events, a persistence in elaborating concepts that began years before, a willingness to describe events in the most clinical terms, a tolerance for great complexity, and a strong sense for situational and individual differences. In marked contrast, the American OD movement reflects more a 'Yank' flavor for 'shooting first and asking questions later', a desire for more simple terminology and concepts, an assembly-line approach to training, a 'here and now' optimism that believes just about any change is possible, a willingness to shrug off or even forget history, a quest for objective 'hard' results, and an enthusiasm to convert people and organizations to an ideal model. (Greiner, 1977, pp. 74–5)

The rise and evolution of action learning in the U.S. followed a similar pattern and fate, as we have seen. Of course, some practitioners integrate several approaches. They also understand the similarities and differences in the theoretical assumptions that underpin these different forms of action learning – but they are, in general, the exceptions.

By the mid-1980s, not just GE, but also many corporations in the U.S. and in "mature" economies were beginning to be swept up by a renewed focus on the rapid rate of change, on the forces and opportunities of globalization and a more ideologically aggressive interpretation of shareholder value. As one of the most admired companies, because of its growth and earnings record, many companies also began to emulate GE's approach to management education and executive development. For the most part, therefore, companies, especially in North America and in the northern hemisphere (but including South Africa and South Korea), when referring to action learning, are describing something that has little to do with the action learning philosophy and approach suggested by its pioneer, Reg Revans. They are really speaking about an "action learning" that has a different foundation – one which has its roots in an interventionist approach to OD that, in turn, is based on the social and behavioral sciences, social activism, and adult education theory – almost all directly associated with U.S. theory and practice.[11] Multinational companies have used (and some continue to use) this and modified approaches to this "Americanized" version. To name a few, among these – besides GE – are Bank of America, Boeing, Honeywell, IBM, Intel, Johnson & Johnson, Lilly, LG, Novartis, Samsung, Standard Bank in South Africa, and there are several direct accounts of their experiences written by company representatives and practitioners.[12]

Action Reflection Learning™ (ARL): Swedish and U.S. variations

In Sweden, and to a lesser extent in the U.S., some consulting organizations use another form of action learning that they call Action Reflection Learning™ (ARL). It is a trademarked term used mainly by two consulting companies, one based in Sweden (MiL) and another in the U.S. Their work involves them with the business community in their region, and with the public sector and not-for-profit sectors as well.

The underlying principles of ARL are discussed in Chapter 17 and we shall not dwell on them here. The fundamental difference between Revans' approach and that of ARL is the very important role assigned to a learning coach in ARL and a "blend" of subject or "programmed learning" in their programs for managers. ARL also clearly stresses "reflection," something which Revans said and wrote about as being in the very nature of his idea of action learning but which ARL has chosen to emphasize, perhaps in reaction to the "Americanized" version of action learning, and executive and management education.

Unlike the U.S. and OD approach already mentioned, it is of interest to note that ARL – as developed in Sweden, in particular – was very familiar with Revans' work, and he even attended some of MiL's annual conferences. Revans was fluent in Swedish (his first wife was Swedish) and he had several supporters who were influential there – among them Lennart Strandler, who was with the Swedish Employers' Association. Revans' work was also translated into Swedish, and his major English-language publisher was a Swede, Bertil Bratt, who also owned the publisher Chartwell-Bratt in the U.K. MiL, however, like the Dutch Action Learning Association (Donnenberg, 1999) evolved on its own from Revans and in close cooperation with some leading Swedish companies, as can be seen from information provided by one of MiL's founders and its President for 32 years, Lennart Rohlin (2009):

The MiL Institute was formed as a not-for-profit foundation in 1 December, 1977. This formal step was preceded by a two year long development process involving about 100 actors from 30 of the largest corporations in southern Sweden (including some CEOs), from the academic world and a few consultancy firms. During this process of co-production several new concepts were developed in cooperation across all borders ("The MiL Model" including "The Actor Model," "The Management Model" and the "Action Strategy for Change and Development"); the longest and most advanced management development program in Sweden was designed ("The MiL Program", 50 days over one year); and the necessary formalities were created together with the stakeholders.

The co-producing process preceding MiL was designed as an open ended inter-organizational Organizational Development (OD) process in which each individual actor has as much say as anybody else, it was a true cooperative initiative where practitioners and academicians worked side by side on equal terms. Eventually MiL came to exist of two main networks, the member corporations and the MiL Faculty with a small full time staff coordinating the whole thing.

When the co-producing phase in 1976 and 1977 have resulted in the new Concepts (eventually named "The MiL Model") and the new program design, several of the actors almost simultaneously mentioned that what have been created was similar to Action Learning. Consequently we invited Reg Revans to one of our meetings in 1977. Although there were important differences to his concept of Action Learning, he embraced and felt stimulated by our work and he made marvelous work in legitimating the approach of ours in the minds of some individuals who still were doubtful about the approach we have created. Later, after having run the first successful MiL program in 1978–79, we invited Reg Revans again.

During the 1980s Reg Revans visited us a few times and it was always very stimulating having him around with his combined supportive and critical mind. He was impressed by the involvement and active support we have managed to elicit among our soon to be over 100 members, mainly large international corporations. He appreciated our basic values of diversity, democracy and inclusion, creativity and innovation. He was especially fond of the fact that we were (and still are) a network of independent actors more than a formal organization and that we were (and still are) not-for-profit.

The first intellectual influences behind MiL are as diverse as the original group of nearly 100 developers. When it comes to learning philosophy and our humanistic values, it would be obvious to mention names such as Piaget, Freire and Kirkegaard, but there are of course also influences from Kolb and other learning theorists as well as Fritz Perls and others from the Gestalt field. Interestingly enough there were not a single individual among the developers with a specialist academic background in pedagogics! And, as mentioned above, few were aware of Action Learning. There were, on the other hand, quite a few with backgrounds similar to mine: strategy, organization and business administration in general. Some influences might have been on a very personal level and not very well known. An example of my own is James Bugental, a Californian psychotherapist whose book Tony Athos put in my hands at Harvard.

The popularity of Action Learning boomed in Scandinavia during the early 1980s and even though there were some important differences between Action Learning and the MiL Model, we went with the boom and started to talk more about Action Learning, which we had avoided during the first years of MiL. The downside of popularity, however, often is that each and everybody jumps on the bandwagon and eventually everything with some components of Action became labelled Action Learning, including initiatives that we did not like to become associated with. So we were just in the process of turning back to our original trade mark on our combined concepts for change, development and learning, i.e. the MiL Model, when we in Sweden in the mid-1980s met with Ernie Turner, Lars Cederholm and some of their colleagues in the U.S. They became interested in setting up a subsidiary in the U.S. based on the MiL Model. We became interested in supporting the formation of an independent organization with which we could have mutually refreshing conversations and perhaps some common business assignments. LIM was eventually formed and in the process we invented Action Reflection Learning, – ARL – as a proper label of the shared learning philosophy and methodology that had originated as the MiL Model.

There was of course also a more factual reason for adding the R(eflection). From the beginning we stressed the importance of Reflection (on Action) as a precondition for Learning.

The ARL concept was then further developed on both sides of the Atlantic Ocean, and sometimes by cooperative efforts. As an example, Victoria Marsick, professor at Columbia University and then member of LIM, was invited on a MiL Scholarship to Sweden to do research on the experiences and effects of MiL Programs in the late 1980s. Together with US colleagues, she went on developing categories of different forms of Action Learning and a lot more. This kind of work made the field develop into maturity far beyond its wild character of the early 1980s.[13]

Detailed descriptions of ARL programs can be found in several sources that are listed in this endnote.[14]

Another variation of action learning, seen less often in the business world than in the public sector, is practiced by Professor Michael Marquardt and his consultancy, the World Institute for Action Learning (WIAL). Despite claims to the contrary, there is no direct link with Revans' philosophy and practice, save a brief, somewhat generic, preface to Marquardt's first volume on action learning and participation in a conference that Revans attended. Like the MiL-LIM approach, WIAL emphasizes the centrality of the "learning coach," and reflection. Both also practice some form of "certification" of these coaches but there does not seem to be any form of cooperation between MiL–LIM and the WIAL (Rimanoczy and Turner, 2008, pp. 145–69; Marquardt et al., 2009, pp. 40–1, 225–7).

Business driven action learning

In 1996, a group of practitioners from multinational companies began to use the term "business driven action learning" (BDAL) to emphasize their business-results focused approach to action learning, and to differentiate themselves from what they saw as the more individual development emphasis seen in other approaches to action learning. They wanted to redress the balance between action and learning, in order to make it clear that action on a company's business challenges was the most important aspect of action learning. In time, the BDAL approach also evolved and moved toward a greater balance between the two. Today it can be said that, if done correctly, BDAL addresses and integrates both individual and team development and learning with organizational learning; that is, with a business-results orientation.

If we were to offer a definition of BDAL it would be as follows:

> Business driven action learning is a philosophy and process, integrating work on critical business challenges with individual, team and organizational learning, at a speed faster than the rate of change, for the purpose

of implementing sustainable business solutions, and the development of leaders and their societies.

Why are business driven action learning programs so popular in the business world? Companies find that integrating work and learning, and learning with work provides them with positive business results, it motivates their employees by empowering them, and does all of this within the context of the organization, the business team and the individual leader (Inglis, 1994, pp. 213–14; Boshyk, 2002; contrast with Revans, 1971, chs 2 and 3).

In short, because of the pace of change and widespread nature of competition in today's world, there is a need for new learning, business and people development, and organizational learning and alignment – and, in these circumstances, action learning found and finds creative and fertile ground. This was well summarized in a note to this author by the late Peter Pribilla from Siemens, head of Corporate Human Resources and member of the Corporate Executive Committee, who noted that in today's world:

> The speed at which a corporation can learn and employ new knowledge is a decisive factor in competition. It is not enough to learn and to work. Learning and working must be integrated. Only then can a corporation be a learning organization. Action learning addresses this challenge very efficiently.[15]

Tying work to learning and learning to work, as well as integrating action with learning and learning to action, is pragmatic and easy to grasp. There is a natural predilection for business leaders to appreciate action (Bruch and Ghoshal, 2004). There are also very clear and immediate returns on the investment in the learning. One can readily see if a team of people has helped a business with a recommended solution or implementation of a solution to a problem or challenge. This was always the case with General Electric under Welch. No "return on investment" (ROI) analysis was ever done as the team recommendations in an action learning program were clear to see, and Welch asked his executive committee to give their reactions to proposals and recommendations immediately and on the spot.[16]

Another reason why action learning is so popular is because respected companies have used action learning effectively and say so, publicizing their achievements and successes in the popular business press or in other publications and forums (Welch and Byrne, 2003, ch. 12).

If understood and done well, business driven action learning has most of the major elements of action learning espoused by Revans, its pioneer. In fact, in the view of some specialists, business driven action learning is seen as being close to Revans' original or "traditional" approach (O'Neil and Marsick, 2007, p. 9) Moreover, all the component parts of a business driven action learning intervention and program are similar to those mentioned by Pedler et al. (2005) for "traditional" action learning.[17]

In principal, as its name explicitly states, BDAL emphasizes the use of action learning *for business*, but it can be (and has been) used in nonbusiness collective activity. In practice, BDAL combines elements from the "Americanized" version of action learning (such as the focus on business results and organizational learning) with the core elements of the "traditional" approach (such as implicit and explicit reflection, personal development and behavioral change).

BDAL also takes a more "ecumenical" or flexible view of some Revans' writings – as, for example, on the issue of the use of facilitators. While being very negatively disposed towards the use of facilitators in regard to action learning and the work with "sets" or teams, it should be noted that Revans did not categorically deny their benefit – and even use in some situations. The following quote from Revans highlights the context when facilitation might be acceptable:

[N]o sets are allowed to become dependent on the tuition of others. Mentorship is always at hand, but it is forthcoming only when truly 'justified'. It is not an 'easy option'. The sets are not allowed to become reliant upon facilitators or advisers either. For the focus is not about *teaching* – it is about *learning* – together. (Revans, 2003, p. viii)

In practice, Revans was also more flexible than his writings would indicate. In the Belgian executive program, interviewed participants recall that he was teaching a great deal, engaging with participants in what he called "P" or programmed learning to a greater extent than is implied in his account of the experience and, certainly, than he advocated in his publications (Dilworth et al., 2010). Likewise, contrary to what he espoused in print, Revans was an active and even interventionist facilitator and set adviser in the General Electric Company's action learning program, according to David Pearce, the person responsible for the program (Pearce, 2009). Over time, Revans also had to adapt to the new needs and requests by companies, and so action learning changed some of the features that he developed earlier – such as, for example, the length of the programs. They became shorter as more of the organization's needs came into play (Clutterbuck, 1976).

However, as with Revans, BDAL does not favor the use of "certified" learning coaches or more active facilitation, because it is assumed, and seen through practice, that executives are loathe to have learning coaches involved in their action learning "sets" and, indeed, programs; that once shown the power of self-managed learning and facilitation – for both themselves and their action learning team – they are more than capable of learning, and certainly in taking action on their learning. The BDAL approach is more in line with "autonomous" facilitation, as described by Heron (1999).

It is often stated that "traditional" action learning involves sets or teams implementing their recommendations on a business challenge. But, while Revans did stress this aspect as an important part of his approach to action learning, he was also very aware that this may not always be possible for some companies or for some management programs. Even in his Belgian experience, he came to an awareness of this reality when he developed the notion of the "welcoming committee" (*structure d'acceuil*) that could also take over the ideas or recommendations and implement them in the company (Revans, 1971, pp. 166, 176). In BDAL programs, the recommendations on business issues and challenges are reviewed by senior executives and sometimes implemented by others in the company, with participants sometimes acting as advisors.

As can be seen in Figure 5.1, another major component part of BDAL is the emphasis placed on engaging "outside-in" elements, including "stakeholders," in the program. This is a direct heritage of Revans and the company and business school visits with his Belgian program participants in the U.S. in 1970, and the General Electric U.S. approach – but deepened and made more comprehensive in practice over the years. This is referred to as the "outside-in" component and involves customers, suppliers, other company experiences and, to a small degree, "subject matter experts" who have knowledge about a particular challenge or issue (Revans, 1971, p. 161; Levy, 2000). In another context, Revans understood the importance of an "outside-in" perspective and it was the foundation of his thinking that the best learning and results came from managers and executives who worked on unfamiliar problems in unfamiliar settings; that is, on business challenges and issues from other companies and with those companies as in the Belgian experience, at least ideally (Dilworth, 2010).

The success factor here is the freedom and ability to listen actively, and ask new and penetrating questions; BDAL, as with Revans, encourages action learners to develop their skill in listening and asking deep questions in much the same spirit as discussed by Revans:

> [A]ction learning shows its strength, not in finding the answers to questions that have already been posed (the role of experts) but in finding the questions that need to be answered (the role of leaders). (Revans, 1980, p. 118; Revans, 1982, on listening)

Another aspect of business driven action learning, like with Revans' practice and thinking, is that reflection on experience is embedded in action learning and does not need to be overly emphasized if done properly – this is unlike other approaches to action learning, such as, for example, "action reflection learning" (Rimanoczy and Turner, 2008) and other consultancies (Marquardt et al., 2009). Critiques of business driven action learning do not, in general, appreciate the degree of reflection that is included in the

Business driven action learning & its components

Levels of action & learning: company, team, & individual levels throughout

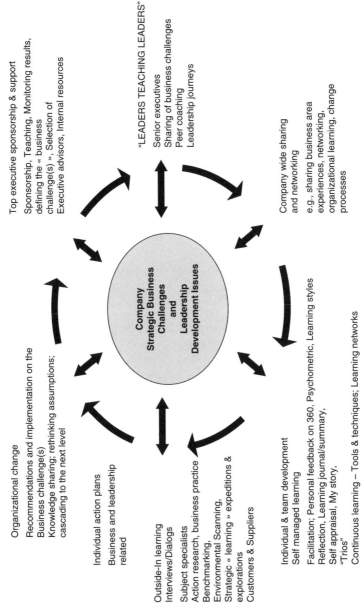

Top executive sponsorship & support

Sponsorship, Teaching, Monitoring results, defining the « business challenge(s) », Selection of Executive advisors, Internal resources

"LEADERS TEACHING LEADERS"

Senior executives
Sharing of business challenges
Peer coaching
Leadership journeys

Organizational change

Recommendations and implementation on the Business challenge(s)
Knowledge sharing: rethinking assumptions; cascading to the next level

Company wide sharing and networking

e.g., sharing business area experiences, networking, organizational learning, change processes

Company Strategic Business Challenges and Leadership Development Issues

Individual action plans
Business and leadership related

Outside-In learning
Interviews/Dialogs
Subject specialists
Action research, business practice
Benchmarking,
Environmental Scanning,
Strategic « learning » expeditions & explorations
Customers & Suppliers

Individual & team development
Self managed learning

Facilitation; Personal feedback on 360, Psychometric, Learning styles
Reflection, Learning journal/summary, Self appraisal, My story,
"Trios"
Continuous learning – Tools & techniques; Learning networks

Figure 5.1 Business driven action learning & its components

practice of this approach and in the best of the "Americanized version" of action learning. They tend to argue that there is too much action and not enough learning. While this may be true of some BDAL company practice, this is not the recommended practice for BDAL. Likewise, what is not usually appreciated is that BDAL incorporates "what is best" in today's approaches to management learning, even though Revans may not have agreed. A good example is the use of business simulations to develop business acumen skills. While adamantly against their use (in his publications) because they do not deal with the realities of business life, in today's business education world some simulations are highly tailored and sophisticated, directly involving company executives who were and are involved in the business situation or problem on which the simulation is based. BDAL approaches, therefore, use simulations as required and other learning approaches that can be viewed as "blended" approaches to executive education. The content of "P," or programmed learning, of Revans' action learning equation has certainly changed over the years from Revans' time, and good business simulations fit into this category. Business cases, however, are another matter and they are not used in BDAL because they are not true reflections of the real complexity and dilemmas of business life. These are represented by adult learners, managers and executives in the room, as Revans (1982, p. 349) stated: "experience is the best curriculum and colleagues the best teachers." A good description of this by a BDAL participant can be found in Chapter 15.

Since the early 1990s, momentum had been growing among some company practitioners in the U.S. and Europe, and a few academics, that "action learning" in the business world had to be more clearly defined and experiences shared. Action learning had come to be seen by these professionals as too focused on individual or team learning, while the organization's business challenges or issues needing exploration and action were downplayed. Business driven action learning was, therefore, interested in focusing the discussion and the practice on results *as well as* on individual, team and OD.

Small groups of practitioners ("partners in adversity," as Revans (1994) would have called them) began to meet to voice and share their concerns and practices and, by 1996, a community of practice emerged around what became known as "business driven action learning." Since that time there have been 14 annual meetings of this community: the Global Forum on Executive Development and Business Driven Action Learning. These practitioners also felt the need to use the best from practices and approaches by other action learning approaches, and so one of the objectives of the community was to engage with and include all approaches to action learning to better enhance learning and business results. Hence, all approaches to action learning at the Global Forum are welcome and take part.[18]

Another aspect of this sharing was the publication of several Global Forum presentations, resulting in the publication of two volumes on experiences with action learning, written by practitioners for the most part (Boshyk, 2000b; 2002). These books also tried to make the case that the house of action has many doors and that we should respect all of them.

The two main questions we shall now address relate to how action learning is being used in the business community today, and the reasons for such usage. We shall concentrate on large global corporations, although there is much that has been undertaken regarding action learning and small and medium-sized enterprises (SMEs) throughout the world with many excellent examples of country-specific experiences. And, as we have mentioned in our introduction, the examples that follow are from the experiences of a highly select group of companies. We do not include business schools in our survey.

Action learning has been, and is being, used for a variety of purposes. One of the most important component parts of BDAL programs, and the starting point for success, is senior executive involvement, because they must see such a program as "their" program. One of the key component parts, therefore, is a business challenge or issue selected and given to participants by senior executives. It is the role of these leaders, in Revans' words:

> to select problems to work on in which management is already interested, that is, problems by which management is seriously embarrassed and of which it is already aware that its existing efforts are unavailing. Thus it is that in mounting any action learning programme the coalition of power must be deeply involved in the choice of projects. It is of no avail that they remit the selection of projects to subordinates, for only if top management themselves are committed to learn will the existential conditions be improved. (Revans, 1980, p. 137)

Participants work on "real" business issues, opportunities and challenges assigned by top leadership to a team of people selected for this purpose and usually organized in a program. Participants are expected to come up with practical recommendations and solutions to the issue, or sometimes several issues.

Companies such as ABNAmro bank, Baxter, BHP, Boeing, Daimler, Disney, Dow Chemical, DHL, DuPont, Eskom, General Electric, Honeywell, IBM, Intel, Johnson & Johnson, LG, Lilly, Motorola, Philips, Rio Tinto (Alcan), SABMiller, Samsung, Shell, Siemens, Standard Bank (South Africa) and Tata, to name a few, have all developed action learning programs with business issues or challenges that relate to one or several of the following themes:

- accelerating growth (Bossert, 2000; Guillon et al., 2000)
- developing strategic plans and actions (Intel, SABMiller)

- discovering future trends and "getting to the future first" (Byrd and Dorsey, 2002)
- clarifying and verifying investment decisions and business planning for board members (Baxter Europe)
- exploring specific business issues and growth initiatives in "mature" and emerging markets around the world (Bossert, 2000; Mercer, 2000a; Isaacson, 2002)
- changing organizations and their direction, sometimes in a turnaround (Freedman, 2000; Hosta, 2000; LeGros and Topolosky, 2000)
- assisting with innovation, integration and alignment of businesses and functions (Bellmann, 2000; Isaacson, 2002)
- developing entrepreneurship (Horan, 2007)
- helping with the development of new products and services (Bellmann, 2000; Bossert, 2000; Mercer, 2000a)
- business and market intelligence.

With regard to the development of people, action learning is seen as being very useful in:

- developing leaders and "high potentials," sometimes in the context of an emerging economy (Braun, 2000; Mollet, 2000; Weidemanis and Boshyk, 2000)
- teambuilding, sometimes with enhancing high performance teamwork (Greville, 2000)
- enhancing networking skills
- developing self-awareness (Philip, 2010)
- leadership and behavioral change (Isaacson, 2002)
- broadening perspectives and understanding of other local, regional and global business practices and other organizational cultures, sometimes through learning consortiums and sometimes referred to as developing "global minds." It is no surprise that action learning was introduced into GE and Boeing at a time when the need for understanding the nature of the global business environment was of critical importance to these companies, in the case of the former in the late 1980s, and the latter in the 1990s (Mercer, 2000a)
- creating a learning organization by aligning learning processes with business needs (Bellmann, 2000)
- developing a competitive and "business-savy" Human Resource group; (Lee, 2002; Tourloukis, 2002).

There are of course, many other uses of action learning in the business world. This is just an illustration of how action learning has now entered the practice and mindset of company approaches to business challenges and opportunities, and to the development of people at the same time.

As for the learning focus, it has been our experience that organizations involved with successful BDAL have incorporated at least three levels of engagement in the program design and content: organizational, team and individual levels. And these, in turn, have tried to address what can be called the "seven dimensions of learning." These are:

1. What am I/we learning about the external environment of our business?
2. What am I/we learning about our organization and business?
3. What am I/we learning about my/our teamwork?
4. What am I/we learning about myself/ourselves?
5. What am I/we learning about the way I/we learn?
6. What am I/we learning about what I/we can use in another context?
7. Who needs to know about my/our responses to the above?

Figure 5.2 portrays the questions associated with these dimensions of learning. We have been discussing action learning *programs* but there are, of course, action learning activities that are not programs in the business world. These can be referred to as action learning "interventions" (if one comes to action learning from the OD perspective and orientation). In one instance, the European executive committee of a global multinational company was deciding on where to invest in Central Europe and, knowing that their direct reports were involved in an action learning program, wanted

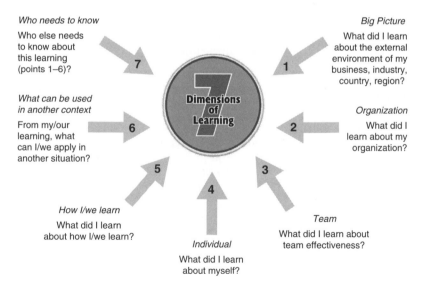

Figure 5.2   7 Dimensions of learning in business driven action learning programs

to try using action learning for themselves. Being eight in number, they were of size that made this manageable (although not optimal), and they embarked on this journey with enthusiasm and a sense of discovery. As a team, they were dealing with a real and critical business opportunity and challenge and, as a leadership team, they were also willing to share their dilemmas. They visited the countries they were considering and talked to many stakeholders, including government officials and local "subject matter specialists," reflecting on their learning and their team interactions with equal focus and enthusiasm.

In another instance, the dynamic CEO of a South Korean company (Hyundai Oilbank) used action learning to turn around the ailing company that he inherited. Using action learning teams or sets throughout the entire organization from the very top to the other layers of the company, he and his team managed to bring the company back to sustained profitability. And, in some circles, the change initiatives at General Electric, Work-Out™ and the Change Acceleration Process are also considered to be a form of action learning. (Davids et al., 2002).

We have so far covered the most well-known action learning approaches to action learning in the business community, both past and present. In the next section, we shall briefly look at the future of action learning in the business world.

The future of action learning in the business community

In Chapter 18, Robert L. Dilworth tackles the issue of action learning's future, so our comments here will be brief and very focused on the future of action learning in the business world. Business driven action learning is tied intimately to a company's strategic priorities, challenges, opportunities and the inevitable dilemmas of choice associated with strategic exploration. Seen from a company and senior executive perspective, *action learning will continue to be used and practiced for the strategic scoping of scenarios and opportunities* as is presently done so effectively at Intel. We see a trend for this approach to be expanded. This, of course, will take on different dimensions and orientations depending on the company and the nature of its operations, as well as its cultural and geographic roots. Action learning in this context will continue to flourish as companies realize that developing strategy with the help of their own intelligent and engaged action learners, who are naturally more aware of alignment and execution issues associated with strategic implementation, will often trump the use of outside strategy consultants, and at a fraction of the cost.

Naturally, the underlying assumptions in such efforts and in such a context are several, and all are based on Revans' theory and practice; that the company sees its and its peoples' strategic advantage as being a learning organization or system learning faster than the rate of change; tying work to learning and learning to work; and trusting the people and the process to know best what to do with seemingly intractable problems; and that individual self-awareness, personal development and growth should accompany all forms of learning and change. These seem to be the characteristics of many leading companies that have a bright and sustainable future – again, an excellent context for action learning as well. The fact that companies and executives will increasingly take more charge of organizational and executive learning, and see it as their responsibility to employees and shareholders, does not auger well for traditional business schools and, while they will always have an important role to play, it is clear that they will have to rethink their offerings and approach (Christensen et al., 2008).

In some companies, we hear the oft-repeated (and sometimes misguided) mantra that "two-thirds of leadership development comes from job experience, about one-third from mentoring and coaching, and a smidgen from classroom training."[19] It is a truism, now confirmed by research, that "learning on the job" is, of course, the reality for most managers, likewise with the development of executives – the difference being that it takes about 25 years to develop a senior executive.[20] However, the research also shows that, while executives learn most from actual experience and "difficult situations," they could learn much better and more efficiently if there were an opportunity and process to help them organize and structure these experiences, either individually and/or collectively. Companies are beginning to see that "learning on the job" can simply be a geographic starting point. A recent article in the *Harvard Business Review* refers to this idea as the "experience trap, using a 'hit or miss' approach to development."[21]

It is important, then, for companies to help structure the experiences and the learning for their executives. Many companies admit a need for this improved structure, both today and in the future. The reality is that there are very few organizations that integrate and tie systematic reflection and a learning process to these experiences and, hence, the learning and development is not as efficient and meaningful as it could be. Because of this weakness, the organization suffers, for it does not fully reap the business benefits that could come from this experience and learning. Action learning can help address this issue.

Corporate universities and coaching departments are adjusting to this "on the job" learning and providing what some companies call "just-in-time" or "quick time solutions" and "on the spot" support for their executives on issues ranging from cross-cultural understanding to specific business skills and specialized knowledge. Companies say they are finding that their executives are asking for more and more *peer-to-peer discussions and collaboration with executives inside their organization* who have gone through similar experiences. This is a more informal process than "coaching," and it is gaining traction in many companies where trust and respect form an essential foundation for collaboration and peer-to-peer learning.[22] This is another situation in which action learning, by its very nature, can help, since the core of Revans' action learning philosophy and practice is about managers and executives as "partners in adversity," helping each other by learning from each other in voluntary "sets" or teams.

This brings us to another trend today: the realization that much development and learning can be gained by executives when they engage with people *outside* their organizations and sometimes outside of the world of business altogether. One example of the former is the growth of inter-*company consortium programs* (sometimes called B2B consortiums) that involve non-competing companies and leaders from these companies. In the past, and to a far lesser extent today, business schools were approached to run these consortiums, or were sometimes even initiated by them. Today, we see a distinct trend to self-organize and run these consortiums without business school involvement. One example was the Boeing-led International Consortium Program that involved companies like ABB, BHPBilliton, Standard Bank from South Africa, Tata and others (Mercer, 2003; Wilmott, 2003). There are now several other major consortiums, including the Global Learning Alliance involving L'Oreal, Wipro, Nissan, Rio Tinto, Schneider and Nokia. There is also a more regional version of a B2B consortium in Singapore, involving the Singapore Exchange and other organizations.[23] It is of interest to note that Revans was very much involved in company consortium learning – be it in the U.K., Europe, the Middle East or even the U.S.

Several companies are concerned about the "high" cost of management and executive programs, and also about engaging as many of their people as possible in action learning. The issue is about whether or not action learning can be cascaded throughout the entire organization and, once again, the answer is "yes" – if Revans' fundamentals are followed – because it is very much about trusting one's people and the internal processes to deliver on action learning's promise. But this hope, in some companies, is also rooted in reality. For example, Hyundai Oilbank in S. Korea and its "action learning" CEO, Young Tae Seo, cascaded action learning throughout the entire organization once he took charge with the mandate of reversing the company's situation.

Action learning in the business community has flourished ever since it was first introduced in the U.K. by Revans about 70 years ago in its experimental phase or, if one prefers, about 40 years ago, when Revans began to call this experience "action learning," providing it with a theoretical and practical foundation along the way. Ever since, it has spread throughout the world in all directions and in all fields of human endeavor, and certainly throughout the business world – the most dynamic and ever changing sector of society. Along the way, "action learning" has been modified to suit different cultures and circumstances, and has even been appropriated to mean something very different from what was intended, especially in the U.S. This reality can also be seen as positive – a sign of its dynamism and adaptability.

Our world will continue to change at a frenetic pace, and there will certainly be no learning without action and no action without learning. Perhaps, in hindsight, "action learning" will metamorphose into something we all can agree with, and perhaps, one day, "action learning" will be seen as having a common ancestry and ethos – but infinite in all directions and making the impact it deserves in creating businesses and societies fit for a sustainable purpose and fit for engaged people.

Notes

It is suggested that this chapter be read in conjunction with Boshyk et al. (2010).

1. See, for example, the trend reports from Executive Development Associates, the most recent one undertaken jointly with Pearson for 2009/2010 by Bonnie Hagemann and Judy Chartrand (2009). Action learning is rated as being in the top three approaches to learning and development.
2. Warren Bennis (cited in LaRue et al., 2006, p. xv):
   > Bennis was asked "What is the most important thing that leaders today need to know in order to be successful?...He said that...leaders today need to understand action-learning and how to apply this unique form of learning in a team setting. He said that, while we are learning a great deal about how to become leaders, we must do much more to understand how to apply what we know within the complex mileau of the real world of with its political, social, and economic intricacies.
3. On Revans' work in the U.K. with business, see Casey and Pearce (1977); Revans (1980; 1983, p. 58; 1984, pp. 48–9; 1985); Barker and Revans (2004). On Revans' work in the private sector outside the U.K., see: Revans (1971; 1974; 1976b; 1978; 1982; 1983; 1987; 1991); Ashmawy and Revans (1971; 1972); Clutterbuck and Crainer (1990, p. 126); Foy (1972); Wieland (1981, pp. 401–2).
4. Some of the more accessible published examples are: Revans (1971; 1972; 1980; 1982; 1983). See also Boshyk et al. (2010).
5. Revans (1982, p. 613, ch. 44). Also note the use of "set advisers" for the General Electric Company program described in Casey and Pearce (1977). According to David Pearce, in interview with Yury Boshyk, September 1, 2009, Revans himself was an active set adviser on the program.
6. Interview with David Pearce, September 1, 2009.
7. On the IMCB, see Wills (1999); and, for other examples of action learning efforts in the U.K., see, for example: Foy (1972; 1977); Casey and Pearce (1977); Coghill (1983); McNulty (1983); Pedler (1983; 1997; 2008); Sutton (1983); Garratt (1987); Inglis (1994); Mumford (1997a; 1997b); Cumming and Hall (2001); McGill and Beaty (2001); Weinstein (2002); Dilworth and Willis (2003); Edmonstone (2003); McGill and Brockbank (2004); Reddy and Barker (2005); Willis (2004); Rigg (2006); Boshyk et al. (2010); Pearce and Williams (2009); and articles in the journal *Action Learning: Research and Practice*.
8. Tichy had no direct experience or understanding of Revans' work and his intellectual and political development because Tichy's inspiration came from entirely

different tributaries, especially from the world of "change agents" that he studied as a doctoral student (among them Saul Alinsky the community activist). Tichy also saw himself as a "change agent" and no doubt seized upon the term "action learning" perhaps due to his activist orientation. See Tichy and Sherman (1993); www.noeltichy.com. Tichy and DeRose (2003) attempt to put Tichy's contributions to action learning and to GE in a larger context.One of GE Crotonville's managers of executive education, Stephen Mercer, was asked to comment on this article, and he stated the following in an email to Yury Boshyk, September 11, 2009:

> ... Connecting Welch and OD is in my opinion incorrect, and attributing the rebirth of OD to Welch is farfetched. This is Tichy interpreting things to re-state that everything we did at GE was an OD intervention. GE did not have an OD organization when I was there, and I never heard the term used in all my years at Crotonville. The expression that Welch "fathers the rebirth of OD," and the "political revolution/social change"...is not believable...Tichy did run Crotonville for two years from 1985–7, but to say that he was brought in to "transform" Crotonville is a real stretch. Tichy did push Jim Noel [another colleague at Crotonville] to introduce action learning, but to say it was Crotonville-wide is simply not true. The only action learning program during Tichy's tenure at Crotonville was the Business Manager Course (BMC). Further, the BMC projects were business focused, and sponsored by Division or Department General Managers. They were NOT cultural change projects. Welch was not even involved in any of the action learning projects until the first China Executive Development Course (EDC) in 1993, and then only because of a chance meeting in the Peace Hotel bar in Shanghai with two class participants, after which he started having the Action Learning project reports presented to the Executive Council. This was more than six years after Tichy left Crotonville. I never heard of the Beckhard Change method, nor am I aware of its use at GE. Tichy was NOT involved in the creation of Work-Out. It was Jim Baughman's brainchild. Tichy was not involved in the creation of the Change Acceleration Program – [Steve] Kerr was. Figure 10.2 is totally inaccurate, and appears to have been altered to support his [Tichy's] OD thesis. The Enrico story is correct. It was after reading this article that Welch directed me to redesign EDC to eliminate outside faculty, and have the initial two weeks prior to the action learning projects be taught by the Executive Council members. It was at this time that I developed the "claim to fame" strategy to get the Exec Council members interested in teaching. The statement that you needed to be a Black Belt to rise to the top is false. The requirement was to be a Green Belt. Further, Tichy had nothing to do with the introduction of Six Sigma to GE. The idea was recommended by an EDC class directed to focus on improving quality.

9. Tichy and Sherman (1993, pp. 130–4). The approach used by Tichy had many elements of OD and was influenced by his study of "change agents" like Saul Alinsky, his supervisor Morton Deutsch at Columbia (who was a colleague of Kurt Lewin, the pioneer of "action research"), his own experience as an undergraduate student at New York Banker's Trust Company (which convinced him that there was much that behavioral science could do for business), the five years he spent working with the Martin Luther King Center in the South Bronx (assisting in developing its neighborhood health center), and finally, "with substantial borrowings from others." Among these, was the experience of the U.S. military's development of "Organizational Effectiveness Officers," a model he apparently

used for his work at GE. (See also Boshyk et al. (2010)). On compressed action learning, see Tichy (2001); Tichy and DeRose (2003); Yury Boshyk interview with Tichy, April 27, 2009.

10. Dixon (1997, pp. 329–30, 335–7).
11. Willis (2004). For another example of "Americanization" in another field, see Cole (1989).
12. For detailed descriptions of some of these programs by practitioners, see Dotlich and Noel (1998); Boshyk (2000a; 2002); Mercer (2003); Wilmott (2003); Horan (2007).
13. Email to Yury Boshyk, February 16, 2009. On other references to MiL, see Yorks et al. (2002, pp. 21–2); Mintzberg (2004, pp. 223–4); O'Neil and Marsick (2007, p. 4); Rimanoczy and Turner (2008, pp. xvi, 137–40); Whitelaw and Wetzig (2008, pp. 183–4). On the MiL story, see also Rohlin (2002).
14. Larsson (1985); Marsick (1990, 2002); Marsick et al. (1992); Cederholm (2002); Pearson (2002); Rohlin et al. (2002); Rimanoczy (2002); Yorks et al. (2002); O'Neil and Marsick (2007); Rimanoczy and Turner (2008); and the MiL and LIM Newsletters.
15. I am grateful to Matthias Bellmann, at the time from Siemens, for providing me with this note from the late Professor Pribilla (cited in Boshyk (2000a), book cover, back page).
16. Mercer (2000a), and in discussion with Yury Boshyk.
17. Pedler et al. (2005) state that the critical elements of action learning are as follows:

    the requirement for action as the basis for learning; working with problems (that have no right answers) not puzzles (which are susceptible to expert knowledge); problems are sponsored and aimed at organizational as well as personal development; the search for fresh questions and 'q' (questioning insight) takes primacy over access to expert knowledge 'p'; action learners work in sets of peers to support, challenge each other ...; profound personal development resulting from reflection upon action' (as cited in Rigg, 2006, pp. 3–4).

18. See www.GlobalForumActionLearning.com
19. John Lechleiter, COO of Eli Lilly as cited in Colvin (2007); and from cnnmoney. com
20. Everhart (2008).
21. Sengupta et al. (2008).
22. de Hann (2005); *McKinsey Quarterly*; The 21st Century Corporation. New York, 2007, especially pp, 36–61. See also, Lank (2006), including the formation of "communities of practice, purpose and interest" (pp. 141–58).
23. For more on this trend, see Wilmott (2003); Bolt and Boshyk (2005); Boshyk (2009).

References

Argyris, C., Putnam, R. and Smith, D. M. (1985) *Action Science: Concepts, Methods, and Skills for Research and Intervention* (San Francisco: Jossey-Bass).

Argyris, C. and Schön, D. (1974) *Theory in Practice. Increasing Professional Effectiveness* (San Francisco: Jossey-Bass).

Argyris, C. and Schön D. (1978) *Organizational Learning: A Theory of Action Perspective* (Reading, MA: Addison-Wesley).

92   *Yury Boshyk*

Ashmawy, S. and Revans, R. W. (1972) "The Nile Project: An Experiment in Educational Authotherapy", A monograph upon which the Fondation Industrie-Université contribution to the 1972 ATM Conference was based (Paris: The Development Centre, Organisation for Economic Co-operation and Development (OECD)).

Barker, A. E. (2004) "Elements of Action Learning", in A. E. Barker and R. W. Revans (eds.), *An Introduction to Genuine Action Learning* (Oradea, Romania: Oradea University Press), pp. 9–207.

Barker, A. E. (2009) Interview with Yury Boshyk and Robert L. Dilworth, February 14.

Barker, A. E. and Revans, R. W. (2004) *An Introduction to Genuine Action Learning* (Oradea, Romania: Oradea University Press).

Bellmann, M. (2000) "Siemens Management Learning: A Highly Integrated Model to Align Learning Processes with Business Needs", in Y. Boshyk (ed.), *Business Driven Action Learning: Global Best Practices* (London/New York: Macmillan Business/St. Martin's), pp. 140–51.

Bolt, J. and Boshyk, Y. (2005) "Using Action Learning for Executive Development", in J. Bolt (ed.), *The Future of Executive Development* (s.l.: Executive Development Associates), pp. 86–99.

Boshyk, Y. (2000a) "Beyond Knowledge Management: How Companies Mobilize Experience", in D. Marchand, T. H. Davenport and T. Dickson (eds.), *Mastering Information Management* (London: *Financial Times*/Prentice Hall), pp. 51–8.

Boshyk, Y. (2000b) "Business Driven Action Learning: The Key Elements", in Y. Boshyk (ed.), *Business Driven Action Learning: Global best practices* (London/New York: Macmillan Business/St. Martin's), pp. xi–xvii.

Boshyk, Y. (2002) "Why Business Driven Action Learning?", in Y. Boshyk (ed.), *Action Learning Worldwide: Experiences of Leadership and Organizational Development* (Basingstoke, U.K./New York: Palgrave Macmillan), pp. 30–52.

Boshyk, Y. (2009) "The Development of Global Executives: Today and Tomorrow", in D. Dotlich, P. Cairo, S. Rhinesmith and R. Meeks (eds.), *The 2009 Pfeiffer Annual: Leadership Development* (San Francisco: Wiley), pp. 108–26.

Boshyk, Y., Barker, A. E., and Dilworth, R. L. (2010) "Milestones in the Evolution of Action Learning", in Y. Boshyk and R. L. Dilworth (eds.), *Action Learning: History and Evolution* (Basingstoke/New York: Palgrave Macmillan), ch. 6.

Bossert, R. (2000) "Johnson & Johnson: Executive Development and Strategic Business Solutions through Action Learning", in Y. Boshyk (ed.), *Business Driven Action Learning: Global Best Practices* (London/New York: Macmillan Business/St. Martin's), pp. 91–103.

Braun, W. (2000) "DaimlerChrysler: Global Leadership Development Using Action-Oriented and Distance-Learning Techniques", in Y. Boshyk (ed.), *Business Driven Action Learning: Global Best Practices* (London/New York: Macmillan Business/St. Martin's), pp. 3–13.

Braun, W. (2009) "Comments on 'Action Learning' in Germany, The Netherlands, Austria and Germany", Otmar Donnenberg (unpublished) in email to Yury Boshyk, February 17.

Bruch, H. and Ghoshal, S. (2004) *A Bias for Action: How Effective Managers Harness their Willpower, Achieve results, and Stop Wasting time* (Boston, MA: Harvard Business School Press).

Burke, W. W. (1987) *Organization Development: A Normative View* (Reading, MA: Addison-Wesley).

Burke, W. W. (2006) "Where Did OD Come From?", in Joan V. Gallos (ed.), *Organization Development: A Jossey-Bass Reader* (San Francisco: Jossey-Bass), pp. 13–38.

Byrd, S. and Dorsey, L. (2002) "Getting to the Future First and the e-Business Leadership Challenge: Business Driven Action learning at Lilly", in Y. Boshyk (ed.), *Action Learning Worldwide: Experiences of Leadership and Organizational Development* (Basingstoke, U.K./New York: Palgrave Macmillan), pp. 110–22.

Casey, D. and Pearce, D. (eds.) (1977) *More than Management Development: Action Learning at GEC* (New York: AMACOM).

Cederholm, L. (2002) "Tibetan Buddhism and the Action Reflection Learning Philosophy", in Y. Boshyk (ed.), *Action Learning Worldwide: Experiences of Leadership and Organizational Development* (Basingstoke, U.K./New York: Palgrave Macmillan), pp. 268–81.

Christensen, C., Johnson, C. W., and Horn, M. B. (2008) *Disrupting Class: How Disruptive Innovation Will Change the Way the World Learns* (New York: McGraw-Hill).

Clutterbuck, D. (1976) "Whatever Happened to Action Learning? While the Traditional Massive Projects Continue, the Future of the Technique Seems to Lie in Less Ambitious Undertakings", *International Management*, 31(11), November, pp. 47–9.

Clutterbuck, D. and Crainer, S. (1990) *Makers of Management: Men and Women Who Changed the Business World* (London: Guild).

Coghill, N. F. (1983) "A Bibliography of Action Learning", in M. Pedler (ed.), *Action Learning in Practice* (Aldershot: Gower), pp. 277–83.

Cole, R. E. (1989) *Strategies for Learning: Small-Group Activities in American, Japanese and Swedish Industry* (Berkeley, CA: University of California Press).

Colvin, G. (2007) "How Top Companies Breed Stars", *Fortune*, September 20.

Cumming, J. and Hall, I. (2001) *Achieving Results through Action Learning: A Practitioner's Toolkit for Developing People* (Maidenhead, U.K.: Peter Honey).

Davey, C. L., Powell, J. A. C., and Powell, J. E. (2004) "Innovation, Construction SMEs and Action Learning", *Engineering, Construction and Architectural Management*, 11(4), pp. 230–7.

Davids, B. N., Aspler, C., and McIvor, B. (2002) "General Electric's Action Learning Change Initiatives: Work-Out and the Change Acceleration Process", in Y. Boshyk (ed.), *Action Learning Worldwide: Experiences of Leadership and Organizational Development* (Basingstoke, U.K./New York: Palgrave Macmillan), pp. 76–89.

de Hann, E. (2005) *Learning with Colleagues: An Action Guide for Peer Consultation* (New York: Palgrave Macmillan).

Dilworth, R. L. (2010) "Explaining Traditional Action Learning: Concepts and beliefs", in Y. Boshyk and R. L. Dilworth (eds.), *Action Learning: History and Evolution* (Basingstoke: Palgrave Macmillan), ch. 1.

Dilworth, R. L., Bellon, D., and Boshyk, Y. (2010) "National Level Experiments with Action Learning: Belgium and Beyond", in Y. Boshyk and R. L. Dilworth (eds.), *Action Learning: History and Evolution* (Basingstoke: Palgrave Macmillan), ch. 5.

Dilworth, R. L. and Willis, V. J. (2003) *Action Learning: Images and Pathways* (Malabar, Florida: Krieger).

Dixon, N. M. (1997) "More Than Just A Task Force", in M. Pedler (ed.), *Action Learning in Practice*, 3rd edition (Aldershot: Gower), pp. 329–37.

Donnenberg, O. (ed.) (1999) *Action Learning: Ein Handbuch* (Stuttgart: Klett-Cotta).

Donnenberg, O. (2009) "Action Learning in The Netherlands, Austria and Switzerland", (February 12, unpublished) and in correspondence with Yury Boshyk, May 15.

Dotlich, D. L. and Noel, J. (1998) *Action Learning: How the World's Top Companies are Re-Creating their Leaders and Themselves* (San Francisco: Jossey-Bass).

Edmonstone, J. (2003) *The Action Learner's Toolkit* (Aldershot: Gower).

Everhart, D. (2008) "Leadership Competencies in Asia: Different from the West?", Korn/Ferry International, 13th Global Forum on Executive Development and Business Driven Action Learning (Seoul, Korea), June 23.

Foy, N. (1972) "The Maverick Mind of Reg Revans", *Management Today*, November, pp. 79, 81, 163, 168.

Foy, N. (1977) "Action Learning Comes to Industry", *Harvard Business Review*, 55(5), September–October, pp. 158–68.

Freedman. N. J. (2000) "Philips and Action Learning Programs: From Training to Transformation", in Y. Boshyk (ed.), *Business Driven Action Learning: Global Best Practices* (London/New York: Macmillan Business/St. Martin's), pp. 123–33.

Garratt, R. (1983) "The Power of Action Learning", in M. Pedler (ed.), *Action Learning in Practice*, 1st edition (3rd edition reprinted in 1997) (Aldershot: Gower), pp. 23–38.

Garratt, R. (1987) "Learning is the Core of Organisational Survival: Action Learning is the Key Integrating Process", in A. Mumford (ed.), "Action Learning", *Journal of Management Development*, Special issue in honor of Reg Revans, 6(2), pp. 38–44.

Greiner, L. E. (1977) "Reflections on OD American style", in C. L. Cooper (ed.), *Organizational Development in the UK and USA* (London: Macmillan), pp. 65–82.

Greville, M.-R. (2000) "Facilitating Leadership Development through High Performance Teamwork", in Yury Boshyk (ed.), *Business Driven Action Learning: Global Best Practices* (London/New York: Macmillan Business/St. Martin's), pp. 191–9.

Guillon, P., Kasprzyk, R., and Sorge, J. (2000) "Dow: Sustaining Change and Accelerating Growth through Business Focused Learning", in Y. Boshyk (ed.), *Business Driven Action Learning: Global Best Practices* (London/New York: Macmillan Business/St. Martin's), pp. 14–28.

Hagemann, B. and Chartrand, J. (2009) *2009/2010 Trends in Executive Development: A Benchmark Report* (s.l.: Executive Development Associates/Pearson's TalentLens Group).

Hanson, K. H. (2000) "Motorola: Combining Business Projects with Learning Projects", in Y. Boshyk (ed.), *Business Driven Action Learning: Global Best Practices* (London/New York: Macmillan Business/St. Martin's), pp. 104–22.

Heron, J. (1999) *The Complete Facilitator's Handbook* (London: Kogan Page).

Horan, J. (2007) "Business Driven Action Learning: A Powerful Tool for Building World-Class Entrepreneurial Business Leaders", *Organization Development Journal*, 25(3), pp. 75–80.

Hosta, R. (2000) "IBM: Using Business Driven Action Learning in a Turnaround", in Y. Boshyk (ed.), *Business Driven Action Learning: Global Best Practices* (London/New York: Macmillan Business/St. Martin's), pp. 76–90.

Inglis, S. (1994) *Making the Most of Action Learning.* (Aldershot: Gower).

Isaacson, B. (2002) Action Learning Beyond Survival: A South African journey", in Y. Boshyk (ed.), *Action Learning Worldwide: Experiences of Leadership and Organizational Development* (Basingstoke, U.K./New York: Palgrave Macmillan), pp. 229–45.

Lackie, G. L. (2000) "Heineken, Shell et al.: Twenty Years of Consortium Action Learning", in Yury Boshyk (ed.), *Business Driven Action Learning: Global Best Practices* (London/New York: Macmillan Business/St. Martin's), pp. 55–64.

Lank, E. (2006) *Collaborative Advantage: How Organizations Win by Working Together* (New York: Palgrave Macmillan).

Larsson, Peter (1985) *Chefer lär chefer: action learning fran ord till handling i chefs utbildningen* (Stockholm: Liber Förlag).

LaRue, B., Childs, P., and Larson, K. (2006) *Leading Organizations from the Inside-Out: Unleashing the Collaborative Genius of Action-Learning Teams* (New York: Wiley).

Lawrence, J. (2009) Interview with Yury Boshyk, February 27.

Lee, T. (2002) "Action Learning in Korea", in Y. Boshyk (ed.), *Action Learning Worldwide: Experiences of Leadership and Organizational Development* (Basingstoke, U.K./New York: Palgrave Macmillan), pp. 249–59.

LeGros, V. M. and Topolosky, P. S. (2000) "DuPont: Business Driven Action Learning to Shift Company Direction", in Y. Boshyk (ed.), *Business Driven Action Learning: Global Best Practices* (London/New York: Macmillan Business/St. Martin's), pp. 29–41.

Lessem, R. (1994) "The Emerging Businessphere", in R. Boot, J. Lawrence, and J. Morris (eds.), *Managing the Unknown by Creating New Futures* (London: McGraw Hill), pp. 109–23.

Levy, P. (2000) "Organising the External Business Perspective: The Role of the Country Coordinator in Action Learning Programmes", in Yury Boshyk (ed.), *Business Driven Action Learning: Global Best Practices* (London/New York: Macmillan Business/St. Martin's), pp. 206–26.

Maital, S., Cizin, S., Gilan, G., and Ramon, T. (2002) "Action Learning and National Competitive Strategy: A Case Study on the Technion Institute of Management in Israel", in Y. Boshyk (ed.), *Action Learning Worldwide: Experiences of Leadership and Organizational Development* (Basingstoke, U.K./New York: Palgrave Macmillan), pp. 208–28.

Marquardt, M. J., Skipton L. H., Freedman, A. M., and Hill, C. C. (2009) *Action Learning For Developing Leaders and Organizations: Principles, Strategies, and Cases* (Washington: American Psychological Association).

Marsick, V. J. (1990) "Action Learning and Reflection in the Workplace", in J. Mezirow et al. (eds.), *Fostering Critical Reflection in Adulthood: A Guide to Transformative and Emancipatory Learning* (San Francisco: Jossey-Bass), pp. 23–46.

Marsick, V. J. (2002) "Exploring the Many Meanings of Action Learning and ARL", in L. Rohlin, K. Billing, A. Lindberg and M. Wickelgren (eds.), *Earning While Learning in Global Leadership* (Lund, Sweden: Studentlitteratur), pp. 297–314.

Marsick, V. J. and Cederholm L. (1988) "Developing Leadership in International Managers: An urgent challenge!" *Columbia Journal of World Business*, 23(4), pp. 3–11.

Marsick, V. J., Cederholm, L., Turner, E., and Pearson, T. (1992) "Action-Reflection Learning", *Training and Development*, August, pp. 63–6.

Marsick, V. J. and Sauquet, A. (2000) "Learning Through Reflection", in M. Deutsch and P. Coleman (eds.), *Handbook of Conflict Resolution: Theory and Practice* (San Francisco: Jossey-Bass), pp. 382–99.

McGill, I. and Beaty, L. (2001) *Action Learning: A Guide for Professional, Management and Educational Development*, rev. 2nd edition (London: Kogan Page).

McGill, I. and Brockbank, A. (2004) *The Action Learning Handbook: Powerful Techniques for Education, Professional Development and Training* (London: Routledge).

McNulty, N. G. (1983) "Action Learning Around the World", in M. Pedler (ed.), *Action Learning in Practice*, 1st edition (Aldershot: Gower), pp. 173–87.

Mercer, S. R. (2000a) "General Electric's Executive Action Learning Programmes", in Y. Boshyk (ed.), *Business Driven Action Learning: Global Best Practices* (London/New York: Macmillan Business/St. Martin's), pp. 42–54.

Mercer, S. R. (2000b) "General Electric Executive Learning Programmes: Checklist and Tools for Action Learning Teams", in Y. Boshyk (ed.), *Business Driven Action Learning: Global Best Practices* (London/New York: Macmillan Business/St. Martin's), pp. 179–90.

Mercer, S. R. (2003) "The Boeing Leadership Center" (unpublished).

Mercer. S. R. (2009) Email correspondence with Yury Boshyk, September 11.

Mintzberg, H. (2004) *Managers Not MBAs: A Hard Look at the Soft Practice of Managing and Management Development* (San Francisco: Berrett-Koehler).

Mollet, G. (2000) "Volkswagen: Action Learning and the Development of High Potentials", in Yury Boshyk (ed.), Business Driven Action Learning: Global Best Practices (London/New York: Macmillan Business/St. Martin's), pp. 152–65.

Mumford, A. (ed.) (1997a) *Action Learning at Work* (Aldershot: Gower).

Mumford, A. (1997b) "A Review of the Literature", in M. Pedler (ed.), *Action Learning in Practice*, 3rd edition (Aldershot: Gower), pp. 373–92.

Mumford, A. (2008) Interview with Yury Boshyk, September (London, U.K.).

Noel, J. L. and Charan, R. (1988) "Leadership Development at GE's Crotonville", *Human Resource Management*, 27(4), pp. 433–49.

Noel, J. L. and Charan, R. (1992) "GE Brings Global Thinking to Light", *Training and Development*, 46(7), pp. 28–33.

Noel, J. L. and Dotlich, D. L. (2008) "Action Learning: Creating Leaders through Work", in J. L. Noel and D. L. Dotlich (eds.), *The 2008 Pfeiffer Annual: Leadership Development* (San Francisco: Wiley), pp. 239–47.

O'Neil, J., Arnell, E., and Turner, E. (1996) "Earning While Learning", in K. E. Watkins and V. J. Marsick (eds.), *Action: Creating the Learning Organization* (Alexandria, VA: American Society for Training and Development), pp. 153–64.

O'Neil, J. and Lamm, S. L. (2000) "Working as a Learning Coach Team in Action Learning", *New Directions for Adult and Continuing Education*, Fall, 87, pp. 43–52.

O'Neil, J. and Marsick, V. J. (2007) *Understanding Action Learning: Theory into Practice* (New York: AMACOM).

Pearce, D. (2009) Interview with Yury Boshyk, September 1.

Pearce, D. and Williams, E. (2009) *Action Learning for Innovation And Change: Welsh Farming Families* (Aberystwyth: Menter a Busnes).

Pearson, R. (2002) "Strategic Change Management at Merck Hong Kong: Building a High Performing Executive Team Using Action Reflection Learning", in Y. Boshyk (ed.), *Action Learning Worldwide: Experiences of Leadership and Organizational Development* (Basingstoke, U.K./New York: Palgrave Macmillan), pp. 282–91.

Pedler. M. (1980) "Book Review of Action Learning: New Techniques for Action Learning by R. W. Revans", *Management Education and Development*, 11, pp. 219–23.

Pedler, M. (ed.) (1983) *Action Learning in Practice*, 1st edition (Aldershot: Gower).

Pedler, M. (ed.) (1997) *Action Learning in Practice*, 3rd [rev.] edition (Aldershot: Gower).

Pedler, M. (2008) *Action Learning for Managers*, 2nd edition (Aldershot: Gower).

Pedler, M., Burgoyne, J., and Brook, C. (2005) "What Has Action Learning Learned to Become?" *Action Learning: Research and Practice*, 2(1), pp. 49–68.

Reddy, S. and Barker, A. E. (eds.) (2005) *Genuine Action Learning: Following the Spirit of Revans* (Hyderabad: ICFAI University Press).

Reinholdsson, A. (2002) "Northern Light: A Survey of Action Learning in the Nordic Region of Europe", in Y. Boshyk (ed.), *Action Learning Worldwide: Experiences of Leadership and Organizational Development* (Basingstoke, U.K./New York: Palgrave Macmillan), pp. 163–72.

Revans, R. W. (1971) *Developing Effective Managers: A New Approach to Business Education* (New York: Praeger).

Revans, R. W. (1972) "Action Learning – A Management Development Program", *Personnel Review*, 1(4), Autumn, pp. 36–44.

Revans, R. W. (1974) "The Project Method: Learning by Doing", in S. Mailick (ed.), *The Making of the Manager: A World View* (Garden City, NY: United Nations

Institute for Training and Research (UNITAR)/Anchor Press/Doubleday), pp. 132–61.

Revans, R. W. (ed.) (1976a) *Action Learning in Hospitals: Diagnosis and Therapy* (London: McGraw-Hill).

Revans, R. W. (1976b) "Action Learning in a Developing Country", *Journal of the Malaysian Institute of Management*, 11(3), December, 8–16.

Revans, R. W. (1977) "Action Learning: The Business of Learning About Business", in D. Casey and D. Pearce (eds.), *More than Management Development: Action Learning at GEC* (Westmead, U.K.: Amacom), pp. 3–6.

Revans, R. W. (1978) "Action Learning takes a Health Cure", *Education and Training*, November–December, pp. 295–9.

Revans, R. W. (1980) *Action Learning: New Techniques for Management* (London: Blond & Briggs).

Revans, R. W. (1982) *The Origins and Growth of Action Learning* (Bromley: Chartwell-Bratt).

Revans, R. W. (1983) *The ABC of Action Learning* (Bromley: Chartwell-Bratt).

Revans, R. W. (1984) *The Sequence of Managerial Achievement* (Bradford: MCB University Press), pp. 48–9.

Revans, R. W. (1985) *Confirming Cases* (Telford: Revans Action Learning International). Republished in A. Barker and R. W. Revans (2004), *Introduction to Genuine Action Learning* (Oradea, Romania: Oradea University Press), pp. 267–318.

Revans, R. W. (1986) "Action Learning in a Developing Country", *Management Decision*, 24(6), pp. 3–7.

Revans, R. W. (1987) "International Perspectives on Action Learning", University of Manchester, Institute for Development Policy and Management, Manchester Training Handbooks, 9 (Manchester: IDPM), University of Manchester.

Revans, R. W. (1988) "The Golden Jubilee of Action Learning: A Collection of Papers Written During 1988" (Manchester Business School and Manchester Action Learning Exchange (MALEx)).

Revans, R. W. (1991) "Action Learning in the Third World", *International Journal of Human Resource Management*, 2, May, pp. 73–91.

Revans, R. W. (1994) "Action Learning or Partnership in Adversity. The Economic Effects of National Spontaneity", prepared by Albert E. Barker. s.l.

Revans, R. W. (2003) "Foreword", in Robert L. Dilworth and Verna J. Willis (eds.), *Action Learning: Images and Pathways* (Malabar, Florida: Krieger), pp. vii–x.

Rigg, C. (2006) "Developing Public Service: The Context for Action Learning", in C. Rigg and S. Richards (eds.), *Action Learning, Leadership and Organizational Development in Public Services* (London: Routledge), pp. 1–11.

Rimanoczy, I. (2002) "Action Reflection Learning in Latin America", in Y. Boshyk (ed.), *Action Learning Worldwide: Experiences of Leadership and Organizational Development* (Basingstoke, U.K./New York: Palgrave Macmillan), pp. 152–60.

Rimanoczy, I. and Turner, E. (2008) *Action Reflection Learning: Solving Real Business Problems by Connecting Learning with Earning* (Mountain View, CA: Davies-Black).

Rohlin, L. (2002) "The Story of Mil", in L. Rohlin, K. Billing, A. Lindberg and M. Wickelgren (eds.), *Earning while Learning in Global Leadership: The Volvo MiL Partnership* (Lund: MiL), pp. 17–22.

Rohlin, L. (2009) Email to Yury Boshyk, February 16, 2009.

Rohlin, L., Billing, K., Lindberg, A. and Wickelgren, M. (eds.) (2002) *Earning while Learning in Global Leadership: The Volvo MiL partnership* (Lund: MiL).

Rohlin, L., Skarvad, P.-H. and Nilsson, S. A. (1998) *Strategic Leadership in the Learning Society* (Vasbyholm: MiL).

Rothwell, W. J. (1999) *The Action Learning Guidebook*. San Francisco: Jossey-Bass/ pfeiffer.

Senge, P. (1990) *The Fifth Discipline: The Art and Practice of the Learning Organization* (New York: Currency Doubleday).

Sengupta, K., Abdel-Hamid, T. K., and Van Wassenhove, L. N. (2008) "The Experience Trap". *Harvard Business Review*, 80(2), February, pp. 94–101.

Sutton, D. (1983) "A Range of Applications", in M. Pedler (ed.), *Action Learning in Practice*, 1st edition (Aldershot: Gower), pp. 65–72.

Tichy, N. M. (2001) "No Ordinary Boot Camp", *Harvard Business Review*, 79(4), pp. 63–9.

Tichy, N. M. (2009) Interview with Yury Boshyk, April 27.

Tichy, N. M. and DeRose, C. (2003) "The Death and Rebirth of Organizational Development", in S. Chowdhury (ed.), *Organization 21C: Someday All Organizations Will Lead This Way* (Upper Saddle River, N.J: *Financial Times*/Prentice Hall), pp. 155–73.

Tichy, N. M. and Sherman, S. (1993) *Control Your Destiny or Someone Else Will: How Jack Welch is Making General Electric the World's Most Competitive Company* (New York: Currency-Doubleday).

Tourloukis, P. (2002) "Using Action Learning to Develop Human Resource Executives at General Electric", in Y. Boshyk (ed.), *Action Learning Worldwide: Experiences of Leadership and Organizational Development* (Basingstoke, U.K./New York: Palgrave Macmillan), pp. 90–109.

Weidemanis, M. and Boshyk, Y. (2000) "Scancem: 'What Did We Earn and Learn?' Emerging Markets and Business Driven Action Learning", in Y. Boshyk (ed.), *Business Driven Action Learning: Global Best Practices* (London/New York: Macmillan Business/St. Martin's), pp. 134–9.

Weinstein, K. (1998) *Action Learning: A Practical Guide*, 2nd edition (Aldershot: Gower).

Weinstein, K. (2002) "Action Learning: The Classic Approach", in Y. Boshyk (ed.), *Action Learning Worldwide: Experiences of Leadership and Organizational Development* (Basingstoke, U.K./New York: Palgrave Macmillan), pp. 3–18.

Welch, J. and Byrne, J. A. (2003) *Straight from the Gut* (New York: Business Plus).

Whitelaw, G. and Wetzig, B. (2008) *Focusing the Four Essential Energies of a Whole and Balanced Leader* (Boston, MA: Nicholas Brealey).

Wieland, G. F. (ed.) (1981) *Improving Health Care Management: Organization Development and Organization Change* (Ann Arbor: Health Administration Press).

Willis, V. J. (2004) "Inspecting Cases against Revans' 'Gold Standard' of Action Learning", *Action Learning: Research and Practice* 1(1), April, pp. 11–27.

Wills, G. (1999) "The Origins and Philosophy of International Management Centres", in A. Mumford (ed.), *Action Learning at Work* (Aldershot: Gower), pp. 30–41.

Wilmott, J. (2003) "Developing Global Leaders: The International Consortium Program" (unpublished).

Wilmott, J. and Wilkinson, L. C. (2003) The International Consortium Program. Available electronically and last accessed November 15, 2009, http://www.penlion.co.za/ns_arti_glo.html

Yorks, L., O'Neil, J. and Marsick, V. (2002) "Action Reflection Learning and Critical Reflection Approaches", in Y. Boshyk (ed.), *Action Learning Worldwide: Experiences of Leadership and Organizational Development* (Basingstoke, U.K./New York: Palgrave Macmillan), pp. 19–29.

6
Action Learning, Community, and Civil Society

Verna J. Willis

Reg Revans saw the early signs and said, just as momentum began to gather, that action learning would be "taken up" worldwide on a massive and diversified scale. This "taking up," largely though action learning derivatives that are more or less faithful to Revans' classic style, visibly spread like wildfire in management development circles. Less noticed, second generation applications are emerging now at a comparable rate across a wide range of global-to-local social and economic development initiatives.

There are reciprocal sides to the story of this rapid and international growth in grassroots reflective learning. Voices across the lands are heard that have never been heard before, demanding the right to determine for themselves what is necessary for their well-being. Funding agencies and aid programs, frustrated by lack of progress, have been forced to realize that, no matter how excellent their intentions and their staffs, they cannot know what people need unless they listen and learn from the people they wish to serve.

Action learning has been tried, and continues to gain reputation as a flexible, durable vehicle for surfacing local knowledge that resides in people "on the ground" trying to cope with unrelenting human challenges. In process, action learning also points to the futility of "wishing development," western-style and with industrial speed, upon less powerful people who have their own destinies in mind, if they only had the time, resources and safety to pursue them.

Introduction

One of action learning's great advantages is that it requires on-site meaning-making, feeding into construction of the roadmaps and strategies for obtaining economic sufficiency, security and civil society. As witness to the truth of this, I cite an example from the Côte d'Ivoire, where an action learning team of faculty members focused upon, and gave incredible energy to, addressing the real problem of power transformer thefts from private homes in the capital city. Several team members had themselves been equal-opportunity victims, literally robbed of power overnight. "Blame the power company" was their first impulse, yet, after engaging in fresh questioning, more than a dozen possible avenues for attacking the problem emerged out of their local knowledge of the situation. Whether they were ever able to work out the proposed solutions and negotiations necessary to carrying out such a community effort I do not know, because my faculty development project ended soon and a political coup was not far behind.

There are several lessons to be learned from this episode:

- Project time limits for making segments of any given society more viable, with or without action learning, are often disconnected from reality. The inquiry and reflection processes of action learning can cut to the core issues very quickly, but the actions, the visible developments, take time. They will tend to occur only if a desire, capacity, and sufficient time to act without penalty are insured.
- Action learning brings out both the strengths and weaknesses of change efforts, even as it transforms "mental sets" and retools thinking to suggest real solutions. It is a forthright way to learn many practical and insightful things that otherwise will not be learned or applied in the future.
- The complications of enacting proposed solutions, or at least trying them out, are often not well-understood. Outsiders cannot map the instances and linkages among these except in partnership with local populations.
- Sometimes all that survives discrete, time-bound enactments is the learning itself, an increase in capacity that informs the future. Thirty-one case study briefs collected from African and Latin American development initiatives testify to this later in this discussion (Taylor et al., 1998).

It is as if all action learning were – once underway – forever in the minds and hearts of those who have engaged in it, ready to be called into service at a moment's notice. It makes visible the uncertainties, the ambiguities, and often the very real disparities in power relations, but it also makes us accountable for what we do about these. Incisive thinking of persons closest to the issue, together with whatever partnerships or resources can be enlisted, may, in combination, prove to be one of the best, most renewable strategies available for crafting new collective and individual realities. Empowerment is one of action learning's best legacies.

Identifying agents of action learning

For the last few decades, governmental and nongovernmental funding agencies have been making grants and contracts for small- and large-scale development projects contingent on involvement of local participants. At the international level, the World Bank and the United Nations are prime examples of this. The development aim is "capacity-building" through various mentoring and partnering arrangements, so that power can be shared and citizens have both the opportunity and the mandate to make the outcomes and processes from their field projects ongoing and self-sustaining. As it turns out, local people are ready to help themselves, if power relationships and working conditions can be brought into balance to make self-help possible. The same contingencies are being established worldwide at other levels of government, in nongovernmental organizations (NGOs), and in local community development efforts where support is often obtained through foundation grants, private subscriptions and contributions, voluntary cooperatives and voluntary service.

As Weinstein (2002) notes, "action learning has become 'fashionable' [so that] organizations of all kinds...claim to be 'doing it.' Many are. But many are not." The momentum of good ideas like action learning is not a guarantee against misconstruing them. Neither is the truth that good ideas coalesce from many different sources in the world society a reasonable excuse for encircling the pioneering work of Revans and subsuming it under other names. But it happens, making it difficult to trace what is being done broadly in the interests of civil society all the way back to the roots of action learning. Nevertheless, I have made an effort to do so, and to concentrate the ensuing discussion on projects and perspectives that I have found, plainly, to have such roots. With the few clarifications that follow, those most familiar with the meanings Revans invested in action learning should find themselves on philosophically and operationally familiar ground.

Participation, a ubiquitous word in the community development and civil society literature, can mean anything from filling out a questionnaire or allowing an interview to the opposite extreme – projects characterized by full-scale, democratic power-sharing. At the very least, participation should mean recognition that "All peoples' time is precious. People should benefit from the time they give to the action learning process" (Mayoux, 2003a, p. 4). Wherever "development" includes an expressed passion for *egalitarian participation*, action learning may be involved, though not always as the ruling impulse or as the carrying process.

Participatory action learning (PAL), participatory learning and action (PLA) and participative rural appraisal (PRA) all are explicitly identified as second generation action learning. Participatory action research (PAR), in many cases, echoes the spirit and intent of action learning as Revans saw it, though filtered through the constraints imposed by standardized methods of research and evaluation. A major difference, as noted elsewhere in this publication, is that PAR, like its forerunner, action research (AR), requires research that becomes *public knowledge*, a permanent artifact in the public domain, whereas action learning may not be asked to "prove anything" beyond the attention given to one real problem, and the genuine learning and action that proceeds from this.

Civil society

Michael Edwards, director of the Ford Foundation's Governance and Civil Society Program, acknowledged that:

> Civil society has become a notoriously slippery concept, used to justify radically different ideological agendas, supported by deeply ambiguous evidence, and suffused with many questionable assumptions ... [Yet] When subjected to a rigorous critique, the idea of civil society re-emerges to offer significant emancipatory potential, explanatory power, and practical support to problem-solving in both established and emerging democracies. (2004, p. vi)

He warned of possible "backlash" that "exaggerated claims" for civil society may engender "to the detriment of progressive social goals and the lives of millions of people across the globe for whom civil society provides a compelling vision in their struggles for a better world. The stakes are very high" (*ibid.*, p. vii).

Edwards offered details of what he calls three "useful, legitimate and incomplete" theoretical positions regarding civil society. These are:

1. analytical models of the various forms of "associational life";
2. normative models of the kind of society that civil society initiatives are supposed to generate; and
3. models of civil society identified simply as "the public sphere."

The first type of model views civil society as a part of society that is "distinct from states and markets." The second type concerns "the realm of service, the breeding grounds of habits of the heart" and of values like cooperation, trust, tolerance, and nonviolence – in short, the associative processes that tend to produce the kind of society people would like to live comfortably and "civilly" within. The normative understanding of civil society prevails whenever there is talk of democratically reconstituting governments and other powerful institutions and practices. The third model of civil society, as Edwards described it, is a society where rational discussions in the public sphere both allow and encourage "active citizenship" in pursuit of "the common interest" (*ibid.*, pp. vii, viii).

Elise Boulding (1988) found the characteristics of civil society to be irreducibly systemic and, on that basis, whatever civil or uncivil elements are embedded in a society become critical indicators of how well or how poorly men, women and children can function in that society. As former Secretary General of the International Peace Research Association, a mother of several children, and a lifelong scholar, Boulding has been deeply involved in world peace movements. She considers emancipatory work among women and children vital in all development undertakings (Boulding, 2003).

Wikipedia acknowledges the power-relations aspects of the concept: "Civil society is composed of the totality of voluntary civic and social organizations that form the basis of a functioning society as opposed to the force-backed structures of a state (regardless of that state's political system) and commercial institutions." Another definition at the same website, from the London School of Economics Centre for Civil Society, states that "in practice, the boundaries between state, civil society, family and market are often complex, blurred and negotiated."

Enormous amounts of energy and resources are currently pouring into the effort to develop and sustain civil societies. The World Bank announces job opportunities for civil society "in various types of development research undertaken by the World Bank and client governments." The Inter-American Development Bank describes its "citizen participation strategy" and outreach efforts. Various intermediate institutes and programs have organized to further the international development work and, using as many as 74 indicators of "the state of civil society," to assess progress in nations diverse in makeup, size, and geography (CS Index).

Community development

Certainly historic longing for civil society, and the struggles to achieve it, lies behind community development efforts that originated primarily – but not exclusively – in democratic societies. According to Wikipedia, "Community development, informally called community building, is a broad term applied to the practices and academic disciplines of civic leaders, activists, involved citizens and professionals to improve various aspects of local communities."

Goals are as various as members of any community may identify, and capacity-building at every point is, and has always been, one of the hallmarks of community organization and accomplishment. Early evidence in Europe of community and capacity-building associations include the appearance of the guilds. Tribal societies have universally provided village or encampment forums for improvement ideas and decision-making. Town hall meetings met such community needs in Colonial America, and this time-honored forum has not disappeared. The rudiments of community formation, planning and development have probably existed throughout human history. They are driven urgently now by population growth and dwindling resources that threaten to dissolve the rural and urban community support systems that exist, and even to block viable replacements.

The U.S. – in its very founding, a revolutionary product of social activism and localism – has a very long history of pursuing "the common good" through civic associations, fraternal organizations, and women's groups (Evans, 1997). Community development has received reinforcement in many countries from various labor movements and their efforts to improve the lives of workers and their families. Local development gathered strength throughout the turbulent readjustments of the post-World War II period, and has found further expression in rural and inner city social and political movements – including the struggle for civil rights of minorities, women, the disabled, and other disenfranchised or "silent" people. Communitarianism, a late twentieth-century point of view, and a movement largely fueled by the work of Etzioni (1995), suggests that individual autonomy and social cohesion can be balanced through policies that reflect community values.

Community development across the globe has generated a sophisticated collection of resource materials and "how-to" procedures. Among these are professional journals, organizing workshops, and manuals detailing empowerment strategies and tactics. Central to all community organizing is the idea of working together, listening to the "voices" in the community, and connecting with funding sources and decision-makers to "make things happen" constructively.

With broadening ecological perspectives a new thread has emerged, entitled "sustainable community development." People from widely different sectors – from homeowners, gardeners and town councils to planning and engineering firms – have been drawn into study of the unexpected consequences of local "development." Their efforts turn on discovering how unsustainability can be predicted in advance of damage to communities and thwarting of quality of life (Lipietz, 1996).

Action learning and "development work"

The extension of action learning beyond the boundaries of management education in business organizations and large public institutions seems to have been happening quietly all along, aided and abetted by Revans himself, and certainly spreading outward from the university and other affiliations he had in the U.K. and abroad. Jones (2004) places action learning and Reg Revans (along with Robert Chambers of the Institute for Development Studies, University of Sussex, England) squarely in the forefront of international development. Jones' prime example appears in an executive summary reporting on Swedish Support to Decentralization Reform in Rwanda. Item 6.12 of this evaluation report notes:

> the District Development component of this Project works through *Task Teams*. As we mentioned in the Introduction, the teams operate according to the *action learning* philosophy, originated by Reg Revans and later

adapted – using a different vocabulary – by Robert Chambers; that groups can learn how to learn and take action from reflecting on their actions and experimenting with new behaviors. This approach has been used effectively by SALA-IDA in Northern Cape Province, South Africa. (*ibid.*, p. 14)

Item 6.14 adds:

In a very brief time (just two years) the work of the teams has produced a variety of concrete, visible benefits. These include the building of two primary schools and repairs to others; the rehabilitation of an important bridge; the provision of small loans to local entrepreneurs to enable them to develop or expand a business; assembling...extensive factual data about districts; assisting farmer associations with improving crop yield and livestock quality; developing a variety of practical strategies for combating the effects of HIV/AIDS; enhancing gender balance; supporting actions, initiated at cell level, to provide clean drinking water to the inhabitants of three cells; and many others. (*ibid.*)

This example is cited not only because of the overt connection to action learning, but also to highlight the details of team projects undertaken. Clearly this is an extensive effort, with many ramifications and with, at least, a five-year funding allocation.

On a minute scale, by comparison, is an action learning field experience that created partnerships between students, a teaching team, and stakeholders in a small rural Native American town in Oregon in the U.S. This project – concerned with "systemic and institutionalized discrimination" among ethnic populations, with resulting community sustainability issues – shows that civil society initiatives are certainly not the sole province of developing countries (Thompson et al., 2004). In the case of Native Americans, reservation "sovereignty" officially confers the power to make decisions for their own communities, but does not specify or guarantee the means with which to do so. Power relations and lack of access to necessary resources have historically and persistently affected the development of Native American institutions and communities.

The critical realism of action learning

Some action researchers in international development practice think of the cooperative exchanges with local people as "animator work" (Gagel, 1995, p. 2) (i.e., generating relationships), whereas the subsequent research work becomes the center of gravity of what gets done. Action learning then becomes a start-up, shortcut process to get people engaged and energized for data collection. This, as Mukherjee (2002, p. 295) suggests, can serve as "a base for scaling up and replication of process" in other locations, albeit with due attention to local issues and sensibilities. PAR specialists generally expect to listen to "voices from the voiceless" (Freire, 1970), and typically merge targeted inquiry with action learning principles to establish whatever level of communication seems pertinent to the research and development objectives.

Perhaps it would be more helpful to think of action learning as a *systemic intelligence* that gathers and operates on behalf of civil society and capacity-building inside the "problem field." The building of local capacity to address local problems is not responsive to shortcuts that endanger "learning with and from each other." Deeper personal commitment and much more on-site sharing of wisdom and work is required. Social realism should teach that "being asked" and "being studied" by (or even with) "researchers" is both wearing and belittling to participants, leading to valid questioning whether, when outsiders come to do "development work," they are really there to pursue private interests and agendas at the expense of the communities. Trust-building is always a major consideration for development practitioners. Fortuitously, trust relationships are a proven natural outcome of genuine action learning.

International development contractors are "tool-users," employing useful technologies from A to Z, from the most simple to the most sophisticated, depending on local people, local knowledge, local power structures, and fears and biases that "come to the table." Those on the ragged edge of development, working with populations previously thought incapable of directly voicing their own needs, are increasingly in demand. The practitioners named in the following section, all outstanding in terms of using action learning, are conscious "paradigm shifters." They work on that ragged edge of critical realism that rejects "quick-fix" solutions. Doubtless, the strengths of these developers are representative of others already in the field or preparing to enter it.

Allan Kaplan, a consultant of the Community Development Resource Association of Cape Town, South Africa, argues that development is non-linear, unpredictable, and results in an "irreducible tension" between what has been and what will be. Development work entails the emergence of critical insights at all levels of human organization, across all kinds of human activities. Kaplan and his colleagues agree that action learning is "a way of life" and that:

> Action-learning is about taking responsibility for ourselves and our world and becoming creators of our lives rather than the victims of circumstances. It involves both individual creativity and the synergy of combining your efforts with others. This opens powerful possibilities for individuals, families, organizations, and communities. No one starts action-learning from scratch. It is already a part of us and we have been

using it throughout our lives. The challenge is to increase the power of our own learning by becoming increasingly conscious and purposeful in using the process ... [then] ... the process builds on itself. (Marais et al., 1997, pp. 71–2)

The principles of inclusion, "accompanying," and finding "speaking partners" are emphasized by these colleagues. For them, facilitation is being a "speaking partner" in action learning interactions, whenever any participant seems to need accompaniment through a personal reflection or learning process. But the fundamental rule is to respect others' rights to "solve problems by themselves and for themselves" (*ibid.*, p. viii).

Kaplan has elsewhere stated that:

Ultimately, development is driven from within, so while a development worker must bring specialist knowledge and skill to an intervention, the final outcome of the intervention is determined by the client ... An effective development practice *accompanies* clients through their developmental stages; one-off interventions and pre-designed packages are quite literally beside the point. (1999, p. 10)

Neela Mukherjee, associated with a Delhi-based enterprise called "Development Tracks, RTC," is another believer that, if the local people are to begin to understand and take action on their own priorities, then the development personnel sent to facilitate this will need to stay in the locality and "learn from and with people" (Robert Chambers, clearly referring to Revans' principles, cited in Mukherjee, 2002). She places a very high premium on the simple act of taking "joint walks" with locals through their communities or with rurally distributed family members to listen, observe and absorb what is going on. She observes that people cannot truly participate without "holding conversations." Mukherjee and others of like mind encourage illiterate persons to use pictorial symbols and diagrams to document problems, their occurrences, their seasons of deprivation (literally, as in food crises), and their wished-for solutions.

From my current reading, nowhere is the complexity of undertaking development work more comprehensively illustrated than in *Participatory Learning and Action* (Mukherjee, 2002). Since practitioners encounter immense ambiguities with every new project, she believes the need is urgent to understand shifting development paradigms, to "deconstruct" mindsets, and acquire new social skills for intuiting and interpreting unfamiliar knowledge systems. Firmly anchored in her own international experience, Mukherjee suggests concrete ways to accomplish this shifting, to appreciate multiple perspectives, multiple world views, and uniqueness of each development possibility. She asks for grounding in realism, resisting "romanticizing of the local," a fallacy that can issue as easily from top-down mentalities with political axes to grind as from participatory and benevolent impulses.

Making notes on work with farmers in Vietnam, she recorded that *no one had ever asked* them for their perspective. An omission that seems even worse is that, often, participants have little to no involvement in evaluation of the impact of development efforts. In the Maldives, where people could read and write, score cards were used to elicit opinions. In illiterate groups where written judgments cannot be elicited, she shows it is possible to use a great variety of ratings and scorings that can be visually represented by countable symbols.

Mukherjee includes a six-chapter compendium of the verbal, visual, analytical, and "joint walk" methods, tools, and strategies she has found helpful for working with largely rural populations and for interfacing with hierarchies of funding and decision-making authorities. Using symbols and graphic representations not only supplies information, but discussions about the pictorial representations also encourage story-telling that helps to identify commonalities and identify the emergence of consensus. While Mukherjee acknowledges the difficulty of reconciling pictorial data collections with verbal reporting requirements and with complex hidden agendas, she sees no alternative when working with largely illiterate, very poor, and often very subjugated populations. When unschooled, easily intimidated and at risk rural people in subsistence societies are asked to give up portions of their burdened time to participate, they go far beyond the usual role of "key informants."

Linda Mayoux (2003a; 2003b; Mayoux et al., 2005), an accomplished linguist who brings that extra skill to her international development work, is also confident of the necessity to build upon local people's own knowledge, interpretive skills, and energies. She is intent upon creating PALs as an interdependent way forward toward sustained development. Like Boulding, cited earlier, Mayoux is attuned to the systemic nature of dysfunctional social and economic patterns, and she has identified action learning as an appropriately systemic way to address the alteration of such patterns.

Mayoux listed five major components of "Grassroots Action Learning: Impact Assessment for Downward Accountability and Civil Society Development." These are paraphrased for brevity:

1. deciding what action learning is, why it can be useful, and what the challenges are that it can address;
2. figuring out what information "grassroots" people need to know and how they can find it;
3. discovering who the grassroots stakeholders are and how they should participate to insure accountability;
4. linking learning with action "from information diaries to change process," and discovering information needs for decision-making (i.e., "networking for empowerment: structures for lateral learning"); and

5. supporting grassroots action learning: roles, benefits and challenges for external agencies (Mayoux, 2003b, unpaginated overview).

Mayoux and staff of ANANDI (the Area Networking and Development Initiatives group) issued a report on their activities as, "a non-political secular organization working with women's organizations and partner NGOs to promote an empowerment approach and gender mainstreaming throughout development activity." ANANDI "helps women from some of the poorest and most marginalized communities in Gujarat [India] to organize themselves for collective action on a range of issues from basic needs and crisis management to gender violence and gender advocacy" (Mayoux et al., 2005, p. 212). This report details the review steps and the pictorial and interpersonal communication tools used in their project. The review was undertaken to insure that the PALs was, as intended, built upon and responsive to the information needs and the action opportunities of participants and their external partners at every point and in every circumstance. "Empowering inquiry" (Mayoux, 2003a) was a first step, to determine who among the stakeholders would represent all others in the review. The representatives then proceeded to envision change and count the costs, appreciate achievements, identify remaining or ongoing challenges, identify strategies for increasing positive changes and reducing negative impacts, finally deciding who would do what next, resolving whatever different views and potential conflicts they might encounter in order to negotiate further change.

ANANDI work addresses a staggering number of issues faced by the girls and women it serves: from untouchable status to drought and vanishing of public lands to personal perils from illness, domestic violence and ancient society-governing, female subordination rules. Where the PALs approach has been piloted, Mayoux and her colleagues believe their participant co-learners have generated vital and reliable data at group and community level, empowering all concerned over both the short and long term of civil society building. It takes imagination to find ways to "data collect" when many of the participants have never held a pen before and are reluctant to do so. But the risk-taking and story-telling of these vulnerable women seems overpowering evidence of their willingness to invest their very lives in social change. Their critical need for brave and astute internal and external development partners is also obvious.

Further examples

Space remains for only a bare listing of projects that have popped up recently in the literature of action learning. Such a list is instrumental in understanding how diverse the uses of action learning are. Projects are identified by title or characteristics and by country.

Particularly instructive are the 31 case briefs mentioned earlier, collected by Taylor et al., (1998). Additional case studies are sought for cross-

Table 6.1   The diverse uses of action learning

Case	Project	Country
1	The community versus the staff	South Africa
6	The chiefs did not know	South Africa
8	The pre-school and the unskilled builder	South Africa
9	Membership control of credit unions	South Africa
13	The sit-in at the city council	Zimbabwe
15	The failures at Chachacha	Zimbabwe
16	Stealing water	Swaziland
18	Clinics on wheels	Dominican Republic
20	Building roads or destroying the forest?	Dominican Republic
21	To fund or not to fund?	South Africa
26	Dropped at the eleventh hour	Namibia
	The crisis of Zamani Carpentry Cooperative	Zimbabwe
29	The donor tried to change the project	Namibia

Note: The case numbers are those used by Taylor et al. (1998); Cases 1–20 assess the quality and effects of participation; cases 21–9 address funding issues.

Source: Selected and adapted from Taylor et al. (1998).

case analysis and training purposes. The 31 already summarized are in two categories: "Exploring Community Participation and Its Significance for Development" and "Exploring the Financial Self-Sustainability of NGOs." Many of these cases end in midstream, with locals, developers or critical decision-makers "not yet decided" over next steps. A few selected titles speak volumes (see Table 6.1).

Both categories are constant headaches in development work. Projects that are well-developed and fully operational may yet fall into disrepair and failure if critical community leaders direct their attentions elsewhere, grow ill, or die. That was the fate of an effective water-sharing project that was undermined when deprived of a respected elder. Other projects have great strength and community commitment, but fail when funding is injected at the wrong times or in the wrong amounts, arbitrarily terminated, or elsewhere deployed.

Table 6.2 presents a sampling of "first world" uses of action learning in civil society includes the following projects; all except one are located in the U.K.

Action learning as a beacon for civil society

Kaplan offers a thesis-antithesis snapshot of the paradigm shift in development from *delivery of resources* to *the developing of capacity*, listing point by point how assumptions and practices are changing (1999, pp. 5,6 and 11,12). A prominent feature of the replacement capacity-building paradigm

Table 6.2 Sample of "first world" uses of action learning in civil society

Organization	Use
Royal Town Planning Institute	For knowledge exchange and professional development, helping group members resolve localized problems.
Praxis Community Projects	A membership base of eight refugee-led Refugee Community Organizations (RCOs) using action learning for structured interaction with policy-makers.
Permaculture Association	Works with groups called "action learning guilds" to help individuals learn to make their lifestyles more sustainable.
National Youth Homelessness Scheme	Cites six unique YMCA/Local Authority partnerships that are involving young people in action learning aimed at reducing the incidence and resulting effects of homelessness.
King's College, London	Women working in universities use action learning to explore remedies for career isolation, lack of role models, and socially imposed expectations that do not match their aspirations.
Youth and Good Governance Workshops	Based on action learning, these workshops are offered by the World Bank Institute as a way to seed ideas of civil society among leaders of the future.

is learning to read the world differently, a way of thinking and behaving that action learners become increasingly proficient in doing. "Reading" how to develop capacity and knowing when capacity is sufficient to protect civil society is exasperatingly difficult, and has its detractors, in part, because it is a skill-set Kaplan says is impossible to "teach." But "old paradigm" delivery of resources, no matter how beneficent, has yet to achieve civil society at home or abroad, and it is evident that something new is needed.

If the old beacon of practice has failed to keep us off the rocks, then a new beacon needs to be found and installed. If "reading differently" is capable of casting more light in the dark, and action learning is itself a "different reading," then surely it is worth a try. Kaplan does not downplay the difficulties of installing the new paradigm:

A reading of development must remain supple, subtle, and nuanced; it must be iterative and gradual; it must be reflective and reflexive. We must penetrate, but softly, so that we can intuit underlying movements; and do so in such a way that the individual or grouping is itself enabled to come to ... awareness and understanding ... The alternative development perspective demands a more developmental approach to building the capacity of its practitioners ... Developmental readings cannot be obtained within the cold and dry parameters of the conventional reporting format; warmer and more human forms must be developed, to support the reading itself. (*ibid.*, p. 17)

Tracing back, it is evident that many, if not most, of the civil society builders who make conscious use of action learning have either studied in the U.K. or learned from someone who did, including those connected with the specific practices noted in this review. Evidence of action learning in counterpart realms in the U.S. seems much harder to come by. For example, it is only recently that U.S. practitioners of organization development (OD) have begun to claim action learning as an OD strategy, perhaps partly because OD action research has been considered a superior way to meet old paradigm demands for "scientific rigor." Action learning almost certainly will become more visible and play a greater role in U.S. civil society in the future.

Conclusion

Action learning is not a technology, as many claim. It is a way of seeing the world. Practitioners of action learning are not so much in a charitable "helping" capacity as in an egalitarian human capacity, being one in company with other learners, none of whom have all the answers to what is needed in any given problem field. Our conversations with developing peoples exchange the wisdom of their systemic worlds and ours. Such exchanges can help prevent the creation of what is not needed or perhaps not in the sequence or the amount needed, or not usable with the low technology available. As Kaplan insists, development work demands that we "facilitate resourcefulness" in full awareness of the fact that we cannot "bring" and impose development – that we can only hope to tap into and assist with the flow of development processes already underway (1999, p. 11). This we will not understand unless we are ready to accept the new paradigm of mutuality and power sharing.

To greater or lesser degree, new ways of accomplishing things are always subject to old paradigm resistance, whether in businesses, governments, civil society, or interstices between. Action learning, by itself, cannot prevent this but, wherever it is seriously undertaken, at least it leaves valuable seeds of regeneration. At best, it illuminates pathways forward. No one has the last word on what giant strides may be taken by investment in learning with and from each other.

References

Action Learning: Learning to Listen – Learning to Learn (A Case Study Action Learning Set) (West Durham Rural Pathfinder, U.K.) Available at www.westdurhampathfinder.com/page/achievements.cfm

Action Learning Ministry Teams", Slide Presentation (Mid-South Christian College, U.S.) Available at www.slideshare.net/Gregwad/action_learning_ministry_teams

Boulding, E. (1988) *Building a Global Civic Culture: Education for an Interdependent World* (New York: Teachers' College Press).

Boulding, E. (2003) Boulding interviewed by Portilla (transcript). Available at www.beyondintractability.org/audio/elise_boulding?nid=2413

Boulding, E. "Civil Society Index and Civil Society Institute". Available at http://CivilSocietyIndex.org/index and www.civilsocietyinstitute.org/what.cfm

Boulding, E. (2007) "Collaborative Working Groups" (Royal Town Planning Institute, U.K.) Available at www.rtpi.org.uk/item/723

Boulding, E. (2004) "Community Development". Available at www.lifelonglearninguk.org/3126.htm

Boulding, E. Communitarianism (five websites). Available at:

http://en.wikipedia.org/w/index
http://plato.stanford.edu/entries/communitarianism/
www.gwu.edu/instituteforcommunitarianpolicystudies
www.infed.org/biblio/communitarianism
www.wordiq.com/definition/Communitarianism

Boulding, E. "Designing an Action Learning Pathway" (Permaculture Association: Britain). Available at www.permaculture.org.uk/mm.asp?mmfile=dipcreatingactionlp

Edwards, M. (2004) *Civil Society* (Cambridge, U.K.: Polity Press/Blackwell).

Etzioni, A. (1995) *The Spirit of Community: Rights and Responsibilities and the Communitarian Agenda* (London: Fontana Press).

Evans, S. (1997) *Born for Liberty* (New York: Free Press).

Falk, R. (2003) "Empowering Inquiry: Our Debt to Edward Said", November. Available at www.larivistadelmanifesto.it/originale/44A20031114.html

Freire, P. (1970) *Pedagogy of the Oppressed* (New York: Seabury Press).

Gagel, D. (n.d) "The Fundamentals of Action-Research in Development Cooperation". Available at www.action-research.de/konzept-english.htm

Giggey, S. (2008) "What is Grassroots Action Learning? Overview of Approaches. GAL Sections 1.2 and 2", REFLECT (Regenerated Freirean Literacy Through Empowering Community Techniques), May. Available at www.reflect.org

Goerner, S. J. (1994) *Chaos and the Evolving Ecological Universe* (Amsterdam: Overseas Publishers Association/Gordon & Breach).

Goerner, S. J. "Job Opportunities for Civil Society". Available at http://web.worldbank.org/WBSITE/EXTERNAL/TOPICS/CSO/0,contentMDK

Jones, M. (2004) "Swedish Support to Decentralization Reform in Rwanda", Report for Democracy and Social Development Department (Stockholm: Swedish International Development Cooperation Agency).

Kaplan, A. (1999) "The Developing of Capacity" (Capetown, South Africa: Centre for Developmental Practice, Community Development Resource Association (CDRA)). Available at http://www.cdra.org.za

Kemmis, S. and McTaggart, R. (2007) "Participatory Action Research", in N. K. Denzin and Y. S. Lincoln (eds.), *Strategies of Qualitative Inquiry*, 3rd edition (Thousand Oaks, CA: Sage).

Leckie, S. (2006) "Using Action Learning to Develop Leaders in the Justice Sector". Available at www.skillsforjustice.com

Lipietz, A. (1996) "Sustainable Community Development", Lecture delivered at the School of Fine Arts in Paris, November 18. Available at www.uwex.edu/ces/ag/sus/html/sustainable_development.html

Marais, D., Taylor, J., and Kaplan, A. (1997) *Action-Learning for Development: Use Your Experience to Improve Your Effectiveness* (Wetton, South Africa: Juta & Co. Ltd and Capetown, South Africa: Community Development Resource Association (CDRA)).

Martin, R. (2007) *The Opposable Mind* (Boston, MA: Harvard Business School Press).

Mayoux, L. (2003a) "Empowering Inquiry: A New Approach to Investigation", Enterprise Development Impact Assessment Information Service (EDIAIS), January. Available at www.enterprise-impact.org.uk/informationresources/toolbox/thinkingitthrough-using diagramsinIA.shtml

Mayoux, L. (2003b) "Grassroots Action Learning: Assessment for Downward Accountability and Civil Society Development", September. Available at www.enterprise-impact.org.UK/word-files/GALContentsOverview.and1.1.dc

Mayoux, L., Andharia, J., Hardikar, N., Thacker, S., and Dand, S. (2005) "Participatory Action Learning in Practice: Experience of a Rapid Participatory Review of ANANDI, India" (published online), *Journal of International Development*, 17(2), February, pp. 211–43.

Mukherjee, N. (2002) *Participatory Learning and Action* (New Delhi: Concept).

Mukherjee, N. "National Youth Homelessness Scheme". Available at www.communities.govv.uk/youthhomelessness/activities/actionlearning

Mukherjee, N. "Participatory Action Learning". Available at www.leap-pased.org/main5.html

Mukherjee, N. "Participatory Learning and Action". Available at www.iied.org/NR/agbioliv/pla_notes/about.html

Mukherjee, N. "Praxis RCOs Workshop News". Available at www.praxis.org.uk/?page=2_11&page3=3&id=8

Reardon, B. (1998) "The Urgency of Peace Education: The Good News and the Bad News". Available at www.soc.nil.ac.jp/psaj/asPrint/e-newsletter/1998/reardon.html

Seerane, M. (1991) "Using Action Research and Action Learning to Develop Project Management Skills in Tertiary Education Students". Available at www.aare.edu.au/01pap/see01666.htm

Swepson, P., Dick, B., Zuber-Skerrit, Passfield, R., Carroll, A., and Wadsworth, Y. (2003) "A History of the Action Learning, Action Research, and Process Management Association (ALARPM): From Brisbane (Australia) to the World through Inclusions and Networks", *Systemic Practice and Action Research*, 16(4), August, pp. 237–81.

Taylor, J., Marais, D., and Heyns, S. (1998) *Action-Learning Series: Case Studies and Lessons from Development Practice* (Capetown, South Africa: Juta and Co. Ltd/ Community Development Resource Association (CDRA)).

Taylor, J., Marais, D., and Heyns, S. (2006) "The School for Social Entrepreneurs". http://socialentrepreneurs.typepad.com

Thompson, R., Peters, K., and Plaza, D. (2004,) "Learning through Listening: Applying an Action Learning Model to a Cross Cultural Field Study Experience in Native America", *International Journal of Intercultural Relations*, 28(2), March, pp. 165–80.

Thompson, R., Peters, K., and Plaza, D. (2003) "Youth and Good Governance. Governance and Anti-Corruption" (World Bank Institute). Available at http://worldbank.org/WBSITE/EXTERNAL/WBI/WBIPROGRAMS/PSGLP/0

Weinstein, K. (2002) "Action Learning: The Classic Approach", in Y. Boshyk (ed.), *Action Learning Worldwide* (Basingstoke, U.K./New York: Palgrave Macmillan).

Weinstein, K. "Women's Action Learning" (Kings College, London). Available at www.kcl.ac.uk/about/structure/admin/equal-opps/training/wal/

Part II
Themes

7
The Practical Primacy of Questions in Action Learning

Marilee G. Adams

Introduction

The centrality of questions in action learning is fundamental for both theory and practice. Reg Revans, the principal pioneer of action learning, a scientist who made important contributions to the fields of management and organizational development, put the search for fresh questions and questioning insight at the core of action learning. He emphasized that questioning insight is the starting point and that people learn very effectively from and with each other, as distinguished from highly formal didactic approaches to learning. His focus was on "learning while doing," with questions accelerating and deepening this process, which also includes self-questioning and reflection. One reflects on what has occurred or what is occurring (reflection in action), which allows one to harvest the learning.

Asking questions invigorates thinking, learning, action and results. Interpersonal questions are used for speaking and communicating with others. Internal questions are used for thinking, learning and reflection within oneself. In either case, one best arrives at effective answers and solutions by route of the best questions. Traveling this route requires resisting the expediency of easy answers and immediate concentration on solutions. Rather, it depends on thought-provoking questions that get to the heart of the matter and can yield more effective answers and solutions, both in the short term and the long term. Reinforcing an "inquiring mindset" in the context of action learning bolsters the habit of questioning and the quantity and quality of questions asked, which can also contribute to generative learning well beyond the experience itself.

Today, the perspectives and processes of action learning, in which question asking is so primary, are widely respected as a powerful approach with objectives such as leadership development, organizational change, team building, problem-solving, raising self-efficacy, and building competitive advantage. While some see action learning as a last resort when traditional methods fail, the practical imperative to develop leaders, managers, and other professionals capable of traveling the route to thoughtful and effective solutions impels many organizations and businesses to engage globally in action learning.

The chapter builds on Revans's premise about the primacy of questions, questioning insight, and curiosity as the foundation of action learning. Curiosity-fueled adult learning – where spontaneity is encouraged – can be strengthened and operationalized by focusing on the question asker, as well as on the question. We begin by exploring the centrality of questions in action learning, and the power and purposes of questions in general. We note the role of internal questions in thinking, reflection, learning and problem-solving, as well as the role of interpersonal questions in communication and collaborative problem-solving. The tendency to value answers more than questions is discussed. We also explore the relationship between questions and their impact on results for both individuals and teams. Enhancing awareness and skills of effective question asking strengthens practical avenues for learning, reflection and collaboration, and also contributes to a greater probability of achieving real-world business results.

Action learning and the primacy of questions

While there are many variations of action learning, there are several fundamental characteristics that Revans associated with it: "the primacy of questioning insight over programmed knowledge, individuals/teams preferably (but not always) assigned to solve problems with which they have little or no familiarity, learning [is] given priority over problem solution, and there is selection of a real problem focus *always*" (Dilworth and Willis, 2003, p. 15). While learning is the first focus, urgency to solve the real problem is what powers the "learning engine."

This focus on "learning while doing" typically occurs within an organizational, system, or team context. In an action learning program, a team uses a key business challenge as a vehicle for intentional learning that often leads to accidental and unexpected learning as well. Practice varies within different schools of action learning, including the definition and involvement of a team advisor or learning coach, the degree of direct focus on learning, the types of learning sought, and whether the team addresses a joint or individual business challenge. Experiential learning focused on the business challenge marks all these endeavors, and may include teams working in simulation situations. (*ibid.*, p.137). While Revans thought that simulations did not meet his standard that action learning should focus on real, even daunting problems, what is "real" today can be found within sophisticated computer simulations and other simulation formats that address real issues in real time. These include those related to homeland security, military operations, and the complex issues facing global organizations.

It is not surprising that Dilworth and Willis cite "the primacy of questioning insight" as the driver of action learning. They note that Revans "repeatedly [made] the point that 'fresh' questions are central to action learning" (*ibid.*, 2003, p.12). Virtually every writer and practitioner of action learning echoes this fundamental theme about the primacy of questions in action learning. For example, Marquardt (1999, pp. 30–1) tells us, "in action learning, questions are not only seeking answers. Rather, they are seeking to go deeper, to understand, to respond to what is being asked, to give it thought. Asking questions is not only a quest for solutions but also an opportunity to explore." Kramer (2007/2008, p. 40) writes that, "The power of action learning comes from the many ways it develops the skills and habits of questioning, listening, and reflection. As in the Socratic method, questions are more important than answers during action learning." Czajkowski (2009) considers action learning "a construct through which participants learn questioning skills." These perspectives on the primacy of questions in action learning are echoed in the following comments by participants and facilitators of action learning programs.

> One of the predominant learnings cited by all participants was the use of questioning insight. They used this learning both in the program and back on the job... questions can move you in a direction that you did not think about because you were in that box and you were not thinking... Now all of a sudden they have a realization and start questioning their initial decision. (O'Neil and Marsick, 2007, p. 142–3)
>
> This jolt – this realization that asking questions is the key to beginning to think, to doing different things, and to doing things differently and learning – is something many participants comment on. (Weinstein, 1995, p. 178)
>
> In essays and self reports, I noticed a pattern that asking questions would bring new understanding. They would get most excited about their own best questions. They would try so hard to come up with questions. These became milestones and landmarks. And yes, you see them developing these questioning and reflection skills all the time. They integrated questioning skills and continued this up until the last process [in their AL experience]. (Willis, 2008)

Revans on learning and questions

The term "action learning" implies intentional learning. Revans notes that this is vital because, "in any epoch of rapid change, those organizations unable to adapt are soon in trouble, and adaptation is achieved only by learning" (Revans, 1983, p. 11). This is as true for individuals as it is for organizations. For Revans, therefore, the goal became accelerating the rate of learning to anticipate, match, and even exceed the rate of change. Revans famously described learning (L) as the result of "programmed knowledge" (P) and questioning insight (Q). Hence, we have his Learning Equation: L = P + Q. While both P and Q are essential, "Revans clearly specifies that the operational start point must be Q. It is Q that expresses the realization that the solution to the problem is *unknown*, or the problem would have been solved already" (Dilworth and Willis, 2003, p. 17, authors' emphasis).

Revans emphasized that, "Q...remains the essence of *true* action learning" (Revans, 1989, p. 102, author's emphasis). He also frequently used "fresh" to describe the most valuable kinds of questions, those unburdened by assumptions and old ways of perceiving. To get to such questions, he wanted learners, whenever possible, to be outside their comfort zone, having to deal with unfamiliar problems, unfamiliar settings, and even unfamiliar associates. He expected that the lack of familiarity would encourage a person to notice long-held assumptions that might no longer work, including some acquired early in life. Recognizing the need to challenge old assumptions and create new ones is the province of transformative learning.

Three interdependent systems of thought and action comprise Revans's formulation of action learning. These he terms "Systems Alpha, Beta, and Gamma," and each has questions at its core, either explicitly or implicitly. In System Alpha, people continually ask themselves and others: "What is happening? What ought to be happening? How can it be made to happen?" In System Beta, people ask questions about "facts" and assumptions, using whatever is revealed in pursuit of new avenues of inquiry and better solutions. System Gamma requires focusing questions on oneself, the kind of reflection required for transformational learning: "it is Gamma that carries the insights. It explicitly requires the action learner to investigate the problem in relation to self, and to examine both self and problem in relation to others" (Dilworth and Willis, 2003, p. 157). Commenting on the importance he placed on System Gamma, Revans wrote that "self-knowledge is gold in the mind" (Revans, 1982, p. 766). Self-knowledge occurs with the willingness to question and examine oneself honestly with reference to mental models, assumptions, intentions, limitations, and places where personal change is deemed desirable.

At any age, young or old, curiosity is the catalyst of questioning and learning. As children, our natural curiosity led to asking questions and learning. Yet, as adult learners, we often need to revitalize our natural curiosity in order to become intentional learners capable of asking questions that can call forth fresh perspectives, answers and solutions. Revans often marveled at the spontaneity of children at play, as they explored and exercised their curiosity. He observed how these traits seemed to be driven out of people by traditional education systems and the stultifying environments in which people work. Revans believed that the empowerment inherent in action learning could rekindle for adults the spontaneity, excitement, and joy of learning that children naturally experience through their curiosity and questioning.

The power and purposes of questions

Focusing on the power of questions in general is germane to this exploration of the practical primacy of questions in action learning. Dilworth comments that while, "Questioning insight and questioning processes are the very core of action learning, people tend not to know what to ask and also to be judgmental instead of curious about the underlying causes of the problem" (Dilworth, 2008). The pervasive, though often unrecognized power inherent in questions led me to write in *The Art of the Question* that, "questions are like treasures hidden in broad daylight" (Goldberg, 1998a, p. 6). The treasure they provide is embedded in every aspect of our lives. Recognizing the unique, profound, and pervasive value of questions may enhance motivation for intentionally developing more skillfulness in formulating and asking them. While every human being *asks* questions, it takes skill and intention to *use* them strategically and effectively. This skill may be continually reinforced and expanded through using questions in action learning to resolve important business challenges.

Skillful and frequent question asking begins with awareness as well as curiosity. In organizational, business, and professional contexts, and in roles such as leader, manager, mentor, coach, consultant, mediator and educator, the value of questions becomes apparent by realizing how many everyday reasons we have for asking them. We ask questions in order to:

- gather information
- lay groundwork for answers and solutions
- think critically, creatively, and strategically
- learn and reflect (including critical reflection)
- uncover and challenge assumptions
- solve problems and make decisions
- clarify and confirm listening
- build and maintain relationships and collaboration
- negotiate and resolve conflicts
- set goals, as well as develop strategy
- create, innovate, and open new possibilities
- catalyze productive and accountable conversation and action.

The importance of questions "versus" answers

This list increases awareness of the multiple and essential functions of questions. Nevertheless, since asking a question implies some level of "not knowing," people are sometimes uncomfortable, reluctant, or even reticent about asking questions at all (*ibid.*, p.3). In fact, Boshyk commented that, "while questions are at the core of action learning and business effectiveness, it's often the case that people are paid *not* to ask questions" (Boshyk, 2008).

If anything, people prize answers, not questions. Unfortunately, valuing answers above questions obscures recognizing that *an answer is the end point of a process*, one that *begins* with a question. Indeed, "We live in an answer-oriented, fix-it-quick world. In the clamor for answers – sometimes any answer – we often overlook quiet distinctions and fresh perspectives that could reveal whole new worlds of possibilities. Moreover, sometimes the conditioned hunt for answers represents a desperate attachment to 'knowing,' and a simultaneous avoidance of any anxiety associated with not knowing, or even appearing not to know" (Goldberg, 1998a, p. 4).

Moreover, sometimes an answer arrived at too quickly or precipitously may itself develop into another problem. The inquiring mindset that participants in action learning programs develop leads them to recognize that effective questions are likely to lead to effective answers and results, ineffective questions may lead to ineffective answers and results, and questions that are missed (often because of assumptions about what is "known") may lead to random and sometimes problematic answers and results. In other words, the zeal for answers may unintentionally compromise the ability to solve problems as well as create new directions and possibilities.

Participation in action learning programs can redirect attention to the power of questions as being at the *source* of answers and solutions, as illustrated by the comments we heard from participants earlier in the chapter. Implicitly or explicitly, they were coming to recognize the value of questions as well as the intrinsic relationship between questions and answers. This relationship is succinctly described by Postman: "all the answers we ever get are responses to questions. The questions may not be evident to us, especially in everyday affairs, but they are there nonetheless, doing their work. Their work, of course, is to design the form that our knowledge will take and therefore to determine the direction of our actions" (Postman, 1976, p. 144).

Postman's point is that questions, including the structure and assumptions embedded in them, frame and direct attention and *action*. As Weinstein (2008) commented, "If I don't ask questions in action learning, I can't make anything happen." This includes questions of others as well as those we ask *ourselves*. In fact, internal questioning is the essence of the thinking involved in problem-solving. We might heed this perspective on the importance of questions in thinking and problem-solving attributed to Albert Einstein: "If I had an hour to solve a problem, and my life depended on the solution, I would spend the first 55 minutes determining the proper questions to ask, for if I knew the proper questions, I could solve the problem in less than five minutes." Focusing one's inquiring mindset on a problem makes it obvious that, if one wants the best answers and solutions, one must *begin* with the best questions.

Questions, learning, and reflection

The emphasis on reflection as intrinsic to learning is embedded in the very fabric of action learning. Reflection, which is replete with questioning, refers to complex and multidimensional operations that are associated with meta-cognition, stages of development, the nature of learning sought, focus on the learner, and the contexts in which this all occurs. Mezirow writes that, "While all reflection implies an element of critique, the term *critical reflection* ... refer(s) to challenging the validity of *presuppositions* in prior learning" (Mezirow, 1990, p. 12, author's emphasis). He also notes that *"Reflection on one's own premises can lead to transformative learning"* (*ibid.*, p. 18, author's emphasis). This observation is consistent with Revans comment that, "the learning process is ... critically about the Self" (Dilworth and Willis, 2003, p. viii). Operationalizing reflection leads to recognizing that asking questions, especially internal ones, is *how* reflection occurs. For Revans, focus on the self occurs within System Gamma. In this context, one might ask oneself questions such as: What assumptions are I attached to? What honestly were my motives in making that comment? What am I missing or avoiding in this situation? What lessons might become available from this mistake if I had the courage to face them?

Linking questions with action and results

For practitioners of action learning, learning itself may be considered the Holy Grail; certainly, all recognize that questions are intrinsic to learning, reflection and development. Others, as we have noted, may worship mainly at the altar of answers and results. For this reason, especially in organizational and business contexts, it is important explicitly to link learning and question asking with real-time business challenges and results. In actuality, every organization, and every individual who works in one or with one, is in the "results business." From this perspective, it is primarily the *benefits* of learning that matter, rather than learning for its own sake. As one executive coaching client confessed, "I wouldn't care much about learning if I weren't convinced I had to in order to get the results I want."

One way of describing the relationship between questions and results is through an illustration, the QDARr™ model. (Adams, 2010, p. 6) In this model, Q = Questions, D = Decisions, A = Action, R = Results, and r = reflection. Here, I use the term "Results" to refer to the "present state"; that is, whatever is now present as an outcome of whatever led up to it. Notice that reflection on Results brings attention back to the Question at the beginning of the equation in a quest to understand any limitations and assumptions embedded within it. Ideally, reflection is an ongoing activity (reflection in action), as the equation indicates. In this iterative process, one can apply the

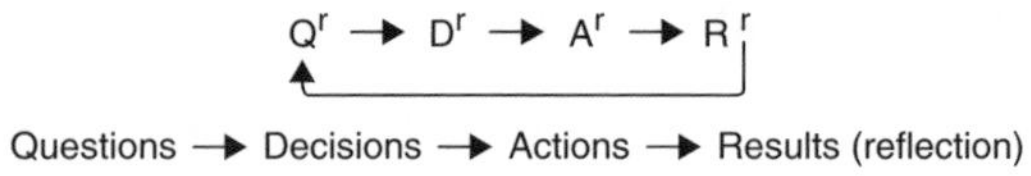

$$Q^r \rightarrow D^r \rightarrow A^r \rightarrow R^r$$

Questions → Decisions → Actions → Results (reflection)

Figure 7.1   QDARr model

Source: Adams (2010, p. 6).

equation in a myriad of situations as a way of deconstructing, understanding and learning from them. It can also provide a way to understand what has contributed to causing a problem, how to reconsider and reformulate the problem itself, and how to resolve it by beginning with a better-construed question.

When a client is looking for change, either organizational or personal, the QDARr model can help them understand how changing their questions can directly impact their ability to influence their results in a positive way. (Adams, 2009, p. 14) In other words, when a new result is desired, identifying and then redesigning the originating question provides a practical "how to" for reconceptualizing and resolving a problem, thus paving the way for achieving the results that are important.

A teaching story illustrates the impact of a new question when a different result is desired. Of course, for the new question to have the desired effect, its structure and the assumptions embedded within it must be reconceived and reformulated, as this example demonstrates. A woman in one of my workshops asked for help with a difficult professional situation. She told us that she loved her career, but conflict with her boss had left her wondering if she should quit her job. When I asked what questions she was asking herself about this dilemma with her boss, she responded with an edge to her voice, "What's he going to do wrong *now?*" and "How's he going to make me look bad today?" Clearly, her current questions would render near impossible any satisfying resolution. In this case, the R represents her conflicted relationship with her boss.

I asked this woman if she would consider asking herself a new question, and suggested, "What can *I* do to make my boss look *good?*" She looked startled, almost confused, by the new query. The thinking and assumptions it represented were clearly outside the mindset or frame with which she had been viewing her boss, as well as herself in relation to him. Nevertheless, she agreed to experiment with the new question.

This is a true story with a fortuitous ending. When I encountered this woman by coincidence a few months later, she gave this report. "Since that workshop, I've gotten a promotion and a raise. The most remarkable thing is that my boss and I volunteered to work on a committee together, whereas before we avoided even being in the same room." Then she added that her husband had noticed a change in her and had even thanked her for not complaining about her boss any more.

This woman was so intrigued about the power of a single question to lead to such far-reaching results that she requested a coaching conversation to discuss it. She was able to engage in critical reflection about her original problem by wondering out loud, "What was I assuming about my boss? How did my judgmental attitude toward him prevent me from assuming responsibility for the conflicts we were having?" She also asked, "Where else in my life do I do this?" and, "How can I become more aware of making assumptions in future situations?"

Now we can return to the QDARr model and use it to deconstruct this teaching story and explore its lessons about the power of questions, especially with reference to outcomes. Clearly, this woman experienced very different Results when her thinking was directed by her "before" question in contrast to her "after" question. Her original Question about her boss ("What's he going to do wrong now?") led to her Decision (probably not conscious) about how to relate to him. That decision surely led to some unpleasant Actions (ways she communicated with her boss), since the Result was their conflicted relationship and her fear about leaving the job she valued so much.

This story emphasizes the importance of focusing on questions first, not answers, if a change, improvement, or new direction is desired. Noting the assumptions embedded in the original question, we can see that it was past-oriented, blame-focused, and outwardly directed. By contrast, the new question assumes a future orientation and a solution focus. Moreover, the new question implicitly required this woman to assume responsibility for her own perceptions, actions, and results. The new question ("How can I make my boss look good?") provided the groundwork for her to make new Decisions about her boss, Act differently toward him, and enjoy the positive Results that ensued.

There are practical ways that an action learning team can use the QDARr model to examine, resolve and generatively learn from their real-time business challenges. Assuming that either limitations or possibilities are embedded in the questions with which the team approaches a problem, they could work together to discover limiting questions and transform them into those capable of leading to the resolution of their business challenge. A team (or individuals on a team) could also use the QDARr model as a guide for collaborative inquiry: "a process consisting of repeated episodes of reflection and action through which a group of peers strives to answer a question of importance to them" (Bray et al., 2002, p. 6, authors' emphasis). They could collaboratively, reflectively and sequentially examine their questions, decisions and actions in light of desired results. They could also create and explore powerful new questions to help them achieve, and perhaps exceed, their goals.

A team discovers missed questions

The inquiring mindset that is reinforced individually and collectively by participating in action learning could also lead a team to search for questions they may have been missing altogether. They might even discover that every question missed is a crisis waiting to happen. Discovering such questions could lead them to approach resolving their business challenge more strategically and comprehensively. In the following example, this search for missing questions helped a team reconceive a problem in a way that led to new directions in thinking and strategy. It also helped them avert potential further problems that could have occurred by responding to the old one too quickly.

This executive team of a large city hospital, also part of a larger hospital system, met to address a serious and mounting problem. Other hospitals within their system were transferring a particular category of patient to them without adequate or timely communication or coordination. This was causing problems with finding beds, providing quality patient care, and increasing stress levels for staff. The team decided the answer was to create a new role for a coordinator and then launched into a discussion about obtaining funding for such a position.

At this point, a respected team member commented that she did not think they had thought through the situation thoroughly enough yet. She suggested they come up with a list of potential questions to explore before jumping precipitously to a solution. Among the questions they had not considered were these:

* What is the formal and informal patient transfer process for this particular category of patient as compared with that of "regular medical patients"?
* Have we adequately communicated the guidelines for this process to staff, both in our hospital and the others in our system?
* What perspectives and suggestions could we get from the nurses who deal with this problem on a daily basis?
* What are best practices in other hospital systems for dealing with similar situations?
* What assumptions are we making and what systemic issues might we discover that would allow us to take patient care to a whole new level?

The team realized that they lacked adequate information for resolving their problem. They also recognized that creating and funding a new role without this information could mask the real problem and potentially lead to even more. In addition, they recognized that a personnel solution cannot "fix" what might be a systems issue. Therefore, they decided to approach the problem by filling in gaps in their understanding of it so they could be more strategic and successful in alleviating this stress for staff, and even reach new levels of quality patient care.

Conclusion

The goal of this chapter has been to make more explicit the implicit, primary and practical power of questions in action learning. More important than any specific suggestions about questions is the meta message about the power and primacy of questions themselves. The typical approach to problem-solving is to search for answers, ideas and solutions. In such situations, questions, when asked, are more for information gathering than anything else. By contrast, participation in an action learning program is a willing immersion in an experience of curiosity, question asking, reflection and learning. Participants naturally inculcate the imperative to consider questions *before* looking for answers.

The context of action learning provides a powerful opportunity for individuals as well as teams to strengthen the inquiring mindset that undergirds being a lifelong learner. This strengthened inquiring perspective helps individuals and teams collaboratively resolve their real-time problems in such a way that new learning also occurs. Over time, the quantity, quality and uses of questions expand. Simultaneously, action learning participants become more comfortable with "not knowing" and with asking questions in general, both of themselves and others.

The potential transformation of participants – from answer-driven problem solvers to more thoughtful, strategic, collaborative and inquiry-based ones – can be seen as the generative gift of action learning. Should any contribution to action learning itself emerge from these perspectives, one focus could be to explore, qualitatively as well as quantitatively, the impact of explicitly sharing practices and perspectives on question asking as a skill and guide to problem-solving, collaboration, learning and personal reflection early in the action learning process. Perhaps useful understandings and positive outcomes would emerge that would further support and extend the growth of action learning, adult education and the generative contributions of both.

References

Adams, M. (2009) *Change Your Questions, Change Your Life: 10 Powerful Tools for Life and Work*, 2nd edition (San Francisco: Berrett-Koehler/ASTD Press).

Adams, M. (2010) *Question Thinking: Theory and Practice* (San Francisco: Berrett-Koehler) (in press).

Boshyk, Y. (ed). (2002) "Why Business Driven Action Learning?" in *Action Learning Worldwide: Experiences in Leadership and Organizational Development*, May (London/New York: Palgrave-Macmillan/St. Martin's Press).

Boshyk, Y. (2008) Personal conversation with Marilee Adams.

Bray, J. N., Lee, J., Smith, L. L., and Yorks, L. (2002) *Collaborative Inquiry in Practice: Action, Reflection, and Making Meaning* (Thousand Oaks, CA: Sage).

Czajkowski, J. (2009) Personal conversation with Marilee Adams.

Dilworth, R. L. (2008) Personal conversation with Marilee Adams.

Dilworth, R. L. and Willis, V. J. (2003) *Action Learning: Images and Pathways* (Malabar, FL: Krieger).

Goldberg, M. (1998a) *The Art of the Question: A Guide to Short-Term, Question-Centered Therapy* (New York: John Wiley & Sons).

Goldberg, M. (1998b) "The Spirit and Discipline of Organizational Inquiry: Asking Questions for Organizational Breakthrough and Transformation", *Manchester Review*, 3(3).

Kramer, R. (2007/2008) "Leading Change through Action Learning", *Public Manager Journal*, Winter.

Marquardt, M. (1999) *Action Learning in Action: Transforming Problems and People for World-Class Organizational Learning* (Palo Alto, CA: Davies-Black).

O'Neil, J. and Marsick, V. J. (2007) *Understanding Action Learning: Theory into Practice* (New York: AMA) (Adult Learning Theory and Practice Book Series).

Mezirow, J. (1990) *Fostering Critical Reflection in Adulthood: A Guide to Transformative and Emancipator Learning* (San Francisco/Oxford: Jossey-Bass).

Postman, N. (1976) *Crazy Talk, Stupid Talk: How We Defeat Ourselves By the Way We Talk and What We Do About It* (New York: Delacorte Press).

Revans, R. W. (1982) *The Origins and Growth of Action Learning* (Bromley, U.K.: Chartwell-Bratt).

Revans, R. W. (1983) *The ABC of Action Learning* (Bromley, U.K.: Chartwell-Brat).

Revans, R. W. (1989) *The Golden Jubilee of Action Learning* (Manchester: Manchester Business School).

Weinstein, K. (1995) *Action Learning: A Journey in Discovery and Development*. London: HarperCollins.

Weinstein, K. (2008) Personal conversation with Marilee Adams.

Willis, V. J. (2008) Personal conversation with Marilee Adams.

8
Process in Action Learning Teams: Similarities and Variations
Michael Huge and John W. Bing

Introduction

This chapter is about process in action learning teams. Edgar Schein (2006) has described process in groups as "how things are done rather than what is done". He further defines these processes as boundary management, problem solving and decision-making, and interpersonal interactions (*ibid.*, p. 287).

We begin by briefly summarizing general conceptualizations of teams and the changing nature of teamwork as an introduction to process on action learning teams. We then differentiate general teams from action learning teams. Rather than being only goal or task centered, action learning teams focus on learning and problem-solving. Though there is certainly over-lap between the goals of action learning teams and other teams, an action learning team may succeed without meeting a tangible goal or benchmark. Action learning teams further differentiate themselves by developing pri-marily from within through critical reflection. These specialized groups often do not have a designated leader. The idea for action learning teams came out of a general movement toward self-directed teams of the mid-twentieth century.

Following this description of the history and evolution of action learn-ing teams, the process within action learning teams is then examined. Key items to investigate within action learning teams include team fundamen-tals, group communication, action learning principles, member develop-ment, and delivering results. To illustrate differences in the application of action learning processes, a theoretical example is given in which two cultures are compared and contrasted as to how action learning may oper-ate differently in certain cultures.

The nature of teams

Teams are a bit like individuals: They have similar characteristics in many respects, but they are different as well. Individuals are born, live and work, and die; teams also are created within an organizational context, work together, and then disband. Like individuals, teams have different goals and can work together with other teams to produce a series of coordinated outputs – as, for example, global teams do in the pharmaceutical industry, often mixing marketing teams with research and development teams with government relations groups and many others.

Teams are unlike other groups in that members of teams have, at some point in their development, common objectives and some agreement on how to reach those objectives.

A taxonomy of teams would provide almost as diverse a list as there are individual's occupations around the world. We have worked with teams from the chemical, information technology, pharmaceutical, manufacturing and other industries, and they are all different – not only by industry, but by level and purpose as well: Board-level teams are very different from factory production teams in many ways but, in terms of communication and human process, there are similarities. Each member of a team has his or her own turf, which they can either share or hoard; each member can communicate openly or hide information to retain power; each can choose to work for the benefit of the team or for themselves alone. And each team also must respond to the outside organizational forces that mold their work and their objectives.

Analysis of teams and teamwork has evolved over time, and especially over the last 20 years, as the process of teamwork has evolved from the old model of coordinating numerous individual tasks, and linear development towards a model emphasizing permeable boundaries within and between teams and individuals in which development is iterative, and in which teams work and succeed in a more intra-dependent manner (Kozlowski and Ilgen, 2006). Instead of numerous discrete goals adding up to the overall success of a project, success emerges from teamwork in a more holistic manner. Work in such teams must then be characterized as adaptive and flexible, ready to change as projects shift scope. Failures of such teams can have catastrophic results in the form of unmet goals, lost productivity and loss of revenue for a company, or loss of efficacy in other organizations. Team members must possess various skill sets, and teams must be capable of achieving multiple goals.

In the most complex organizational structures, teams interlock with each other like gears in a watch. If the watch is well-tuned, time moves fast, and so does productivity; if not, time and productivity are lost. Finally, teams are also sometimes given tasks that are either impossible or very difficult, such as the development of a compound from the laboratory to an approved drug in the pharmaceutical industry. Few compounds move successfully from laboratory to market, but this does not make those teams who fail to develop such a drug less successful – on the contrary, those teams which "kill compounds" quickly, rather than have them die a slow death in the regulatory process, will save the company money.

Action learning teams as a distinct subcategory of teams

Certainly one of the outputs of a taxonomy of teams must include action learning teams as a subspecies, as they are quite distinct from other types of teams in certain critical and specific ways. Action learning teams can also be quite different from each other.

First, as distinct from other types of teams, action-learning teams are focused on two objectives: learning and problem-solving. For action-learning teams, these interwoven objectives alone distinguish them from other types of teams. On no other type of team is individual learning considered an objective in itself although, on some teams at some points in their development, team member learning and development is sometimes a part of team development and productivity.

Dilworth (2001) has described the salient distinctions between action learning teams and other teams as follows:

1. The problem to be addressed by the set (or team) is real and in great need of address. It is not fabricated in any way.
2. While it is expected that a solution to the problem can be developed and acted upon, the larger yield is learning itself. The real problem becomes the fulcrum on which critically reflective learning processes occur. The goal from a human resource development standpoint is to develop people who are capable of leading, problem solving, working effectively in teams, and thinking critically in building the long-term strategic capabilities of the organization.
3. Action learning must lead to action (Marquardt, 1999). "Merely producing reports and recommendations for someone else to implement results in diminished commitment, effectiveness, and learning" (p. 33).
4. Emphasis is on questioning inquiry (the "Q" in the parlance of Reg Revans) as opposed to excessive dependency on "P," standing for programmed instruction (Revans, 1983, p. 11). Revans argues that in a rapidly changing environment we should begin with the "Q" (what is happening, what ought to be happening, and how do you make it happen?).
5. The set has no assigned leader and customarily operates as a self-directed work team with responsibilities shared.
6. Emphasis can be on moving learners away from what they already know, assigning them to work on problems that no one in the set has any great familiarity with. This can lead to fresh questions (the "Q" factor) and a re-examination of basic underlying assumptions. In this format, members of the action learning set are usually assigned a common problem to deal with. In other approaches, the individual set members may have individual problems they work on that are taken from their respective workplaces. In the latter case, the problem will probably only be familiar to the set member studying that issue (unless an entire natural team is

committed to problem solution), thus creating an environment conducive to questioning inquiry.

One can look at this distinctiveness in another way. Generally, teams which neglect individual learning but reach team goals are seldom perceived as failures. Action learning teams, however, which fail to foster individual learning and development but reach certain external objectives will, under Revan's general approach, fail as action learning teams. "Action Learning couples the development of people in work organizations with action on their difficult problems. It is based on the premise that there is no learning without action and no sober and deliberate action without learning... Action Learning makes the task the vehicle for learning" (Pedler, 1997, p. xxx).

Revans has noted that the business enterprise is a learning system; that many businesses seek experts and approaches from the outside to spur learning; but that action learning "must seek the means of improvement from within, indeed, from the common task" (Revans, 1997, p. 44). He goes further by saying that the signature learning that occurs in action learning groups comes neither from outside sources alone, nor from other group members, but from ignorance. "It is recognized ignorance, not programmed knowledge, that is the key to Action Learning: men start to learn with and from each other only when they discover that no one knows the answer but all are obliged to find it" (*ibid.*, p. 5).

Further, action learning teams are generally leaderless groups. Are they, in fact, teams or, rather, groups? Because action learning teams have a shared objective of promoting learning and problem-solving, and they share a common process for reaching those objectives, they fulfill the definition of a team: a group which uses common methods to reach common objectives.

Revans established the practice of action learning on the principle of self-directed teams, which was developed around the same time as T-Groups (or sensitivity training) and D-Groups (or developmental groups) which, in their origin, were similar to action learning teams. Development groups were also leaderless groups developed in the 1960s, which focused on problem-solving and individual development. Development groups were a part of the instrumented training movement developed by Robert R. Blake, a psychologist at the University of Texas (Wight, 2009).

Examining process within action learning teams

Process on teams in general has been shown to be important to reaching team and organizational objectives. The relationship between process and performance in individuals has been well researched. Employees require knowledge, skill, information, competencies, resources, motivation and incentives to perform tasks, and will fail to perform tasks to the extent that these elements are missing or less than optimal.

This same relationship (between process and performance) exists on teams. At the most basic level, it is almost a tautology to observe that dissatisfied team members will contribute little to team productivity and that, therefore, team productivity is related to the level of satisfaction of team members. It is, of course, obvious that satisfaction is not the only metric that relates to team productivity, and even if it were, there are many components which make up "satisfaction" (Bing, 2006).

The following are examples of the relationship between process and performance on teams:

1. Empirical research focusing on IT firms in Belgium and the Netherlands (Hendrich *et. al.*, 2002) have identified factors which correlated significantly with insufficient adaptability of project planning. Among those factors which significantly correlate at the *p* <.05 level are:

   (a) agreements in meetings are not implemented
   (b) insufficiently well informed about each others' activities
   (c) insufficient visibility of the management team in the firm
   (d) decisions have to be revised repeatedly.

2. A McKinsey survey, which examined differences between high and low performing top management teams, noted: "The most effective teams, focusing initially on working together, get early results in their efforts to deal with important business issues and then reflect together on the manner in which they did so, thus discovering how to function as a team" (Herb et al., 2001, p. 34). The pattern of action, reflection, change, action (sometimes called experiential learning, and related to action learning) is enhanced when the reflective phase is based upon recent metrics which indicate exactly what problems and successes the team has undergone and what needs to be changed to improve team performance. "Structured self-discovery and reflection must be combined with decision making and action in the real world; the constant interplay among these elements over time is what creates lasting change" (*ibid.*, p. 41–2).

3. Atul Gawande (2002) notes that "Learning is ubiquitous in medicine, and yet no one had ever compared how well different teams do it." After an extensive study of teams that were introducing a new heart operation, "the researchers found striking disparities in the speed with which different teams learned. All teams came from highly respected institutions with experience in adopting innovations and received the same three-day training session. Yet, in the course of 50cases, some teams managed to halve their operating time while others improved hardly at all. Practice, it turned out, did not necessarily make perfect. The crucial variable was how the surgeons and their teams practiced." The most successful surgeons picked their teams, kept them together, scheduled the new operations so

that learning would be reinforced, and debriefed after each operation. The less successful surgeons used different teams and held no debriefs.

In 2004, Dilworth and Bing developed an assessment to investigate the effectiveness of process on action learning teams. This assessment grew out of action learning's fundamentals, and the action-learning team dimensions assessed are as follows:

I   Team fundamentals

- Level of involvement by all members: Are all members contributing to the work of the team?
- Distribution of work within the team: Is the work evenly distributed, or are one or two team members carrying the load?
- Time available for work on team's activities: So some members have time problems in working with the team?
- Clarity of the team objectives: Are the objectives of the team clear to all members?
- Clarity of individual roles and responsibilities
- Measures for effectiveness of the team in place (both task accomplishment and member development): Are the team members satisfied with how they are being measured?
- Identification of barriers standing in the way of the team's work: Do the team members see barriers? Do they see the same ones or different ones?

II   Communications

- Group communications: Are communications within the team effective:
- Level of trust within the team: Is the level of trust at a high or low level?
- Ways of identifying conflict on team established: What is an acceptable level of conflict and how is that identified?
- Ability of team to resolve problems when they arise: Are conflict-resolution approaches understood and used?
- Extent to which team has been open to a diversity of views: Is there an imposed uniformity of views or is there an openness to diversity?
- Effective monitoring of group process by the team: Is the team capable of monitoring their own process?
- Team effort to improve process: Is there an effort to improve ineffective or counterproductive processes?

III   Action learning principles (i.e., action learning basics in place)

- Effectiveness of team's initial orientation: Was the initial orientation sufficient to launch the team to act on its own?

- Wide distribution of leadership: How dispersed is leadership?
- Time being taken by team for reflection: Is this critical process honored?
- Quality of support by sponsoring organization: Is there support and, if there is, is it sufficient?
- Usefulness of involvement of the external advisor/learning coach: If the action-learning process involves a coach, is the intervention appropriate and effective?
- Unfamiliar problems encountered: Are unfamiliar problems a part of the action learning processes?
- Unfamiliar settings encountered: Do the problems being considered take members outside their areas of competence?
- Team and management expectations that recommendations will be implemented: Is there a belief among members that their actions and recommendations will find support?

IV   Member development (i.e., learning and personal growth)

- Increase in skills and capabilities
- Degree of learning on this team versus other learning experiences: Does the action-learning experience provide new learnings, or greater learnings, than comparable group work?
- Degree to which experience on this team meets learning needs
- Degree to which experience has enhanced level of self-confidence
- Extent to which learning experience has helped identify gaps in skills, knowledge and abilities.

V   Delivering results

- Relationship of team effort to strategic goals of the organization: Does the work of the team closely relate to organizational goals?
- Extent to which experiences of this type can improve the learning environment in the organization: Do members believe that their experience will contribute to wider learning?
- Extent to which experiences of this type can improve productivity in the organization.

The assessment that was based on these dimensions (Bing, 2003) was derived from earlier team research conducted on teams outside the action learning field as well as on the basic tenants of action research – that action research teams should be self-directed; contain a diversity of views, backgrounds and approaches; use an unfamiliar task; result in member development; and provide results to the sponsoring organization.

Process as mediated by culture on action learning teams

Human values and processes vary in different national cultures. This is also true of action learning. Revans wrote, with respect to some of the earliest action learning programs, that the managers, "perhaps for the first time in their professional lives" were "able to relate their managerial styles (how to set objectives, evaluate resources and appraise difficulties) to their own values, their own talents, and their own infirmities" (Revans, 1997, p. 9). Here, he may have been referring to personal versus institutional values, but values are also the basis of cultural distinctions (although, of course, talents and infirmities are not). If values differ widely between cultures, then one would have to expect that the processes that are developed on teams made up of individuals of different national backgrounds, or of teams that are nationally congruent, also will be different.

Will the transformative possibilities that action learning fosters be different in different cultures? This is likely to be true, but it is also likely that the concept of transformation will apply wherever action learning occurs – for the collective ignorance referred to earlier, and the necessity to overcome that ignorance through creative efforts, exists in all places where humans interact. As Revans wrote: "The central thesis – that responsible action is our greatest disciplinarian as well as our most sympathetic helper – will appear in every light, in every setting and in every culture" (*ibid.*, p. 13).

The Hofstede dimensions

The following analysis applies the work of Geert Hofstede to an analysis of how action learning may fare in different cultures.

Hofstede (2001) has identified five dimensions that distinguish between national cultures. They are:

1. *Individualism*: The degree to which individuals act alone for their own interests or in concert with others for the benefit of the group;
2. *Power distance*: The degree to which inequality is tolerated in a culture or organization;
3. *Uncertainty avoidance*: The degree to which uncertainty is preferred in a culture;
4. *Masculinity–femininity*: How the distribution of sex roles in a society is managed, with strict gender differences, or with blurring of differences;
5. *Long- and short-term orientation*: Whether a culture prefers short- or long-term approaches to work and problem-solving.

How could one predict the differences in process on action learning teams based on these dimensions and on Hofstede's results in various cultures? In the following discussion, keep in mind that national cultures contain various degrees of difference in subcultures *within* their borders, and that there are also differences based on age, occupation and, sometimes, gender. So, these results must be considered to be applicable at the national level, at the mean of the entire population, and should be modified for subgroups within the culture.

How will these cultural differences play out on action learning teams (assuming that the teams are representative samples of those countries, similar to Hofstede's samples)? Will the action-learning teams have similar team processes?

Let's look at an example. Note that these comparisons are based on the research of Hofstede and are, therefore, conjectural; further research will need to establish whether behavioral differences along these lines are observed in action learning teams.

In this example, we will use the process of the three areas described by Edgar Schein (2006). These are:

1. Boundary management
2. Problem-solving and decision-making
3. Interpersonal interactions

Action learning teams in the U.S. compared with teams in South Korea

I have selected two very different cultures as examples of how national cultural values may influence the behavior of action learning teams.

According to Hofstede's research, U.S. teams have very high levels of individuality, relatively low uncertainty avoidance scores (indicating a low need for certainty), slightly below-the-mean power-distance scores, above-the-mean levels of masculinity (preference for task over quality of life and process issues), and a short-term orientation.

Korean teams that share Hofstede's Korean national scores have a low individualism score (a much higher tendency to integrate work into groups), a high-range uncertainty avoidance score (i.e., a high need for certainty), a relatively high power-distance score (i.e., a high tolerance for unequal work roles), a low masculinity index (meaning values of process and quality of life are more predominant), and a long-term orientation.

Boundary management

Group boundary management is likely to be very different with Korean or U.S. team members.

The U.S. team will likely develop sharp discussions on approaches, with each individual member exerting their preference. A group solution will not necessarily be sought, at least initially. At the same time, their short-term results orientation may force a fairly rapid and contentious approach – especially because a "masculine" approach prefers development of goals over group process. A lower preference for power distance means that a natural hierarchy of members is less likely to develop – for example, the oldest person on the team would not necessarily be granted any special respect.

The approach of such a team is likely to play out in back and forth discussion. One can imagine a meeting of such a group in which each member asserts their own idea as the best solution or approach. As debate continues, individuals vie for leadership roles in the group as a means of persuading others of the superiority of their own idea. The relationship of the action learning team to the organization which created it is likely to be initially one in which the group *asserts* its approaches and rights as much as one in which the group listens to how it should carry out its task. Only when it learns of its collective ignorance, as Revans puts it, will such a group begin to work with a sense of humility. So, initially, such a group would test its boundaries with the organization and individuals.

By contrast, the Korean action learning team would have a natural preference for working as a group, and those that would assert individual approaches would not gain respect. Their more feminine approach would require more time on group process, discussion, and consensus building, and their higher need for certainty would also increase the planning quality for their work on the action learning team. However, their very group approach would likely reduce the amount of time required to reach consensus, as there would be little to no time spent on individuals jockeying for position or status within the group. Furthermore, their respect of authority (power distance) would likely make the team less "flat" than their American colleagues. An initial hierarchy would exist from the inception of the group, based on previous status roles or longevity with the company. A longer-term orientation would allow for more time to reach consensus, if necessary, and more flexibility in achieving goals. The long-term orientation dimension may also impact the vision of the group, as problem-solving and group learning would likely be more focused on "flexible adaptation to new realities" (Hofstede, 2009).

The Korean team, acting natively as a group rather than a collection of individuals, may well reach out more actively to listen to their set instructions, the boundaries of their group's mandate, and how they are to communicate, because of the Korean values of respect for balance (the higher score on femininity). Because of their respect for authority, more attention will be paid to the instructions for establishing the team (or "set") and for communicating its progress to others. At the same time, this respect for authority and established instruction could also stifle some types of creative or "outside the box" thinking.

Problem-solving and decision-making

This area of team process is most critical to success on action learning teams. How our Korean and U.S. teams handle this may be quite different.

U.S. team members will likely compete more than their Korean counterparts for the limelight, for leadership, given their higher individualism.

Approaches on the U.S. team may include brainstorming sessions in which any and all ideas are welcome. As various ideas are put forth, individuals will champion their own solutions or support worthy solutions put forth by others. Debate may be heated. Though such an environment can lead to gridlock and tension, it may also serve as an arena for emergent thinking, whereby an initial idea is criticized, reviewed, and merged with other ideas in an effort to arrive a novel solution. Koreans, on the other hand, will, in a mixed nationality group, tend to be more quiet; and, in a group of their peers, tend to seek consensus. Given their proclivity for group decisions, consensus will come more quickly than for their American counterparts. In the initial phase, this preference for consensus will offer a more supportive environment for original ideas. Group members will spend less time fighting for their own ideas and more time considering the merits of competing solutions. At the same time, the Korean need for certainty and respect for authority may give senior group members an upper hand in the collaborative process. Younger or newer employees may downplay, or even withhold, their own ideas in deference to more respected colleagues. What will take longer in the Korean group is the planning process. Given their high need for certainty, getting the planning right is very important. So, although consensus will come quickly on objectives, planning will take longer.

Interpersonal interactions

Interpersonal interactions on these two abstract action learning teams will be different as well, as the nature of a group's interpersonal interactions overlaps a great deal with their problem-solving styles and overall group orientation. Take, for example, the issue of critical questioning and critical reflection, so necessary on action learning teams. Americans generally do not hesitate to ask sometimes direct questions of people above them in the hierarchy and to their peers, no matter the age difference. As previously mentioned, the "flatness" of such an American group could possibly allow for more ideas being suggested and considered. Any subsequent debate of ideas or approaches is likely to involve most or all of the group, as individuals from all levels of a company hierarchy will feel at least a modest level of comfort in contributing to the group and questioning the ideas of other group members. The risk of social penalty in such a low power-distance group is less than in a group that considered seniority and hierarchy to be more important, as is the case with typical Korean teams.

Members of Korean teams would be more likely to follow conversational norms that adhere to company and social hierarchies. In other words, those with a lower status would be much less likely to question or criticize the ideas of those with a higher status, due to a fear of subsequent social cost associated with violating interpersonal norms. Koreans will often wait for guidance from the oldest or most senior person in the room (they are often the same), and this may restrain the freedom necessary to ask probing, critical questions.

While the effect of process on action learning teams does have some universal characteristics and outcomes, there may also be cultural differentiations along the lines of the example given. Whether these cultural differences may affect action learning teams in a positive or negative way is not our judgment to make in this context, but it does suggest important conceptual and practical questions.

Conclusion

Process in action learning teams is a special case of process in teams in general. In this review, we have looked at how processes in general teams, and in action learning teams, share similarities and display differences. We noted that action learning teams came out of the general self-directed team approaches developed in the middle of the last century. We reviewed specific action learning team process dimensions and the kinds of questions that can reveal differences in process on action learning teams. We also looked at how processes on teams are influenced by the cultures in which they are embedded.

Teams are important to the effectiveness of contemporary organizations. Action learning teams are now an accepted and preferred approach to learning and problem-solving in an increasing number of organizations. We have reviewed how process modulates such teams, and what factors make for more effective and valuable experiences for individuals, teams and organizations.

References

Bing, J. (2003) The Action Learning Team Process Questionnaire Developed by Robert L.Dilworth and John W. Bing. Available at http://www.itapintl.com/tools/altpq.html
Bing, J. W. (2006) The Relationship between Process and Performance on Teams. Available at http://www.itapintl.com/facultyandresources/articlelibrarymain/the-relationship-between-process-and-performance-on-teams.html
Dilworth, R. L. (2001) "Mapping Group Dynamics in an Action Learning Experience: The Global Team Process Questionnaire", Proceedings of the Academy of Human Resource Development Annual Conference (Tulsa, Oklahoma) February 28–March 4, 2001.
Gawande, A. (2002) "Annals of Medicine: The Learning Curve", *New Yorker*, 77(55), January 28, pp. 59–61.
Hendrich, Boone, C. and den Brabander, B. (2002) "Team Composition and Organizational Performance: An Empirical Research of IT Firms in Belgium and the Netherlands", EURAM presentation, May 9–11 (Stockholm School of Entrepreneurship, Stockholm, Sweden).

Herb, E., Leslie, K., and Price, C. (2001) "Teamwork at the Top", *McKinsey Quarterly*, 2, pp. 32–43.

Hofstede, G. (2001) *Culture's Consequences: Comparing Values, Behaviors, Institutions and Organizations Across Nations*, 2nd edition (Thousand Oaks, CA: Sage).

Hofstede, G. (2009) Personal Communication (email) to John Bing.

Kozlowski, S. W. J. and Ilgen, D. R. (2006) "Enhancing the Effectiveness of Work Groups and Teams", *Psychological Science*, 7(3), pp. 77–124.

Marquardt, M. (1999) *Action Learning in Action* (Palo Alto, CA: Davies-Black).

Pedler, M. (ed.) (1997) "Introduction", in *Action Learning in Practice* (Brookfield, VT: Gower), p. xxx.

Revans, R. (1983) *ABC of Action Learning* (Bromley, U.K.: Chartwell-Bratt).

Revans, R. W. (1997) "The Enterprise as a Learning System", in M. Pedler (ed.), *Action Learning in Practice*, 3rd edition (Aldershot: Gower), pp. 41–7.

Schein, E. H. (2006) "Facilitative Process Interventions", in Joan V. Gallos (ed.), *Organizational Development: A Jossey-Bass Reader* (San Francisco: Jossey-Bass), pp. 286–308.

Wight, Albert (2009) Personal Communication (email) to John W. Bing.

9
Action Learning and Organization Development

W. Warner Burke and Debra A. Noumair

Among most practitioners in the world of organization development (OD) there is a bias for learning and reflection, to *think* about what we are doing, and attempt to understand and make sense out of what we are doing (see, for example, Schön, 1983). Better yet, is to discuss this thinking with a colleague or two, to gain as much perspective and insight as we can. We practitioners love to "bounce ideas off one another."

There may be an even stronger bias among us, however – a bias for *action*. We use the words "learning" and "reflection" quite frequently in our OD language, but we probably use the word "action" even more. After all, OD is based on an *action* research framework (French, 1969), and we have now combined our biases with the notion of *action* learning. We love learning but, just as much or more, we love to make things happen – to take action. The coming together of action learning and OD is therefore a natural.

Problems of definition

From the beginning stages in the late 1950s to current times, OD practitioners have experienced a number of different forms about what really is the true nature and definition of the field. Early on, OD was not much more than team building and a process of "opening up" a system to get actual problems on the table so that action could be taken that might make a real difference. But the practice expanded. By the late 1960s, when the Addison-Wesley series of books on OD emerged, the field included conflict management, a larger system perspective (i.e., beyond teams), process consultation and management style. Later into the 1970s, OD included work redesign, career dynamics, double-loop learning, organizational structure and data-feedback processes. And the 1980s brought to our attention stream analysis, power dynamics, reward systems, organization design and advanced versions of process consultation. Finally, in the 1990s, we learned about diversity, business teams, total quality, labor–management dynamics, organizational learning, network organizations, changing organizational culture and work-based learning – a link to action learning.

With this sizable list and array of activities supposedly falling within the rubric of OD, the field became ever more difficult to define and seemed to have lost its way (Bradford and Burke, 2005). But not entirely. A common set of values seems to provide some glue for OD practitioners such as humanism – feelings are legitimate sources of data, conflict should be surfaced and managed, there should be a spirit of inquiry and the provision of choice. Moreover, in addition to numerous texts on OD, we now have a thick handbook (Cummings, 2008).

While not as pervasive perhaps, action learning as a field has gone through similar transitions. As originally conceived by the British physicist, Reginald Revans (1980) – at about the same time as OD emerged in the 1940s and 1950s – action learning was a process of inquiry, particularly when traditional knowledge did not provide answers to tough problems. It was a shift from dependence on current expertise to questioning – not as a single individual, potential learner but, rather, within a small group where inquiry could be in the form of exchange and a collective effort at seeking solutions to seemingly intractable problems by pushing boundaries and questioning what was accepted knowledge.

From an OD perspective, action learning has been seen as essentially a process of what Argyris and Schön (1987) labeled as "double-loop learning" in contrast to "single-loop learning." That is:

Single-loop learning is fixing a problem, accomplishing a task, whereas double-loop learning is solving a problem and learning more about the problem-solving process itself. OD practitioners can make the mistake of acting on the belief that they really do not need to know the content, the product or service of the organization; whether it is a potato chip or a computer chip really doesn't matter. After all, OD is about process. But how organization members talk and interact at work differs depending on whether they are producing potato chips or computer chips, and this difference creates a distinctive process for each work setting. OD practitioners therefore must learn more about this interaction of content and process and intervene accordingly, showing a work team how the nature of the task affects their work processes. (Burke, 2008, p. 29)

This consideration of action learning defines the activity as one of combining process with content and how important this is for OD practitioners, yet, by seeming to equate it with double-loop learning, the emphasis is still more on process; that is, learning how to solve problems as a small group by focusing on the problem-solving process itself and learning how to improve it. Many would argue, no doubt, that there is more to action learning than double-loop learning.

Another activity that has been equated with – or, at least, seen as an aspect of action learning – is the process of "after action review" (AAR), apparently originating in the U.S. Army (see, for example, an article by Darling et al., 2005). The focus is initially on the past – examining a previous project or set of activities from the perspective of goal(s), what was attempting to be accomplished or achieved, what went well, what did not go well, and what can be learned so that mistakes will not be repeated – and then on the future, in terms of how can the people involved apply what has been learned to future, similar projects and activities.

AARs have been questioned regarding their implied promise of learning. Past mistakes can, indeed, be identified, but it is rare that future performance is enhanced. In other words, the contention is that little is learned after the fact. Yet, it is also contended that learning does occur – in the moment, as it were; in the midst of battle (*ibid.*, 2005) and during the action learning sessions themselves via exploring issues in depth and receiving personal feedback (de Haan and de Ridder, 2006).

If it is true, as these authors argue, that an increase in overall performance is rarely attained, then the learning that does occur is at the individual level and therefore somewhat idiosyncratic. Gaining collective wisdom may be very difficult to achieve, at least by way of after action reviews.

Perhaps double-loop learning and AARs are limited cases of action learning, and the more "normal" way of defining the process is when small groups (usually cross-functional and heterogeneous) within an organization come together to work and attempt to solve organizational problems that:

(a) have been neglected for one reason or another;
(b) have been reluctantly tackled due to their complexity if not enormity; or
(c) may be too politically hot to handle.

These small groups usually work on one problem or the other, not all tackling the same problem at the same time. They meet periodically and, in the interim, collect and analyze data to bring to the next meeting for further analysis and deliberation. Experienced facilitators work with each group to help the group members understand how their process enhances or impedes their work, and how each member contributes or not by providing individual feedback from all other group members. The facilitator must understand group process, of course, but also know something about the content as well – the exact nature of the task and what constitutes progress. The learning comes from seeing how the group process interacts with the task(s), and the overall content is about the potential for new products and/or services, about a different business model, the deeply rooted organizational culture that needs changing, exploiting the organization's brand in new and different ways, or a problem of a similar nature. Also relevant is how well the group's process contributes to effective problem-solving. For examples of this way of conducting action learning, see the book by Dotlich and Noel (1998).

We have briefly considered three kinds of activities, all of which having been associated with definitions and examples of action learning. Which is truly action learning? What exactly is OD? Perhaps it is not critical to define action learning precisely, as long as appropriate action is taken in the service of enhancing organizational effectiveness, and organizational members learn how to do this kind of work even better in the future. And perhaps it is not critical to define OD precisely, as long as culture and other important organizational dimensions are changed in the service of enhancing overall organization effectiveness.

Comparing action learning and organization development

Although action learning and OD have some distinctive qualities and characteristics, there may be more similarity and overlap between the two than there are differences. For a comparison of action learning and OD in summary form, see Table 9.1. As can be seen from this summary comparison, the differences may be more a function of emphasis and focus whereas, overall, they are fundamentally much the same. Let us consider a brief statement or two about each of the four comparative dimensions presented in Table 9.1.

With respect to *purpose* for both action learning and OD, it is about growing and developing capacity for learning and change. For action learning, the focus is on the individual and small group; for OD, the focus has a multilevel emphasis, especially on the system as a whole.

Goals can easily overlap, if not from time to time be exactly the same for both action learning and OD. In any case, the goals for action learning are primarily to solve tough problems and to learn more about problem-solving along the way; for OD, it is more about large-scale, planned change toward greater effectiveness and adaptability for the overall organization.

Methodologically both action learning and OD are concerned with the application of knowledge – action learning emphasizing inquiry and information exchange, and OD emphasizing multiple approaches and interventions.

And, finally, with respect to *practitioners' expertise*, both action learning and OD are about the ability to link theory and evidence with practice – action learning being based largely on group dynamics theory and research, and OD based largely on open system theory and research from organizational psychology and organizational behavior *writ large*.

As noted earlier, there are more similarities and overlap between action learning and OD than there are differences and discrete activities. Action learning can easily be conducted in the service of some large-scale change effort in an organization and OD, after all, is not just about change but also

Table 9.1   A comparison of action learning and organization development

Dimension	Action learning	Organization development
Purpose	To enhance organizational members' capacity for inquiry, problem-solving and learning (whether individually or in small groups).	To expand an organization's capacity for leading and managing change.
Goals	To provide new solutions to tough and complex organizational problems and to learn more about effective problem-solving while doing so.	To initiate and implement organization change efforts in a planned and systemic manner that is led from the top yet involves organizational members in the process, resulting in significant and lasting change.
Method	Applying knowledge of group dynamics to activities in both small and large group settings to ensure that inquiry, challenge of traditional expertise, information exchange and effective problem solving occurs.	Applying behavioral science knowledge to activities at all organizational levels to ensure that change goals provided by change lenders are clear, organizational members are involved, resistance and conflict are resolved, and momentum is sustained.
Practitioners' expertise	Application of small group theory, adult learning theory, knowledge regarding the interaction of content and process, knowledge of feedback processes, and knowledge about problem-solving skills at both individual and group levels.	Application of open system theory, culture change theory, change leadership, organizational diagnostic and intervention methods, action science, and change management (i.e., dealing effectively with unintended consequences of interventions).

about learning – note the sub-title of Burke's (1994) text on organization development, "A process of learning and changing."

To illustrate these similarities and overlap, we will now describe a case that involved conducting a course on OD – a practice course consisting primarily of experiential learning – that led to highly relevant action in a complex system.

A special case of action learning

At Teachers College, Columbia University, we offer the Eisenhower Leader Development Program (ELDP), a joint Masters Degree Program with the United States Military Academy at West Point. The ELDP is intended to provide education and training to Army officers who are preparing to work as Tactical Officers in the U.S. Corps of Cadets at the USMA, West Point. It should be noted that most of these ELDP students hold the rank of Captain and enter the program fresh from Iraq and/or Afghanistan. The following description defines the role for which most of them are being educated and trained to fill:

A Tactical Officer (TAC) is the legal Company Commander of a Cadet Company comprised of about 130 men and women and the primary developer of these cadets at the USMA, West Point. The TAC officer assists each cadet in balancing and integrating the requirements of the physical, military, academic, and moral-ethical programs. The TAC officer trains and coaches the cadet chain of command to establish and sustain high unit standards and behavior essential to a cohesive company environment. TAC officers inspire cadets to develop effective leadership styles through role-modeling, counseling, teaching, and training. TAC officers also present formal and informal instruction to the company, implement special development programs for individual cadets as needed, and they are responsible for all company administration. (Teachers College, 2009)

One of the required courses in the ELDP is *Practicum in Change and Consultation in Organizations*, hereafter referred to as "Practicum." Practicum is intended to provide students with an introduction to the practice of consultation and planned organizational change through the application of behavioral science concepts and tools. Assuming some basic knowledge of organizational behavior and theory, the course addresses issues of how to gather information about organizations in order to diagnose and facilitate change, to increase effectiveness, and to foster the capacity for learning and development over time. The focus is on understanding organizations through the development and use of diagnostic models and self-as-instrument in conjunction with specific change technologies during all phases of consulting to organizations.

In the ELDP, Practicum was offered in the summer following a year of coursework in the program, and coincided with the beginning of ELDP students taking up their roles as TAC Officers. We tailored the course for their special circumstances and condensed the course into five modules, two upfront on the content of organization change and consultation, and three opportunities to meet while they were engaged in organization consultation with the temporary organizations that comprised summer training at West

Point. This meant that each TAC Officer was required to consult to a temporary organization of cadets engaged in military training. While it was challenging to be in two roles (one as continuing ELDP students, the other in the beginning stages of exercising their responsibilities as TAC Officers), especially two roles that were both unfamiliar to them, the newly minted TAC Officers made effective use of peer and faculty coaching. They were surprised to discover what a powerful impact OD consulting could have on a social system; and that resistance was to be expected, and managed. This learning required the TAC officers and us (faculty) to make adjustments along the way. We learned that we were not solely teaching an applied class; we were intervening in a powerful social system, the United States Military Academy.

We used an emergent design as a way to manage Practicum for this group of students. Because they were in dual roles, the way we had originally set up Practicum was not feasible; therefore, we engaged in redesign work in which we incorporated Practicum into their responsibilities as TAC Officers during the summer. Rather than frame their OD consulting project as something separate from their work and in addition to their roles, collecting data and developing a diagnosis of the temporary organizations they were overseeing became part of what it meant to be an effective TAC Officer. We asked them to expand their thinking from considering 130 cadets as individuals to considering these young men and women as a collective unit with a culture that could be understood, and that this understanding of the unit as a whole would lead to more effective individual and collective performance. We met periodically with the TAC Officer students as a whole class, and provided space for each of the consulting teams to report out on their experiences. We provided supervision on their consulting work as well as inputs on relevant content areas. At the end of the summer, we conducted an AAR and recommended that, going forward, they routinely conduct Before Action Reviews (Darling et al., 2005), building on their learning from this experience and using it to inform how they approach OD consulting at West Point in the future.

Practicum 2, the follow-up course offered in the following fall semester, was a 2-hour seminar based on topics from the curriculum at Teachers College and the United States Military Academy. Courses with similar content were grouped together into five sessions:

1. Adult learning and coaching;
2. Organizational psychology and understanding behavioral research;
3. Leadership and military leadership and professional military ethic;
4. Group dynamics, intercultural communication, and conflict resolution;
5. Organization dynamics, organization culture, and Practicum in change and consultation in organizations.

Groups of three TAC Officers (continuing to maintain their student roles) took responsibility for each one of the class sessions. The purpose of the class sessions was to provide an opportunity for TAC Officers to reflect on their learning in the ELDP, and to consider the links between the academic side of the program and their work as TAC Officers; in essence, to integrate theory and practice (learning and action).

The first group of students used *Discussion as a way of teaching* (Brookfield and Preskill, 2005) to design the class session. They began with an introduction in which they identified the focal point of the discussion, such as similarities and differences in coaching and counseling, and used an exercise known as "rotating stations." For each one of the courses listed for the class session, the leaders identified topics and reflective questions for their peers to respond to at corresponding stations. They then organized themselves into rotating teams and spent ten minutes at each station in small group discussion, followed by 15-minute report outs to the whole group. The class session ended with an opportunity to reflect on the small and large group discussions, and the identification of key learnings and action steps related to implementation with their cadet companies. Following are two examples that illustrate the kind of action learning that occurred in Practicum 2.

Example 1

When reflecting on learning in Group Dynamics, TAC Officers used a group as a whole perspective (Wells, 1985) to understand different subgroups at West Point, such as athletes and the more academically oriented cadets. Through this lens, they understood that each subgroup contained certain characteristics – that is, being stereotyped – and, as a result, were viewed as "less than" other groups. Neither athletes nor more academically oriented cadets were viewed as capable in multiple domains, and therefore expectations of them were lowered. Through discussion, TAC Officer students considered that such categorizing and stereotyping was a form of scapegoating that they could interrupt by applying their learning to their work with cadets. The class session ended with a list of actions that TAC officers could take and an agreement to check in periodically with each other to compare notes and make adjustments to their strategies, as needed.

Example 2

In the class session that focused on the leadership courses, the important insight that occurred focused on rifle training. This rifle training was new to both the TAC Officers and the cadets. It concerned, for example, learning to shoot at close quarters very quickly (as in heavily populated urban areas) and on the run, rather than lying on the ground and slowly taking careful aim – the traditional form of rifle training. The TAC Officers described being on the rifle range in this new context and, therefore, rather than undertaking the traditional mode of training, they engaged in a discussion about what they were trying to accomplish (the new modes of combat) and what they needed to do to achieve their objectives. This was a new way for them to approach their work and a different way of thinking; they traced this innovation in thinking to their learning in the ELDP and, specifically, to the courses at Teachers College, the "civilian" component of their graduate education (e.g., how adults learn). For them, it was about taking responsibility for their actions and thinking before doing and thinking while doing; they came to describe it as reflection-in-action, similar to the manner in which Schön (1983) refers to it, because, prior to the ELDP, they tended to act and reflect afterwards. In some sense, they incorporated BAR's and AAR's into their ongoing work (Darling et al., 2005).

Action learning did not end with Practicum 2; it extended to the TAC Officers ongoing work at West Point in several different forms:

Example 3

The TAC Officers who participated in Practicum 2 decided to extend the biweekly sessions beyond the semester and graduation and without faculty oversight, in the form of monthly brown-bag lunches. They viewed these ongoing sessions as an opportunity to incorporate their new learning into their work as TAC Officers – in their words, to engage in guided reflection, coaching and development of TAC Officer best practices based on theory and practice from the ELDP and ongoing work with cadet companies.

Example 4

Several TAC Officers began to act as internal OD consultants, engaging in consulting projects with various constituencies within the USMA. What became apparent was the new lens through which they viewed the applicability of their skills and, in part, their organizational roles. They were now able to identify OD projects before their "clients" identified them as such, and they were able to facilitate learning and action for those they worked with and for themselves.

Conclusion

Examples 3 and 4 provided a "special case" of action learning; that is, it was not typical of action learning. Dotlich and Noel (1998) and Tichy and Sherman (1993) provide examples largely from the corporate sector that conform more closely perhaps to the usual way that action learning has been conducted and understood. In addition, the examples from these two sources from the 1990s probably fit more closely with OD – as described in Table 9.1. What we have attempted to illustrate with our case, however, is that action learning – and organization change and development, for that matter – can take many forms.

Finally, at the risk of oversimplification, the U.S. Army stereotypically is all about action, and the University – again, stereotypically – is all about reflection. Putting the two stereotypes together gives birth to a special case of action learning and an element of OD.

References

Argyris, C. and Schön, D. A. (1987) *Organizational Learning: A Theory of Action Perspective* (Reading, MA: Addison-Wesley).

Bradford, D. L. and Burke, W. W. (eds.) (2005) *Reinventing Organization Development* (San Francisco: Pfeiffer/Wiley).

Brookfield, S. D. and Preskill, S. (2005) *Discussion as a Way of Teaching*, 2nd edition (San Francisco: Jossey-Bass).

Burke, W. W. (1994) *Organization Development: A Process of Learning and Changing*, 2nd edition (Reading, MA: Addison-Wesley).

Burke, W. W. (2008) "A Contemporary View of Organization Development", in T. G. Cummings (ed.), *Handbook of Organization Development* (Thousand Oaks, CA: Sage), pp. 13–38.

Cummings, T. G. (ed.) (2008) *Handbook of Organization Development* (Thousand Oaks, CA: Sage).

Darling, M., Parry, C., and Moore, S. (2005) "Learning in the Thick of It", *Harvard Business Review*, 83(7), pp. 84–92.

de Haan, E. and de Ridder, I. (2006) "Action Learning in Practice: How Do Participants Learn?" *Consulting Psychology Journal: Practice and Research*, 58, pp. 216–31.

Dotlich, D. L. and Noel, J. L. (1998) *Action Learning: How the World's Top Companies are Re-Creating their Leaders and Themselves* (San Francisco: Jossey-Bass).

French, W. L. (1969) "Organization Development: Objectives, Assumptions, and Strategies", *California Management Review*, 12, pp. 23–34.

Revans, R. (1980) *Action Learning: New Techniques for Management* (London: Blond & Briggs).

Schön, D. A. (1983) *The Reflective Practitioner* (New York: Basic Books).

Teachers College (2009) Teachers College Columbia University Organization and Leadership Department website. Available at http://www.tc.columbia.edu/o&l/ newsletter.asp?id=M.A.+Program+For+West+Point

Tichy, N. M. and Sherman, S. (1993) *Control Your Destiny or Someone Else Will: How Jack Welch is Making General Electric the World's Most Competitive Corporation* (New York: Doubleday).

Wells, L., Jr. (1985) "The Group-as-a-Whole Perspective and its Theoretical Roots", in A. D. Colman and M. H. Geller (eds.), *Group Relations Reader 2* (Washington, DC: A. K. Rice Institute), pp. 109–26.

10
Action Learning and the Learning Organization: Building Learning Capacity in Individuals, Groups and Organizations

Judy O'Neil, Karen E. Watkins and Victoria J. Marsick

Moving to healthy, open organizations has been a fundamental aim of organization development (OD) since Kurt Lewin's (1951) early work contrasting authoritarian and democratic groups. Later, Rensis Likert's System 4 framework (1967) offered a set of dimensions or organizational capacities that enable the organization to learn from its environment, people and markets. Recent focus on creating learning organizations led to the evolution of a number of interventions that help organizations embed these critical capacities. Perhaps no other intervention has the potential of action learning to build capacities at the individual, group and organizational levels.

This chapter examines the relationships between concepts of the learning organization and action learning. We examine them from the perspective of the dimensions of the learning organization (DLOQ) (Watkins and Marsick, 1993; 1997) – our assessment instrument developed from work and research suggesting that a strong learning culture is built around learning practices, structures, processes and norms at the individual, group and organizational level. Learning is manifested through seven dimensions: create continuous learning opportunities; promote inquiry and dialogue; encourage collaboration and team learning; create systems to capture and share learning; empower people towards a collective vision; connect the organization to its environment; and provide strategic leadership for learning. Studies have established a correlation between these learning organization dimensions and knowledge and financial performance across profit, nonprofit, business and government sectors (Watkins, 1998; McHargue, 1999; Ellinger et al., 2002; Hernandez and Watkins, 2003; Sta. Maria and Watkins, 2003; Watkins and Marsick, 2003; Yang, 2003; Yang et al., 2004; Davis and Daley, 2008). Using action learning to develop these learning dimensions thus holds great promise for building capacity for organizational learning.

We begin by outlining our approach to action learning. We then offer illustrations and case examples from our work that show how action learning enables organizations to initiate changes in the learning culture. In our final case example, we show how we have used our learning organization assessment to initiate and frame an action learning intervention.

Our approach to action learning

When we discuss and practice action learning, we mean an approach to working with and developing people that uses work on an actual project or problem as the way to learn. Participants work in small groups to take action to solve their problem and learn how to learn from that action. A learning coach usually works with the group in order to help participants learn how to balance their work with the learning from that work (O'Neil and Marsick, 2007). In our practice of action learning, we have found that this approach is a powerful strategy for creating learning organizations because it addresses the dimensions at all three levels – individual, team and organizational.

Reg Revans, the 'father' of action learning (1983), provides an antecedent to our experience in his discussion of 'exchange options'. In this discussion, he points out that there are two kinds of projects and two kinds of settings for an action learning program – familiar and unfamiliar. While the four combinations of options – familiar project/familiar setting, familiar project/unfamiliar setting, unfamiliar project/familiar setting, unfamiliar project/unfamiliar setting – can all be appropriate for an action learning program, he advocated for a design that used an unfamiliar project in an unfamiliar setting. Revans thought this design would provide the opportunity for the deepest learning at the individual, group and organizational levels. The following ideas and stories provide examples of how action learning can impact learning at all three levels.

Individual level of the learning organization

At the individual level, the first dimension is to create continuous learning opportunities. In this dimension, one of the key activities we look for in an organization is work that is designed in such a way that people can stop and learn from problems, challenges and mistakes (Marsick and Watkins, 1999). In our action learning codesign work with clients, we advocate for program designs that can help participants learn how to stop and learn from their action learning problem and transfer that process back to their workplace.

Codesign and continuous learning

The main design element that impacts this dimension is the length of the program and timing of the sessions. While there is no ideal length, we believe that some of the best designs for promoting continuous learning opportunities are ones in which participants meet intermittently over an extended period of time. This kind of schedule provides participants with the opportunity to balance work on the project with learning, to experiment, to try out new actions and behaviors, and to test out theories about the project and organization. The action learning projects/problems often change and evolve as participants recognize that complex problems are not always what they first appear to be. Some examples of programs designed to promote continuous learning opportunities are shown in Table 10.1.

The second dimension important to a learning organization at the individual level is to promote inquiry and dialogue. The skills represented in this dimension enable people more clearly to present their own thinking, better listen to and understand others, and probe beneath the surface of problems (*ibid.*, 1999). One of the best ways this dimension is developed in an action learning program is through a process we call "action learning conversations." This process makes use of questioning insight, the raising and challenging of assumptions, and encouraging the reframing of action learning projects/problems.

Table 10.1 Action learning program designs

Organization	Design length
PSE&G	½-day orientation (1 interim week)
	2-day session (2 interim weeks)
	2-day session (Teams also met during interim time as needed)
Berlex	3-day session (1 interim month)
	1-day session (1 interim month)
	1-day session (1 interim month)
	1-day session (1 interim month)
	1-day session (1 interim month)
	2-day session (Teams also met during interim time as needed)
Invensys	3-day session (2 interim months)
	2-day session (1 interim month)
	2-day session (1 interim month)
	2-day session (Teams also met during interim time as needed)
VNU	3-day session (3 interim months)
	3-day session (6 interim months)
	3-day session (3 interim months)
	3-day session (Teams also met during interim time as needed)
Global Pharmaceutical Company	3-day session (2 interim months)
	1–1½-day session (2 interim months)
	1–1½-day session (2 interim months)
	2-day session

Action learning conversations at the Global Pharmaceutical Company

The Global Pharmaceutical Company's action learning program was a global program designed for executive development and to aid the organization with integration after a large merger. The codesign used individual problems chosen by each participant and offers some examples of how action learning conversations contribute to inquiry and dialogue in an organization. As a global organization, the company is made up of employees from many different cultures. A participant in one of the action learning programs started out with a problem that he thought was being caused by cultural differences: "How are the cultural issues getting in the way of changing the way operations are being performed in one of my factories?" Questions like "How much of this problem actually exists and how much has to do with your assumptions about this culture?" led him to begin questioning and testing his own preconceived assumptions. By the end of the program, he had realized that the problem was not based in cultural differences, but in the way the factory was being run. The action he took to remedy the situation was quite different than he would have taken before his action learning conversations.

The Executive Vice President of Human Resources for the company in a European country presented the following problem to his team, "How can I develop my senior management team to manage their learning better?" He went on to explain that his senior team of seven people, which included the marketing company president and himself, achieved good results last year but were not good at sharing their knowledge and expertise with others in the company. He had shared his concerns with some of his peers but was afraid to raise the issue publicly. Complicating the issue was the fact that some of the directors did not get along. "The marketing director 'hates' the other directors." He felt they all needed to cooperate in order to ensure that the business would continue to be successful. Some of the questions asked in the action learning conversation included:

- Where did the success last year come from if there was this lack of cooperation?
- Do all the directors behave this way? Do they behave this way all the time?
- What is your evidence that this behavior is not good?
- Is the behavior open or hidden?
- Have you figured out how you are contributing to the problem?

Some of the assumptions raised were, "I assume personal ambition is a factor" and "I assume this is considered to be an acceptable way of working." Based on reflection on the questions, assumptions and reframes offered, the vice president reframed his problem to "How can I help the senior management team recognize that their dysfunctional behavior will eventually harm the marketing company?" He decided that he needed to take the explicit action he had been avoiding and discuss the issues with the president and management team (O'Neil and Marsick, 2007).

Team level of the learning organization

At the team level, the key dimension is to encourage collaboration and team learning. This dimension refers to the sharing of continuous learning within groups (Marsick and Watkins, 1999). Action learning can provide many opportunities for the development of this dimension: contracting about how work will be done within the team to build the trust needed for learning; "P" learning, like the Honey–Mumford Learning Styles Questionnaire, to build a richer understanding of the strengths and weaknesses in a team; team building activities to develop better team dynamics. One of the most effective ways action learning contributes to this dimension is through the encouragement of the use of reflection. Although reflection is personal in nature, by introducing a process during the team meetings to encourage participants to share some of what they may have been thinking privately, ultimately reflection helps teams become more aware of their collective actions and what they could do to become more productive (O'Neil et al. 2008).

Action Learning at VNU

In 2003, VNU – parent company of ACNielsen and Nielsen Media Research – launched the Explorers Program to develop emerging leaders in its North American businesses. The program, codesigned with Partners for Learning and Leadership, supported VNU's organization goals to develop future executives to have a broader understanding of all its businesses and to identify future leaders (O'Neil and Marsick, 2007). The VNU program provides a good example of how reflection can lead to team learning. In one of the programs, it became apparent early on that one of the teams was struggling with their work, while another was doing quite well. An analysis of learning coach notes revealed that a key difference between the two teams was the use of reflection.

The initial reflection questions posed by the learning coaches to the teams in their early calls were focused on team process: "What's been the most important thing you've learned as a team? Based on your reflections, what do you think you need to do next?" A few members on Team A responded with immediate resistance to the reflection. Other members answered the questions, but time spent with resisters precluded any discussion, a usual part of reflection. Team B seemed more open to the concept of how reflection might be helpful and responded by noting, "We've already changed our minds; continue to evolve; there are differing roads to our project con-clusion." Another member said, "I like things to fit, but realize it's okay I don't know where we're going yet."

In the next team calls, Team A skipped reflection due to lack of time. With less than five minutes to go, the call leader suggested that the dis-cussion around the project question was really a reflection question. The group acknowledged that the coach probably would not like that view of reflection. Team B continued to include reflection in their calls, began for-mulating their own reflection questions, and began using reflection to help individual team members identify where they would like to make changes. One question posed to this team was "How well is your decision process working?" Each took a turn responding, and one member took a slightly dif-ferent approach. He asked if they were really getting good at reaching con-sensus or were they just being apathetic? As the Devil's advocate for the call, he had raised some questions earlier to help the team think about alternate approaches and now used the reflection time to revisit that role.

Figure 10.1 illustrates how the project work progressed as Teams A and B continued to use reflection in their work. We defined a productive meeting as one that started on time, team members attended as planned, team roles had been decided in advance, and the call leader was prepared. An agenda was published ahead of time and the team either discussed the majority of items or opted to table those that were not essential to making a decision during the call. Finally, there was sufficient time at the end of the call for a brief reflection.

As the teams moved further into their projects, there were a few break-throughs for Team A. On April 5 one of the call leaders asked if others were able to identify common themes around their discussion, and if there were

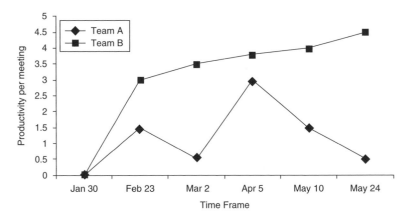

Figure 10.1 Plotting the use of reflection over five months

consensus on some of those areas. However, a few weeks later Team A was unable to build on the success of the meeting from April 5. The project which was presented in October was finally pulled together the evening before the presentation. While the team members did have interesting content, they were not able to combine their work into a coherent thesis.

By contrast, Team B continued to evolve the use of the reflection to explore implications for their project moving well beyond the process questions they had addressed at the beginning of the project. As they got deeper into the project, they began to challenge themselves by asking, "How can we continue to keep ourselves open to a variety of options for solutions as we gather data?" Their responses included the need to continue to ask good questions, to be Devil's advocates, and the fact that they are still "naïve" (their word) about their topic and how that will help them. The willingness to adopt reflection as a team practice, and then to continue to build on the possibilities that evolved with each meeting, contributed to a highly productive virtual team environment. As Figure 10.1 suggests, Team B was able to create a high-performing team and concluded the program by presenting a well thought-out project that had gone beyond the sponsor's original mandate (O'Neil et al. 2008).

Organization level of the learning organization

At the organization level, the key dimensions we identified are: create systems to capture and share learning, make systemic connections between the organization and its environment, and provide leadership for learning. Work done in the public health domain illustrates several of these dimensions.

Action learning in a local public health department

There has been a marked increase in the availability of training for the public health workforce in the last number of years. However, it is increasingly clear in the work of one public health training center that the training event is only a portion of the work needed to develop and maintain a prepared, skilled and effective public health workforce (Watkins et al., 2008). In an unpublished study, organizational barriers were identified as an impediment in one local health department in the transfer of training to the practice of new skills in the work environment. To understand how to develop more effective workforce training, the public health training center began to examine organizational capacity as a factor that would influence not only individual learning, but also how effective an organization is in carrying out its mission. The concept of a learning organization was used by the public health training center as a framework for understanding organizational barriers to workforce development.

A large state public health department training center worked with Karen Watkins and Judy Milton to assess the learning culture using the DLOQ in four diverse public health departments. Results indicated a number of areas of strategic leverage – where even small changes had the potential to improve the overall openness and learning capacity of the organization. Initially, a workshop was held with key leaders from throughout the state to introduce the idea of a learning organization and to share findings from this study. One of the departments that had been very active in encouraging a learning organization framework elected to continue this work by sharing findings for their department and introducing the idea of action learning as a strategy to promote change in the culture. The department was in a primarily suburban area, and had a reputation as an innovator among its peers. A workshop was held with key managers across all divisions. Results from the DLOQ indicated a number of areas that were below the average based on our national database. Of particular interest were the areas of empowering people towards a collective vision and improving knowledge performance, since these were the areas in which the department had scored lowest.

A workshop was held to share findings from the survey including high- and low-scoring items in each dimension, to learn about action learning, and to set objectives for continuing work together in face-to-face and virtual formats. Participants spent the day learning the tools of action learning and received a workbook that introduced a number of action learning tools. Groups met over the next four months and concluded with a video teleconference, in which groups made recommendations to improve the learning culture to the head of the agency and received feedback from him and from Watkins and Milton. While there was no facilitator in each small group, attempts were made to guide their work through the stimulus questions on the website and through the worksheets in their workshop notebook. These worksheets were also posted on the virtual conference center. Some groups shared information virtually; most did not.

During the workshop, participants were asked to brainstorm what actions might build organizational capacity within each of the seven dimensions of a learning organization. Participants were given five colored dots and asked to vote on the highest priority issues, and action learning groups were formed to focus on the four highest priority recommendations. In terms of individual learning, participants focused on "promoting dialogue and inquiry" and noted that a significant need was for leadership to "make clear when a decision is made and why." In the area of "encourage collaboration and team learning," participants showed greatest enthusiasm for the recommendation that support be given for "like-classification teams to meet for support and to enhance productivity." At the organizational level, one group recommended that they institute "cross-training by previous person in a position" to "create systems to capture and share learning" and to prevent the loss of expertise when people leave. A final group focused on the dimension of "making systemic connections between the organization and its environment" and distilled from a recommendation that staff "be in

Table 10.2 Local public health department action learning teams

Problem	Recommendations	Feedback
Group 1: [Individual level] Promote dialogue and inquiry		
It is not always clear that a decision has been made or what the decision is.	Change agenda template for management team meetings to include a section entitled "Decisions and Directives Issued" that will be archived with team minutes in a web folder accessible to all managers.	Will this action prevent questioning of decisions? One possibility is that the rumor mill that questions decisions is focused more on decisions that are more gray – things managers think are desirable but are nevertheless optional? How will this approach provide clarity in this situation? Is it a realistic goal for all management decisions to be unquestioned?
Group 2: [Group or team level] Encourage collaboration and team learning		
People and programs within the department are working on similar issues but are not communicating and collaborating.	Increase program awareness across divisions and establish workgroups that focus on strategic plan outcomes.	What would this structured collaboration look like and how is it different from current cross-functional teams?
Group 3: [Organizational level] Create systems to capture and share learning		
How can we prevent the loss of expertise and experience when people leave or change jobs?	Develop a training manual, provide cross-training, schedule a transition period, provide mentors and supervisors to step in when needed.	What resource or system barriers might prevent implementing this approach? How will supervisors know when to step in?
Group 4: [Organizational level] Making systemic connections between the organization and its environment		
How do we avoid burn-out and over-use of employees?	Survey employee skills, conduct time studies, equalize work load, review county hiring practices, and eliminate silos so others can assist and relieve.	One assumption the group identified is that people see this as an individual rather than a system problem. To what extent might this perception limit the organization's willingness to implement these recommendations? How will these strategies address the problem?

a position where they are happy and have appropriate skills" – a focus on preventing burnout.

Groups were self-guided though a process of question-storming (a process similar to brainstorming, but using questions instead of statements, developed by Marilee Adams, 2004) to redefine the problem, stop and reflect, identify underlying assumptions, reframe the problem, gather data and results, and recommend next steps. In the final reporting sessions, recognizing the brevity of their work to date, groups were asked to restate the problem as they had now defined it and to make a recommendation for next steps to begin either to continue to understand the issue or to address it. Table 10.2 gives group summary data and facilitator feedback.

The action learning groups identified primarily soft skills issues – and groups wrestled with trying to figure out what would have to change in order to impact these communication and role overload issues. One important outcome of this work was greater understanding of how behaviors in management team meetings impact the overall learning culture. The DLOQ offers public health department leaders guidance on where strategically to target change efforts, and action learning provides a means to encourage management learning and development while implementing these targeted changes. For example, mission performance in public health is an area of great strategic leverage; despite resource constraints, leaders can count on high levels of dedication and motivation when they empower staff and align them towards a clear vision.

Conclusion

While an organization can take many routes to develop a learning culture, these case examples illustrate the ability of action learning to help drive this development. The literature shows that action learning can take many forms (O'Neil and Marsick, 2007), but our work has demonstrated that there are certain elements that contribute to making action learning a powerful tool to enable organizations to influence their learning culture.

These case examples illustrate how the organizational problem focus of action learning groups, together with the focus on individual learning, reflection, and group dynamics, contribute to making action learning a powerful tool to enable organizations to influence the learning culture. There need to be design elements that enable participants to question and challenge the premises of their own thinking. Groups need sufficient time and facilitation to be productive in this work, and – most importantly – guidance and a focus on reflection. Organizations need the data and understanding to recognize where to target their action learning change efforts to impact learning at the organization level.

What the findings from this work mean for our understanding of planned change is that the culture that is most conducive to fostering change and development is one in which the leaders embody and model learning. In addition, people are empowered to take requisite action towards a commonly shared and understood vision, systems are in place to capture and share learning, and connections are made between the organization, its stakeholders and its environment (Watkins and Marsick, 2003).

References

Adams, M. (2004) *Change Your Questions, Change Your Life: 7 Powerful Tools for Life and Work* (San Francisco: Berrett-Koehler).

Davis, D. and Daley, B. (2008) "The Learning Organization and its Dimensions as Key Factors in Firms' Performance", *Human Resources Development International*, 11(1), pp. 51–66.

Ellinger, A. D., Ellinger, A. E., Yang, B., and Howton, S. W. (2002) "The Relationship between the Learning Organization Concept and Firms' Financial Performance: An Empirical Assessment", *Human Resource Development Quarterly*, 13(1), pp. 5–21.

Hernandez, M. and Watkins, K. (2003) "Translation, Validation, and Adaptation of the Spanish Version of the Dimensions of the Learning Organization Questionnaire", *Human Resource Development International*, 6(2), pp. 187–96.

Holtzhauer, F. J. (2001) "Improving Performance at the Local Level: Implementing a Public Health Learning Workforce Intervention", *Journal of Public Health Management Practice*, 7(4), pp. 96–104.

Lewin, K. (1951) Field Theory in Social Science: Selected Theoretical Papers, in D. Cartwright (ed.) (New York: Harper & Row).

Likert, R. (1967) *The Human Organization: Its Management and Value* (New York: McGraw Hill).

Marsick, V. J. and Watkins, K. E. (1999) *Facilitating Learning in Organizations: Making Learning Count* (Aldershot, U.K.: Gower).

McHargue, S. (1999) "Dimensions of the Learning Organization as Determinants of Organizational Performance in Nonprofit Organizations", PhD dissertation (University of Georgia).

O'Neil, J., O' Grady, H., and Ward, R. (2008) "Action Learning: Using Reflection for Learning, Development, and Performance Improvement", *OD Practitioner*, 40(3), pp. 18–23.

O'Neil, J. and Marsick, V. J. (2007) *Understanding Action Learning* (New York: AMACOM).

Revans, R. W. (1983) "Action Learning Projects", in B. Taylor and G. Lippitt (eds.), *Management Development and Training Handbook*, 2nd edition (New York: McGraw-Hill), pp. 226–74.

Sta. Maria, R. and Watkins, K. (2003) "Perception of Learning Culture and Concerns about the Innovation on Use of Innovation: A Question of Level of Analysis", *Human Resource Development International*, 6(4), pp. 491–508.

Watkins, K. (1998) "Measuring Organizational Learning and Performance: Findings from the Dimensions of the Learning Organization Questionnaire", Keynote address at the Sixth Annual International Conference on Post-compulsory Education and Training (Griffith University, Queensland), Australia, December.

Watkins, K. E., Milton, J., and Kurz, D. (2008) "Diagnosing the Learning Culture in Public Health Agencies", Proceedings of the Eleventh Annual European Human Resource Development Conference (Lille, France).

Watkins, K. E. and Marsick, V. J. (1993) *Sculpting the Learning Organization* (San Francisco: Jossey-Bass).

Watkins, K. E. and Marsick, V. J. (1997) "Dimensions of the Learning Organization Questionnaire" (survey) (Warwick, RI: Partners for the Learning and Leadership), www.partnersforlearning.com.

Watkins, K. E. and Marsick, V. J. (2003) "Summing Up: Demonstrating the Value of an Organization's Learning Culture", *Advances in Developing Human Resources*, 5(2), pp. 129–31.

Yang, B. (2003) "Identifying Valid and Reliable Measures for Dimensions of a Learning Culture", *Advances in Human Resources*, 5(2), pp. 152–62.

Yang, B., Watkins, K., and Marsick, V. (2004) "The Construct of the Learning Organization: Dimensions, Measurement, and Validation", *Human Resource Development Quarterly*, 15(1), pp. 31–56.

11
Action Learning and Action Research
Verna J. Willis

What can be gained by making a distinction between *action learning* and *action research*? The question is more than rhetorical. It can make a world of difference which approach you use, depending on your purpose. Further, if you should choose action learning, it can make a world of difference which particular "brand" you select, depending on how you view human beings and how comfortable you are with the assumption that they have capacities to self-direct their learning and their work. My contention is that action learning and action research are not identical, not even "blood brothers" – if for no other reason than that they spring from different origins and traditions. They do not share the same orientation towards the world. Having had "classic" experiences of both, I conclude that the difference between them is more significant than most people realize, and that misperceptions diminish the strengths of each.

A few important fundamentals

First, it makes sense to acknowledge a source of much confusion. Today, the marketplace is awash with people-influencing tools, popularly called "action technologies." There are some basic likenesses and a few notable differences among them. Each "technology" is accompanied by jargon that seeks to identify itself as separate from every other. This makes distinguishing characteristics between action learning and action research even harder to fish out of the waters. In various combinations, these tools (e.g., "open space," "force field analysis," "guided reflection") find their way into programs dominated by consultant-led organizational change interventions and expert coaching – whatever the label given to the programs. For the most part, the tools are fashioned from principles of applied social and educational psychology. A key feature is asking participants to think about what they say and do in contexts that affect other people, and to reflect upon what they might say and do differently for different results. Changed behavior of individuals and organizations is therefore the anticipated outcome of using "action technologies." In some cases, when a cluster of tools is used over and over in approximately the same configuration, the whole configuration is called an "action technology," as in Action Reflection Learning (ARL), Appreciative Inquiry, and so on. Regardless of how useful these "technologies" are, it becomes analytically necessary to peel away the layers of them to arrive at the core features of action learning and action research. Stripping elaborate tools out of the analysis and laying aside claims for superiority of any particular approach makes it more likely that "research" can be seen to stand on its own as the distinguishing, case-study-oriented core of action research. Likewise, "learning" can stand forth as the unadorned heart of action learning, making reference to a vigorous and exciting human process that occurs in natural settings among human beings with common concerns.

Sifting through dozens of definitions of action research online, in biographical materials, scholarly journals, prominent books on the subject, handbooks of naturalistic inquiry and the like (e.g. Denzin and Lincoln, 1994; Dick, 1999 and 2001; Gummesson, 1991; McGill and Brockbank, 2004; O'Brien, 1998; Stake, 1995; Wadsworth, 1998; Reddy and Barker, 2005; Raelin, 2008; Whyte, 1991), I have selected two excerpts from different sources that seem to me the most straight-to-the-point descriptions of action research and its researchers:

> Action research is inquiry or research in the context of focused efforts to improve the quality of an organization and its performance. It typically is designed and conducted by practitioners who analyze the data to improve their own practice (*North Central Regional Educational Laboratory,* www.ncrel.org).
>
> Action researchers "see the development of theory or understanding as a by-product of the improvement of real situations, rather than application as a by-product of advances in 'pure' theory." (Carr and Kemmis, 1986, p. 28, cited also in Wikiversity Action Learning article). This is a means to generate ideas (theory) that are relevant *locally* – to the people who are involved in the research, and to the environment in which it has taken place. (Wikiversity, en.wikiversity.org)

My own definition of action learning is, I trust, equally straight to the point:

> Action learning is a process of reflecting on one's work and beliefs in a supportive/confrontational environment of one's peers for the purpose of gaining new insights and resolving real business and community problems in real time. (Dilworth and Willis, 2003, p. 11)

Some facets common to both action learning and action research are striking. One is that "real situations" are sites of localized activity, and another is the faith that participant involvement insures that something important will be gained. A third commonality is that people actually in those real situations participate in the work of inquiry and meaning-making, as "co-researchers" and/or "co-learners."

However, individually "hard-wired" as we are to our preconceptions, we may filter out from these definitions any notion of a playing field where people engage in collaborative, open-ended and leaderless inquiry. If this happens, then what is left is only a playing field where experts of some kind will be needed to show the way and to insure that processes like "research" and "social interaction" are sanctioned and authoritative. We will then lump action learning and action research together as parts of one formal piece, sharing the same leader-dependent territory. This perception may, in turn, tempt us to assume that differences, if any, are not important and that it is perfectly acceptable to "mix and match" – or, to use another homespun metaphor, "blend and puree" – at will, and call what we are doing in action learning or action research by whatever label we think is most novel or most in vogue.

Because we have become so accustomed to what I call the effect of "teacherliness," so thoroughly used to the exercise of lecturer or change-agent expertise to reform organizations and individuals, it is easy to begin to doubt that we can do very much on our own to reform our circumstances or ourselves. But, in classic action learning, we learn that we cannot hand the baton to anyone else. Action learning means "doing change" autonomously. When this realization comes into play, distinctions between action learning and action research become most visible.

It is *classic action learning* and *classic action research* that I will be comparing throughout this discussion. By "classic," I mean action learning and action research as they were in the original, as they were described when they were first named and began to be understood as such in common parlance. To recover the classic requires tracing a bit of history.

Pioneer figures and their orientations

Action research is, by nature, interventionist. It is fact-finding (like all research) with the goal of improving specific practices (like teaching or managing). It involves challenging assumptions that may be of long duration, and it socially conditions people to relate differently to their own practice and to one another. Groups of participants are trained to listen and express sensitivity towards others and their beliefs and values. The "pioneer" name most associated with action research (for he named it) is psychologist Kurt Lewin. From a time beginning in the late 1940s, when he was called upon to design psychosocial interventions for the purpose of enhancing minority inclusion in organizations, a long train of inspired practitioners has followed in his footsteps. Most certified organization development specialists, at least in the

U.S., are his intellectual heirs and understand their interventions – regardless of what technologies they use – to be classic action research. Action research is conducted on a case-by-case basis, but it is intended to contribute to overall development of theory and practice that induces social/behavioral change. Interviews and survey instruments figure prominently in the data collection and analysis. Advance planning and careful structuring are considered imperative, for the results must be taken seriously. Consultants are well aware that they are putting their professional reputations on the line with every new client situation.

In *participatory action research* (PAR) – found commonly among teachers, public agencies, and community action groups in countries around the world – fund-generators who serve as consultants may set in motion a series or collection of projects. Teachers, nongovernment organization (NGO) workers, and community residents generally confine themselves to narrowly targeted goals, though expectations for end products may change in midstream. They actively establish their own priorities and plan their own actions, checking to see what is happening at relevant intervals and making corrections as they proceed. They tend to evaluate their progress both formatively, (i.e., to make adjustments as they plan and work) and summatively (at the end of their projects). In the course of their investigations, participants may experience insightful, emotional moments and personal growth akin to the intense transformational moments that occur in action learning. But the emphasis in participatory action research is on cognitive and operational changes, understanding better than before what assumptions they have made, how things in the environment actually work, and how actions and attitudes may be adjusted.

Action learning is by nature nondirective and noninterventionist, trusting that people as social beings are generally motivated to self-organize and to work and play collaboratively, contributing all they can in unpretentious ways to the common good. The "pioneer" name most prominently associated with action learning (for he named it) is Olympic athlete, physicist and educator-critic Reginald Revans. Though he began from boyhood to work out the principles and processes he thought most conducive to intensive and effective learning at individual and organizational levels, it was in the late 1930s that he began to envision and use "questioning circles" and "learning with and from each other" as a system of *action learning*. During the crises of the "Battle of Britain" war years – when so much was at stake in survival, productivity, and postwar recovery – Revans found himself increasingly in agreement with his economist colleague at the U.K. National Coal Board, who believed that leaders must "give a man a chance to utilize and develop his faculties; to enable him to overcome his egocentredness by joining with other people in a common task; and to bring forth the goods and services needed for a becoming existence" (Schumacher, n.d., p. 5).

Over the years, Revans' ideas about cooperative inquiry and unconventional problem-tackling have obviously taken root and been seized upon by many practitioners. He meant, literally, that in order to become wise about anything, we must make our minds receptive to *news of difference* that we notice in the world, exactly as if we were curious little children. To adults, this often sounds counterintuitive. People with hard-earned expertise seem to have particular difficulty with the idea of suppressing expertise for the sake of discovery, in the working out of the learning equation. The action learners themselves come to welcome a holiday from structure and expertise, repeatedly citing the incredible "freedom to learn" that is unleashed by absence of an authority figure, and by the unexpected largesse of using their own imaginations and devising their own procedures in team (set) activity. Choosing the least restrictive format for inquiry and critical reflection was something Revans hoped all action learners would do, in order to turn up their own creative capabilities to top speed and effectiveness. Team members on their own are extraordinarily high-performing because they have no choice if they are to get anything done.

Bateson (1979, p. 29) declared that "news of difference" is a basic requirement for all learning. Toddlers learn the news that a dog is not a cat and that red is not blue, because they receive distinguishing information through liberal use of senses, action trials and hearing what others say. Revans understood that such "news" is acquired in adulthood primarily in real-time interactions with others and in questioning what we think we know constantly throughout our lives. Since getting to know ourselves is part of the discriminating process, and a lifelong task at that, developing self-knowledge is implicated constantly in all classic action learning (Revans, 1988).

Few action learning proponents – particularly in the U.S. – seem to have recognized the influence of general systems theory (GST) on Revans' thinking. He was historically and certifiably "on the ground floor" with others in the global meta-scientific movement that encouraged crossing disciplinary boundaries and investigating any universe of systems holistically. The notions of boundary-less organizations and cross-functionality are descended directly from general systems theory, and Revans was turning these systems concepts into practice long ahead of most. Systems thinking found its way into action learning as a matter of course, and is woven subtly throughout Revans' writings and discourse.

Further, little attention has been paid to the scope and depth of his reading and understanding in dozens of subject areas. His bookshelves were as eclectic as any I have seen. Such breadth and depth allows the extraction of nuggets of wisdom from innumerable sources. I believe that one of the inimitable strengths of classic action learning is that Revans went for the core of things, not for their embellishments, and he encouraged others to do so.

While Revans said often that we must pick up the rate of learning to match or exceed the rate of change, he did not believe that the key to learning effectiveness lay in carefully tiered, predictable, shortest-route Triptik maps and tour guides. He desperately wanted us to drop the "speakers' platform" and "circles-with-arrows" images that we scribe for ourselves to make us more comfortable about what to expect, what to think, how to think it, in what sequence. In the hard sciences he came from, nothing was that reliable. Certified experts remained experts for a day, for, even on the day that followed, they might find their truths and certainties drastically unconfirmed. Expertise did not impress Revans; willingness to test assumptions and embrace new learning did. It is no wonder that, in his view, no one had final answers and that all our learning should, with humility, be considered tentative.

Humility, tentativeness, and strictest honesty as well as inquisitiveness are hallmarks of classic action learning. This makes it very genuine, if not always easy to sell to organizations that want only a little truth, a great deal of certainty, and rapid-fire quick fixes. I wrote down what Revans advised one day, warning us not to claim to be sleight-of-the-hand magicians of problem-solving:

> Do not run away with the idea of totally eliminating a problem. (Revans, 1996)

The lesson stays with me. I do not imagine that what I am writing now will "totally eliminate the problem" of confusing messages about action learning and action research. There is no denying that some people reading this (perhaps many people) will not get "news of difference" from these background remarks, or from my sharing of experience and my readout of factors that distinguish action learning and action research. They may disagree at will with my cognitive outlook, though they have fewer grounds to quarrel with what I say I have experienced.

Exemplars for comparison of action learning and action research

Classic action research seems today to be basically unaltered from its origins, except for increased participation in the research itself and for an expansion into a wider range of settings that include isolated parts of the Third World. *Classic action learning* has not been so well treated in the past half century. It has seemed defenseless against piecemeal adaptation, ill-fitting insertions, transliteration to suit multiple purposes, and even snide debunking of both the original process and its originator. Kember (2000) offers one possible explanation for the relative obscurity of action learning that persists even today:

> Of the two, action research has been written about much more, which is hardly surprising since research normally leads to published outcomes, whereas learning rarely does. Action research is therefore quite well defined compared to action learning (p. 21)

I take issue with his last sentence. What seems to me to be the crux of the matter is that people inquiring into the nature of action learning have too often taken a quick look, perhaps found themselves with unfamiliar expressions in unfamiliar territory, and as a result may have innocently imposed skewed interpretations of what Revans was defining. Then, too, as in any published author whose work evolves, they may have found contradictions and chosen to construct a version that seemed closer to their own point of view. Others have felt that they could take some ingredients, add extras from outside, and create a richer blend (O'Neil and Marsick, 2007; Rimanoczy and Turner, 2008). Nothing prevents anyone from making these alterations, but substitutions and blends taste different from original recipes, and variants called "action learning" will not have the same flavor as classic action learning.

Revans' writings are cited so briefly and so infrequently that I have come to wonder if many who undertake explanations of action learning have relied solely on one or two of his publications, or have not read him in the original at all. It is possible, on the other hand, that those who have read carefully have chosen to dismiss his ideas because they seemed simplistic or, on the other hand, too difficult and complex to implement.

The following examples illustrate:

1. deliberate misappropriation of the name "action learning";
2. two practitioners' crystal clarity about their terms, purposes, and potential outcomes;
3. a classic case of Lewin-style action research; and
4. a classic case of Revans-style action learning.

The stories in the examples are true, but narratives are stripped-down to the core of what each exemplifies. A fifth story has no known outcome.

Example 1

Kember (2000) described at length the effects of 50 projects to improve teaching and learning in seven educational institutions in Hong Kong. Though all the projects were specifically based on "the theory and practice of action research," the title of the endeavor was "The Action Learning Project (ALP)." We are told that the reason for this was "to obtain funding from a body that did not fund 'research.'" This was justified as "tactically appropriate" (p. 21).

Tactically appropriate or not, such name switching is acceptable only if one assumes that action learning and action research are completely interchangeable. But Kember and his colleagues did know that this was not the case. It seems that the farther away action learning is yanked from its moorings, the easier and more expedient it becomes to define it any way we choose. The next example challenges Kember's earlier assertion that action learning is "ill-defined" as compare with action research.

Example 2

Corley and Eades (2004) had no difficulty understanding differences between action learning and action research, and using the separate strengths of each. In two universities in Liverpool, England, they used action learning as a work-based instructional strategy in degree-granting postgraduate programs for senior practitioners in Personnel and Development, and Human Resource Development. They also employed a standard brand of participatory action research that involved the learners themselves in a collective identification and assessment of what went well and what did not, to determine what might be changed. At intervals throughout the programs, Corley and Eades gathered data and feedback from the students, and then studied data from focus groups and interviews when courses were finished. The goal was congruent with traditional action research: to improve practices for the next round of these programs.

Example 3

In the academic years 1969–70 and 1970–1, I participated in a five-year action research project headed by researchers affiliated with the National Training Laboratories (NTL). The project was directed towards improving campus life at five separate universities across the U.S. Each campus team – composed of faculty, students, and administrators – was coached in group dynamics and human relations T-Groups (sensitivity training groups), and then the teams set out to identify and assess relationship and interface problems that plagued the different campuses. We did both short- and long-term "trial and error" experiments in tension reduction and recognition of various needs and perspectives. One successful effort at my campus was a student-staffed Help Center, backed up in crisis cases by counseling professionals. At appropriate intervals, our seasoned NTL facilitators engaged us in data collection on our projects and processes. Reports were written by these facilitators concerning the successes and failures of our processing and our outcomes. These activities were never represented to us as anything other than action research, even though we felt and learned a great deal from our research efforts and our common/uncommon experiences with the other four teams.

Example 4

In the mid-1990s, I took part in a two-week action learning effort to assist two merging hospitals in the U.K. with "thinking-through" what the merger would mean in several operational areas. Participants were assigned to teams to insure variety, but each team self-organized and set its own ground rules. Some declined any facilitation. At least one team felt free to welcome the client into the team as often as she could get away to join them. Revans was, among others, available for consultation if problems arose. He lived in the same dorm we did for the duration of the program. Such informality led to many vital conversations. In the general view of participants, this egalitarian action learning experience was far less "conducted," more open to inquiry, more transformative and insight-producing than any previous experiences of a similar kind.

Example with an unknown end

There is a further complication which illustrates the additive – not necessarily integrative – nature of variants from both classic action research and classic action learning. Downstream of action research, along came an extension called "action science," (Argyris et al., 1985) which concerns itself with research about perceptions and attributed meanings in interpersonal verbal exchanges, with identifying types of learning, and with differences between what we espouse and what we practice. This is certainly not irrelevant to the current discussion, but would, if pursued, go beyond the purpose of this chapter. Aspects of action science have now made their way into both action research and some omnibus brands of action learning. Events in these arenas tend to be characterized by the steady presence of "coaches" (facilitators) who intervene in the small group sessions whenever they judge it to be helpful. The freedom so cherished by advocates of classic action learning is certainly conditioned by these contributor-presences. The unknown end of this story is whether, in such facilitated venues, classic action learning can remain uncompromised. It's not that the presence of facilitators/coaches is hostile; it is simply that they are there, soft-pedaling the participants' obligations and opportunities to struggle with the real, un-facilitated world. It is a question of whether facilitation "fits" with the avowed intention to deal with real situations in real time. It is also a question of whether adults can or cannot be trusted, given time and each other, to figure things out for themselves without help. Revans himself repeatedly asked us to recognize that facilitated teams are not really a part of the scheme of *classic action learning* and, in fact, are antithetical to the worldview embodied in action learning as he envisioned it.

Easy lessons from the examples

1. Things are not always what they seem or what they are called.
2. Some people believe there is a difference between action learning and action research, and act upon this belief.

3. Classic action research draws most heavily upon the social sciences, psychology in particular, and on traditional survey research methods. Interpretive license allows researchers to use interviews, participant observation, reflection and other data collection strategies to obtain qualitative information. The purpose is to use the information to suggest improvements in what people do and how they do it, usually within a specified range of responsibility.

4. Classic action learning may use any of the data collection methods that action research may use, but the emphasis is on wide-open learning of wisdom, a "commodity" other kinds of learning venues are hard pressed to deliver. In action learning, there are huge strides in the development of self-esteem and self-efficacy, willingness to start from positions of ignorance and move towards creative and collective competence, ability to do things never done before, courage to act and take the full consequences, and motivation to manage monumental amounts of work in very short time periods in the midst of other responsibilities. Action learning somehow inspires us to "take the bull by the horns" and "try anything once" but not repeat the same mistakes twice over. Knowledge is gained; wisdom arrives by way of reflection.

5. We can address issues and find workable solutions in any venue and by many different methods, but issues and problems tend not to stay solved. Technologies are not the whole answer, and perhaps not even the best answer. They can produce the illusion of "progress" where there is none. There are flexible-brain training advantages in low-tech, nothing-to-work-with, have-to-come-up-with-something situations. Here is a metaphor I think Revans would have liked: Without any help, children can play wonderfully creative sandlot baseball and may learn more than they ever could in supremely well-coached, well-uniformed Little League. All persons are creative in their own unique ways, and Revans wanted us out creating differences in the sandlots of the world.

Charting "news of difference" between action learning and action research

Every item in Table 11.1 should be considered either news of difference or news of likeness, but the likenesses have to be so identical as to be indistinguishable, thus appearing in both columns. As you would expect, there are only two columns – one headed *classic action learning*; the other headed *classic action research*.

I make no claim that Tables 11.1 is unassailable. Tables are taxonomic, and it is unwise to accept any taxonomy as final truth. Too many new things can be discovered to wipe out our taxonomic assumptions. Boxes never tell the whole story, though they may make premises less obscure.

Table 11.1 Characteristics of action learning and action research

Classic action learning	Classic action research
Utilizes small-group activity	Utilizes small-group activity
Has felt need to know	Has felt need to know
Is implicated in action; seeks to solve problems with new mental models	Is implicated in action; seeks to solve problems through research findings
Values autonomy and spontaneity; relies on members' realms of meaning and experiences	Is participative and interactive; encouraging and summarizing multiple contributions
Uses little to no "facilitation"; generates just-in-time, as-needed volunteer leadership	Relies on expert process consultation, intervention, guidance, and facilitation
Places high value on self-organizing as an inventive inquiry system, a learning system, and a real-world work system	Is organized programmatically by those familiar with a range of general to specific organizational and community cultures
Acknowledges ignorance in order not to rely on routine, ready-made solutions	Seeks to improve social practice by changing it
Honors but is not intimidated by complexity; is challenged to legitimize new insights	Relies extensively on a variety of experts and decision-makers for authority to proceed
Values experiential learning	Values experiential learning
Ventures into the unknown deliberately	Seeks to address skill deficiencies
Asks for critical reflection about self, others, and social organization of work in the world	Asks for critical reflection about practice; seeks refinement of theories
Tilts toward learning to be more forthright and authentic; to undertake potentially risky actions with courage, honesty and integrity	Tilts toward research but expects authentic, self-critical participation directed toward dispelling false assumptions
Acknowledges validity of differing points of view; invents collaborative, non-linear strategies for continuing work	Conceptualizes iterative cycles for testing and applying results of research to a target aspect of practice
Is profoundly invested in finding uncharted ways to accomplish the "impossible"	Is profoundly invested in bridging the gaps between theory and practice
Is profoundly invested in creating better organizations and a better world	Is profoundly concerned to solve problems in human relations and communications

The items listed in Table 11.1 are by no means exhaustive, but perhaps they sketch a landscape of differences that deserves further scrutiny. I have made confident assumptions on the basis of what I have learned from Revans and others, and what I have experienced directly during more than a decade of action learning. Assumptions are always open to testing through further study. I view Revans' publications as a deep well of thought that may best be researched through textual and literary criticism, and I am not aware of any efforts that have been made in that direction. That would be my choice as a means to improve precision on the classic action learning side of the chart, along with a parallel effort to refine the elements on the side of classic action research. Referring to an earlier metaphor, I reiterate that differences are significant: dogs are precisely not cats and red is precisely not blue. Like objects, systems of thought are not precisely alike. Each has systemic integrity and purposes that set it apart from others. It is our loss if we, in any way, in our passion for inclusion, dismantle such systems and the verity within them.

All we ever have are the collective outcomes of whatever meaning-making processes we have individually and collectively used to learn and to undertake action. Both action research and action learning are meaning-making processes. We may never agree on relative merits, but we can certainly take cues from those who use both, for different purposes.

References

Action research (n.d.) Excerpt from Wikiversity, en.wikiversity.org

Argyris, C., Putnam, R., and Smith, D. (1985) *Action Science* (San Francisco: Jossey-Bass).

Bateson, Gregory (1979) *Mind and Nature* (New York: E. P. Dutton).

Carr, W. and Kemmis, S. (1986) *Becoming Critical* (Lewes: Falmer Press).

Corley, A. and Eades, E. (2004) "Becoming Critically Reflective Practitioners: Academics' and Students' Reflections on the Issues Involved", *Human Resource Development International*, 7(1), March, pp. 137–44.

Denzin, N. K. and Lincoln, Y. S. (eds.) (1994) *Handbook of Qualitative Research* (Thousand Oaks, CA: Sage), pp. 206–7, 301, 333–9.

Dick, B. (n.d.) "Action Learning and Action Research" [briefly compared]. Available at www.scu.edu.au/schools/gcm/ar/arp/actlearn.html

Dick, B. (2001) "Action Research: Action and Research", in S. Sankaran, B. Dick, R. Passfield and P. Swepson (eds.), *Effective Change Management Using Action Learning and Action Research* (Lismore, NSW: Southern Cross University Press), pp. 21–7.

Dick, B. (1999) "Sources of Rigor in Action Research: Addressing the Issues of Trustworthiness and Credibility". Available at www.latrobe.edu.au/aqr/offer/papers/BDick.htm

Dilworth, R. L. and Willis, V. J. (2003) *Action Learning: Images and Pathways* (Malabar, FL: Krieger).

Gummesson, E. (1991) *Qualitative Methods in Management Research*, rev. edition (Newbury Park, CA: Sage).

Kember, D. (2000) *Action Learning and Action Research: Improving the Quality of Teaching and Learning* (London: Kogan Page).

McGill, I. and Brockbank, A. (2004) *The Action Learning Handbook* (London: Routledge).

O'Brien, R. (1998) "An Overview of the Methodological Approach of Action Research", pp. 1–18. Available at www.web.net/robrien

O'Neil, J. and Marsick, V. J. (2007) *Understanding Action Learning* (New York: American Management Association).

Raelin, J. A. (2008) *Work-Based Learning*, rev. edition (San Francisco: Jossey-Bass).

Reddy, S. and Barker, A. E. (2005) *Genuine Action Learning: Following the Spirit of Revans* (Hyderabad, India: ICFAI University Press).

Revans, R. W. (1988) *The Golden Jubilee of Action Learning* (Manchester, England: Manchester Action Learning Exchange).

Revans, R. W. (1996) Quotation from notes taken during discussions with Revans at University of Salford, UK.

Rimanoczy, I. and Turner, E. (2008) *Action Reflection Learning* (Mountain View, CA: Davies-Black).

Schumacher, E. F. (n.d.) Cited in en.wikipedia.org, p. 5 of 7.

Stake, R. E. (1995) *The Art of Case Study Research* (Thousand Oaks, CA: Sage).

Vaartjes, V. (2005) "Integrating Action Learning Practices into Executive Coaching to Enhance Business Results", *International Journal of Evidence Based Coaching and Mentoring*, 3(1), Spring, pp. 1–17.

Wadsworth, Y. (1998) "What is Participatory Action Research?", pp. 1–20. Available at www.scu.edu.au/schools/gcm/ar/ari/p-ywadsworth98.html

Whyte, W. F. (1991) *Participatory Action Research* (Newbury Park, CA: Sage).

12
Future Search as Action Learning

Marvin R. Weisbord and Sandra Janoff

If "action learning" is "a form of learning by doing," then "future search," to borrow a phrase from the pioneer social psychologist Kurt Lewin, means "doing by learning." This may be a distinction without a difference, since learning and doing seem to us inextricably linked. Future search derives from action research, a key legacy of Kurt Lewin's. However, future search represents a significant departure from its action research roots. It has become a kind of hybrid large group amalgam supporting many traditions, including that of action learning.

Kurt Lewin's legacy

Weisbord (2004) traced the principles behind future search back to the 1930s and Lewin, the "practical theorist," father of action research, refugee from Nazi Germany, originator of field theory, seminal figure in human relations training, and mentor of the colleagues who, in turn, inspired us. Together with members of Future Search Network, we have sought for decades to modify Lewinian action research to cope with the pace of nonstop change and increasing cultural diversity.

We define action research as a joint inquiry into a situation in which researchers and subjects share a stake in learning and take responsibility

Illustration 12.1   Kurt Lewin, progenitor of Future Search

for their actions. The purposes are twofold: improving the situation, and creating knowledge about improving social change processes. Lewin sought to use action research as a way to "unfreeze, move, and refreeze" systems. He believed that confronting people with dissonant diagnostic data would encourage cultural change that could then be stabilized ("frozen") at a higher level of functioning. In a fast moving world, however, people have little time for diagnoses that hold only momentarily; hence the need for methods that enable people to participate in systems improvement in "real time," learning for themselves rather than from a consultant's conclusions.

Despite many parallels among action research, action learning, and future search, action research historically differed from both action learning and future search in a significant way that is worth noting. Lewin was at heart a researcher who practiced "topological psychology," a discipline based in geometry. He believed that the intensity of forces acting within and upon his subjects in social situations could be measured. Force field analysis, a problem-solving tool taught in management courses, was among his innovations.

Lewin sought to subject social situations to scientific experiments, emulating as best he could the physical sciences. During World War II, for example, he teamed with anthropologist Margaret Mead to find ways to change American eating habits. The goal was to free up scarce meats for the armed forces. Their experiment involved Iowa housewives. The control group heard an expert tout "variety meats" (e.g., Spam) as equally nutritious as prime rib and much more patriotic to serve. The experimental group heard the same lecture. However, they were asked to discuss it among themselves and make public what they chose to do. When the researchers followed up, they found (surprise!) that those who made their decisions in dialogue were more likely to implement the program.

They also found that declaring their decisions aloud reinforced the women's resolve to act. Thus was born the theory of "participative management" (Weisbord, 2004). The Lewin–Meade findings became a key part of future search practice. Participants do their own data analysis, engage in continual dialogue, and draw their own conclusions. The meetings usually end with people sitting in a circle, those who wish to do so making public the personal actions they will take.

Lewin's experiments led to many variations on the action research theme. In the late 1970s, for example, Marvin Weisbrod was invited to organize a leadership training program for physicians in a medical research laboratory. He proposed a two-step process grounded in action research. During a two-day diagnostic workshop, the physicians would sample various tools – personal style instruments, organizational surveys, conflict management, problem-solving and decision methods. They would assess their own needs and write their own "prescriptions" for the training phase. A three-day workshop would then be designed, based on their wishes for further study. The group embraced this joint inquiry with enthusiasm, and, contrary to our experiences with externally-imposed training, they put great energy into learning and applying new skills.

As you can see, there are elements of both action research and action learning in this example. Indeed, at the level of principles rather than procedures, the methods have much in common.

A short history of future search principles

Thus, if you want to understand future search, you need to go back to the origin of its principles. You will see that these parallel action learning in several respects. For example:

> 1st principle: Get the "whole system" in the room (defined by us as stakeholders who collectively have among them *authority to act, resources, expertise, information,* and *need*).

Simply calling such a meeting is often a radical change in itself that makes possible other changes previously thought impossible.

> 2nd principle: Explore the whole system before seeking to fix any part of it (also framed as get everyone talking about the same world or "think globally, act locally").

People create a portrait of the whole that no one person could draw alone. No action is attempted until all are talking about the same world, one that includes everyone's perceptions of both the system and its environment.

> 3rd principle: Focus on the common ground and desired future, treating problems and conflicts as information, not action items.

By putting conflicts and problems on the back-burner, we make possible discoveries that are unlikely when 80% of the time is spent on 20% of the issues difficult to resolve.

> 4th principle: Have people self-manage their own small groups and take responsibility for action.

Future search consultants avoid doing anything for participants that they are capable of doing for themselves.

The first experiment leading to these principles was run in 1938–9 by Kurt Lewin (1948) with graduate students Ronald Lippitt and Ralph White at the State University of Iowa. They set out to test Lippitt's hypothesis, based on his undergraduate experience as an outdoor group leader, that democratic leaders got higher commitment and better results than autocrats.

Working on arts and crafts projects with local boys' clubs, Lippitt and White led their groups in democratic and autocratic styles for six sessions at a time. Lewin recorded the boys' behavior with a movie camera. Statistical analysis of incidents of flight, fight and apathy demonstrated the superiority of democratic leadership behavior. Lewin and Lippitt coined the term "group dynamics" to describe the effect of a leader's actions on group satisfaction and performance. Their research set the stage for a "leadership style" industry that continues to this day.

Lippitt went on to develop group problem-solving techniques for setting goals, brainstorming, prioritizing and testing solutions. In the 1950s, using audio tapes of strategic planning meetings, Lippitt concluded that group problem-solving depresses people. So, he devised methods to elicit "images of potential" that would stimulate positive energy. Instead of asking what was wrong and how to fix it, Lippitt asked what futures people preferred and what they were willing to do to get there. This work led to visioning exercises and appreciative methods widely adopted decades later.

In the 1970s, Eva Schindler-Rainman (a community development consultant) and Lippitt (1980) ran 88 large workshops based on focusing on the future. These events built on earlier experiments showing that people were more likely to implement decisions they had helped to make. Each meeting involved a cross-section of the community from all walks of life, as many as 300 people at a time. The pair found that having "everybody" involved in planning their own future led to many innovative, long-lasting programs.

From the Lewin/Lippitt/Schindler-Rainman research we derived two principles, getting the "whole system" in the room, and focusing on a system's future and common ground rather than managing conflict and solving narrow problems piecemeal.

We also drew on studies from Great Britain. During World War II, the social scientist Eric Trist, another exponent of Lewin's work, teamed with psychiatrist Wilfred Bion to create an innovative selection process for British Army field officers. They placed candidates in leaderless groups and posed field problems with clear goals requiring skill in balancing self-interest and group interest. The best candidates, who later proved successful in battle, knew how to get people cooperating for the common good.

This early experiment with self-managing task groups was reinforced by real-life observation when, in the late 1940s, Trist's student, Kenneth Bamforth, visited a coal mine where he had once worked. He saw teams of multiskilled miners working underground in leaderless teams. By every measure, they were more productive than those in old fragmented systems where miners were closely supervised and specialized only in one job. This validated the potential of broad, general knowledge and self-management (Weisbord, 2004).

In the 1950s, Trist was joined in England by a young Australian social scientist, Fred Emery – another devotee of Lewin. They sought to apply the lessons learned in coal mines to business strategy planning. In a historic conference with the newly-formed Bristol-Siddeley aircraft engine company they drew for their meeting design on the research of social psychologist Solomon Asch (1952). Asch had shown that, when people talk about a world that includes all their realities and experience their psychological similarities, they are more likely to accept each other's views, enter into real dialogue, and commit to mutual action plans (Trist and Emery, 1960).

To bring the "Asch conditions" alive, Trist and Emery had the executives immerse themselves in global and industry trends before looking at their company. In effect, they elevated the dialogue to a context inclusive of each executive's understanding of the "environment." The group had little conflict, showed high commitment and, indeed, went on to develop a new, more efficient aircraft engine. Emery and Trist called their innovative meeting a "search conference" (Weisbord et al., 1992). From their work we also derived two future search principles: having people talk about the same world – one that includes all their perceptions; and having people self-manage their own small groups and take responsibility for action.

Thus, the name "future search" honors all the pioneers who influenced us; "future" referring to the Lippitt and Schindler-Rainman collaborative futures conferences, "search" to the pioneering efforts of Emery and Trist.

Future search as a learning model

By now, the similarities between action learning and future search should be obvious. Action learning takes place in small groups, perhaps eight to 12 people meeting periodically over weeks or months. Future search usually involves 50 to 80 people in a single event lasting two-and-a-half days. However, much of the work is done in groups of eight or nine, analogous to action learning "teams" (sets). Action learning tends to be problem-centered; future search is system-centered, the system being a community or an organization. However, we believe there is nothing inherent in either method that would inhibit a group's choosing to focus on a system or a problem.

Action learning groups solve the problem, study their own behavior, and improve their problem-solving skills. Future search groups study their system, discover common ground, and create action plans for improvement. Although future search groups do not study their own behavior, they often transform their system's capability for action. No one tells them that is what they are doing. They do it as a function of the method.

For many years, we have followed a generic future search meeting design embodying the above principles. The procedures are culture free, allowing people to tap into their own experiences and vocabulary. As a result, the method works pretty much the same way in Western cities or African villages (Weisbord and Janoff, 2000). The design calls for a large group working in one

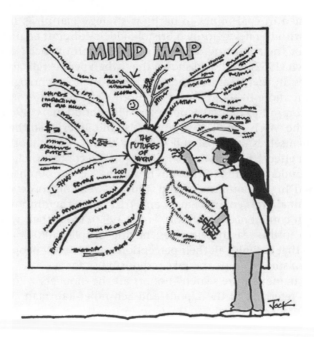

Illustration 12.2   Don't just do something, stand there!
Source: Illustration by Jock Macneish from Weisbord and Janoff (2007).

room on the same agenda. The purpose is always the future of "X." Groups spend about half a day in each of five phases: past, present, future, common ground, and action planning. Participants educate one another to what they know, believe, and want. Together, they develop a rich understanding of the connections among themselves, their community or organization, and the world they live in.

We usually start with lunch on Day 1 and end the afternoon of Day 3. Action planning is put off until mid-morning of Day 3, when everyone has a picture of the whole that none had at the start. The design employs simple, well-known techniques – time lines, a mind map, brainstorming, preferred futures and action planning methods. All, however, are placed in service of the underlying principles. (Many other techniques might serve. We use the ones we know and love.) At each step, people build their own data base, talk it over in small groups, report their conclusions, and engage in a whole group dialogue.

Over the years, we have added a few new wrinkles; for example, a "reality dialogue" in which a whole group confirms its common ground; and procedures for translating common ground statements into action plans for concrete policies, programs and systems. Participants require no training.

Most consultants with group experience can learn to use the method successfully.

A philosophy and theory of facilitating

We advocate a nonintrusive form of democratic group leadership that makes a group's taking responsibility more probable. We do not urge people to do or say anything except what they volunteer. If you study only the meeting design, you may miss this key point. Our philosophy is that every person is doing the best they can with what they have. In groups diversified by culture, ethnicity, gender, education, class, race and hierarchy, no one can figure out what every person needs anyway. So, we do not seek to diagnose deficits or to teach people unfamiliar skills. To change the world, we start with the meeting at hand, learning to accept others the way we find them. We work with whatever "styles" people bring to the table. The glue that binds people is the task. So, we seek to head off any behavior that might divert a group from its core mission. (For more on how we do this, see Weisbord and Janoff, 2007).

Future search as a cross-cultural phenomenon

One aspect of future search that has bemused us for many years is the spontaneous appeal of this learning/doing method among diverse cultures. At the time of writing, Future Search Network members (and many others) have applied the core principles equally well with the aboriginal peoples of Australia; the Inuit of the Arctic; the U.S. Army; business firms; government agencies; schools, colleges and universities; hospitals; museums; NGOs; charities and foundations; and in inner cities, towns and rural areas in Austria, Bangladesh, Botswana, Canada, Denmark, Ethiopia, England, Germany, Great Britain, Hungary, India, Iran, Israel, Mexico, Nepal, the Netherlands, Norway, Poland, Russia, Singapore, Sweden, South Africa, Thailand, and the United States.

People have improved water quality through future search in Pakistan; demobilized child soldiers in the Southern Sudan; made business plans in Spain; cut factory costs in Brazil; developed women leaders in Siberia; and fought AIDS in Senegal, Nigeria and Ghana. These are just a few of hundreds, probably thousands, of examples. We now go on to describe in detail what people did in one situation that had at first seemed hopeless. It provides many clues to conditions under which future search is likely to succeed: a compelling task, committed leaders, sufficient time and scrupulous attention to principles.

Case study: Children of Southern Sudan

Southern Sudan's six million people live in one of world's poorest and most chronically underdeveloped areas. They lost a generation of children to a brutal North–South civil war that began after independence from Great Britain in 1956. The area also has endured decades of intermittent hostilities among its own many tribes. By the 1990s, more than a million people had died from war and famine, and thousands more from preventable diseases.

For many years, the political debate on Sudan's future tended to focus on whether development in the South could only follow a peace agreement. Meanwhile, the situation for children grew worse. They had lost homes, schools, families and freedom. Thousands, some as young as 11 years old, had been conscripted to fight by various militias.

Against this background, Sharad Sapra, a medical doctor directing UNICEF's Operation Lifeline Sudan, decided on a bold move on the anniversary of the UN Convention on the Rights of the Child. He would convene a cross-section of Southern Sudanese adults to see whether they could put their tribal differences aside and find common ground for the sake of the children. As his vehicle, he chose future search, a process he had experienced in Bangladesh, and later used successfully in Iran to relieve the plight of street children.

The event we will describe was held in Nairobi, Kenya, in November 1999. This is as good an example as can be found of cross-cultural action learning driven by a dedicated leader and a compelling task. Participants were recruited from many parts of Southern Sudan and from Sudanese emigrants in Africa and Europe. The group included health care workers, NGO activists, elders, teachers, tribal chiefs, women, administrators and academics – a unique gathering of people who under normal circumstances would never meet. They were invited to leave their political differences behind and create, through dialogue, a dream for their children six years hence, in the year 2005.

Sapra's vision for the meeting went further. He wanted the voices of the children heard, not just invoked second-hand. Hence, he decided that Southern Sudanese children should have their own future search prior to the adult event. The children would develop their future vision and bring it into the adult meeting.

Thus, some 40 youngsters, aged 13 to 17, joined by their teachers, flew into Nairobi in November 1999 and were taken by bus to a conference center outside the city. None had ever flown before. Most had never seen a hotel, experienced television, or used knives and forks for eating. Nearly all had suffered displacement and separation from families. Some had been wounded as child conscripts in the war. For many, this was the first time ever that they had met youngsters and grown-ups from other regions and tribes in an atmosphere of calm and hope.

During their own meeting, the children earnestly entered into dialogue with one another. They made vivid the extent to which they all had suffered from war. Though poorly educated, every young person had something positive and unique to contribute to a shared vision. Their message was focused and clear. They wanted peace, access to health services and a normal family life. Above all, rather than haphazard lessons conducted under trees, they wanted to learn in real schools.

The children approached their tasks with great maturity, humor and tolerance for each other's views. Nowhere was this more evident than during a debate about how to pick ten of their number to represent them in the adult conference. Some held that the ones most capable of articulating a common vision should be chosen, others that each region or ethnic group should be tapped. Their discussion was intense and lively.

Then, the children – never having experienced democratic decision-making – fell back on what they knew best. They insisted that Sandra, who was leading the meeting, choose among them. They were surprised and frustrated when he refused, saying he believed they were capable of deciding for themselves. A long discussion ensued. At last, the group concluded that the fairest solution was for each of the five diverse groups that had been meeting together to pick two members. That way all groups would be represented. In the end, they picked more boys than girls and did not include all regions. Having done it themselves, however, the young people felt heard and well-represented.

The adult future search began on an emotional high. Several participants had not seen one another for a decade or more. Many had never met at all. They were overwhelmed by the children's opening presentation of what their short lives had been like. The young people dramatized, in a way that position papers and statistics could never reveal, how they had been traumatized by war and now yearned for peace, reunion with families, and normal schools.

The future search methodology was new for most participants. Indeed, but for Shapra and a few of his staff, those with the most future search experience were the children. It took some time for the adults to grasp that this event was not for presenting papers, analyzing data and going over the futile ground covered in so many prior conferences.

People learned, at last, that the meeting depended on everyone bringing their own experience into the room, just as the children had – whereupon they embraced the conference tasks with great will and enthusiasm. Given the deeply painful past they shared, including bitter conflicts between ethnic groups in the room, the ease with which everyone focused was gratifying to all. The fate of their children provided the common bond.

Adults validated the children's stories. Every person present had suffered trauma and loss as a result of the war. Personal tragedies – the deaths of children, parents and siblings; bombing of schools; fleeing in terror from attacks – all were recounted. People described their feelings of helplessness when they were unable to provide for their families during famine, and their inability to give adequate health care and schooling to the children. But they also told of initiatives of which they were proud; and it became apparent to all that they were trying, under daunting circumstances, to improve their children's lives.

Political issues could not help but intrude. When the adults were on the verge of blaming each other for their problems, it was the children who kept them focused on what that had brought them to this place. Working in small groups, the adults went on to create their own dreams for their children's future. They, too, specified peace and reconciliation as key priorities, along with education and health services. The adults also identified an additional responsibility they felt for securing a better future: good governance, with accountability structures respecting human rights.

Results and critical factors

As with all such meetings, some left skeptical that anything more would come of the conference. Said one articulate 14-year old at the end, "We charge you, the adults, not to leave all these good ideas here in this Safari Park Hotel!" Many took up the challenge. Some expatriates formed a task force to develop curriculum materials and deliver textbooks to villages. Another group set out to increase the pool of educators by identifying community members with teaching skills. A third group planned training courses for agriculturists and farmers. The health care professionals committed to train health workers and to help local citizens erect new health centers. The conference ended with many public commitments.

Fortunately, given UNICEF's infrastructure and the dedication of Sapra and his staff, things did not stop with good intentions. Seven months later, Sapra asked us to return to Nairobi to train 54 Sudanese NGO staff members, from both the North and the South, in future search. A week later, four of the trainees from the UNICEF/OLS staff went into Southern Sudan to a village recently bombed by government forces, and ran a future search on demobilizing child soldiers. It included school children, parents, teachers, religious leaders, NGOs, village and tribal chiefs, and, most significantly, local authorities and commanders from the Sudanese People's Liberation Army (SPLA).

In February 2001, in the largest effort of its kind ever undertaken in Southern Sudan, UNICEF announced that it had airlifted more than 2500 child combatants out of conflict zones and into safe areas where they could be returned to civilian life and have a chance to trace the fate of their families. By 2003, the number of demobilized child soldiers had passed 11,000.

In the original future search of November 1999, the children had dreamed an impossible dream: peace by 2005, a peace driven by education. Indeed, school construction began right after the adult conference. By 2002, there were more than 50 schools, including two boarding schools for girls, tripling in one year in those areas the number of young women in school.

There was more to come. In January 2005, the Government of Sudan and the Sudanese People's Liberation Movement signed an agreement declaring peace between North and South Sudan for the first time in decades. In an email to us, Sharad Shapra wrote that the children's 1999 call for peace by 2005 had created the energy and will among the adults to make that happen.

Whatever the explanation, the coincidence in timing was stunning. The region was no longer at war and people were seeking to rebuild their society. (It is important to note that this conflict had different roots than that of Darfur in the western part of Sudan. Also, not unexpectedly, there were further tensions between North and South following the peace treaty. The issues were many and complex, including historic hostilities among southern tribes and not just with the north).

Learning from a learning event

We take three lessons from this story. First, the future search helped children learn that their views count and that they could make a difference in their own lives. This was reinforced when their theme – peace through education – influenced the adults to act. Second, these future searches challenged the paradigm that development can happen only after peace has been declared. Third, there is an unending tension between light and shadow in the human psyche, and learning to manage it is a task that will never be completed. Southern Sudan remains a difficult and dangerous place. It is also true that thousands of children are no longer forced to risk their lives for causes they do not understand. The new schools and health centers built since 1999 really do exist.

It was Sapra's contention that developmental activities could fertilize the ground for reconciliation. "Peace," Sapra has said, "is not an event, it is a behavior. Most conflicts start because of disparities and competition for resources. They may present themselves as ethnic or religious conflicts, but in reality it is the disparity that is the triggering factor. Education, therefore, becomes the most important tool for peace. It provides an essential alternative to war." (See Future Search Network (n.d.)).

Crossing cultures is counterintuitive, unless...

We come at last to a question we have been asking since the moment in the early 1990s when we learned that future search, without any intention on our part, was making its way around the globe. Why this easy crossing of cultural boundaries in Asia and Africa of a method devised by the offspring of Europeans? Well, we have no proof but many speculations. For one thing, people work entirely with their own experience. They need learn no theories or skills they do not already have (though they may not know that they have them).

Future search makes systems "thinking" experiential. People improve their systems by experiencing the part each person plays in the success of the whole. Thus, anybody can participate. Indeed, the more diverse a group, the better the experience. Given an important shared task, people discover that their common stakes overshadow the mistrust they sometimes feel for those who are different.

Oddly enough, each culture finds in future search aspects of its own traditions. Native Hawaiians, for example, see future search as bringing to life the unity of mind, body and spirit. Business executives like the emphasis on personal initiative, responsibility and teamwork. Chinese bureaucrats highlight family cooperation for the good of the whole. Religious groups as diverse as the Unity Church, the Jewish Reconstructionist Federation and American Baptist Convention have identified key values of their faiths in the practice of future search. It may be that in a world of technology run amok, economic uncertainty, and nonstop social change, people use future search to reconnect with universal needs for mutual respect and community going back thousands of years.

Conclusion: A comment on the "future"

Our focus on the "future" is actually a philosophical choice. We affirm that people who put their energy into supporting one another to get what they want are more likely to have it. Despite the name, everything in future search, including images of a desired future, happens in the present. The past that we explore in detail exists now, in memory. The present that we describe from firsthand experience recedes instantaneously into the past. The future lives on in us only in the present. We believe the future is now. It arrives as we talk about it and dissolves moment by moment into the past.

Thus, whatever we do in a future search meeting is consequential and existentially valuable at that moment. We have been, by turns, astonished, awed, delighted and humbled to discover the extent to which actions have rippled out in time and space from a single meeting. (See www.future-search.net, Weisbord and Janoff (2000) and Weisbord (2004) for numerous examples).

While few future searchers do formal research, the Future Search Network has for many years supported an ongoing study – the "Ripple Project" – to find out what people are capable of doing after a future search that they could not do before. A number of doctoral theses have been written on the subject. Nearly all validate the observation that those who stick to the principles and put enough time into the meeting are likely to succeed beyond those who do not. Oddly enough, this verifiable fact has little influence on the thousands of meetings people love to hate.

Though we bend a knee to the altar of learning, we must acknowledge that not everybody learns, especially from other peoples' experiences. In the end, no matter how much we (you, they) learn about what works and what does not in human affairs, and no matter how hard we struggle to communicate what we find, each generation has no choice but to learn – by acting – all over again for itself.

References

Asch, S. (1952) *Social Psychology* (New York: Prentice-Hall).

Emery, F. E. and Trist, E. L. (1973) *Toward a Social Ecology* (New York: Plenum).

Future Search Network (n.d.) "Children of Southern Sudan", 30-minute DVD. Available from Future Search Network, www.futuresearch.net

Lewin, K. (1948) *Resolving Social Conflicts: Selected Papers on Group Dynamics,* in G. W. Lewin (ed.) (New York: Harper & Row).

Schindler-Rainman, E. and Lippitt, R. (1980) *Building the Collaborative Community: Mobilizing Citizens for Action* (Irvine: University of California). Available from ENERGIZE, 215 438–8342.

Trist, Eric L. and Emery, F. E. (1960) "Report on the Barford Conference for Bristol/Siddeley Aero-Engine Corp.", 10–16 July, Document 598 (London: Tavistock).

Weisbord, M. R. (1987) *Productive Workplaces: Organizing and Managing for Dignity, Meaning and Community* (San Francisco: Jossey-Bass), ch. 14.

Weisbord, M. R. (2004) *Productive Workplaces Revisited: Dignity, Meaning and Community in the 21st Century* (San Francisco: Jossey-Bass/Wiley), chs 20 and 21.

Weisbord, M. R. and 35 co-authors (1992) *Discovering Common Ground* (San Francisco: Berrett-Koehler).

Weisbord, M. and Janoff, S. (2000) *Future Search: An Action Guide to Finding Common Ground in Organizations and Communities*, 2nd edition (San Francisco: Berrett-Koehler).

Weisbord, M. and Janoff, S. (2007) *Don't Just Do Something, Stand There! Ten Principles for Leading Meetings That Matter* (San Francisco: Berrett-Koehler).

Part III
Perspectives

13
Action Learning through the Lens of Action Learners

Robert L. Dilworth, Verna J. Willis, Karen M. Videtec, Mariana Garban, Lillie Graham Sapp, Marvin R. Weisbord, Fran Szabo, Judy O'Neil, Victoria J. Marsick, Karen E. Watkins, Sandra Janoff and Isabel Rimanoczy

This chapter looks at action learning from the perspective of a participant. Each of the contributing authors in this chapter has experienced action learning in some form as a learner. Some of them have also managed action learning initiatives. Their comments prove that there are varying perspectives on action learning. The first four contributors (Dilworth, Willis, Videtic and Garban) either met Revans or worked with him closely. Dilworth and Willis, in particular, spent much time with Revans. Two of the longer contributions can be found in Chapters 14 and 15 of this volume.

My friend Reg
Robert L. Dilworth

Walking toward the air terminal building in Tallahassee, Florida, I heard my name announced over the loudspeaker system – "Paging Lex Dilworth. Please come to the Lost and Found Department." On arriving there, I found Reg Revans with a cluster of female airline employees around him. His flight had arrived very early and they had seen the 84-year-old gentleman wandering around the airport. The airline staff had brewed him some tea and he was regaling them with stories. They were obviously enthralled and not pleased when I took him away.

This was my first meeting with Reg. He carried a thin valise that seemed to be bulging at the seams. He had no other baggage. As I came to know him, it became evident that this was his method of operation. No matter how long the visit – one day in this case – he always confined his gear to one small bag.

On arrival at his hotel room to freshen up for dinner, he immediately opened up his valise. It was filled with books and papers, but almost nothing else. He began laying out the various papers on the bed and talked for four straight hours about action learning. It was interesting, fascinating and brilliant. I finally suggested we go to dinner before all the restaurants locked up for the night.

He ate almost no dinner, and I found over time that this was the way he operated. He continued to talk about action learning. He was giving me a cram course. While my doctoral studies at Columbia had exposed me to action learning, my knowledge was quite thin. One of my former professors, Victoria Marsick, had offered me the chance to have Reg come to Tallahassee to speak to state employees.

The next day, just before Reg was to address middle managers and senior managers from across Florida's state government, a senior official from the Department of Labor and Employment Security approached me and said: "Do you really expect these bureaucrats to sit and listen to an 84-year-old Englishman talk to them about action learning, something they know nothing about? It will be a huge flop, and I will bet you the best steak dinner in the State of Florida that this is what is about to happen." I took the bet. From what I had seen of Reg's power of articulation and high energy the night before, there was little doubt in my mind that this fellow had it wrong. I did have to admit that these bureaucrats were pretty dry folks and not known for bursts of innovative thinking.

Revans spoke for 45 minutes, and the question-and-answer period exceeded the time allocated because of the high audience interest. When a halt was called, everyone stood up and gave Reg a standing ovation. The official who had bet with me ended up taking me to Bern's Steak House in Tampa – one of the best steak houses in the country – and I ordered the biggest steak on their menu.

This began a warm friendship and close collaborations with Reg. At later gatherings where he spoke, including an Academy of Human Resource Development Annual Conference in New Orleans, where I introduced him, people would have a perception that someone of his age could somehow not be expected to perform. He would prove them wrong every time. He had the energy of a much younger man, probably a carry over from his days as an Olympic athlete.

He visited me for a week in Richmond, Virginia when I was on the faculty in the School of Education at Virginia Commonwealth University. I had a team of six graduate students – an "action learning set [team]" formed for the occasion – work with him all week. His close friend Albert Barker in England had sent me an email and asked me to go easy on him in the scheduling. I ended up scheduling Reg for 18 events that week and he thrived on it. He inspired the students to set up an International Center for Action learning in Richmond. A week after he left, they presented me with their business cards. They had taken him seriously. He also asked them to go to Bologna, Italy to a conference and present their views on action learning. They pooled their money, the school contributed a small amount of money, and they went.

Traveling on the power of Reg's inspiration, the students continued to meet for two years and began some initiatives of which he was very proud. One of the six students, Donna Vick, was given the first full scholarship at the Revans Center for Action Learning and Research at the University of Salford, She earned her doctorate there and then joined the faculty.

There were many other occasions when I saw a man in his eighties, and then nineties, continue to make a contribution. There was the First Congress on Action Learning and Mutual Collaboration in Heathrow, England in 1995, which inspired some international effort. In 1996, Reg spent two weeks with me and 31 graduate students from Canada, the United States and Australia at the University of Salford, a program that David Botham, the Revans Center Director, and I had organized. Reg was 89 by then. I remember him sitting on the lawn outside the school surrounded by a circle of students. He kept inspiring people.

He had asked that I write "a better book" on action learning, as he called it, and he kept after me. The book appeared in 2003, coauthored by Verna Willis, another collaborator with Revans. The last words by Revans to appear in print are contained in his Foreword to that book.

You might say that I discovered a great deal in that Lost and Found Department back in 1991.

Every time I talked to Reg in the latter years of his life, he would begin with the following comment, "All the world is discovering action learning." Per usual, Reg was right! He richly deserves to be called the "Father of Action Learning."

Experiencing action learning (my thoughts)
Verna J. Willis

During my first brush with action learning, listening to Revans, I knew at once that here was something very different, refreshingly divorced from the taxonomic world of instructional design and expert-driven teaching/learning events so common in organizations today. I felt a live spark of reconnection to the past joy of learning in a one-room country school – where questions flew, no fierce competition among the disciplines prevailed, all kinds of learning were valued, and it was perfectly acceptable to know, and be recognized for knowing, things that the big kids and even the teacher did not.

I heard Reg insisting that, *in genuine action learning, the autonomy of the learner is explicitly restored to the learner,* and that sounded right to me. This was not, and is not, trivial; it still evokes intense emotional response from me. Though formally well-taught by others, I have always associated learning with matters we have to discover, sift and examine for ourselves, both in privacy and in community. A contrary notion is afoot in many programs calling themselves "action learning." There is favor for strict, often subtle, control mechanisms for what I believe Reg intended should be more like the natural play of curious, questioning minds and hearts that together seek and trade new insights and try out new "answers." I do not think it is accidental that workers tell us they value autonomy above all else in the workplace. There may well be a quintessentially human need for spontaneity, straightforwardness and a lack of interruption in the midst of working, learning and knotty problem-solving.

By the time I began action learning in a team (set), decades of "doing" human relations, team-building, teaching and corporate training duties had left me disheartened – haunted by the ease with which young and older adults alike shed responsibility for their own learning. However, when I "action-learned" in comradeship with people I did not know, who arrived in London – at the Action Learning and Mutual Collaboration Congress at Heathrow, England in 1995 – with a variety of national perspectives, I began to see new ways for groups and individuals to reach a deeper learning. This international team work was a successful experiment for me, though I did not yet see how I could enact real action learning in my university classrooms.

After several months of reflection – and a chance remark of Reg's – I was finally ready to take the risk of launching action learning in graduate education. What worried me most was whether I could find work sites with genuinely significant problems that human resource development (HRD) students would be allowed to tackle. But I did. The best reward from reading reflective essays at course-end was a comment from a Master's student finishing her instructional technology degree, a girl who had "wandered into the course." She said that, for the first time in all her college experience, she had at last felt "free to learn."

Many graduate action learning teams later, the project course had become the capstone of the MS HRD program, replacing a comprehensive examination. Each action learning team made high quality final presentations, proposing implementable actions to their impressed client organizations. Transformations were obvious: from wary and uncertain team members, to confident action learning advocates.

Six students accompanied me to the Revans Center in the U.K. to work through action learning on merger issues confronting Manchester hospitals – A seminar on action learning in 1996. To be included by the organizers in this two-week endeavor and to take a later research role in examining results from reflective writings of the students from three countries were unforgettable experiences. Upon return to the U.S., I enlisted a cadre of graduate volunteers, half of whom had never experienced action learning, to code and analyze the identity-removed reflective essays. A predominance of personal growth and transformational statements were found. Clearly, action learning challenged assumptions, changed perspectives and, as determined from later contacts, changed lives. Clients had a new, multi-viewpoint field of options, too.

Action learning in Australia was another pivotal experience, as at the University of Ballarat several academicians sought to discover whether we could collaboratively develop some form of joint degrees that featured action learning. Later, the efficacy of action learning was underscored for me by trading insights with British colleagues, including Reg, at the Revans Center during a long study leave. It was a great privilege to read at will in the Revans archives, including an unpublished manuscript he had laid aside, and to come to grips "after school" every night with the life-changing-ness of action learning, sitting alone with books and thoughts in a room on campus at Salford University.

Adventures in action learning
Karen M. Videtic

New to the world of "action learning" and a "rookie" with regard to the language, concepts and principles of double-loop learning and reflective listening, I anxiously headed off to the First World Congress on Action Learning (1995) with several of my fellow graduate students and our professor Lex Dilworth. Excited to be in London, and intrigued by a new way to create dynamic classrooms with more than books and case studies, I began a path that would change my life forever. What a fateful adventure!

Visiting the House of Lords; discussion groups with people from India, Australia and Canada; an opening address from a Member of Parliament – and yet, the highlight of this trip was interacting with Reg Revans, an irreverent scholar and the father of action learning. Exposed to a wide range of concepts and principles, my head was spinning with the possibilities that could infuse real learning into my classroom at Virginia Commonwealth University. I wanted... no needed more experience with action learning, so, when offered the opportunity to study at the Revans Centre at the University of Salford in the summer of 1996, I enrolled in the course immediately.

From the first day of this summer program, I was immersed in the "real thing": action teams, reflective thinking, double-loop learning and so much more. Our teams were diverse culturally, academically and professionally. Our discussions were lively and we were presented real problems to be solved in real time. Friendships grew, laughter emoted and the adventure continued. Principles and theory became concrete, and I was anxious to test my new knowledge.

During a conversation with Neil McAdam, an academic from University of Ballarat in Australia, he casually asked if I might consider teaching at their "Uni" using the action learning principles. Could this be true? Could this summer adventure in action learning get any better? Evidently, it could!

Through negotiations and a great deal of support from both sides of the world, I headed off to Ballarat to teach several courses in their School of Business, guided by a process that must include diverse teams, real problems, taking action and learning. Assigned a graduate level course on "Buyer Behaviour," I struggled with uncovering a real problem that the graduate students could embrace. The problem had to be both real and relevant if this "action learning" was going to work. I had to find something that all the students might share, and the university itself was the one common denominator. Since this was a marketing class about how consumers made decisions, it seemed appropriate to explore the effectiveness of the University of Ballarat's own promotional campaign.

Charged with evaluating and improving the recruitment efforts of undergraduate students, the nine graduate students enrolled in the Buyer Behaviour class quickly brought their diverse backgrounds to play. This "action team" was comprised of professional firefighters, a chemist, several international students and a few local government administrators. From the first day that they were given the "problem," they were energized and mobilized! It was hard to keep them in their seats and focused. The ideas, the conversations, the opinions had to be harnessed. So, this was what Reg Revans was talking about!

As part of an executive degree program, the students had weeks between course meetings, so they met with me often to discuss how to tackle this problem and just where to begin. They started with a plan that assigned different team members with different responsibilities. First, the action team developed a set of questions with the help of a fellow professor that specialized in market research. They asked undergraduate students why they chose Ballarat, and they tried to determine their customer base. They asked new freshman which of the advertisements for University of Ballarat had appealed to them, and had those adverts influenced their decision to come to Ballarat. The questionnaire also asked why they had chosen this university. The responses were rich, and the action team redesigned an entire promotional campaign based on the data they received – but their job was not over. They then had to present their findings and suggestions to the Chancellor of the University.

The last week of classes was tense for all of us. The action team perfected their PowerPoint presentation, and rechecked their statistics. They practiced and I asked tough questions. They were ready, and those nine students had gained knowledge and experience that they could never have found in a traditional classroom. Their learning came from solving a real problem in real time, and with the possibility of a real outcome.

Faculty and administration including the Chancellor attended their presentation, and were engaged and quite possibly "amazed" at the solutions developed by these graduate students. The Chancellor commented that they would like to receive all of their research and work so the university could implement many of the suggestions that had been made that day.

Did we meet the principles of action learning Reg Revans had spoken so eloquently about just last summer? We had met the criteria of a diverse team of individuals of varying age, ethnicity and professional backgrounds, and we had tackled a real problem in real time. The students had been reflective and action oriented, and, above all, sincere in their efforts to "solve this problem." As the action learning coach, I was committed to not only the outcome but the process, and the learning that I hoped would take place through thought-provoking questions and reflective listening.

And, as this Australian adventure ended, I realized that my students had not only learned volumes about consumer behavior, but they were also immersed in leadership development, team-building and creative problem solving. And for me, I also left with new knowledge: about self-reliance, risk taking, independence, the value of family and friends, and the impact that action learning can have on one's life.

Thanks Reg...for the memories.

A view from Romania

Mariana Garban

It was the spring of 1990 when I first came in contact with Professor Reg Revans and action learning. He was invited to Iasi by some academics from Iasi Polytechnic Institute, as an extension of his visit to the Clinic on Lung Diseases where I was then a student. The audience consisted of 50–60 students and professors.

Reg lectured us about the Hospital Internal Communications (HIC) Study that covered ten London hospitals in the 1960s. Per usual, we clapped our hands politely and presented flowers. This time it was different! There were discussions. I felt like a long-forgotten language was trying to come out of my mind...and I asked to speak. My English was poor but Professor Reg understood and clarified my questions and invited me to the same table with Professor Mihaescu and other professors from the Polytechnic Institute.

This began a friendship that lasted until Revans' death in 2003. We students from the Lung Clinic in Iasi and Professor Traian Mihaescu created some action learning teams. We also discussed Reg's letters to us, as well as our collaboration between students and professors. One year later, Dr. Mihaescu founded the *EEMJ* (*East European Medical Journal*), creating a vehicle for information and communication in the East European medical world. Reg wrote the first article and gave us his encouragement. He referred to this as "platonic action learning."

We had contacts with medical managers from Wales. They shared their experiences with action learning. We also had our first contact with doctors from the *British Medical Journal* and they shared their activity and training, and encouraged us.

My course work finished in 1991, and I returned to the Vaslui County Hospital as a specialist doctor in lung diseases, working mainly in the field of tuberculosis (TB) with poor patients. We had minimal medical resources with which to treat them.

Correspondence with Reg continued, and he connected us with doctors who had participated in the HIC Study, including Margaret Ullyat. She gave me further encouragement, sharing her experience. Her favorite question was "Why do we have to repeat our mistakes?" Our medical system suffered a financial collapse after the December 1989 Revolution. In all letters received by me from abroad, they told me to try and identify the "emergencies"...but at the time everything was a survival emergency (beginning with medical drugs; technical equipment; diagnostic facilities; patient accommodations – like beds, blankets, food).

One bright spot was the fact was that TB drugs were assured by a very good national team that was struggling to eradicate the existence of TB in Romania.

In 1994, I received an invitation from Professor Reg and Lord Butterfield to join the Heathrow team that was organizing the First International Congress on Action Learning and Mutual Collaboration, with Reg in the middle of the action. It was a strong cooperative effort. The Congress was held in 1995. Participants came from around the globe (Australia, Asia, the Americas, Europe and Africa). It was work, communication, action and much learning under the oversight of Revans.

In July 1995, Janet Craig a lifetime partner and friend of Professor Revans invited me to her home in Edinburgh, Scotland. Reg had traveled to Edinburgh to be with us. Every day Janet had an agenda, including meetings (local members of the action learning club were meeting every week at Janet's home). Some important figures from the local National Health Service participated. ... Reg and Janet seemed to know everyone from everywhere. Every morning, papers were read and discussed.

Coming home, my colleagues and I tried to survive and overcome our local challenges.

On being appointed as medical director of a Departmental Hospital in 1998, I had discussions with my patients, empowering them to help solve the problems. They ended up performing many services for which there were no funds. It was action learning at work.

In sum, Reg Revans had a very important impact on my life, allowing me to practice action learning in ways that helped my patients.

Action learning for a lifetime
Lillie G. Sapp

In 1996, I met Dr. Reginald Revans, who is widely recognized as the father of action learning, which means Learning = Programmed Knowledge + Questioning Insight (L = P + Q). I was a part of a cohort of graduate students from several universities, from Virginia to Australia, studying abroad on the subject of Human Resource and Development internationally. We implemented action learning into our project of helping two hospitals with their organizational realignment process. The project turned out wonderfully, and has continued to be utilized in the organization. Both hospitals were able to remain open, and very few people lost their jobs; one hospital as the legacy and the other as the cutting edge in cardiology.

When I first laid eyes on him, Revans reminded me of Dr. Einstein. One day, a group of us students were sitting on the grass as Dr. Revans was slowly walking by, and one of the students presented a question to him. He stopped to answer him, and we all became very engaged in a conversation with him. We had to get him a chair to sit down. It was like sitting at the feet of Gandhi as he spoke to us with such conviction and reverence. Then he stated, "If anyone thinks he is wise become a fool, that he may become wise." He asked us where we would find this quote. No one responded, and I remember raising my hand slowly and saying, "In the Bible." He answered, "Yes in 1 Corinthians 3:18." Giving the right answer to a question from someone so wise was reaffirming. My self-esteem was raised to a height it had never known. I looked to my future with possibilities and great expectations not just for myself, but my children, family and friends. I incorporate action learning theory, (L = P + Q) into everything requiring an answer.

Working at the U.S. Army Management Staff College as a Faculty Curriculum Designer, I utilized the action learning process to build a new foundation with the curriculum design team. Together, we built a new course using Inquiry Base Learning methodology, and the first stage "Advance Course" is being held up as the model of the Civilian Education System for the Army worldwide. Methodologies may come and go, but action learning is continuous and saturates your life to remain forever. "Action learning" as a strategic process generates collaborative learning; transforms workplaces, schools, universities, communities, organizations, and governments. In my experience, the utilization of this process has changed individuals and groups, creating local and global change for the achievement of a more equitable, just, joyful, productive, peaceful and sustainable society.

Learning by doing, doing by learning
Marvin Weisbord

My passion is hands-on learning. I have worked as a photographer, teacher, magazine writer, business executive and consultant, and have aspired to be an amateur pilot, woodworker and jazz pianist. Teaching photography at Penn State in the 1950s, I got students who had never used a camera to create photo essays in the style of *LIFE* and *LOOK* – taking, developing, printing, laying out, captioning and mounting their own pictures. In the 1960s, having read Douglas McGregor's *The Human Side of Enterprise*, I started self-managing work teams in a business forms company. I saw productivity go up 40% and convinced myself that there was no necessary tension between economic success and engaging work.

Steeped in this belief, I started consulting to companies and medical schools in 1969. After a decade in business, I had concluded that all change projects are experimental. Change means doing something you never did before. I had clients before I knew what to do. I went to skill-building workshops and acquired a theory base for what I had been doing intuitively – "experiential learning."

Action research became my practice of choice. My modus operandi was to take a theory that I could ground in my own experience and turn it into a client problem-solving experiment. Eventually, I built collaborative action research projects from the work of McGregor, Rensis Likert, of Michigan's Institute for Social Research; Eliot Jacques, a theoretician of bureaucracy; Dale Zand, who once headed NYU's management school; plus all the people Sandra and I mentioned in our future search chapter. In 1969, I began consulting with Women's Medical College on a systemic planning process that would address, mission, structure, program and budget all at once. We included medical and nursing faculty, students, managers and board members on planning teams. We devised an organization plan based on the research of Paul Lawrence and Jay Lorsch described in their seminal book *Organization and Environment* (1960). Paul and I became friends, and we spent much of the 1970s adapting his theory to academic medical centers.

From this work came my most memorable learning adventure. I had observed early on that physicians and scientists had little taste for organizational development practices based on collaborative group and interpersonal skills. Most were autonomous professionals with narrow expertise and no patience for administration. They also were "hands-on" types, for whom I had a lot of empathy. They liked "hard data."

That Lawrence and I could give them copious survey-based statistics on the nature of their medical centers got us in the door. Going from data to action was another matter. At one school, after extensive feedback, the Dean and department head asked for our recommendations. We proposed that the group discuss how they wanted to manage the medical center, in particular those areas requiring coordination. "Thank you very much!", said the Dean. "We will consider that." Then he adjourned the meeting. At another school whose Dean was more open to learning, we ran a retreat for 100 people. More than half the group were physicians and scientists. After a few hours of going over our data in small groups, a noted neurosurgeon made an ostentatious exit, pausing at the door to announce loudly, "It's a waste of my time to discuss these matters with students and nurses!"

By contrast, in 1978 I was invited by Bill Spiser, a physician running the University of Maryland's new primary care program, to help set up a joint training program for graduate physicians, nurse practitioners, clinical pharmacists and hospital administrators. The plan was to run the program first for faculty members, then make it a regular requirement.

The planners had a diagnosis and prescription – a heavy dose of personal, interpersonal, group and organizational dynamics. I was to mix up and deliver the medicine. Part of the expectation was that, with my years of working in medical centers, I would know how to overcome inevitable resistance. I was, by then, savvy enough to resist being labeled a resistance expert. If we intended to teach collaboration, then we needed to start by collaborating.

I proposed to the planners that the five-day faculty workshop be run in an action research mode. We would make no assumptions about the content. Instead, we would offer the faculty sample theories, lectures, instruments and experiential exercises at each level – personal, interpersonal, group, system. The faculty – experts in their own specialties – were to try out and help us evaluate the relevance of each unit for the graduate training program.

Our private hypothesis was that they would go for the conceptual large systems stuff and dismiss much of the rest. The first clue about how wrong we were came on the third day. I had described what we had learned about task conflict in medical centers and how it might be handled – denying, avoiding, smoothing, bargaining, confronting. Group members talked over the concepts, then one said, "Why are we studying this stuff in the abstract? We have a lot of conflict right here. We ought to be working on that!"

By the seminar's end, the faculty had declared nearly all the content relevant, with the headier systems material low on the list. Several offered to write case studies based on actual incidents in their hospital as the basis for role-playing and problem-solving. We ran the program for several years, collaborating with faculty from each medical profession. It was a big hit and had considerable impact on the way professionals handled conflict, ran meetings, and cooperated in caring for patients.

My experiences with action learning

Fran Szabo

I was no stranger to action learning principles, as I had first been exposed to the theories in the late 1980s through the American Society of Training and Development (ASTD) conferences and publications. But when I was approached as the Chief Learning Officer at a Fortune 500 company about using this approach to grant degrees to employees, I was a bit skeptical. My previous degrees had been rather traditional, one from the University of California at Davis and one from the University of San Francisco. I did not see how the unstructured environment and award of credit for past experiences could possibly result in a degree. So, I decided to enroll to earn my degree through this theory of action learning to better understand how it was possible.

I became quite a believer in the principle, more so than I had been in the past. I had an incredible experience. Being able to apply my learning immediately was a passion for me. I worked with five other individuals who shared a similar challenge. We all were working in companies that promoted and hired managers into positions responsible for millions of dollars with little or no training. Even though the members on my learning team were not earning a degree, we worked together extremely well, fostering a great plan to train these managers for our individual companies as well as learning and supporting each other.

I am not sure I realized the value of learning from my peers. I now know that learning from and with each other was a key factor. After studying adult learning theory for years, I think it is not necessarily true. I believe that as adults, we learn the same way that we did as children. I never learned the principles of sharing and respect for others through a classroom. That learning was gained from experience. Bouncing ideas and behaviors off others is how children and adults learn best.

I often share an example with action learning students about my experience in my undergraduate calculus class. I sat in an auditorium with 150 other students staring down from the seats at the professor, who read from his book. While he was brilliant, it took me two times to complete that course with a passing grade of "D". People tell me that I use those principles in my everyday life, but I still do not understand how I have applied them. My experience with action learning allowed me to apply my learning immediately to my work and life. The reflection process in action learning has changed how I approach life. I realize that I learn and share learning with others every day. I now spend time reflecting on my learning every day.

For people who travel a great deal and are not able to conform to a consistent classroom schedule, this is a great solution. However, the effort takes a great deal of discipline. I found that there were people enrolled in the program for more than five years without completing the degree. I found myself taking a little over 24 months for my Doctorate degree, which should have been completed in 12–18 months. A good coach/advisor is necessary. My coach gently nudged me to keep going. I know others in the action learning program were not as fortunate and, hence, have not completed.

When I was initially approached to adapt this degree program, it had already begun as a "grassroots effort" with little record-keeping or tracking. As I came up to speed about how to sponsor a corporate university degree program, I found the need to stop it for a time in which the company could enact a little structure, policies and record-keeping. During this time, I studied educational systems around the world to understand that the United States views degree programs a little differently. It continues to be a challenge to educate "traditionalists" that this method of schooling is more beneficial than the standard forms found in the United States. I have found that I can better convince executives in other countries about the value of action learning.

After advising the graduation of over 50 students in action learning, I find myself still working to convince executives about the value of this program. I believe that, if these executives could become more involved in the program, even reading a career review or attending an external review, they would become more supportive. Career and external reviews continue to be the most rewarding part of advising an action learning degree program.

Our experiences in action learning
Judy O'Neil, Victoria J. Marsick, and Karen E. Watkins

Judy's first exposure to action learning was at Teachers College, Columbia University, through her work with Victoria, who assumed various roles as teacher, mentor and eventual business partner, and who helped Judy launch her first program at AT&T. While Judy was at Teachers College, she had one of her most significant experiences and, she believes, contributions in the world of action learning through dissertation research on the role of learning coaches. There had been little previous research on this important role, and her study of the work and wisdom of 23 practicing learning coaches in the United States, England and Sweden provided findings on external and internal influences on their work, the kinds of interventions they employed to create situations to help participants learn, and the theoretical "schools" of action learning. Since 1996, Judy has implemented, managed, facilitated, researched and/or consulted on action learning programs for over 25 organizations, governments and universities; and written substantially about her research and practice in this area, as more fully described in the authors' descriptions.

Victoria discovered action learning through a colleague, Lars Cederholm, who was connected with MiL Institute, Sweden, and who invited Victoria and others to practice action learning as a new consulting group, Leadership in International Management (LIM). Victoria recounts these formative experiences in Chapter 17. Victoria's research into MiL Institute's initiatives – combined with her own research and practice of informal learning from experience for individuals, groups and organizations – has shaped her view of action learning. Victoria is especially interested in deep learning and fundamental change, and in helping people learn through action and reflection in many different cultures and contexts. Recent work on a yearlong action learning program (with Judy O'Neil and colleagues in Bermuda) has reawakened her interest in global voices and the understanding of learning and change – which she thinks are well pursued through action learning.

Karen discovered action learning through Victoria and through her work with action research, action science and organizational development. In the mid-1980s, she asked Dr. Chris Argyris to come to the University of Texas

(UT) at Austin to work with faculty to learn action science so that they could teach it to their students as part of his legacy. Karen's own research and that of a number of doctoral students became grounded in action science concepts. She read most of what Argyris had written; worked action science cases with students and practitioners; and explored ways to both teach these ideas and to extend the framework into her work with Victoria Marsick, exploring informal and incidental learning in the workplace and later on creating organizations that can learn. Karen had a long-term interest in Kurt Lewin's work as foundational to the field of human resource and organization development. With Annie Brooks, she edited a book on action technologies, comparing action research, action learning, action science and participatory action research. When Karen moved to the University of Georgia she added a study abroad experience and a virtual approach to using action science. It was not until Karen's work with Partners for Learning and Leadership, a Consultancy, that she began to incorporate action learning in both consulting and instruction. She eventually again added an online approach to her use of action learning, culminating in a minicourse in action learning taught with faculty in five universities – three in the U.S., one in Australia, and one in England. This work became the focus for research on virtual group dynamics and virtual group facilitation.

My action learning experiences
Sandra Janoff

I lived the "Action Learning" principles years before I learned to put the words in caps. My formative professional experience was in the mid-1970s amidst the social turbulence that started in the 1960s. Doors were opening for experimentation in the U.S. educational sector. I was hired as one of 12 educators who were charged with creating an alternative high school for 200 students. These students, many rebelling against authoritarian structures, refused to go to their traditional schools.

Because this program was funded by the Philadelphia School District and its surrounding suburban districts, this was the only voluntary urban-suburb public high school that existed in this country. We adults were very young, green, hopeful, creative and, for twelve years, had the resources and autonomy to build our "learning community." We taught high school content in an environment with flexible structures, democratic decision-making, reflective learning and openness for inquiry, risk taking and course correcting.

The experiment informed us all – students, parents, staff, teachers, contributing schools, community people and so on. As I noted, we knew nothing about open systems, action learning or Kurt Lewin. Learning from doing and doing as we learned just made sense to us. The experiment lasted ten years, until traditional district leadership closed it down in 1984.

The next phase begins in 1985, when I went to graduate school at Temple University in Philadelphia, PA. I wanted a program with flexibility and scope so that my Ph.D. would enable me to work in both organizational and clinical worlds. It comes as no surprise that the program I chose was originally called the Center for Group Dynamics and had been founded by David Jenkins, a colleague of Kurt Lewin's. There, I formally learned the theory and practice of action learning and open systems thinking, and its application in organizational and therapy groups. I was also involved in the Society for Field Theory annual meetings and I was privileged to meet first generation Lewinians, from Europe, Russia and the United States.

Phase III is my years of collaborating with Marvin Weisbord in the world of future search and the Future Search Network, our learning laboratory for making the world a better place, one meeting at a time.

Revans' legacy

Isabel Rimanoczy

I never met Revans in person, but I met him through his writings, the stories people tell about him and through the impact he has made beyond his lifetime. I think the most significant aspect of his legacy is that he pushed the idea of trusting people's knowledge, of trusting the power of stopping and reflecting, exchanging thoughts with each other in a respectful way, in order to find new ideas and solutions. He turned the stage lights away from experts and lecturers, and turned them onto the regular people, suggesting that we pay attention to the huge depository of knowledge that was available there. This is something that I find relevant and revolutionary, up to this very day.

Experience of action learners

I want to share a story in two scenes.

Scene 1

Scene 1 takes place in Europe, as a leadership development program for a global team of executives, back in 2001. I was a learning coach for one of the teams, and also had been randomly assigned a few individuals to provide individual coaching support. One of them, who I will call Klaus, was not very happy with the idea of having a coaching conversation. He explained to me that he did not think it could be of any value, that he was a very concrete and pragmatic person who just liked to solve problems without much talking about them, because ultimately experts knew how to tackle challenges of their own domain. He attended the whole program, and at the closing circle he said something like "I am beginning to see that reflection has a value."

Scene 2

A few weeks ago I received an email from Andrew.

> Many years ago I received a training given by LIM. It was a training to learn how to cooperate with different cultures, practised via a company project. We worked on this project for 6/7 months, ending in a presentation. I was and I still am very positive about the training. It has changed my way of thinking profoundly. I found it interesting to look at people in this different way.
>
> Some time ago I noticed that there was a gap of understanding in the organization, between management and floor workers. I heard their complaints and asked "what are you going to do about this?" So I started with six people who wanted to do something. We called the project "How to get influence on your environment" with the aim to bring the two levels together. I gave them the opportunity to surface their well buried ideas and wishes. It was clear that they knew exactly what the department was missing. We decided to go on with two major items for two groups. We described the projects and supported ideas with figures. In doing this we found out that it is not so easy to realise your ideas. We learned a lot, but the biggest advantage was that we could realise our hidden ideas. When the project progressed other people got interested and even the management showed interest. We are now starting to finalise one project and the other one is successfully implemented. The whole exercise took 8 months.
>
> What are the results of this initiative: There is talent and ideas at the extremes (working floor) of an organization. By developing this you can create better understanding and motivation. Recognition is not a problem anymore. The project is highly effective.

Andrew continued the email describing the challenge he was now facing, sharing his reflections and asking for coaching.

What this story in two scenes tells me is that, through the program in which he participated, Klaus was able to change his mental models; incorporate reflection into his life; become a change agent in his environment; inspire and lead others into different ways of communicating; and promote dialogue, creativity and learning exchange. He is showing with his daily behaviors that; when people are given an opportunity to speak up and exchange thoughts, magical things happen. He has learned it for himself, and now cannot stop spreading the word.

14
From the Frying Pan to the Fire – And Back Again: An Action Learning Story from General Electric

Stephen R. Mercer

Part I: The frying pan

The flight from New York to Paris turned out to be a busy one. It was late June 1988, and I was one of a group of 40 executives from General Electric (GE) who were heading to INSEAD, the French business school in Fontainebleau, for the kick-off of a new version of GE's four-week action learning based Business Management Course. This was the first ever "Global BMC" held outside the United States, and the objective was one of sensitizing GE's executives to the opportunities and challenges of competing in the growing global marketplace. Paolo Fresco, GE's Senior Vice President (International) had finally convinced the CEO that the world was larger than the continental United States and, although GE was known to have a global presence almost since its inception, we should be looking to expand our non-U.S. business dramatically. Since Fresco was one of the few non-U.S. executives at the top of the company, he perceived the need to develop what he called "global brains" in the U.S. born and educated executive ranks. That he was correct in this need was illustrated by the fact that a significant number of the participants in this Global BMC did not have passports until they were notified of their selection for the program. The reason that I was aware of this was that I was on the staff of GE's Leadership Development Institute (known as Crotonville), and my colleague, Jim Noel, was running this program.

The flight was busy because the faculty at INSEAD had assigned a significant amount of readings and case studies to be prepared in advance, and, like most of the other participants, I had been "too busy" to do much of the reading, figuring that I could do it on the flight over. What a joke! By the time the cabin crew had finished serving drinks, dinner and after dinner refreshments, there were only a few hours left to try to grab some sleep before our early morning landing in Paris, drive to Fontainebleau, hotel check-in and opening session at INSEAD. Thankfully, the reading helped put me to sleep, but I did not get through much of it.

The program was divided into two major segments. The first two weeks would be held at INSEAD, and their faculty had put together an intensive series of sessions designed to jolt us into an awareness of the geopolitical and business situation in Europe. The second two weeks would be spent working on three live business projects sponsored by GE business leaders, and targeted on developing business opportunities in Europe. At the conclusion of the program, the project teams would present their findings to the sponsoring business leader and his/her management team.

The BMC business project approach was a unique one. The participants in each class were divided into six teams. There were three projects undertaken by each class. Two teams were assigned to each project, a Red Team and a Blue Team. In preparation for the project work, three consultants from GE's internal Marketing Consulting Operation had worked for three months (one with each of the sponsoring businesses) to pull together the information and logistics needed to facilitate the project team's intensive work during their two weeks activity:

- A "problem statement" outlining the project issue and a set of deliverables that the business was looking for
- A comprehensive briefing book containing all pertinent correspondence and other documentation related to the project issue
- A designated project contact from the business, who would undertake a complete project briefing and be available by phone or fax during the two weeks of project work (remember – no cell phones or Internet access in 1988)
- A schedule of 50–60 interviews/meetings/dialogues with outside stakeholders (customers, suppliers, potential partners, industry experts, academics) with knowledge and opinions on the business issue, to be conducted during the third week of the program.

But why two teams on each project? – partly a logistic issue, and partly an issue of getting multiple perspectives. The logistic issue was that to run the program cost effectively, and to maintain an annual throughput of 120 or so BMC graduates, we needed a class size of 36–42 participants. The ideal team size, based on our experience, was six or seven; any larger than that became unwieldy with respect to team dynamics and interaction. That meant six teams per program. Conducting six projects was an administrative nightmare, as well as a significant burden in generating six appropriate issues for each of three programs each year. The solution was to use three projects and put two teams on each project. The teams would be briefed together on the issue. They would then break out into their two separate groups to plan their project approach, develop initial hypotheses, and develop their questions for the outside stakeholder meetings. The outside meetings would be conducted in pairs – one person from each of the two assigned teams. They would therefore need to pool their questions and decide how to best manage the meetings. At the conclusion of the interview week, they would pool their notes, but then would return to their respective teams to analyze the data, develop conclusions, develop alternatives for solution, and make a final determination of recommendations. The process was therefore:

- Briefing together
- Plan separately
- Gather data together
- Analyze separately.

The result of this approach invariably was that each of the two teams took a different route to their conclusions and recommendations, even if the recommendations were similar. This helped eliminate the phenomenon of group-think. When the teams presented to the sponsoring business, even if the recommendations were similar, the routes to getting there were usually different, and created an opportunity for in-depth discussion. If the recommendations were different, there was the opportunity for a debate of the opposing views, and the development of stronger commitment to the solution ultimately selected.

The two weeks at INSEAD were a blur. It seemed that we were nonstop from the time the plane landed until we were sent off to do our project work. The initial challenge of finding the *location de voitures*, recalling how to drive a stick shift, and navigating from the airport to *L' Aigle Noir* hotel in Fontainebleu was not as daunting as it could have been. Even making it to the opening session that afternoon at INSEAD was fine, despite only three hours' fitful sleep on the plane. The INSEAD instructors were good. Once we tuned our ears to the accented English (from a very multicultural faculty, from a variety of countries) and got over our embarrassment at our ignorance of things European, the discussions were quite lively and challenging. Many of us had been through case method instruction at U.S. schools, so the teaching methods were not that different from our prior experiences at business schools. We quickly got into the routine of the long morning espresso break, where the classroom discussions continued informally, and the surprise of finding wine and beer in the cafeteria for lunch. The breaks also offered an opportunity to interact with MBA students and other business people, primarily from European companies, attending INSEAD executive programs. It was good to get out of a GE-centric environment, and interact with faculty and students who could represent the viewpoints of some outstanding multinational companies and European small businesses. By the end of the two weeks, we had developed a healthy respect for the challenges and issues faced by companies forced to go global to grow – companies that could not rely on large home markets like the U.S. to sustain them forever. Now it was time to venture forth for our project work.

The first step in working on the project was reviewing the problem statement. The project I was assigned to was being sponsored by the President of GE Information Services Company (GEISCO). We were to take a look at GEISCO activities in Europe, and recommend a strategy for growing the business. This was to include looking at their current segmentation focus, and suggesting whether it was the best approach for future growth. I was on a team with six other GE executives – a diverse mix of people from across the various GE businesses. One business, however, was conspicuous by its absence from our team. There was no one from GEISCO on our team. This was in keeping with the "iron rule" for GE's action learning projects – that no one from the business being studied was permitted on the team. The reason for this was that our past experience had demonstrated that, when people from the project business were on the team, they tended to dominate the discussion and constrain the possible solution set. We wanted a broad look at the problem, and we wanted people to be able to ask the "dumb questions" that often revealed the road to a creative solution. The absence of a GEISCO person did not, however, result in a dearth of discussion dominators. It became apparent from our first meeting that our team had a number of strong and opinionated personalities, and it was going to be quite a challenge to drive toward consensus with this group.

After individually reviewing the problem statement, we got together as a team to share our initial impressions, and to prepare a set of questions for our meeting with the project briefer from the business. At the meeting, we received the comprehensive briefing book, and were given a presentation elaborating on the contents of the book. A lively discussion ensued, during which I am sure we did not endear ourselves to the briefer, who it turned out was also the project contact on whom we would be relying for the next ten days as we went out into the field for our outside meetings. Not very smart on our part. The last part of the briefing consisted of a review of the outside meetings we would have. It was a tight schedule. We would each be dealing with around four meetings each day for four days, which would total over 100 meetings between the seven of us. Normally, the meetings would take place over a five-day period; however, as was typical in 1988, the "global" schedulers had forgotten something. The scheduling of the BMC was usually carefully done to avoid key U.S. holidays and three-day weekends like Memorial Day, Independence Day, Labor Day and Thanksgiving Day. An exception was made for this first Global BMC. Since the Europeans obviously did not celebrate American Independence Day, this program started before July 4, and the participants gave up this holiday for the honor of being in the first global session. What was overlooked was that July 14 was Bastille Day, and everything in France would be shut down right in the middle of our project work. At least we would get to see the parade.

Our team spent the weekend preparing our questions for our "interviews" with the outside resources, and deciding how we would divide up the interviews, which had been carefully prescheduled by the BMC planning team. There were a few open slots in the agenda for us to schedule other meetings if we felt someone could shed light on the issue. It would be up to us to fill these in. We also set up a communications system, antiquated by today's standards, but critical back then. We would be traveling all over Europe for our meetings, and it was crucial that we be able to share across the team the key things we had learned, and be able to have our team mates explore new avenues opened to us as a result of our meetings. One person was designated as "the Scribe" for each day. Each of us would call in to the Scribe at the completion of our day's activities with a summary of key findings, and suggested new questions or ideas. The Scribe would summarize everything, and then fax the summary to each of us so we would have it for our next day's meetings. Cumbersome, but it worked.

The week of meetings was exhausting. The schedules were tight, and we were rushing from one meeting to the next with little time to reflect on what we had heard. Our note-taking skills grew exponentially as the week progressed. The Bastille Day break was welcome, as it gave those of us in France a chance to catch our breath and do some summarization of what we were all hearing. The meetings were fascinating. There was some concern initially that we would be imposing on the people that had agreed to meet with us. Nothing was further from the truth. They welcomed us with open arms, impressed with the investment that GE was making in the program, and happy to see that the company was serious about listening to their opinions. Suffice it to say, we got an earful from everyone we spoke with. And for those of us lucky enough to have had some dinner meetings scheduled, we were introduced to some very fine wines.

If we thought that the week of meetings was tough, we could not have anticipated how tough the several days of analysis and report writing would be. Recall what I said earlier about strong and opinionated personalities. The discussion was brutal. We were debating a radical departure from the current GEISCO focus. The majority of effort was being placed in the Financial Services sector. Our data was indicating that the competition in that segment was fierce, with European GEISCO competitors fighting it out with us vigorously. In our opinion, the ability to grow profitably was going to be severely constrained. We had discovered what we thought was a promising new area – Trade and Transportation. Information technology could be a huge opportunity for such industries as trucking, rail and various retail trade companies. This was a radical departure from the current strategy, and would be a risky recommendation to make. Some on the team wanted to go for it, while others wanted to play it safe with a more toned-down recommendation. We battled into the wee hours, and finally the "Go For Its" prevailed. We carefully crafted our presentation. Now the question was: Who will be the presenter?

It was here that politics came into play. Almost everyone on the team was from a business operation. Although most of my career at GE had been in business operations, I was now "corporate," assigned to Crotonville. The team decided that if the recommendations were too controversial, and any-one needed to be sacrificed, it should be "the corporate guy." I was elected the presenter by a vote of six to one – you know who cast the "one" ballot. A cardinal rule of the Presentation Skills Course is never to give someone else's pitch, so it fell to me to burn the midnight oil revising the style of the slides to better fit my style, without losing the integrity and intent of the presentation.

The next day was the Day of Reckoning. We would be presenting our find-ings and recommendations to the President of GEISCO, and to Paolo Fresco, the Senior Vice President for International for GE. I would be making the presentation, and my team would (I hoped) be backing me up when the going got tough. My biggest fear was that, when a difficult question came up, my teammates would all be ducking down to tie their shoelaces, leaving me to sway in the wind. We were attempting to anticipate difficult ques-tions, and had assigned each person on the team an area of expertise, so I would not have to worry about doing the presentation, managing the time and answering all the questions. It was a smart move. Once the President saw which way we were going, the questions came thick and fast, and he got very defensive. It was not looking good for me.

For a while, I felt like a tennis player blocking rocket balls from a super-ior opponent. In fairness, my teammates did their best to back me up, but the pounding was incessant. Finally, Fresco spoke up. He looked at the GEISCO President and said: "I don't think you are listening to what this team is saying." It was like a weight lifted from my back. The tone changed. The discussion became interactive and incisive. We were able to discuss our rationale for the change in strategy, and gradually, grudgingly, got some acknowledgement that perhaps we were on to something. By the time we were finished, we got what I considered to be a great compliment. Apparently, the President had recently retained one of the big consulting firms to do a study of the business, taking many months, and at a price tag of over US$1,000,000. He now told us that our report and recommenda-tions, done over a two-week period, was every bit as good, if not better, than that study.

I do not remember much about the graduation dinner, but I am sure that the wine flowed freely, and a group of tired, but smarter, GE executives were quite pleased with the outcome of their four-week odyssey. We were return-ing home with a much richer understanding of business outside the U.S., and were ready to be missionaries for the future of the Global BMC.

Part II: The fire

If I thought the flight to Paris was busy six months ago, there was no comparison to this flight to Moscow in January 1989. My reward for being a participant in the first Global BMC was that I was now assigned to a team of three, responsible for planning and delivering the second Global BMC. This program was an extremely ambitious one. We would be sending teams to three emerging economic powers – Russia, India and China. I would eventually lead the China contingent, but for now the team of Jim, Jarobin and I would travel together to each of the target countries to do the initial scoping of the feasibility of the program. Jarobin was an NBC executive, fluent in Russian, and with quite a few contacts there. We spent much of the flight picking his brain, and strategizing how to work with the GE team in Moscow to convince them that "we were from Corporate, and we were REALLY here to help them." After we were finished in Moscow, it was on to Delhi, and then to Beijing for our initial meetings with the GE Country Teams located in each city.

We had our hands full in each location. At that particular time, the GE Country Teams might as well have been on Mars. We had significant business in each country, but the Country Teams were like remote fiefdoms – pretty much calling their own shots – and rarely visited by top ranking executives outside of the International Sector other than for the obligatory periodic flyby to show the flag, get a quick briefing, and for the spouses to do some sightseeing. The exception might be a visit for the signing of a huge order, say for power turbines or aircraft engines. What we were proposing for the BMC was that 12 GE execs would be coming to each country for three weeks, during which they would travel around to key locations and meet with local customers, partners, academics, politicians and business leaders. The teams would perform an overall country analysis, and would evaluate specific business opportunities in each country: power systems in Russia, medical systems in India, and major appliances in China. Does that sound threatening to the Country Team?

It took all our collective persuasive skills in each country to bring the Country Team on board. Not only was there a nagging suspicion on their part that some neophyte executives would come in and either misinterpret the situation or upset a customer, but, on top of that, the in-country people would have to work with us to set up the outside meetings, and they would not be allowed to accompany the BMC teams to the meetings. We would be getting our own translators and excluding the Country Team from the meetings in an effort to get the local people to open up to us if there were any problems. It took Fresco's intervention to make sure that we got full cooperation, as well as our assurance that we would share all our findings with the Country Team first, before reporting out to Fresco and the business sponsors.

On completion of this first visit, it was decided that Jarobin, of course, would handle Russia, Jim would take India, and I would handle China. I had met Tom, the Asia Pacific Vice President on a previous visit to the region, and had hit it off well with Chuck, the China Country Manager, so this seemed like the best plan. There followed a flurry of phone calls, faxes, and several visits to China and Hong Kong, during which we selected a local consulting firm to help us with the initial orientation of the China team, and also with the setting up of the "outside in perspective" meetings.

Working with the consultant and the Country Manager, we developed an approach for maximizing the exposure of the teams to the evolving situation in China. At the time, there were three major economic areas:

- Beijing, the Capital city, where the key governmental agencies controlling the economy were located
- Shanghai, the traditional financial center, and the base of western powers entry into China
- Guangzhou, in Guangdong Province, adjacent to Hong Kong, and the location of Special Economic Zones created to spur business development.

Our plan was to convene in Hong Kong for several days of overview briefings on the history, culture, the political situation and the economic situation in the People's Republic. We would then split into two groups. One group would travel to Guangzhou and spend a week studying the Special Economic Zones and the developing business situation there. The second group would travel to Shanghai and spend the week studying the situation in that part of the country. Both teams would then fly to Beijing for a final series of meetings with government officials and business leaders there.

There was one other minor issue that we had to deal with. In the spring of 1989, there was significant unrest in the student population protesting against the government, and there were the beginnings of student demonstrations in Beijing. We had already committed to the program, and were in the process of setting up the outside meetings with Chinese ministry officials, businesses and academics. Cancelling the program would create a "face" issue, if the student protests were to fade away. On the other hand, if the protests were to become serious, we would have to cancel, and we would be left with 12 executives with nothing to do for the project portion of the program. We came up with a contingency plan. Working with the GE Country Teams in Japan and Korea, we set up a series of contingency meetings with China experts and companies doing business in China. If we were to cancel the China visit, we would send one team to Japan and one team to Korea to do the project from the outside looking in.

The program started off well enough. In late May 1989, we met in Hong Kong for the initial orientation briefings, and then split into the two groups. One group flew off to Shanghai, and I stayed with the second group, which crossed over to the Kowloon side and took the train to the border with the People's Republic of China (PRC). We were on our own – the consultant had kissed us goodbye at the Kowloon train station – and we would be traveling without an interpreter until we arrived in Guangzhou. Now our adventure was about to begin.

The PRC border at the Shenzen Special Economic Zone (SEZ) was fenced – not to keep people in, but to keep people out. The SEZ was beginning to prosper, with many job opportunities opening up, and the government was trying to control "immigration" from other areas of the PRC. We already had train tickets to Gangzhou, procured for us by the consultant. We were cleared through the border checkpoint, and waiting for the train to depart, when one of the participants discovered that he had lost his train ticket. Panic ensued. Finally, I decided to give my ticket to the participant, and buy another one for myself at the train station. If you have ever seen a queue in China, you know what I was in for. The ticket line was pandemonium. By the time I got to the ticket window, I learned that the train was sold out, and I would only be able to get a ticket for the next train.

When I returned to the group of participants and informed them that they would be traveling on their own to Guangzhou, and I would join them later, traveling on the next train, the second panic ensued. These executives, fearless in running their businesses, were paralyzed by the thought of traveling on their own in a strange land with funny looking pictures for a language. They implored me to find a way to get on the train with them. We agreed that I would try to fake it on to the train with my ticket for the next train. When boarding time came and I tried to board with the bogus ticket, of course, the train conductor tried to stop me. I say "tried," because that was when the third panic occurred. The participants, desperately afraid that they would be left on their own to fend for themselves on the train journey, formed a flying wedge and carried me past the conductor and on to the train. They then formed a human wall between me and the train conductor to prevent him from throwing me off the train. I thought that we were about to cause an international incident, but fortunately the one or two young People's Army soldiers called by the conductor decided that it was not worth their effort to deal with 13 obviously deranged Americans. They let me stay on the train, and we departed for our destination.

The train journey was comical. We had, of course, as traveling GE executives, been booked in the reserved seat section. I, of course, traveling on a bogus ticket, did not have a seat. I unceremoniously parked myself on my luggage in the middle of the aisle. It was at this time that the innate kindness of the Chinese people towards strangers in their midst came to the fore. Initially, they laughed and joked at the six-foot-four-inch foreigner sitting awkwardly astride a suitcase in the narrow aisle. Then, out of thin air, there miraculously materialized a small folding stool, which was offered to me to sit on in the narrow aisle. We had a grand old time for the rest of the train journey.

The initial part of the program in Guangzhou went well. The GE local staff, including Chuck, the Managing Director of GE China, met us at the hotel, and we had an orientation on the political and economic situation in the area. We also got a cultural overview, which, on the first evening, included a trip to a local restaurant where the creatures on the menu were featured live in cages and tanks in the front window. The initial series of interview and discussion meetings with the local business and political people started on the next day, and would proceed for several days. My plan was to break away from the Guangzhou group after a few days, fly to Shanghai to be with that group for the last few days of their visit, and then accompany them to Beijing.

On the morning of June 3, I got up at the crack of dawn to go to the airport to fly to Shanghai. Even at that hour the terminal was jammed, and it seemed as if I was the only foreigner there. I fought the crowd to get to the check-in counter, picked up my boarding pass, and proceeded to the gate area. The gate area was a large waiting area with the various gates and final check-in locations around the periphery. As I approached the gate marked on my boarding pass, I noticed that my flight was not posted on the display panel over the Jetway. This was not unusual, since we all know that multiple flights depart from the same gate. What was unusual was that the display panel was blank. As I looked around the waiting area, I noticed that ALL the display panels were blank. Furthermore, the large display panel on the main wall, listing all flights, departure times and gates, was also blank. This was strange, but I assumed it was some kind of temporary electrical problem, and stood by for more information.

The time for my flight departure was approaching, and still all the displays were blank. I pushed through to the check-in counter and asked about the flight. "Flight delayed, flight delayed," I was told. As the planned departure time passed, the answer was still "flight delayed." The waiting room was getting more and more crowded. The display screens were all still blank. I was starting to get a bit concerned. No flights seemed to be leaving, and the situation started getting very confused. The local Chinese, who were able to communicate with the gate attendants, started scurrying from one gate to another. I had no idea what was going on, since my Chinese language skills were virtually nonexistent, and the gate attendant's English was minimal. I could not find out any information about my flight.

A few hours passed with no flights leaving and the waiting area filling to the point where it was almost impassable. Finally, it appeared that flights were being called, but still all the screens were blank, and all I could find out about my flight was "Flight delayed." I was not getting any hard information. As I looked forlornly at my boarding pass, I realized that all the boarding passes were marked with a different colored stripe. Mine was brown. I looked around my immediate area and located a Chinese gentleman clutching a brown-striped boarding pass. I approached him, and pointing at his boarding pass, showed him mine. Although neither of us spoke the other's language, we were able to use our body language to convey our frustration at the situation. As we compared passes, I verified that his was for the same flight as mine, and resolved to "tail" him to assure I would not miss my flight. I did this for some time until finally, with the screens still blank, I saw him react to an announcement in Chinese and scurry off to a gate on the opposite side of the waiting area. I was hot on his heels and, some time later, found myself on board my flight waiting for takeoff. When the flight finally took off I looked at my watch and calculated that we would not reach Shanghai until 11:00 pm or later. I had been scheduled to arrive by noon to meet with the BMC Shanghai team. With no access to a phone in the waiting area of the terminal – and, of course, no personal mobile phone in 1989 – I had been unable to communicate with them. I would find them at breakfast tomorrow.

When the flight landed and I walked out of the terminal, I got my next shock. The area was deserted. No taxis, no buses. The people on the flight had almost all dispersed to waiting cars, and it appeared that I was stranded. I wandered out into the parking area, and under the dim light of a lamp post noticed a group of people getting into the back of a truck. Was this a public conveyance? I rushed over calling "Taxi, taxi." After a few moments of pointing and hand gesturing, as well as the production of a sufficient quantity of currency and me saying "Hilton Hotel" several times, I was waved into the back of the truck and we were on our way. I had no idea where I was going to end up. Once we got off the main road from the airport and started through the city, we seemed to be taking a very circuitous route. A few times, as I looked out the back of the truck, I saw piles of burning tires in the roadway. I had no idea what was going on. Finally, we turned a corner and were heading up the driveway to the Hilton. I can only guess at what the bellman was thinking as the rickety truck pulled up at the entrance, and a blue-suited Westerner hopped out of the back with his luggage.

The telephone in my room jarred me awake. Strange – I had not requested a wake-up call. It was Chuck, the Managing Director of GE China, who had stayed with the team in Guangzhou:

"Steve, is the team all right? What is going on there?"

"I guess so, Chuck. I didn't get here until after midnight. I haven't seen them yet. Why do you ask?"

"Haven't you seen the news?"

"No. I just told you I didn't get here until midnight. I just checked in and crashed."

"Turn on the TV news. There are huge student demonstrations in Tian An Men Square. The government is moving troops in to quell the demonstrators. Your Beijing leg of the program is off. We are pulling the Guangzhou team out and returning to Hong Kong. You have to get the Shanghai team out of the country NOW. Get them back to Hong Kong!"

I was stunned. No sooner did I hang up the phone than it rang again. It was Tom, the Asia Pacific Vice President:

"Steve, are you crazy? You actually went to Shanghai yesterday? I want you and the team out of there IMMEDIATELY!"

I hung up the phone and sat there for a minute processing data. There were six participants plus myself here in Shanghai, as well as two local Chinese members of the GE China staff, Edward and Bessie. (The Chinese staff in those days almost all took on Western "first names.") My job would be to get myself and the participants out. The local Chinese staff would have to be left behind. I called the switchboard and started contacting everyone, asking that we meet in the breakfast area. I walked to the window, opened the curtains, and looked across to the street below. A pile of tires was burning in the middle of the street.

A somber group met in the breakfast area later that morning. Everyone had been doing their best to keep informed regarding what was happening. Edward and Bessie looked shaken. They had been fortunate enough to get a good job with an elite Western company, and now they saw everything slipping away. GE was pulling all expatriots out of China. The locals had no idea whether the pull out was temporary or permanent, and no idea what would happen to them. We quickly formulated an "escape plan." Edward checked with the airport. Some planes were still flying – especially those leaving the country. We had a vehicle at our disposal – a minibus that was being used to transport participants to their interviews. We would all pack and meet as soon as possible, take the minibus to the airport and see if we could get a flight out to Hong Kong.

The ride to the airport was hair-raising. We had to take a very circuitous route around various street blockages and the ubiquitous burning tire piles. We rode on the sidewalk more than once. Finally, we arrived at a nearly deserted airport, and rushed to the ticket counter to inquire about flights to Hong Kong. An Airbus was minutes from departure. There was no way we could make the plane on time. I started negotiating with the ticket agent. I learned that the plane was nearly empty. I needed seven business class tickets. He made a quick phone call, and turned back to me.

"How will you pay for the tickets? We will not accept credit card right now."
"How about cash?", I responded.

He dialed the phone again.

"Hold the plane."

Fortunately, I had learned that traveling in places like China and Russia at that time it was a good idea to fortify myself with a respectable quantity of cash money for unanticipated situations. I opened up my shirt, reached into my money belt, and counted out good old U.S. dollars for seven tickets.

It was a somber farewell we said to Bessie and Edward. We had no idea what would happen to them, and it pained me to have to abandon them like that. We rushed to the gate where they were actually holding the plane for us, the doors closed, and we taxied to the runway for liftoff for Hong Kong. On arrival there, we would implement our carefully crafted contingency plan to send the teams to Japan and Korea to complete their project. The whole atmosphere for the project had now completely changed.

Epilogue: The frying pan again

I could start this epilogue with another flight. In December 1989, we took the China team back to China to "finish the job" after our hasty departure during the Tian An Men Square incident. Their report, after we had returned, cautioned GE against hasty action, predicting that things would settle down despite everyone's repulsion at what had transpired on that day in June. They turned out to be correct in their assessment. We would have to deal with the paradox of a rapidly developing economy tied to a dominating government. In the months following June 4 and the GE pull-out, the expatriots slowly returned to resume their positions in China. By December, things had settled down enough that we felt we could bring the BMC China team back to complete the interviews/discussions that we had earlier planned for the program. They did this successfully, and presented a supplementary report to the business sponsor.

My action learning story following this has been a rich one:

- At the end of 1989 I assumed full responsibility for BMC action learning. At the same time, the Executive Development Program, GE's highest level program, targeted at newly appointed and potential Vice Presidents, was converted to a business driven action learning program managed by my new boss, Dick Kennedy.
- In 1990 we did two domestic and one Global BMC. The Global BMC was done in former East Bloc countries of Czechoslovakia, East Germany, and Yugoslavia. It was at this time that I met Dr. Yury Boshyk, then on the faculty at IMD in Lausanne, and began a collaboration that would last for 15 years. Yury and I were able to pull off this Eastern Europe BMC only because no one ever told the bumblebee that it was not designed to fly.

The piece of the Berlin Wall that we chipped out during one of our planning visits still hangs on my wall at home.

- In 1991 all BMC were converted to Global, and we did two programs.
- In 1992 both BMC and EDC were fully converted to Global programs, and we did a full complement of three BMC and one EDC.
- In 1993 I assumed full responsibility for all action learning programs, including both EDC and BMC. We took EDC back to China, where a chance meeting at the bar in the Peace Hotel in Shanghai between the visiting CEO and two EDC participants resulted in the CEO asking that the EDC teams report their findings to the next Corporate Executive Council meeting. The CEC was comprised of the top 30people in the company – the CEO, Vice Chairmen, Business Unit Presidents, and top Corporate Staff.
- In 1994 all BMC and the EDC were converted to action learning. The CEO took ownership, and I worked with him to select and define the projects. All programs were scheduled around, and reported out to, the CEC. After a couple of these reports, we had to modify the Red Team/Blue Team approach. The CEO's attention span was too short to sit through six project presentations, and invariably the last couple of teams up were cut short. We resorted to having the two teams do a combined presentation for a few programs, then ultimately resigned ourselves to only having three teams of 12 participants, and letting them deal with the unwieldiness and interpersonal issues.
- The BMC and EDC programs became key strategic tools for the company, addressing key issues facing the businesses and the Corporation. Among the major results of BMC/EDC business driven action learning programs were:

  - the creation of GE Capital India
  - the Growth BMC, which recommended that each major business redefine its served market so that its current market share was only 10%, and grow it from there
  - the Quality BMC, which resulted in the Six Sigma program at GE

- Within a few years, we had completed programs in over 50 countries on five continents. We had been in Russia shortly after the burning of the Russian White House. We had been in Mexico during a currency crisis and devaluation of the peso. We had been in Turkey during an earthquake. It was joked that when I called a Country Manager to inform him/her that a BMC or EDC was coming to their country, they first protested vehemently, fearing some doomsday event, and, when they were overruled, they immediately took out catastrophe insurance.

In 1998, I departed GE to join the Boeing Company and help build and launch the Boeing Leadership Center in St Louis, Missouri. After a couple of years, we were able to introduce global action learning to Boeing, with the Global Leadership Program, in which I was again privileged to work with Yury Boshyk. We then finally achieved a dream that Yury and I had discussed for many years with the launch of the International Consortium Program. This was a global action learning program undertaken by Boeing in partnership with three other global companies: ASEA Brown Boveri (Switzerland), BHP Billiton (Australia), and ABN AMRO Bank (the Netherlands), and targeted for top executives at Vice President level in each company. Each program was jointly planned by representatives from the four companies. Each program had an overarching theme to which all companies had agreed, and each company team brought an action learning project selected by the CEO under the umbrella of the theme. The ICP gave us the opportunity to open a good number of executives' eyes to the world of global business by sharing best practices across world-class companies, and by having their project work critiqued by first-class business people from these companies.

It was a long journey from the airplane to Paris in 1988 to the satisfaction of seeing the International Consortium Program finally come to fruition in 2001. Many lessons were learned along the way:

- Top level buy-in and committed business sponsors with real projects are critical to success.
- The best projects are "customer facing," giving the participants an opportunity for dialog with outside stakeholders. New business development or customer service based projects are particularly good.
- Although many will disagree, I believe that short duration, full-time commitment projects work much better than long duration "do the project while you are doing your job" projects.
- Teams of people that exclude members from the business sponsoring the project are superior to teams that include people from the business. "Newbie" teams are more creative, do not get bogged down in minutia, and are more likely to ask the "dumb" questions that people from the business are reluctant to ask.
- Do not give teams a template for their final report, or show them reports from previous sessions. They are then much more likely to come up with a creative way of displaying their findings and recommendations that fits better with the project.
  It was a journey well worth taking.

15
My Experience with Business Driven Action Learning

Alasdair Philip

Business driven action learning proved to be a turning point in my personal and professional development. I was introduced to it during an employer-sponsored development course called the International Business Leadership Program (IBLP). With 30 colleagues from six different business units and 14 countries descending on South Florida for nearly two weeks, this required a significant financial investment from my employer. I anticipated 11 days of challenging work, professional growth and team building, but underestimated the impact of the IBLP, as I did not understand the power of business driven action learning.

As the title implies, learning is central to business driven action learning. It encourages learning as a continuous, intentional, focused and, perhaps most importantly, personal journey. Accordingly, our course prework included a Learning Style Questionnaire (LSQ) from www.peterhoney.com. The LSQ gave me insight into my personal learning style and how I balance the four styles of activist, pragmatist, theorist and reflector. During our initial introductions, participants shared learning styles. Doing so accelerated the integration of how the styles impact our own ability to learn, how we help and hinder the learning of others, and how we work with others. We also completed the Caliper® Profile and received comments from colleagues through the 360° Feedback process. These tools were included to further our self-knowledge and were integral to our overall learning, but the LSQ provided the foundation for my experience of the IBLP, and proved a springboard for my development since. However, it was the context provided by business driven action learning that gave the LSQ fertile ground in which to take root.

Our team was confronted with a business challenge and, as is the norm with business driven action learning, it was a real and complex business problem facing our organization. In this case, on the first day our CFO challenged us to recommend how to organize 'shared services' across our enterprise. As an organization with over 500,000 employees across six continents, generating US$70 billion in revenues and following the integration of over 200 mergers, creating the best possible model for delivery of common services such as risk management, legal, purchasing, IT and other business critical functions is vital. Effective shared services can deliver cost savings, improved service execution, and help provide the glue that binds an organization together across functional silos. However, our organization wanted to improve shared services in terms of cost, performance and collaboration. The intricacies of our particular business challenge reflected some of the challenges that faced our team: managing internal stakeholders and their different priorities across multiple business units and cultures. Given the scale of our enterprise, complexity is part of our business by default, and this was also reflected in our group. Creating our proposal while working in a compressed and intense environment required us to confront challenging subjects including people, our own assumptions, competing business priorities and cultural differences. Therefore, in order to manage the people and the challenge, it was critical to follow a process.

The process unfolded in logical steps, bringing order to an intense challenge. The schedule seemed to follow a pattern where we first understood our internal environment, then fanned out to explore our external environment and how it related to our business before returning us to our internal environment again, but this time with a significantly different perspective. After we met our colleagues and the course leaders, the business challenge was introduced by our CFO. We were then taken through a series of sessions about the foundations of learning, our organization, "outside-in" perspectives (on our company and the business challenge), our external environment, value creation and leadership. Eleven days later we finished with our business challenge presentation to the CFO, completing the circle.

Foundations of learning

We spent time understanding the LSQ, how it shapes our ability to learn, how we lead, and the concept of after action learning reviews (AALRs). This post-action review process asks you to reflect on what the objective was, what actually happened, what was learned and, crucially, who needs to know what we learned. AALRs were built into the daily schedule, reinforcing the learning experience and allowing for periods of reflection, something our group agreed they did not normally make enough time for. The process of 'learning to learn' and how our learning style can help and hinder the learning of others was particularly important. This allowed us to learn more about ourselves, how we work in teams, and significantly increased our effectiveness.

Our organization

The schedule took us through a variety of interactive presentations by senior global executives. Aimed at broadening our understanding of our various business units, corporate services and strategic priorities, these sessions enabled our learning by connecting the information to the business challenge. Doing so enabled the team to quickly overcome the 'silo' mentality that was prevalent at the outset of the course. This silo mentality appeared largely as a reaction to the relative complexity of our business. We have undergone significant organizational change, and many of us had retreated to the perceived certainty provided by strongly identifying with our business unit of origin. Without broadening our perspective, we could not complete the business challenge in a meaningful manner. Likewise, without the business challenge, the learning opportunity would have been significantly reduced. This symbiosis was a thread running through the program; each part of the schedule reinforced another, reflecting the interconnectedness of our business environment.

"Outside-in" perspectives

Balancing the expanded knowledge of our internal world, "outside-in" perspectives on our company and how others approached our business challenge were woven into the course. These perspectives were gained from executives from companies such as HP, APAX Partners (a private equity leader), and J&J, as well as 20 customer dialogue sessions tied specifically to the business challenge. Some team members were not in customer facing roles, so developing a discipline to seek an "outside-in" perspective was difficult at first. However, it became a touchstone that further broke down the internal silo mentality by bringing people together and supporting team development, a core objective of business driven action learning.

Our external environment

"An eye on the 'outside'" is essential for global leaders. Each day we learned about trends impacting our external environment – such as regulatory issues, the environment, demographics, globalization, the knowledge era, and other geopolitical developments leaders have to face. This further emphasized the importance of integrating what is happening beyond our organization and locale to our business challenge.

Value creation

Understanding value and identifying its levers underpinned two highlights of the course: the business simulation and a value creation presentation. The latter was delivered by Zehavit Cohen, Managing Director of APAX Partners, the world's fourth largest private equity firm. Most of us would not have chosen to spend five hours on the intricacies of financial performance and the markets on a Saturday morning when the sun was out and Miami's beaches beckoning, but no one would have wanted to miss this engaging and dynamic speaker. She clearly connected the principles of value-based decision-making to our current business environment and the business challenge.

The business simulation challenged five teams to run a company over two days. The objective was to deliver the most value over three years and success was predicated on our ability to apply what we had learned in a team environment Reflecting the real world, the impact of our decisions about factors such as resource allocation and pricing, was shaped by the decisions of our competitors. One of the most important lessons for me was in understanding how the learning styles of each person on the team impacted everyone else. My team had a combustible mix of six "type A" personalities with two core learning styles; activist and theorist. These styles can conflict as one is prone to action, and the other to gathering information. This led to some other teams later admitting they thought our styles would fail to work together, particularly given the time constraints.

Three years were compressed into three two-and-a-quarter hour sessions, with feedback and results from the previous year in between. Our team quickly matched learning styles to our organizational structure, agreed a decision-making process, and a strategy focused on value creation and the external environment. Key to our doing so was to integrate each person's learning style into our decision-making process. For example, the activists allowed more time for information exchange, explaining the underlying thought processes behind their 'gut' feelings, while the theorists learned to reduce their reliance on facts and accept they had to make decisions with less information that they were comfortable with. This allowed the activists to make better informed decisions, the theorists to come to faster conclusions, and the team to focus on the value drivers of the simulation. By valuing and being flexible to everyone's styles, we brought the team to the fore, generating more financial returns than any other IBLP business simulation team had to date.

Leadership

Naturally leadership is integral to a course entitled the International Business Leadership Program. However, rather than just emphasizing behavioral characteristics of leadership, our inquiry was also about what areas good leaders are focusing on. Areas such as how to support a learning organization and the cultural change required for a value mindset were then connected to the business challenge. While the sessions dedicated to leadership were highly valuable, the leadership shown by our colleagues, both good and bad, throughout the 11 days proved equally instructional. The action driven agenda allowed us to explore our leadership styles in different situations but the AALRs and peer-to-peer sessions created a reflective environment allowing us to learn at a deeper level than any other leadership course

I have attended. This balance, repeated each day, helped me build the discipline to carry the lessons forward beyond the course.

The impact on one's personal development cannot be overestimated, assuming the person is ready to do the work. The IBLP taught me a considerable amount about my strengths and weaknesses of which I was not aware, and how to work with both. Being in a peer group environment for an extended period of time, I was better able to understand my impact on others, both positive and negative. This has allowed me to take energy from areas of 'strength' and refocus it on areas that need strengthening. By doing so, I hope to contribute more to my organization, and to my direct team, by increasing my effectiveness.

The magic of business driven action learning comes from integrating team and individual learning with a relevant business challenge in an atmosphere that supports reflection. The approach accelerated my learning significantly and has impacted my approach to work since, most notably in my ability to support the development of a learning organization. Be it expanding my engagement with mentoring programs, collaborating on cross-business unit initiatives or the introduction of the LSQ to numerous colleagues, my personal rate of learning and that of my team, continues to grow.

In summary, by aligning the needs of the business with the development of its emerging leadership, business driven action learning can appreciably impact the leadership pipeline at any organization. In a world where effective succession planning and talent development continue to grow in importance, business driven action learning should be considered integral to developing a culture built to prosper in an increasingly complex world.

16
Making Space for Reflection in Action Learning

Geert R. Egger

Reflection: Careful thought, or an idea or opinion based on this.
Thinking quietly about something.

Longman Dictionary of Contemporary English

Debate is still going on as to what exactly qualifies as an action learning program. Practitioners from different cultures, with a different organizational focus, and with different types of experiences hold different opinions and have different reservations on the topic. So, common ground regarding what minimum requirements or basic principles qualify as an action learning program remains to be defined – if that is indeed possible.

I am fully aware that many people who work with action learning may be reluctant to create or adhere to too rigid a definition of the concept. The risk of boxing in action learning instead of letting it grow is obvious, and the concern is understandable. On the other hand some clarification of, or arrival at a common understanding of, the "core" of action learning – irrespective of whatever practical forms it may take – should be welcomed. If this is not done, the strong and beautiful substance of action learning may become so diluted that the very uniqueness of the concept of action learning floats away.

The author of this chapter, however, candidly anticipates that if ever such a set of minimum requirements is defined, it will at least contain the element of reflection as a key parameter. A program without reflection space and reflection on learning is hardly ever to be considered an action learning program in the general opinion of neither theorists nor practitioners. Ensuring *space for reflection* needs to be taken into account when designing and conducting proper action learning programs.

Luckily, this can still be observed in practice – within business driven action learning as well as within other forms of action learning. In most cases, the professional organizers and action learning practitioners *do* pay great attention to building in platforms and opportunities for reflection in their various programs.

So, what is the problem?

The short answer is that the possibilities for making space – or even defending space – for reflection have come under severe pressure in the last decades if compared with the ideal notions originally emphasized in action learning by, for instance, Reginald Revans. At least two megatrends, in my mind, have contributed in building-up that pressure – one of them an "outside-in" trend, the other an "inside-out" trend with regard to the practices of action learning.

The "outside-in" trend

The "outside-in" trend is *a general societal trend*: the overall transition from modern to postmodern lifestyle and, thereby, a whole new "rhythm" of society. When Revans conceptualized his pioneering work back in the middle of the twentieth century, nobody yet had had any everyday experience with computers, the Internet, cell phones, music videos, jet-planes and so on.

Some may argue here that societal megatrends are better described at more abstract levels, focusing on major forces of change. I am inclined to agree with the thinking of the French philosopher Michel Foucault, who pointed to the complex architecture of artefacts as being the unique molder of mindset and markers of change. So, allow me to stick to artefacts as physical evidence of the transition from modernism to what has, for lack of imagination, been characterized as postmodernism.

So, in short, since the days of early action learning work, the speed or rhythm of societal processes has increased tremendously. Fewer and fewer continue to appreciate spending up to three cinema-hours in watching the slow storyline being built up in the Julie Andrews musical "Sound of Music" from the 1960s. More and more prefer to have the three-minute music video playing itself on their personal iPod Nano – exactly when and where they want.

This may be considered a banal example, but it contains the broader societal mindset shift which another French philosopher, Jean Baudrillard, described as the desire to cut out the long building-up of things and the desire to eliminate what is standing in the way, for the only thing that really matters is the "peak." Postmodernism is a hectic drive for peaks, and you tend to want more and more of them, more and more quickly.

Because of this trend, if your task is to make space for reflection in action learning in the first decades of the new millennium, then you are presented with a severe challenge. You will be under pressure from people and settings, which are no longer that inclined to just stop, take time, stay silent, turn inwards, build up – merely for the sake of obtaining perhaps even troublesome insights.

The "inside-out" trend

The "inside-out" trend which simultaneously has put reflection in action learning under pressure is a more internally triggered development within the action learning community itself. It is a common experience since the 1980s that more and more action learning initiatives and practitioners have managed to establish good collaboration with the private business segment, conducting business driven action learning for clients.

For very good reasons, large business corporations have adapted some of the main principles in action learning – the very notion of learning in action is appealing to a sector with a high emphasis on productivity and output. And, in recent years, the need for innovative business approaches has further focused attention on what action learning can offer, such as the concept of business driven action learning, inspired by Yury Boshyk's work. This has become a well-known and highly appreciated approach.

Private business, as an environment for action learning processes, poses some specific challenges to the work. Private business is not just about good productivity, tangible output and innovative processes. It is also about making organizations more lean by pruning them, continuous cost control, profitability requests, improving the company value to shareholders and the tremendous importance of the next quarterly result. At the same time, action learning participants in private companies are often the ones with extra talent and potential (i.e., those with the highest ambitions, the strictest goal orientation and the toughest competitiveness).

All of this adds up to an action learning environment in some companies, where the ideal balance of solving a task while at the same time learning from and reflecting on the process is challenged in the acid test of daily business life. The short-term company horizons, the intense performance orientation and the aggressive career ambitions sometimes create environments where action learning initiatives will have to deal up-front with the challenge of actively preserving the reflection elements, despite the company's subconscious inclination to sacrifice this if under pressure. "This is not very business-like," I was once told by a business client, when arguing for the importance of keeping time and space for reflections in an ongoing action learning process. His perception is, of course, wrong but, nevertheless, expresses an immediate – dare I say un-reflected – thought process shared by some business peers.

On top of this, I have in the last six to seven years experienced what you may call a "classical" action learning flow with a duration of four to six months on-the-job that can be hard to implement in the more and more rapidly moving businesses of today. The organizational stability is not always there over longer periods, the top management impatience is obvious (almost embedded in the positions), and the business priorities sometimes change overnight. Also, the challenge of working virtually in globally distributed action learning teams has not yet found its proper solutions – at least, not in my experience.

Hence, over the years, some of us have continuously experimented with radically pruning and boiling down the action learning ingredients while

Table 16.1 The lab week[Typesetter: Set this table as in original.]

	Monday "Taking off"	Tuesday "Collecting"	Wednesday "Exploring"	Thursday "Condensing"	Friday "Evaluating"
Morning	Introduction to Business Problems/Management	*Morning roll call and Learning Log I	*Morning roll call and Learning Log II	*Morning roll call and Learning Log III	Presentations Q&A and Evaluation by Management
	Working in Action Learning Flows	*Teams at work*	*Teams at work*	*Teams at work*	
	*Experience transfer (other sets → now)				
	Lunch	Lunch	Lunch	Lunch	Lunch
	*Team composition: strengths and weaknesses	*Teams at work*	*Teams at work*	*Teams at work*	*Group experiences and Learning Log IV
			*Team optimization (including feedback)		and
	*Team rules defined				*Feedback preparation
Afternoon					*Individual feedback
					Review and closing
	Dinner	Dinner	18.30→	Grab-and-go available	*To follow:*
Evening	*Teams at work*	*Teams at work*		*Teams at work*	*(Individual follow-up talks and feed back)*
	*Team optimization	*Team optimization			Action Lab Inc.©

Note: An asterisk indicates built-in spaces for reflection.

still trying to preserve the main benefits from this unique way of learning. The current result is what I prefer to call an "action lab intensive," in this case a process with focus on only five days – or 100 hours – of fully committed action learning with selected in-company participants.

Obviously, when committing yourself to only five days of intense action learning – within the business segment and in the postmodern era – then you are really putting the challenge to its edge: Can you at all make proper space for reflection under such conditions? Nevertheless, I will take the challenge of the question while using the five-days action lab intensive ("the lab week") in private business companies as my reference point (see Table 16.1).

When going through the following review of possible tools and practices in ensuring reflection, I owe a great deal to Robert L. Dilworth, who some years ago pointed me to possible paths to follow via his article on nine important avenues. My current status is only a current status. It is evolving. Many other practitioners may have better suggestions and other experiences. If so, please contribute to the debate.

For the sake of a good overview, allow me to deal with each tool/experience under the headings of (a) the pre-lab week phase; (b) the lab week phase; and (c) the post-lab week phase.

Making space for reflection

The pre-lab week phase

1   Participants in action learning programs are often screened and selected by management based on an assessment of their current performance and their future potential. But what are the parameters used for assessing future potential? Mostly, they are about potential for crawling up the ladder (e.g., defined in a set of management competencies, such as a results orientation, personal drive, and a business mindset). *Additional screening parameters* that might be added relate to areas that can be the subject of debate, like emotional intelligence, transformational leadership style, or personal leadership qualities. People rated high on things as "self-awareness" (the ability to recognize and understand their moods, emotions, and drives, as well as their effect on others), "self-regulation" (the ability to control or redirect disruptive impulses and moods), and "empathy" (the ability to understand the emotional makeup of other people) tend to be more open and appreciative of the reflective elements in action learning programs.

2   Ensure that individual preparation talks are carried out with each selected participant in due time before the lab week. Often a 360-degrees assessment and/or a special personality analysis has been carried out, and this forms the basis for the *participant's discussion with a Program Official* or

a qualified person from Human Resources on the person's strengths and weaknesses, as well as possible ongoing development areas. The reflections can then be tied into learning opportunities during the upcoming lab week, hence constituting a kind of mental preparation for the intense activities in the pipeline and a consciousness around what the participant may want to bring to the table.

3   A solid anchoring of the action learning program with the line of business is key. This is especially important with respect to the top management sponsoring the program, and will give up a valuable resource for a full week. It is also important with respect to the participant's own direct manager who will be coaching the participants continued ongoing learning. A clarifying discussion between participant and immediate manager prior to the lab week often takes place, and is normally about *aligning mutual expectations* to the participant's learning opportunities ahead.

The lab week phase

4   Before the lab week starts on Monday morning, all participants have been encouraged to familiarize themselves with the thinking behind action learning in relevant *pre-reads* (e.g., through reading Dilworth (1998) – a fine article called "Action Learning in a Nutshell"). This gives most readers a pretty good idea of the basic thinking, but most participants still do not know what is going to happen before they have been introduced to the business challenges they are supposed to work with and the framework of the week.

5   The *business problems* that the teams will address during the lab week have to be well prepared. In dialogue with top management, it is important that the problems are of strategic importance and of obvious value to the business, if solved. In order to stimulate reflection on the topic, it is also important that the challenges have no obvious "digital" solution (yes/no) but, instead, call for some out-of-box and out-of-comfort-zone thinking. In a large biotech company, for instance, the challenge was phrased: "Suggest two conceptual scenarios for a second-generation bio-fuels business model and how to implement in XX Inc." In a global IT company the challenge went: "Identify strategic drivers on how XX Inc. can reach +YY USD billions in revenue in five years." As anybody will acknowledge, the action learning teams have no chance of coming up with a fully substantiated solution within only five days. Best case scenario, one can hope for a good mix of "fresh thinking" and "business relevance" that may lead to further investigation and testing after the lab week.

6   Before the action learning teams are formed on Monday – and before things start getting out of "control" – I recommend the use of an *experience*

transfer session. What works well in my opinion is to invite one or two former participants from other companies who have tried a lab week like this, and who are willing to share their own reflections on what went well, what did not, and why. Interestingly enough, former participants are very eager to do this and very often share reflections of a high quality – not least on the process and learning aspects of the assignments.

7   In preparation for the forming of action learning teams on Monday morning, it is beneficial to provide the participants with a *simple profiling tool* stipulating their own normal way of acting/working in teams. There are many profiling tools are available, such as MBTI or the LSQ, but, in a condensed flow like the lab week, I normally ask participants to profile themselves as a combination of some of Belbin's nine team roles: the specialist, the plant, the monitor-evaluator, the coordinator, the team-worker, the resource investigator, the completer, the implementer and, finally, the shaper. Of course, we all hold some preferred combination of those roles, but the tool makes them reflect on their traditional team behavior/roles and comes in handy throughout the week as a point of reference for the team as it develops and as a handy adjustment tool when hidden resources have to be put in play.

8   As a final preparation on the reflection part before the action learning teams are finally formed and begin work, I have experienced the value of introducing a one-page template, where participants are reflecting by themselves what they would consider to be *success and failure* during the lab week with regard to the business challenge given, the team established and their own learning. Having accomplished these preparations, it is finally time to form the teams and get started.

9   However, the action learning facilitators will normally stress the importance of what is called *the good beginning*. The good beginning is simply about taking your time to align the teams properly, instead of just rushing into the task-solving right away. Normally, teams actually do spend a couple of hours in sharing their self-assessed team profiles, in mapping a joint team profile and concluding how to optimize the strengths of the team and possibly mitigate the weaknesses. Also, thorough discussions of success and failure, as well as alignment of the joint ambition level take place. Last, but not least, most teams take their time to formulate their game rules for the week ahead. Of course, you will find a few team members here and there who cannot really see the value of such a lengthy clarification discussion at the beginning. They are eager to get started "for real". However, experience shows beyond (my) doubt that taking time for a quality "good beginning" significantly reduces the likelihood and severity of later "panic crashes" during the lab week. In addition to this, it is worth mentioning that several participants after a lab week have explicitly stated that NOT taking proper

time for "a good beginning" on Monday was one of the root causes for not delivering to expectations on Friday.

10   What will happen from Monday afternoon towards Friday is basically unpredictable and very team specific. As action learning facilitators, you do have an excellent opportunity to study and observe the process at close range, since you are normally residing at the same site as the participants – day and night. On the other hand, as a facilitator you are not supposed to interact directly with the teams unless called upon. Yet, you still have the challenge of making room for reflection along the way. My experience has been that the regular conduct of so called *team optimizations* during the week can serve that purpose without disturbing the team process unnecessarily. Every evening from 10 pm to 10.30 pm a facilitator will sit in with the team and facilitate a discussion on what has worked well today, what maybe has not, their individual concerns right now, and what can be improved/changed with respect to tomorrow's team work. When comparing this with trimming your sailing boat for tomorrows "rough waters," it is generally accepted by participants as a constructive, yet unfamiliar, session. After only one or two sessions, you often see teams applying the method in their own team optimizations at critical points.

11   The only other mandatory session during the lab week is what I call the morning "roll call." Here, the teams in play are kindly asked to brief the other teams in a structured form on their status and current work – thereby calling for some reflection and possible mutual help and inspiration. The session is, furthermore, used for individual reflections in the participants' own *learning log*. Writing to yourself what you have actually learned during the previous 24 hours related to the topic, the stakeholders, the team, and yourself is valuable in keeping focus on the reflection part, as well as for capturing learning on the fly. The learning log reflections will be summed up and used for the individual follow-up talks after the lab week.

12   On Wednesday's team optimization, it is now time to introduce the individual feedback element to the team, if not already opened up. So, on Wednesday it is no longer just about "trimming the boat" but also about "trimming the crew." An informal, yet structured, *feedback round* is conducted, where everybody gives and receives feedback on what is especially appreciated in the individual's contribution, and what could the individual do more/less/different with regards to the remaining two tough days ahead.

13   Right from the beginning, the teams are fully aware that their output will be evaluated against on Friday's presentations to top management. One of the four key criteria is the quality of the team process conducted, and it is a stated requirement that the team's presentation must contain a few minutes of *reflections on the team process* and the learnings in the team as an

integrated part of the final presentation made to top management. I have heard from other practitioners that top management is really not always that interested in listening to such "process-stuff." In my experience, this is no longer the case in most places. Especially when you are dealing with talent pools of various kinds, top management is genuinely interested in the participants' ability to meta-reflect on their own "journey."

14 Ideally, the actual *business solutions* presented by the teams to top management on Friday should contain reflection elements. What has been our line of thinking? Why have we defined the scope as we have? Why have we chosen this solution instead of that. Often, top management itself is constructively provoked by what is presented and starts new routes of reflection themselves. The key message to the bio-fuels challenge (touched upon in paragraph 5) was basically that the company's current strategy was wrong and that a totally different implementation path should be taken. That path is, today, fully integrated in the business operation. The challenge on the very ambitious revenue goals of the IT-company (described in paragraph 5) was answered by the identification of and business case around a fully new customer segment/product placement. Top management acknowledged – with slight admiration – that they themselves had been outperformed by their own talents. The business case is now part of the company's strategy. Of course, not all solutions are as well received as the two cited but, from a larger learning and reflection perspective, you cannot win them all. You have to take chances in dealing with your business challenges and sometimes end on thin ice. As a top manager once elegantly fed back to a lab week team with a less than brilliant business solution: "You cannot think if you are sure that you are right" – thereby acknowledging the other very valuable aspects of action learning.

15 At the final feedback session on Friday evening – after the presentation to top management – the participants are given enough time to prepare their individual feedback in writing to each of the other team mates. Here, the participant also will receive feedback from team mates on the exact same nine Belbin roles as the participant conducted a self-rating on during the Monday morning. The comparison of own initial self-assessment and colleagues' "real-life" assessment often calls for useful reflections on perceived image versus behavioral action. The verbalization of the final feedback is still about what has been experienced by others during the week but, as a part the forward-looking portion of the feedback, participants are encouraged to provide ideas and proposals for the receivers *continued job development* – hence providing a bridge out of the lab week.

The post-lab week phase

16 In the weeks between the closing of the lab week and the date for their individual follow-up talk, the participants receive a template where they

are kind asked to *sum up their different types of learning* and input during the process. Basically, what is done is to extract and conclude upon their learning logs and the applicability of their learnings to everyday work-life. Also, the input from the team-profiling and the individual feedback received is reflected upon, before the template is returned to the facilitators prior to the face-to-face talk. In the templates, you often witness very fine reflections on self and others, as well as mature post-program week conclusions which could not have been made during the hectic week itself.

17   The *individual follow-up talks* normally take one to two hours. The participant, together with the facilitator(s), discusses and focuses on the various learning aspects of the process. The facilitators then provide individual feedback to the participants: what was observed during the week, what seemed to be reasons for this and that, what might be some potential focus areas for the future and so on. The feedback is made in writing as well, and has to be agreed to by both parties as fair and to the point. Finally, the discussion will focus on what can be done with respect to job development by the participant in the period ahead, and concrete actions are filled into the individual development plan (e.g., job-swaps, business briefs, peer-coaching, mentorships, own "feedback-boards" and so on).

18   After the individual follow-up talk, the participant is encouraged to have a renewed discussion with their direct manager, where they can jointly go through the learnings obtained, the feedback received, and the development plan outlined. Hopefully, and in most cases, the individual development plan then comes to constitute a mutually agreed guiding tool for the participant's ongoing development, and will be reviewed and adjusted in connection with the annual target setting with the manager.

19   Finally, in making space for reflection I have had good experiences with setting up so called reunions, where all teams will meet for a joint one-day session a year after the lab week. Here, a great deal of reflection will take place on what has happened since their last meeting with regard to job and competence development, why or why not, and what was captured at the time that is still in the mind and so on. Also, a revisit by top management is an option, addressing the status/fate of the various team suggestions presented the previous year.

Conclusion: A final reflection

Making space for reflection in action learning can be a tough job these days. But for the individuals participating, as well as for the output produced and the top management involved in action learning programs, the proper reflection space cannot be thrown away without also losing the true "differentiating differentiator" in the postmodern learning environment.

Reflection provides a unique opportunity to build more nuances and emotional intelligence around someone's own personality. Reflection is a work approach most likely to produce smarter output with higher innovation. Last, but not least, reflection as a key competence in a company's leadership pipeline is the best guarantee for top management that the company will be able to create true engagement amongst a progressively more self-reliant and individualized workforce in the postmodern era.

This chapter has argued that reflection should be a key characteristic of any program claiming to be action learning. There may be other such key characteristics to be discussed, and perhaps even be able to build consensus around. The author would welcome any contribution to this ongoing debate.

References

Baudrillard, J. (1999) *The Defence of the Real* (New York: Sage)

Belbin, R. M. (2004) *Management Teams: Why They Succeed or Fail*, 2nd edition (Oxford: Butterworth-Heinemann).

Bolt, J. F. (ed.) (2005) *The Future of Executive Development* (Executive Development Associates Inc).

Boshyk, Y. (ed.) (2000) *Business Driven Action Learning* (Basingstoke: Palgrave Macmillan).

Dilworth, R. L. (1998) "Action Learning in a Nutshell", *Performance Improvement Quarterly*, 11(1).

Dilworth, R. L. and Willis, V. J. (2003) *Action Learning: Images and Pathways* (Malabar, FL: Krieger).

ITAP International (n.d.) *Creating Opportunities for Reflection in Action Learning.* Available at www.itapintl.com

Foucault, M. (1979) *The Order of Things: An Archaeology of Human Sciences* (New York: Routledge).

Goffe, R. and Jones, G. (2006) *Why Should Anyone Be Led by You?* (Boston, MA: Harvard Business School Press).

Goleman, D. (1998) *Working with Emotional Intelligence* (New York: Bantam Books).

17
Action Reflection Learning: Tales of Two Journeys

Isabel Rimanoczy and Victoria J. Marsick

In this chapter, the authors recount stories of how they came to value the interactive role of reflection and action so much that they – and colleagues at sister organizations the MiL Institute in Sweden (MiL) and Leadership in International Management (LIM) in the United States – coined the term "action reflection learning" (ARL) for the work that they do. In action reflection learning, the role of the set advisor, as laid out by Revans, is modified in that this person (often called a "learning coach") actively supports explicit reflection in order to help people learn more explicitly from their experiences. Cunningham (2003, p. 6), in a tribute to Revans, recalled "one conversation with Reg" about the legitimacy of intervening in this way "to assist and not to dictate." Reg countered, "You are like the dog chasing a motorbike and believing you are making it go." Reg's comments prompted Cunningham to pursue "a Ph.D. to explore Reg's challenge" in which his "research conclusions were an explicit rebuttal of Reg's stance." Be that as it may, many followers of Revans conclude that Reg's views are substantiated by their experience. We have experienced highly self-directing groups in which learning coaches play little, if any, role in valuable reflective learning from experience and innovative, and fresh questioning. But we have also experienced the contrary; that is, groups – perhaps influenced by mis-educative early life experiences – that found it difficult to learn or to reflect in and on action (to use concepts introduced by Schön (1983)) despite the willingness of the team (set) advisor to step aside and play a nondirective role in order to encourage people in the group to take charge of their own learning.

Revans argued that reflection is a natural human act – one that does not need, or benefit from, the help of a facilitator. However, Raelin and Marsick (2006) argue that it may not be easy to incorporate reflection in many U.S. workplace action learning programs for a variety of reasons (e.g., the rapidly changing environment, time constraints, and organizational cultures that value obedience over questioning and action over thinking). Conger and Benjamin (1999), who researched action learning in leadership development programs, concluded that an essential ingredient for successful leadership development is multiple opportunities for reflective learning. They noted that "better-designed programs powerfully blend reflective learning experiences with the pressures and deadlines of a significant undertaking" (*ibid.*, p. 223). Better-designed programs build many opportunities for reflection into programs, rather than saving it for a one-off presentation at the end of the program. And finally, in better-designed programs, "reflective learning opportunities are not only targeted at what was learned through the projects themselves but also on the personal approaches and styles of the individual team members" (*ibid.*, p. 224). Unfortunately, they also concluded that such reflection does not always happen.

The stories of the authors of this chapter will show that the learning coach can provide just-in-time support and tools to help people in action learning programs better reflect and learn from their experience. Sometimes, this happens as "P" learning using a "teaching" hat, and sometimes it happens just by modeling learning or asking questions or setting a task for the group that supports their own self-directed understanding of the experience. In those cases, we believe, the role of the learning coach might effectively go beyond that advocated by Revans.

Thus, the authors of this chapter have many times seen leaders embrace the value of action reflection learning because they personally experienced its power, especially in nonroutine situations when they faced ill-structured problems that called for fresh ways of seeing, thinking and acting. In this chapter, Victoria and Isabel tell their own stories of having encountered action reflection learning and how that changed their practice.

Victoria Marsick's story

My journey into action reflection learning began in the mid-1980s. I hired a Swedish organization development (OD) consultant, Lars Cederholm, to help me with a stress management intervention I was guiding when I worked at UNICEF. Not long after that, I left UNICEF and joined the faculty at Columbia University, Teachers College. Lars and I remained friends. Lars introduced me to action learning when he, Lennart Rohlin – who was founder and president of MiL Institute (MiL) – and other OD consultants presented on their work at the Organization Development Network conference in New York City. Lars invited a group of OD and leadership development consultants to meet his Swedish colleagues and consider whether to introduce MiL's brand of action learning in our own work in the U.S. That was the origin of the LIM consulting group.

To learn more about action learning, I used a small professional development grant to journey to Sweden to meet and interview many of the clients and faculty of MiL. Unbeknownst to me at the time, my own foray into an unknown environment talking with people about an innovative learning approach was not unlike a key principle behind MiL's work. Perhaps because of Sweden's seafaring heritage, it was not unusual in a MiL action learning program to take a team-building trip to another country (as core staff and/or with participants in a program) in order to engender fresh questions about a challenge – much as I did by spending time as a participant observer at MiL programs and talking to many of the people connected with MiL's programs. MiL graciously supported my research, opened program sessions and staff meetings up so I could observe and talk with participants, made arrangements for visiting past participants at their offices, provided me with translators when necessary, and supplied office space and other accommodations.

My goal was to tell the stories of people I met so that our potential clients in the U.S. could better understand action learning. Looking back on an article based on this research (Marsick, 1990), I found that MiL's programs helped executives learn from their experience by:

1. working through a process of finding the right problem to be addressed;
2. examining a problem from multiple perspectives;
3. learning to challenge taken-for-granted norms';
4. learning a process of consultation;
5. gaining insight into the dynamics of the groups in which they work;
6. gaining insight into oneself as a manager (*ibid.*, p. 54).

MiL did not call special attention to the idea of reflection by name in the 1980s, but the hallmark of its programs, that led to the learning strategies identified above, was always some form of reflection, whether explicit or embedded in tacit ways into activities and conversations. Sometimes, for example, they asked leaders to go out in a new culture and find out what leadership meant to musicians, cooks, or people on the street. One evening they took over as waiters at a well-known restaurant to better understand customer service, and were surprised when friends and neighbors did not recognize them because they merely saw them as "servants." Another cold night, leaders hiked in the wilderness and shared a cabin overnight near a pond with a "smelly, tattered bum" (who was a MiL faculty playing that part) to challenge the way leaders might make meaning of the bum's rather persuasive ideas, even though he apparently came from a lower social class.

Learning coaches used an action research approach, so participants often found themselves visiting other companies to get an outside perspective on their issue and interviewing a wide variety of stakeholders. Questions and reflective discussions were key to opening up new points of view, as, for example, in an insurance company when a project group found itself unable to help the company's executives see what the project group then understood:

> They didn't know what the problem was so just at the time when these (executives) were going to leave, (the facilitator) asked them to sit for half an hour and listen to the [project] group. He asked the group to reflect on the conversation thus far while the executives listened to them [project group], in a kind of fish bowl, where no one could interrupt. After half an hour, he opened discussion up to everyone and found that both sides could see things differently from before. (*ibid.*, 1990, p. 55)

MiL differentiated itself from other Swedish leadership development groups by challenging participants to think critically and independently, even when this meant pushing against norms. For example, one woman told me about how, in the consumer cooperative project on which she worked, the group turned around the initial framing of the problem the coop faced, which headquarters described as "a lack of courage on the part of retail store owners" but which turned out to be caused more directly by bureaucratic policies and procedures that "did not allow them [store owners] to take full control" (*ibid.*, pp. 55–6). After interviewing store owners and facilitating a feedback session for owners and headquarters' staff, "headquarters said that the store owners could do anything they wanted, so long as it was legal." Empowered by this process and supported by the project group, store owners challenged headquarters' ways of working (e.g., by ordering "a popular beer produced by a competitor, which they had delivered with publicity," even though they thought this might anger headquarters – which it did! (*ibid.*)). The project group surfaced and helped managers explore "sacred" views that stood in the way of stated goals.

Building reflection into action learning in the U.S.

We used what we learned from this research in our early work before action learning was commonly adopted by U.S. companies. As time went on, LIM became more explicit and intentional about adding reflection to programs we designed and coached. I had long been familiar with David Kolb's (1984) experiential learning designs. We then met Bernice McCarthy, who adapted Kolb's work, and we spent time learning with her so we could incorporate reflection into our action. We designed sessions to help participants first describe and examine their own experience, then relate that to what was known about a topic, and then act upon these new insights.

We also learned from Chris Argyris and Don Schön (1974), with whom I experienced action science that helps people change dysfunctional behaviors and unwanted outcomes by adding double-loop learning to their repertoire that helps managers reframe challenges. And we learned from Jack Mezirow (1991), who writes about transformative learning that also helps adults identify and rethink fundamental views and beliefs that govern how they see and act on their worlds.

As we got our work going, I and a few other researchers – writing under the name of ARL Inquiry – began to study LIM's programs to further examine the nature of action reflection learning. Several of us built on this and other research to develop a pyramid that we use to distinguish among different kinds of action learning programs based on the fundamental learning theories that underlie how participants learn from their experience (Yorks et al., 1999; O'Neil and Marsick, 2007). The first level in the pyramid – tacit models of action learning – engage participants in challenging activities in programs that also rely on expertise and facilitated activities that structure how participants engage in their learning. The second level follows the more rigorous action research approach that Reg Revans (1971) designed, in which teams of peers engage in systematic question-driven inquiry into a challenge. The third level involves experiential learning, often based on work by David Kolb (1984), in which reflection is used to drive personal development and learning how to learn, along with task accomplishment. The fourth level emphasizes critical reflection and questioning of the status quo of the kind described in MiL's approach. Each level builds on prior levels. Choices are made about the best model to use in a given situation, based on a fit with the purposes of the program and the culture of the organization/community in which learning takes place. As one moves from the tacit to the critical reflection levels, individual learning inevitably causes more "noise" in the system that can be leveraged to surface and reflect collectively on how things are done in order to transform individual and system actions.

When reflection does add power

I have come to appreciate that reflection looks different for each person. An extrovert reflects by talking to someone, while an introvert needs quiet time. A colleague and former CEO, Willie Pieterson, had his driver take him to the East Side of Central Park in New York City every morning and pick him up on the South side of the park, so he could reflect while walking. (His staff knew not to disturb him when he got to the office until after he could write down the ideas gained from the walk.) School superintendents and principals tell me they get little solitude but they are able to reflect in the shower, while driving to work, or in the midst of otherwise hectic decision-making. In one action learning program with a public utility, my colleague Judy O'Neil said that one man, whose work involved fixing pipes and wires, claimed that he would rather eat ground glass than reflect! She gently suggested that he need not participate beyond his comfort zone and, by the end of the program, he did, indeed, take time to think and share his reflections.

At first, many participants think that reflection will be touchy-feely; but most of them find by the end of the program that they appreciate real performance gains from the time they gave themselves to take stock and learn from their own experience. I have come to agree with human development scholars Bob Kegan (1994) and Eleanor Drago-Severson (2004) – that reflection requires the ability to move beyond a black-and-white view of the world. Kegan notes that everyone is not able to reflect; but that this capability (and others) can be nurtured by providing both challenge and support, specifically by nudging people to begin to think for themselves and ask questions about their worlds. Action reflection learning is a powerful way to help people become more able to think and work capably in our very complex world! And so, I conclude that when adults can direct their own learning, and do not need help to engage in reflection and questioning of the kind that Revans advocates, then the learning coach should, indeed, step out of the way. But I also think learning coaches can add value when they help people stop and slow down thinking in order to dig more deeply into points of view that may be dysfunctional, or otherwise impediments to fresh insights. Learning coaches may use reflection to probe power dynamics and other subterranean values, beliefs or dynamics that shape conversations in unconscious ways. Learning coaches, however, need to reflect on when and how they intervene, in order to better support the members of the group and not to put themselves in the limelight.

Isabel Rimanoczy's story

It was May 1994 when, as a leadership development trainer and consultant in Buenos Aires, Argentina, I signed up for the European Foundation for Management Development (EFMD) conference in Copenhagen, which included a pre-conference event in Klippan, in southern Sweden. Organized by the MiL Institute at their campus, this latter event brought together line managers, consultants and academics and, to this day, I remember the presenter at one of the sessions, Eva Arnell, who reported on a leadership development program she had implemented. "One day a line manager participant in this program came to see me and I asked him how the program was going. He replied, 'It's great! We're making wonderful progress! I just cannot understand why you are connected to this program, Eva! Because it is not training.'" She smiled as she shared this conversation with us, saying it was one of her professional highlights; people at that organization had always seen training as separated from "real life," so this comment had a special meaning to her. They were clearly now learning in a different way.

This vignette, among many other memorable experiences and exchanges during the event, made me extremely curious about the approach MiL used, called action reflection learning. I had never heard of it but it intrigued me, because I had recently been struggling with the problem of how to connect learning with the "real world" of business and, thus, make relevant and lasting the learning experiences I designed for my clients in Argentina. I had not so far found the answer. Was it just possible that I could find it in this tiny Swedish so many miles from my home?

Journey of exploration

The Internet was just gaining steam at this time, and I began a sporadic email exchange with LIM, the U.S.-based partners of the MiL Institute, asking for articles or books to read to learn more about action reflection learning. There was not much literature available though, except for some anecdotal stories but, as I heard these stories, I became even more intrigued. I felt I had to gain deeper insight into action reflection learning, to try it out for myself, and so I gathered a small group of colleagues in Buenos Aires, and invited Ernie Turner from LIM to Argentina to train us, and share his experience and knowledge. Training us was a real challenge, almost a paradox. Action reflection learning had its roots in the late 1970s in Sweden, as a reaction to the way management development programs were taught at business schools. There was a small group of intellectuals who believed that business needed more than managers, and that leadership was not taught through finance or marketing courses. It involved a mindset, attitudes, values – the whole person, not just the intellect. Besides, individuals had a great deal of knowledge already. When was that tapped into? It was difficult for people to connect with their own knowledge when they had to listen to a lecture. These were some of the reflections that pushed the Swedish pioneers to experiment with a "different approach" to teaching; more precisely, a pedagogic approach focused on learning more than on teaching.

One consequence of these deliberations was that the Swedish practitioners began to try out different ways to connect the participant to the learning. They followed what we call a "constructivist" approach, where creativity was the only boundary. To give an example, participants at their leadership development programs received a textbook the first day, entitled "Leadership." When they opened this hardcover book, however, they found all the pages blank. The message was revolutionary and it was clear!

Given this intriguing – and, for us Hispanic consultants, novel and unstructured approach to learning – I was at a loss to see how a "training of action reflection learning coaches" would be possible. We could readily grasp some fundamental aspects of the action reflection learning methodology – such as how many participants should ideally work together with one coach, how many times they should meet, for how long and so on. But things turned muddier when we, the Hispanic coaches-to-be, asked why, what and how. Why do you work with small groups and large groups alternately? What do you specifically do, as an action reflection learning coach? How do you intervene and why? And when? In retrospect, we Latinos were not constructivists. We were more used to gurus, to experts, to top-down teaching and authorities sharing their knowledge. Our experience was that, if we wanted to learn, some expert would have to be the source of learning!

Parenthetically, I have seen some further interesting developments in the application of action reflection learning methodologies that relate to national culture. In the U.S. the LIM organization found it helpful to develop frameworks for institutionalizing knowledge about action reflection learning. They wrote a set of guidelines, processes, even a handbook for action reflection learning coaches. Conversely, their Swedish colleagues, did not see a need for "handbooks" and they believed totally in the constructivist paradigm that lay at their foundation.

Over time, the action reflection learning practitioners experimented with different applications of action reflection learning and, in so doing, broadened and deepened its relevance and fashioned it into a new learning methodology. At first, the focus of action reflection learning had concentrated on developing leadership competencies, but then the practitioners looked at other areas of application. They began applying action reflection learning: to team development for both intact and *ad hoc* teams; to integrating a new leader into an intact team; to managing a transition in leadership; to supporting post-merger integration; and to developing young talent. On another front, they changed the duration of the action reflection learning based intervention, anywhere from a single session lasting a couple of hours to sessions lasting several days. And the context also varied. Action reflection learning was used not only in training or development programs, but also to design interactive sessions at conferences, to design meetings, or as a methodology for individual coaching sessions. In the course of this transition of action reflection learning into a varied and comprehensive learning methodology, it differentiated itself from other forms of action learning.

Where is action learning in all this?

This was a question I asked myself many times, as did others. Given all this experimentation with approaches, what did action reflection learning actually represent? What was its core? What did it look like in different situations? Were there any commonalities among what practitioners were doing in different geographies and contexts? How could one get one's mind around the philosophy of action reflection learning? In 2005, I decided to explore this question and began a research project to identify if there were any common elements used by practitioners and, if so, what they were.

I thus initiated some qualitative exploratory research, surveying 23 practitioners from different geographic locations who had all participated in the design or delivery of at least two action reflection learning programs between 1995 and 2004. As a result of this study, I was able to identify 16 common elements that characterized the action reflection learning interventions – independent of their context and the purpose of their design. Figure 17.1 presents the action reflection learning elements that I and my

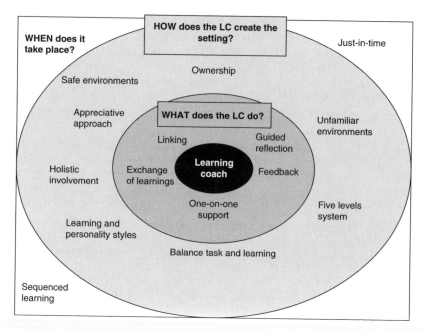

Figure 17.1   The action reflection learning elements

colleagues identified, organized in three clusters:

Cluster (a) Elements related to WHAT the learning coach does

1. Guided reflection
2. Linking
3. Feedback
4. One-on-one support
5. Exchange of learnings

Cluster (b) Elements related to HOW the learning coach prepares the setting

 6. Safe environments
 7. Appreciative approach
 8. Holistic involvement
 9. Unfamiliar environments
10. Ownership
11. Balancing task and learning
12. Learning and personality styles
13. Five-levels system

Cluster (c) Elements related to WHEN it all takes place:

14. Just-in-time
15. Sequenced learning

And at the center of this, WHO sets up the learning environment

16. The learning coach

Furthermore, with my colleague Boris Drizin from São Paulo, Brazil, I took one more step; we closely examined the elements and asked ourselves a series of questions. Why do practitioners purposely create ownership of the learning among the participants? Why do they involve the learner in setting the learning goals and in recommending the content of the learning? Why do the coaches choose, first, to observe the learners in action, and thus wait before introducing a concept, learning tool or a process? Why wait until the individuals are struggling? Why do the coaches not teach first and then help individuals apply what they have heard? Why do the coaches stop the flow of the task and switch to focus on the process, and then back again? Why do the coaches use so many questions, and why are they so reluctant to share their expert answers with the learners? We found the answers in the underlying assumptions, some examples of which are presented in Table 17.1.

We realized that these assumptions were present in a number of different conceptual frameworks, theories and schools of thought. They were not new, although they were mingled together in this approach – perhaps for the first time. We sought for months to find a cohesive statement that could encompass the theories involved, describing the underlying foundations of the elements. We finally came up with ten statements that we called "principles." Table 17.2 presents the ten principles.

No wonder it is powerful

When one considers how the intuitive and collective knowledge of practitioners around the world assembled so much valuable wisdom and knowledge, it is no surprise that the result is a powerful learning methodology. True, the constructivist spirit did not stop at the otherwise traditional academic practices, and did not mind combining a behaviorist paradigm with a humanistic perspective, but the learners did not seem to be in danger because of this, or even to mind.

As for the connection with action learning, I believe it was a key trigger for the early Swedish practitioners, who experimented combining learning with "real work projects," grouping learners into small teams, using inquiry and learning exchange, and designing sequenced meetings over a period of time. Then they and their U.S. colleagues explored new frontiers,

Table 17.1   Example of three action research learning elements and the underlying assumptions

Element: Taking ownership for one's learning

Operational description:
To allow the involvement of the learner in setting the learning goals and recommending contents

Assumptions:
- When individuals have an active role in setting their learning agenda and the contents, or in influencing the way the contents are transmitted, the learning is more effective
- Active involvement of the learners creates a positive atmosphere for learning
- Individuals who set their learning goals are more motivated than those who have no input into their learning agenda.

Element: Just-in-time learning

Operational description:
To wait until the learner needs a concept, question, intervention or tool. (This could more properly be called "just-in-time interventions".)

Underlying assumption:
- Individuals learn best when the teaching is timely and connected with a challenge they are currently facing, when they are experiencing difficulties and welcome some help or input.

Element: Linking

Operational description:
To connect what is being learned with other scenarios, to transfer it, to encourage individuals to adapt and apply it, to extract concepts and conclusions of higher level of abstraction

Underlying assumptions:
- When individuals become aware of what they are learning, the next step is to consider how it could be applied in different situations
- Through conscious projection of the learning into other contexts, the individual is able to convert an anecdotal event into a concept that can be adapted to new situations
- By establishing the connection between a current learning and other possible applications, the learning is further assimilated and it becomes easier to remember.

experimented with other designs, applications, settings and interventions. The "R" in ARL that indicated intentionality in introducing reflection into the action learning practice may have been a good rationale back in the mid-1980s. However, it was certainly in the core of Reg Revans' breakthrough concept – that individuals had a great deal to gain if they took time to collectively reflect and challenge each other. Revans disliked the intervention of a facilitator in this process, because he wanted to avoid an interference

Table 17.2 Principles underlying action research learning

Principle	Definition	Examples of theoretical foundation
Relevance	Learning is optimal when the focus of the learning is owned by, relevant to, important and timely for the individual.	J. Dewey, L. Vigotsky, K. Lewin, P. Freire, R. Revans, Cunningham, Murdoch, Wilson, J. Lave, J. Raelin
Tacit knowledge	Knowledge exists within individuals in implicit, often unaware forms, is under- or not fully utilized and can be accessed through guided introspection.	Socrates, Zen Buddhism, S. Freud, M. Polanyi, T. Nonaka
Reflection	The process of being able to thoughtfully reflect upon experience is an essential part of the learning process, which can enable greater meaning and learning to be derived from a given situation.	Socrates, J. Dewey, K. Lewin, D. Kolb, J. Van Manen, Habermas, C. Argyris, D. Schön
Uncovering, adapting and building new mental maps and models	The most significant learning occurs when an individual is able to shift the perspective by which they habitually view the world, leading to greater understanding (of the world and of the other), self-awareness and intelligent action	P. Freire, Korzybski, C. Argyris, D. Schön, P. Senge
Systemic	We live in a complex, interconnected, co-created world, and, in order to better understand and tackle individual and organizational issues, we have to take into account the different systems and contexts which mutually influence one another and affect these issues.	F. Capra, Tarnas, von Bertalanffy, J. Forrester, P. Senge
Social learning	Learning emerges through social interaction and, therefore, individuals learn better with others than by themselves	K. Lewin, Bandura, R. Revans, L. Vigotsky, J. Lave, D. Cooperrider, Whitney, P. Gergen, Wenger
Integration	People are a combination of mind, body, feelings and emotions, and respond best when all aspects of their being are considered, engaged, and valued.	Rogers, Maslow, W. Reich, Perls, Campbell, Wilber
Self-awareness	Building self-awareness through helping people understand the relation between what they feel, think, and act, and their impact on others, is a crucial step to greater personal and professional competence.	S. Freud, W. James, C. F. Jung, Myers-Briggs, Goleman, B. McCarthy, Mumford
Repetition and reinforcement	Practice brings mastery and positive reinforcement increases the assimilation.	Skinner, Stevanovich, Tchakhotine, Pavlov, W. James, J. Dewey, Watson, Thorndike, D. Kolb, Bandura, Ausubel
Facilitated learning	A specific role exists for an expert in teaching and learning methods and techniques which can help individuals and groups best learn.	K. Lewin, Maslow, Roger, R. Revans, D. Kolb, Piaget, Knowles, Mezirow, D. Schön, Schein

that could disrupt the natural process of social learning, forcing onto the team members contents or a direction that they were not choosing. In this sense, the role of the action reflection learning coach takes a step outside the original thinking of Revans. The action reflection learning coach is a combination of facilitator, coach and instructor – the three hats having a common characteristic, which is the learning transfer. Whether the learning coach is introducing a just-in-time tool, offering a "stop-reflect" to pause and ponder what is happening, or codesigning a session, there is always an explanation of what he or she is doing and why, in order to share in transparency and, therefore, convert each intervention into a learning opportunity. Because of the intentional learning transfer, participants tend to pick up tools and processes that make their sessions richer, which allows them to take turns wearing the "facilitator," "coach" or "just-in-time teacher" hat. The ultimate goal of the action reflection learning coach is empowering the participants to take on the new learned roles, and this could be seen as going back to what Revans dreamed of: a self-managed team, except now with some new tools, processes or skills learned on the way.

It is possible that the need to give it a different name from action learning came from realizing that, with so many variations (number of participants, learning settings, duration of the learning session, role of the learning coach and so on), what they were doing was no longer, quite, "action learning." One way or another, I believe the journey has come full circle – yet, in a spiral. Nurtured in action learning ideas, it has moved into other territories and has now returned as a learning methodology that can enrich the practice of action learning coaches, as they explore the principles and elements, and may be useful to them as a checklist to see if there is something else they could consider in their action learning designs and facilitation. I cannot wait to see what will come out of this next!

References

Argyris, C. and Schön, D. (1974) *Theory in Practice: Increasing Professional Effectiveness* (San Francisco: Jossey-Bass).
Conger, J. A. and Benjamin, B. (1999) *Building Leaders: How Successful Companies Develop the Next Generation* (San Francisco: Jossey-Bass).
Cunningham, I. (2003) "Reg Revans – An Appreciation", *Training Strategies for Tomorrow*, 17(3), pp. 4–6. Retrieved from ABI/INFORM Global.
Drago-Severson, E. (2004) *Becoming Adult Learners: Principles and Practices for Effective Development* (New York: Teachers College Press).
Kegan, R. (1994) *In Over Our Heads: The Mental Demands of Modern Life* (Cambridge: Harvard University Press).
Kolb, D. A. (1984) *Experiential Learning: Experience as the Source of Learning and Development* (Englewood Cliffs, NJ: Prentice-Hall).
Marsick, V. J. (1990) "Experience-Based Learning: Executive Learning Outside the Classroom", *Journal of Management Development*, 9(4), pp. 50–60.

McCarthy, B. (1987) *The 4Mat System: Teaching to Learning Styles with Right/Left Ode Techniques* (Barrington, IL: EXCEL, Inc).

Mezirow, J. (1991) *Transformative Dimensions of Adult Learning* (San Francisco: Jossey-Bass).

O'Neil, J. and Marsick, V. J. (2007) *Understanding Action Learning* (New York: AMACOM).

Raelin, J. A. and Marsick, V. J. (2006) "Where is the Reflection in Action Learning?" Academy of Management Annual Symposium, (Atlanta, Georgia).

Revans, R. (1971) *Developing Effective Managers: A New Approach to Business Education* (London: Longmans).

Rimanoczy, I. and Turner, E. (2008) *Action Reflection Learning: Solving Real Business Problems by Connecting Earning With Learning* (Palo Alto: Davies-Black).

Schön, D. A. (1983) *The Reflective Practitioner* (New York: Basic Books).

Yorks, L., O'Neil, J. A., and Marsick, V. J. (eds.) (1999) *Action Learning: Successful Strategies for Individual, Team, and Organizational Development, Advances in Developing Human Resources*, 1(2) (San Francisco: Barrett-Koehler/Academy of Human Resource Development).

18
Looking to the Future of Action Learning
Robert L. Dilworth

Introduction

The chapters contained in this volume demonstrate that action learning can occur in a wide range of contexts and environments. Action learning also blends smoothly with other management approaches, including organization development (OD) and future search conferences, both of which are addressed in this volume. It also fits comfortably with organizational learning and transformative learning. In the case of transformative learning, where fundamental changes of perspective can take place, it seems to be a rather common occurrence in action learning related initiatives. Participants can feel empowered, and experience a feeling of greater self-confidence, having taken on a significant and real challenge and successfully dealt with it. In the process, they can find that they were able to draw on inner resources that they did not realize they possessed.

In looking to the future of action learning, we adopt a broad-gauged and strategic point of view, as we consider the practice of action learning ten years from now.

Companies are the client organizations that we principally have in mind, but we also extend our reach to the public sector as well. One of our significant reference points is traditional action learning and business driven action learning, each sharing many of the same characteristics, especially the emphasis on problem-solving, learning, reflection and results.

Not everyone will agree with our assumptions or the suggested future for action learning that we depict. However, we believe that the focus needs to be at the strategic level, addressing the major dimensions of the challenges we face, rather than getting bound up in techniques, typologies and rigid design specifications. If we can arrive at some consensus around broad issues, then the specifics can begin to fall into place. That can lead, in turn, to a somewhat different view of action learning than is currently in vogue.

There is no absolutely fixed way of practicing action learning. It can take many forms. Reg Revans emphasized this. When you hear someone say that they are experts and have the one best way to do it, you need to be on our guard. We do not make that claim. However, we do make the argument that when action learning is failing to live up to its promise, it is often the product of rigid guidelines and hesitancy – because of perceived risks – to unleash the full power of action learning. The way to unleash the power of action learning is truly to empower the participants, and that departs sharply from traditional training approaches, where the participant is often in a passive role. We also believe that the most basic of Revans' precepts, some of which have largely fallen from view, now need to be revisited. They can have a place in action learning's future. We address them here. At the same time, we are not slavish in precisely adhering to what Revans espoused. The world is changing rapidly, and we point to the need to make greater use of virtual teams in the practice of action learning. Globalization makes that necessary. We also hold that Revans' exclusion of sophisticated computer-driven simulations from the realm of action learning needs to be reconsidered. As we will outline, it can fill an important niche and deliver a level of learning that is consistent with action learning initiatives that are entirely grounded in a real problem that needs to be resolved in real time.

The strategic view

A key aspect of strategic thinking and futures planning is to begin with some fundamental questions. What will be the range of the forecast? Will it be ten years, 20 years, or some other projection? What will the future state look like? What is most significant about it? What makes it relevant? What is different about it? What assumptions or planning factors are involved? What resistances can be anticipated, and how can they be ameliorated or overcome? Significant resistances are usually a certainty in undertaking major change. The changes can run cross-grain with vested interests, produce shifts in power and influence, and they can even be perceived as job-threatening.

One vehicle that can be helpful in sorting through the resistances is force field analysis, a simple model that was developed by Kurt Lewin. It compares "driving forces" (what can help bring about change) with "restraining forces" (forces that can either impede progress or block change), and the perceived relative strength of these forces. Such an analysis can lead to adjustment of the future state that is envisioned.

We will set the range of our forecast at ten years, for the purposes of discussion in examining the future of action learning. There are certain things we know about the future ten years out. From a business standpoint – and it is likely to influence the practice of action learning, management approaches, and how businesses are organized and operated – the pace of change can be expected to accelerate. That acceleration will be brought about, in part, by the vast global economic upheaval evident in 2009. This will cause a monumental shakeout of institutions worldwide. Some companies will not make it through this extremely challenging period. Others will be transformed by it. It will make it even more difficult to remain competitive, making any approach that can help the organization survive, including action learning, that much more important to pursue.

It seems apparent that the environment ten years from now will be even more challenging than the current one. Globalization will have advanced further, and international competition will be even fiercer than it is now. Telecommunications will be an even greater force. A workforce that is well-educated and highly skilled will be even more essential. There will also be more emphasis on working in teams, getting close to the customer and having employees who can think for themselves, show leadership (at all levels in the organization, not just at the top), know how to problem-solve, and have well-refined communication skills. They will also need to become adept at operating in cross-cultural environments.

The basic context

Action learning, whatever form it takes, cannot be separated from the context and culture in which it occurs. To master the kind of intense environment we can expect to see over the next ten years will require some major shifts in the contextual framework that exists in 2009 in the U.S., as well as elsewhere in the world – that is, if businesses plan to survive and be successful.

You cannot have a highly-skilled adult workforce if they come out of school lacking in functional literacy and basic skills. This is especially the case in an economy in the process of rapid transition, where high-level skills become more and more important.

Shortfalls in the secondary education systems roll over into adulthood when young people seek employment. This is a serious problem in the U.S., and there are other countries experiencing similar problems. The problems related to acquiring well-educated people for the workplace is not new. They became particularly acute as technology advanced. The Office of Technology Assessment in the U.S. Government (1990, p. 7), noted that:

> Many American firms have found training employees for new technology more difficult than anticipated. Many workers need to upgrade their skills before they can handle other training.

Put another way – and directly relevant to the technological environment in which we can expect to find ourselves ten years from now:

> American manufacturing and service workers have the skills for yesterday's routine jobs. But these workers will need new skills to function well

in the more demanding work environments that increasingly characterize competitive industries able to provide high-wage jobs. (*ibid.*, p. 1)

While written in 1990, this quote could have been written yesterday. Companies find themselves unable to obtain the high-quality workers they need, especially people who are well-educated in math and science. This is true even in an economic downturn, when the number of jobs shrinks and unemployment rises.

Meeting the challenge

When individuals arrive in the workplace, the training provided can mirror our school systems – essentially, one-way communication. However, many companies have been traveling in the direction of a new paradigm for years, and their numbers are now growing rapidly – in part, because traditional training approaches are often found to fall short. The focus is shifting to experiential learning, and action learning in particular. Interest in action learning has been expanding rapidly around the world, but as occurs during any period of rapid growth of a management or learning approach, the formulation and implementation of action learning programs can leave much to be desired.

We will now turn to some examples that seem timeless in their relevance, some of them rooted in the past, that can point the way to what is possible now, and what can be considered for the future state of action learning.

General Electric and its workout technology

In terms of enlightenment and doing it right, there is no better example than General Electric (GE) and its use of action learning, a core management and learning strategy within the company since at least the late 1980s. What is especially significant about GE is that the Chief Executive Officer (CEO) himself, the legendary Jack Welch, identified the problem and then led the charge to correct it. He made a practice of devoting considerable attention to executive education and development, centered on GE's premier corporate university at Crotonville, New York. He even met with each class of students at length in what was called "the pit" at Crotonville, standing at the center of a tiered business school-type classroom. He wanted to inculcate a specific set of values in molding the corporate culture – among them empowerment, encouragement of initiative and innovation, and working to support and develop the capabilities of its leaders and managers. By every measure, the corporate university seemed to be meeting very high standards and accomplishing that. Later, GE established three overarching values to govern the way they would operate; self-confidence, speed, and simplicity.

Executives would come away from the Crotonville program steeped in the company's vision for the future, and in full support of the corporate values. However, feedback from employees after return to their workplace indicated that they found it business as usual. Initiatives could be blocked, and it could be a matter of oppressive control rather than empowerment. Welch decided to change that, and his vision was to make the entire company like Crotonville in terms of living by GE values every day. To do that would require a major shift in the way they developed talent within GE. In 1988, Welch suddenly experienced an epiphany that enabled him to embody his whole understanding of business in a single, very practical idea. It was a big idea, the sort of transformative thought that comes along only once or twice in a lifetime (Tichy and Sherman, 1993, p. 196).

The workout "technology" was born. As time went on, Welch gathered several very talented people around him to build the methodology and then quickly deploy it throughout GE. They included Jim Baughman and Steve Kerr. They were highly-skilled consultants and had experience in crafting OD strategies for organizational change. It was clear to them that this was an action learning approach.

There are some practitioners of action learning outside GE who do not consider the workout to be action learning. They miss the essence of what happens, and the extent of its motivational and transformative power in terms of individual employees and the organizations within GE in which workouts occur – which means virtually every organization in the corporation. It was executed wall-to-wall. A few senior executives, who were making the numbers in terms of profitability and performance, but had not been practicing GE values in terms of empowerment of their people, were publicly fired by Jack Welch. That vividly demonstrated the depth of Welch's commitment to get the necessary changes in place.

The best way to address the action learning properties of the workout approach is to examine the way a workout unfolds and the dynamics involved. Dilworth had significant exposure to workouts, using a version of it in his military organization only about a year after the program was launched at GE. He had to improvise at that point, drawing from early reports in newspapers and other publications. Later, in 1992, and then again in 1994, Dilworth was privileged to work with two early pioneers of the workout at GE – Mary Ann Von Glinow and Clyde Keller – in bringing the workout approach to a large corporation and large state agency. He also had an opportunity to get to know Steve Kerr.

We will now provide a general overview of a workout, together with commentary about the actual dynamics that occur. We will be referencing some of the description information developed by Dilworth and Willis (2003, pp. 64–6). The workout in our example extended over three days, had 32 participants, and was the template used for the major corporation. It can be considered true to the GE workout philosophy and approach, and was guided by an expert in the GE methodology.

It is safe to say that the 32 who had been selected by top management to participate had not worked together in this way before. To compare this with practices at GE, it was not uncommon to assign an issue area to the group that was quite different from what they were confronting in their jobs every day, and resolution of the issue was important to the competitiveness of GE. Steve Kerr referred to it as "unnatural acts in unnatural places" (Kerr, 1992). This part of the design directly conforms to two things that Reg Revans, the principal pioneer of action learning, considered highly important. First, the problem needed to be real and complex, even daunting. This was an absolutely fundamental crucible. If the problem to be addressed were not real, it was not action learning. Second, Revans encouraged placement of individuals in teams where they had to confront unfamiliar problems in an unfamiliar setting. He wanted them out of their "comfort zone." Steve Kerr was, in effect, saying the same thing another way.

Revans wanted to separate the participants from their expertise, because it caused them to reconsider their underlying assumptions, build new ones, and deal with new challenges. This tended to lead to fresh questions and could be an avenue for breakthrough thinking, solving problems that experts had not been able to resolve. Table 18.1 presents an abbreviated view of how the workout unfolded:

To sum up the workout process, there is no question about empowerment of employees if the workout process has been set up properly and the expectations are clear. Dilworth witnessed a workout where the leader indicated that he would approve a recommendation, but defer implementation until April, rather than put it in place in January. The group did not buy his rationale and began stomping their feet and chanting January, January! The leader quickly acceded to the point and made it January.

Because of the success of the workout program at GE, where a high percentage of team recommendations usually ended up being approved, and with great benefits accrued by GE, it became fashionable to try and replicate this GE technology in other companies. Other CEOs would ask Jack Welch for advice on using the workout in their companies, and he would tell them, "Make sure your corporate culture is robust enough to handle it." That was good advice.

Those who suggest that the workout does not constitute action learning can contend that another shortfall is the absence of a reflective component. This seems a specious argument for several reasons. First, a workout can be a transformative experience for those participating. It causes new thinking and can inspire greater self-confidence. Reflection is inherently a part of any process that causes significant transformative learning to occur. Participants are doing what Donald Schön has referred to as "reflection in action." There is also some follow-up to a workout, including coordination with champions for the implementation of given recommendations.

Table 18.1   An abbreviated view of how the workout unfolded

Day 1	• Participants assemble early in the morning.
	• The senior corporate leader briefly addresses the group, expressing full support for the process, and then leaves.
	• The work-out process is explained.
	• The overall team is now broken down into teams of eight people (in effect, action learning teams), based on a team composition scheme decided on ahead of time. Each team meets in a separate room with a facilitator. The facilitator jump starts the process and then, to the extent possible, fades back and assumes more of an observer role.
	• Each team is fully empowered, has no designated leader, and is asked to arrive at two to four proposals related to the issue/problem to be addressed.
	• Each proposal is entered on one overhead transparency using a grease pencil. Entries on the form include Issue, Symptoms, Recommendations, Benefits, Action Plan, Potential Obstacles and Champions (not confined to the work-out team itself).
	• Team begins to refine each proposal into a form that could be presented for decision in three to four minutes.
Day 2	• Team rehearsals continue.
	• In the afternoon each of the four teams presents their proposals to the entire group of 32 and the facilitators. One of the facilitators acts as a Devil's Advocate in playing the role of the senior manager to receive the decision briefing. All proposals must be approved and embraced by the entire group in order to be cleared for presentation. Therefore, the entire group stands solidly behind every proposal to be presented.
Day 3	• Teams do their final tune up in getting ready for their presentation.
	• The leader arrives for the presentation of proposals and decision making.
	• The lead facilitator maintains tight time discipline during the presentations (up to 20 proposals may be presented for decision within a two-hour time frame). It is an intense, high energy, session.
	• As the proposals are presented by each team spokesperson, the leader must reach a decision then and there. It is not for leaders who are faint at heart. There are only three choices open to the leader:
	– Approve the proposal
	– Reject the proposal, but only for cause
	– Defer the proposal, but there must be a reason, and delay must be resolved quickly, usually within thirty days. The leader is asked to write his decision on the overhead slide and sign it in grease pencil on the spot. It becomes a contract.

Those who argue that the time is too short for the experience to be considered action learning need to compare the accrued meeting time of a workout team with the cumulative time built up by other action learning teams that may only meet twice a month for two-hour periods. In three days, the workout can involve the number of hours that might be accrued by another type of action learning team in four to six months. The difference is also in the intensity of the experience and the continuous learning that occurs over three days. There are no intermittent periods of down time.

Florida Power & Light (FPL)

This is another case of best practices in terms of approaches that can be related to action learning. What is interesting here is that FPL never, to our knowledge, used the term "action learning" in relation to the initiative that will be described. We will make the point later, in addressing the perceived future state for action learning, that what happens is much more important than the label one assigns. There are at least four parallel examples we can think of that reinforce this point. The first is behavioral economics and its importance. It was a distinctive piece of the field of economics, but now it has increasingly become a mainstream part of the field of economics. The second is artificial intelligence (AI), which was separate and apart, at the outset, from mainstream computer programming. AI and expert systems are now an embedded part of computer technology. We see it in computer games, cell phone technology and even relatively simple devices that we use daily. The third is the application of OD in the U.S. Army. At one time, the Army had a school to train "Organizational Effectiveness Officers (OESOs)" (a synonym for OD), and there were over 2000 OESOs in the Army. The school no longer exists and the OESOs are, for all practical purposes, gone. Why? What constitutes OD has essentially become main stream in the Army. It is embedded.

The last example, FPL, relates to quality management. There is great emphasis on quality management today, whether in the form of total quality management (TQM) or Six Sigma, which GE helped pioneer. Serious practitioners of quality management can say that "Any company that feels a need to display signs announcing that they are practicing quality management probably doesn't understand quality." It is now mainstream management. You do it. You cannot be competitive without having quality management principles engrained in your production processes.

In the 1980s, FPL was trying to work its way out of a persistent problem. Roughly 10% of the power generated by the company ended up being lost between the point of generation and the customer. Repeated efforts to solve the problem had been unsuccessful. FPL now tried something different. They called together a small group of employees from across the company – about the size of a typical action learning team – to work on the problem. They had never before done any trouble-shooting of a major problem, and brought different skills to the table. It was not a group of power generation experts *per se*. There was no team leader designated. The team was set free to do what they could do, each an equal in the undertaking.

The team was able to finally frame the principal drivers of the problem. Some of their findings were not what had been expected. One significant contributor to the problem they found to be birds on power lines. There are thousands of miles of power lines in Florida, and there were millions of birds. They were shorting out power lines with their feces and biting into the insulation on the wires. That was, to say the least, a surprising revelation.

Dilworth had the pleasure of hearing the team brief the results. They were outlining their experience as part of a program at Qualtech, a subsidiary of FPL that was marketing approaches to quality management. The team had obviously bonded, and they were very proud of their achievement. They had even given themselves a name, and wore T-shirts emblazoned with it – "The Drips." After the presentation, there was a luncheon, and Dilworth ended up seated next to the presenter that day. He told her how impressed he was with what the team had done, and commented that it would probably mean a promotion for her at some point. Her response was unexpected. She said, "I may get a promotion along the way, but please understand something. That is not the most important thing to me. What is important to me is that when I run into a senior vice president of the company in the hallway, they greet me by my first name."

The FPL example would have made Reg Revans smile, because it incorporated so many of his principles of action learning. The team was empowered, it was egalitarian (everyone left whatever mantle of authority they might have enjoyed on the doorstep), and the team members were dealing with a problem that was unfamiliar to them, and far beyond the scale of anything they had worked on before. It was also certainly a real problem that had been extremely daunting. The company needed to solve it.

As in the case of the GE workout, there are those who say that this is not an example of action learning. One of them – a person who has been engaged in action learning for many years – when asked why he felt that way, said, "It just isn't action learning." He could not provide any specifics. Part of the problem appeared to be that the people who comprised the team had received no orientation in action learning. They had not been certified to engage in action learning, and there was no facilitator hovering over their shoulders during their meetings "to make sure that they did it right." To that kind of criticism we respond, "Wild flowers can even be prettier than cultivated ones at times." There is no doubt in our minds that FPL was engaged in action learning.

The key element to be taken away from this example probably comes from Revans' philosophy. He believed that no one is the expert on how action learning should be orchestrated. He simply asked that there be certain key ingredients in place and, with the exception of a distinctive emphasis on reflection, they were all there in the case of the FPL initiative: true empowerment, equality within the team, a real problem of great complexity and magnitude to solve, support for the team and what they would deliver, small team size, and letting the team operate without constant interventions by an external facilitator. Revans would make the point repeatedly that the dynamics of action learning are not complex, except as those with MBA's tend to make them so. Some are incredulous about how a template so simple in conception can work so well. It is about allowing people to explore and demonstrate initiative. It is a microcosm of democracy. As General George S. Patton, of World War II fame, would say: "Let the troops show initiative, and they will surprise you with their ingenuity." That happened at FPL.

Union Carbide (now a part of Monsanto)

In the 1990s, Dilworth served as one of the learning coaches during an action learning program at Union Carbide. What was instructive about the program is that it led off with a weeklong simulation exercise to get the teams up and running. This was a very realistic and difficult exercise, and it was global in scope. During the exercise, there would be a need to coordinate actions with company operations in other countries. While the persons playing these roles were in the next room manning a phone bank, these coordination calls were very authentic, down to highly believable foreign accents on the phone.

Following this week of dealing with a highly sophisticated simulation, the teams settled in to work on the real problems they had been assigned. Team members came from across the company and from a variety of countries. It was very international in character. Team members had usually never worked together before, and they were not necessarily conversant in the problem area that had been assigned (e.g., a chemical engineer having to joust with issues related to marketing of company products). The Honey–Mumford Learning Style Questionnaire (LSQ) was used to alert team members to their differing learning styles, across the spectrum of activists, reflectors, pragmatists, and theorists – categories related to the research of David Kolb. This was helpful in understanding and moderating team dynamics.

Here is what can be taken away from this example. Revans decried the use of puzzles, simulations, or anything else that is fabricated in the place of a real problem. However, in this case the simulation exercise proved to be a powerful stimulant in building team norms – how the team members would work together. That allowed them to launch, with minimal milling around and confusion, when they began addressing the real problem that they had been handed. Simulations can be a very effective complement to action learning, short of being a surrogate for a real problem in the learning process.

The Union Carbide example lines up well with Revans' precepts. Teams were empowered, all team members operated as equals, there was no designated leader, they were confronting unfamiliar problems, and the facilitators did not intervene continually in the process. Revans objection to use of case studies, business games and other simulations was articulated in this way:

> These are normally based on narrow edited descriptions by anonymous writers of unknowable conditions. (Revans, 1983)

Revans objected to simulations on the basis that they were not real and products of the past. In the case of Union Carbide, this was simply a tune-up exercise, but there is now a larger point to make. Revans' commentary has lost some of its relevance over the years, given the power of some of the sophisticated computer simulations now available. Simulations, as we will discuss in presenting our view of the future state of action learning, have come of age.

A second lesson is in use of the LSQ to get a gauge of the learning style profile for a team. The irony here is that one of the developers of the instrument, Alan Mumford of England, is also an action learning practitioner, and yet there are practitioners of action learning in England that would never accept use of any instrument with action learning teams. There can be a belief that it might detract from the purity of the action learning process. The fact is that learning style instruments can be quite helpful, whether it be the LSQ, the Myer–Briggs Temperament Inventory (MBTI), or some other recognized instrument for surveying learning styles.

The issue of problem diagnosis versus implementation of solutions

Having examined the General Electric, Florida Power & Light, and Union Carbide examples, the issue of problem diagnosis versus implementation of solutions needs to be addressed. This issue can also stand in the way of arriving at an improved future state for action learning. It is sometimes a point of rather sharp contention, and even viewed as a conundrum or dilemma. Some will cite it as an example of an incongruity and inconsistency in Revans' philosophy and precepts related to action learning.

On the one hand, Revans tells us that it is desirable to have people work on problems with which they are unfamiliar. But how can they then be asked to translate their diagnosis into implementation? Technically, they lack the required skills. The main idea of having people with little or no expertise tackle unfamiliar problems can, in and of itself, seem counterintuitive to business professionals, who have been educated to believe that the way to solve complex problems is to assemble a team of experts. Revans argues that the lack of familiarity is what allows people to get outside the box and solve the kind of complex problems that experts may have repeatedly failed to diagnose. That is what happened in the case of Florida Power & Light. Dilworth can cite a number of instances of the same phenomenon being demonstrated.

Revans' beliefs in the case of having people take on unfamiliar problems centers on the strength that comes from the action learners not having expert knowledge, As such, they are not blocked by long-held assumptions and ask "fresh questions," questions that an expert probably would not have asked. They are not entrapped by habitual patterns of thought. This can be a path that leads to breakthroughs in solving the problem. Some practitioners of action learning debunk this logic, contending that the action learning team must be able to diagnose the problem and implement the solutions. As proof of principle, they can cite Revans' dictate that "There is no learning without action, and no action without learning." In other words, it is not action learning unless the action learning team is involved with both diagnosis and implementation.

What they miss in their argument is that diagnosis includes action. The action component is not confined to the implementation phase alone. Revans did recognize that this is an area that needs to be addressed. In the Belgian experiments that he was responsible for in the mid-1960s, he provided coverage for the implementation once a diagnosis was determined. His approach was to create a "framework of welcome" in the receiving enterprise. Once the diagnosis was determined by someone who was a nonexpert, a second action learning team within the client organization was assembled to deal with the implementation. The person doing the diagnosis helped to seed this team as it began its work. This approach seems to have worked rather well.

There is another phenomenon that Dilworth has documented that has not been covered in the general literature of action learning until now. What he found is that nonexpert action learning teams, assigned a joint problem to diagnose with which they had no prior familiarity, could move beyond the diagnosis and assume responsibilities for implementation – even when there was no expectation that they would or could do so. The question becomes, how could they implement solutions when they technically lacked the expertise?

What caused this phenomenon to occur? There seem to be several factors in play. First, when you assign very smart people to diagnose a problem, even when it is outside their normal range of expertise, they are liable to surprise you. Second, there is the matter of engagement. The team can become intensely engaged and motivated, and it can bond around the need to stand together in solving a difficult problem. What is outlined next is an actual example of the effort moving from diagnosis to implementation as a smooth and natural evolution. This is an example of a team working far outside their comfort zone. No one on the team had any background what-soever related to the problem being addressed.

The project involved a one hundred year old U.S.-based recycling company in Roanoke, Virginia. In partnership with a Spanish company, they were setting out to disassemble over 1300 locomotives, with parts either to be treated as scrap or used to reassemble locomotives that could be shipped to developing countries with less stringent air pollution standards than those in the U.S. They were going to launch a new start-up company to handle this work. It was new ground for them and they wanted help in recruiting the necessary workforce and developing interview protocols for the selection process. The action learning team quickly recognized that they could not come up with recruiting strategies before the jobs were engineered, job descriptions written and qualifications determined. Therefore, they donned hard hats like construction workers and walked the two-block long disassembly line that was being brought together. They asked many questions, interviewed company employees, and examined what was to occur at each station. They not only arrived at job descriptions and qualifications, they provided ideas on how the disassembly line was to be set up. They then built a recruiting plan and the interview protocols. But they went beyond that. They wrote up the administrative procedures for the human resources personnel, and built a training plan once the new employees were on board. It was not just diagnosis. They ended up turnkeying the implementation.

The bottom line is that Revans' precept of assigning action learning teams to solve unfamiliar problems needs to be followed whenever possible. The implementation can be dealt with but, if you do not diagnose the problem, implementation has nowhere to go. That was certainly the lesson from Florida Power & Light.

A partnership between Google and Proctor & Gamble

The *Wall Street Journal* (2008) reported that Google and Proctor & Gamble (P&G) would begin exchanging executives. Each company has been hugely successful, but they also have vastly different corporate cultures. Google is known to be freewheeling, and P&G has by comparison a highly rigid culture. It was unheard of for either company to let outsiders examine their competitive practices first hand, even sitting in on key decision-making sessions of the other company. But there was much to be gained by each party. P&G was one of the biggest advertisers in the country, and Google was the premier company in terms of advertising on the web, something that P&G was still developing. It became apparent very quickly that there were significant potential benefits for both companies if they were more collaborative – even operating as partners.

You may ask, "What does this have to do with action learning?" The answer is "a great deal." Revans, who pioneered action learning for over 60 years, viewed exchange of executives between companies as a powerful way of leveraging learning and building competitive advantage. He used it as a fundamental part of the action learning program that came to be called the Belgian Experiment in the late 1960s. It was one of the government sponsored approaches for increasing the industrial productivity of the Belgian economy. During the program, roughly 40 senior executives were exchanged, each was asked to deal with a major problem in another company, and in an area in which they had no expertise or familiarity. That, of course, was the case with the employees of both Google and P&G, in that they were asked to enter a corporate culture that was essentially foreign to them.

At times, the GE programs came to include action learning team members who worked for competitors, as well as suppliers and customers. The principle here was essentially the same as in the case of the Google and P&G swaps. There was perceived value in learning from each other in given areas. Baxter, a health care company based in Evanston, Illinois, provides another interesting example of such synergy.

Baxter has had a practice of training its competitors in ways that can be profitable for each party. In fact, a large percentage of their training dollar can be devoted to training the employees of competitor companies. Baxter trains the competitor in certain Baxter products so that the competitor can more effectively sell their own products. Why? It is not a giveaway program by Baxter. They have gaps in their product line, specialty niches that are filled by competitors. If Baxter can help round out its own product by enhancing the ability of competitors to cover their niches, then, overall, Baxter sales stand to be increased.

There has been some history of using this technique in the public sector. Some years ago the Governor of Maryland had an exchange program. It involved department heads swapping jobs for a month, and the rule was that the person temporarily filling the position in the other department had full responsibility and accountability. The person replaced could have been on Mars. He or she was not to be used as a resource during the period of the detail. The person sitting in the position had to muddle through and take the necessary actions. In one instance, the person who had been sent to the Department of Prisons for a month found himself facing a prison riot. He had to deal with it. The track record was interesting. There were very few dropped balls, and the executives learned a great deal through this "baptism by fire."

A suggested future state for action learning

What we are providing does not tip its hat to any given model for practicing action learning. It drives deeper than that. However, it does in large measure reflect the basic governing precepts of action learning that have already been covered, which we feel need to be in play whatever model is selected. We believe that part of the problem in getting to meaningful advances in action learning, and this translates to larger learning yields and more potent business results, is hampered by the "rice bowl" mentality – my model is the correct one, and everyone who is planning to practice "true" action learning has to line up on our template and our way of thinking.

This is most apparent in certification programs for learning coaches/advisors, the implication being that if you do not hold the certificate – which in our view can be an oversimplification in the extreme – you are not cleared as one capable of either developing or guiding a legitimate action learning program. One program advertises that within two hours, if you take their one-day certification program (at a significant cost), you will experience the power of action learning. It can be a case of the blind leading the blind.

We now present the principal components in the future state for action learning as we view them.

Principal component 1

The CEO, as was true of GE, not only needs to be supportive of action learning, but must understand it. It cannot be mere "lip service."

To Jack Welch at GE, action learning – the workout, the Change Acceleration Program (CAP), and later the Leadership, Innovation and Growth (LIG) Program – was not a side show or paste-on program. They were mainstream management initiatives. Welch made the comment at about the point when he moved the company into ubiquitous use of the workout, that his first ten years as CEO had been devoted to the "hardware" – refining the structures and operating procedures – and the rest of his time as CEO would be focused on the "software." By software, he meant development of people.

Getting the CEO on board is not easy, especially since Human Resource Development departments in companies can view action learning as a form of threat. They may want to keep things predictable, and they can be driven by metrics, like the number of people trained, rather than the learning that was realized.

Principal component 2

Action learning must be learner-centered.

This really goes without saying. People are what produce the business results. And yet there can be a fixation with the team advisor/learning coach, as if that person is the key to everything. Some models of action learning even map it that way. The learner is the key, and constraining the learning journey by incessant intrusions by a coach in the team process can be highly unproductive and frustrating.

From an adult learning perspective, being learner-centric builds independence of thought and problem-solving ability, rather than the dependency that occurs when you constantly "crutch" the learner with what can be unwelcome and unnecessary "assistance" from a learning coach.

Principal component 3

The problem must be real, extremely challenging, and something that the organization truly needs resolved.

The essentiality of a real problem was of great importance to Revans. In a number of action learning programs today, the problems are really not all that challenging. There can be an interest in making them safe and pretty much risk-free. Any unpredictable outcomes are, for all intents and purposes, ruled out. Think of the workouts. They are challenging, and certainly unpredictable. They are a robust form of action learning

Principal component 4

We need to shift to teams that are given a joint problem to solve.

Action learning teams in business – or higher education for that matter – where each team member brings a separate problem to the table tend to be dysfunctional for several reasons. First, there is no common vesting in the team. The team does not usually bond as strongly as a team pursuing a joint project/problem. Second, the difficulty of the individual problems can be quite uneven. Third, because you are dealing with up to six individual problems, the meeting time of the team gets eaten up by report-outs and updates. Finally, it can be a poor choice when operating in Asia and some other parts of the world, where the culture expects group activity and not individual initiatives.

Principal component 5

The action learning team must truly be empowered.

For some of the reasons already highlighted, this can be difficult to achieve, and yet there is nothing more essential. Managers can be very reluctant to give up control. The fact is that it often does not happen, leading to a rather "hollow" expression of action learning. *True empowerment can be a glaring shortfall in action learning programs today.*

Principal component 6

Get people out of their comfort zones.

As Revans would repeatedly state, the higher forms of learning come from having people work in unfamiliar settings on unfamiliar problems. It causes them to move to "fresh" questions, because the old ones probably do not work. It can mean that new assumptions need to be framed. *This particular precept can be almost entirely overlooked or purposely ignored by action learning practitioners today.* As GE has proved, having people do "unnatural acts in unnatural places" can be highly productive and profitable. Revans considered this the true province of the learning organization.

Principal component 7

Globalization requires that we think virtually.

We need to think in terms of teams meeting in cyber space, making full use of the web. Our large global companies have such coordination and teamwork engrained in them. It needs to become a part of our thinking when constructing action learning programs. Those who have tried it know that it works.

Principal component 8

Leaderless teams are the way to go.

Each member of the team is a leader. This is not a case of advocating anarchy. When you bring a team of employees together – and it does not need to be only mid-level or senior executives – they bring a great deal of experience to the table. It may take a "shake down" period to smooth out team processes, because not all may have had experience working in teams before, but they will almost always come together quickly as a team. When you are chasing a major problem, and have an alligator by the tail, so to speak, you quickly fold into a team dynamic that draws on all the knowledge and expertise within the team. Revans would refer to this as "partners in adversity." There is no more powerful tonic than sinking or swimming together.

Principal component 9

The facilitator, learning coach, team (set) advisor, or what ever you choose to call them, should not adopt an interventionist mode of operating.

No precept of Revans has been more widely ignored, and this, in turn, can trample empowerment. The learning coach has an important role in jump-starting the process, and then helping the process along at key milestone points. You see this in the case of the GE workouts. The role of the learning coach is an important one, but after the process is rolling, the learning coach becomes a fly on the wall. There is a minimum of interruption or intervention. This stands in sharp contrast to action reflection learning and similar orientations that emphasize the omnipresence, omnipotence and frequent "push backs" of the learning coach.

In a broader sense, the learning coach or outside management/learning consultant can be instrumental in explaining action learning to senior executives in a company, and then conducting workshops or other activities to help the action learning modality take root. It is not a case of the learning coach or consultant not having an important role. The issue is around the nature of the role and whether it helps or hinders the action learning process.

Principal component 10

As an action learning program matures, it should become embedded in the business and management processes of the organization.

We see this at GE. Employment of outside facilitators was important at the outset, but then the company quickly moved to create an internal group of facilitators. Today, you would have to say that action learning has become engrained in the way they do business.

Principal component 11

Selective application of action learning precepts in the absence of a fully developed program is okay.

Action learning does not need to be all or nothing. In some cases, it may prove impossible to gain support for a full-blown program, yet it may be possible to benefit from some of the precepts. Exchanging business executives between Google and P&G is another example. Once a given precept proves itself, there can be an appetite to go further, perhaps leading to a more comprehensive action learning program.

Principal component 12

Judiciously used, simulations, especially sophisticated computer-driven ones, can provide benefits that are compatible with true action learning.

Today, such simulations can be highly relevant and real – whether it relates to contingency planning for breaks in the levies encircling New Orleans, continuity of business operations in a major corporation in responding to a natural disaster, Homeland Security issues, or military strategies in dealing with specific threats. This represents a departure from the absolute dictate of Revans that simulations simply are not action learning.

Principal component 13

Critical reflection needs to be encouraged, but not through an interventionist mentality, where a learning coach frequently stops activity in the team to discuss learning and reflection.

Interruptions can do more harm than good. It can disrupt the dialogue and thought flow within the team. The reflective component can be dealt with more effectively by means other than continuous spur-of-the-moment interruptions. The best approach is to set aside time to discuss the learning that is occurring and consider ways to develop critical reflection, which ends up being a skill set that many business executives do not possess. This is where a good learning coach can earn their money.

Some ways to develop critical reflection skills (which is a level deeper than much of the reflection that occurs) is to use learning logs, especially those that are based on critical incidents, with the learner asking him or herself when they were most distanced, when they were most engaged, when were they most puzzled, when they felt most affirmed.

The reflective component of action learning is where you harvest the key learning that has occurred before it has a chance to decay. This is strategic in nature, because it not only builds the capacity of the learner to tackle future problems, but it can also serve to build the competitive advantage of the business enterprise.

Principal component 14

Questioning insight needs to be emphasized as the start point for action learning, rather than beginning with past reports and problem-solving.

This is yet another fundamental precept of Revans that ends up either being ignored or largely diluted. It is counterintuitive to the way businesses operate.

The time pressure can lead to hasty problem-solving, not really examining what is happening in any depth. An in-depth up-front questioning process can even be viewed as a waste of time – "Let's get on with it!" A solution is selected and implemented that may quickly sour or fail to live up to expectations. Anyone who has been through the process understands the value of the questioning insight. Revans would list three basic questions: What is happening? What ought to be happening? How do we make it happen?

When the FPL team met, it did not make much sense to anchor themselves to past solution paths. They had not worked. They had to look for fresh questions.

How do you take these 14 points and build a bridge that can have them in place ten years from now? The first part would seem easy. All of these components are known today, even though not all are being followed. The biggest hurdle is changing the psychology around the way action learning is practiced. Some of the practices travel out of limited expectations by design, in order to avoid making waves and creating potential risks. Life is a risk and the world of business – and, certainly, globalization – contain risks. Therefore, to practice action learning that is essentially risk-free and timid in its application does not provide a robust experience. It can hamstring action learning, robbing it of its fundamental strengths and potential. GE can provide an importance reference point here, because the company emphasizes stretching to grow, testing the metal, and it is willing to take judicious risks in the process.

Conclusion

Running through the precepts just outlined – what we view as the future building blocks of action learning – is a common thread. It is the need to break away from practices that impede rather than facilitate action learning. We refer to them as "half-way" expressions of action learning. One of the common shortfalls is lack of true empowerment. There can be a fear of setting the action learners free to explore nontraditional avenues for solving a problem, even when the traditional approaches have proved to be a failure.

The problem itself can be "half-way, real but nonchallenging." This is usually the product of playing it safe, simply going through the motions of action learning. Having people work out of their comfort zone on unfamiliar problems in unfamiliar settings, and with unfamiliar associates, can be viewed as counterintuitive and too risky. But that is a potent way to foster learning and find solutions to pressing problems. It is a core precept of Revans that is almost universally ignored.

Perhaps the most significant suppressant of true action learning is the omnipresence of a learning coach/advisor external to the action learning team. There are those who absolutely believe that it is necessary that the learning coach manage the learning, be present at team meetings and do "push-backs" at will to pinpoint learning that is occurring. In the process, they interrupt the processes of the team and can disrupt the learning that is occurring, not to mention the disruption of problem-solving activity. The persistent interventions of a learning coach violate the most basic principles of adult learning theory, including the need to promote independence of the learner, as opposed to creating a dependence on an external facilitator to make sense out of what is happening. It also ignores the collective intelligence and experience of the action learners.

To break away from this paradigm of nonrisk taking and diminution of the learner will require more than rearranging the deck furniture. It requires an overhaul of the way action learning is approached. Those who practice interventionist approaches to action learning have built a lucrative niche out of offering what are, ultimately, often badly adulterated versions of action learning

We feel that the future state for action learning that we present, in terms of the 14 components, represents a close fit with the way businesses operate. You see that in the GE example we provided. When the senior executives of a company personally come to understand the nature of action learning, rather than turning it entirely over to human resources departments to explain and engineer, we feel that what we propose will be found to be much more in tune with our challenging times then the "safe" versions of action learning now so much in evidence.

References

Dilworth, R. and Willis, V. (2003) *Action Learning: Images and Pathways* (Malabar, FL: Krieger).
Jim Lehrer News Hour, PBS, 20 March, 2009.
Kerr, S. (1992) Conversation with Robert L. Dilworth.
Office of Technology Assessment, U.S. Congress (1990) "Worker Training: Competing in the New International Economy (OTA-ITA-957)" (Washington, DC: U.S. Government Printing Office).
Revans, R. (1983) *ABC of Action Learning* (Bromley, U.K. Chartwell-Bratt).
Tichy, N. and Sherman, S. (1993) *Control Your Destiny or Someone Else Will* (New York: Doubleday).
Wall Street Journal (2008) "A New Odd Couple: Google, P&G Swap Workers to Spur Innovation", November 19.

Appendix: Robert L. Dilworth: His Life and Legacy (1936–2009)

Verna J. Willis

Brigadier General Robert Lexow Dilworth, coeditor of this volume with Yury Boshyk, passed away unexpectedly on June 6, 2009, when he suffered a fatal heart attack. Fortunately, he left to us a brilliant example to follow and a vibrant legacy to draw upon, although we are also left with much that he envisioned still to do. In this, he is like Reg Revans who, before Lex, carried the flag for action learning while he lived and gathered up a growing group of committed people to carry on his work. Both men worked tirelessly and unpretentiously in preparation for the years ahead, challenging those willing to learn with and from each other, and championing their best efforts.

General Dilworth – who also held the distinguished title of Associate Professor Emeritus from Virginia Commonwealth University in Richmond, Virginia – has been known to all his friends and many of his professional contacts and acquaintances as simply "Lex." He viewed himself as an ordinary man doing ordinary things, with extraordinarily hard work and attentiveness. The fact that he was by no means ordinary is beside the point; if he made extraordinary contributions, he was sure that everyone else could do the same. He wanted to be called Lex, and we will do this, knowing that he would not set himself above anyone, face-to-face or in print, and risk ruining a possibly rewarding friendship. He made friends with great gusto, and with limitless appreciation of who each person had been, was, and yet might be.

Lex took five years (until 2002) to organize and write his personal history from records and recollections of the first 65 years of his life, more than 31 of which were devoted to his active service in the U.S. Army. If one adds to that the years he spent in college in the reserve officers' training (R.O.T.C.), plus a prior period when he briefly belonged to the Air Force Reserve, Lex spent more than half of his life to that point in preparatory and active military service.

Lex titled his privately held memoirs the "Reflective Mapping of a Soldier's Life and Times." While he was writing his 2008 book, *The Fogs of War and Peace: A Midstream Analysis of World War III* with his Israeli colleague, Shlomo Maital, Lex told us that he then realized – perhaps as never before – how much his soldier's life had influenced the evolution of his thinking and acting in the world. No small part of this was the experience of living and working in widely different cultures in his overseas postings. There was also a major shift in his worldview in the months immediately after his Army retirement in 1991, when he simultaneously took on a civilian job in Florida and began his doctoral studies at Teachers College, Columbia University, commuting between these new "postings."

A few references to his life before he received his R.O.T.C. officer's commission in the U.S. Army in June, 1959 may help us to see how Lex lightheartedly and youthfully became engaged in his military career. It appears that he found a real home in the Service, made life-long friendships there, and contributed far beyond what was required of him to be "a good soldier." This is the pattern he set for all of his adult life: friendship and giving, personal discipline and impeccable accountability, and wondrously generous support to others so that they have been empowered to give their best as well. The words of the Army slogan, "Be all that you can be," were not empty for him.

Lex's mother and father, Linda Lexow and Robert Oliver Dilworth, were born around the turn of the twentieth century, married in 1925, and Lex was their only child. Growing up in Chicago was apparently not a happy time for him, for he has titled that section of his memoirs "The Dark Years," and says that, although his mother (estranged from his father) held him "at the center of her life," he lived what felt like a chaotic and insecure childhood. It was not until he and his mother moved south for "The Miami Years (1952–5)" in high school that Lex began to come into his own sense of worth. Though he never forgot childhood friends from Chicago and visited them regularly, it is in Florida that he grew more confident as a social individual who, for the first time, called himself "Lex" to his friends, and let that stand for his core identity.

One high school mathematics teacher, Sarah McClendon, made a particularly lasting impression. Even though he did not star in her classes, she saw both his potential and his needs. She obtained tickets for him so he could attend his senior prom, was instrumental in helping him obtain a college scholarship, and wrote in his yearbook "*Keep a gain.*"

For him, he said, this translated into a personal mantra: "The key to life is to stay ahead." From then on, this has obviously meant to him that if he tried, he could always gain just a little more, do just a little more, be just a little more than ever he *thought* he could. He learned to expect the same "keep a gain" from others, and has always helped them pick themselves up if they have fallen short of doing so. Thus, it is not by accident that he has inspired and nurtured so many people who have happened to enter his sphere of influence or who have sought him out.

Lex grew up in an intensely patriotic and politically energized era, when Franklin D. Roosevelt was President. People were planting "victory" vegetable gardens, even in urban areas, to supplement food supplies for civilians and military alike in a nation at war. Lex's father grew one. Americans were all-consumed with winning World War II, and honoring those who sacrificed their lives to fight it. Lex was well acquainted with economizing and earning his own money for everything he craved, working at typical jobs for youngsters in those days. He had a newspaper delivery route, and earned money for a new bicycle by sweeping floors in the barber shop below the tiny apartment where he lived. Later, he worked as a movie usher, a bellhop and at diverse summer jobs – whatever he could pick up for pocket money. Ever the entrepreneur, he soon figured out ways to do various kinds of trade-offs for profit.

One summer, during high school, he went back to Chicago and worked with his father as an electrician's apprentice. He tells us in his memoir that he learned a valuable lesson there. When a new air conditioning installation did not work in the former Palmolive Building (now the Playboy) during a ceremony called especially to celebrate its completion, specialists were flown in to fix the problem. An electrician's apprentice asked if he could help, crawled under the installation, found a switch that had not been turned on, and everything worked. What Lex learned from this was to "always involve everyone."

A budding strategist and determined implementer of his strategies, Lex seems at an early age, unsuspected by almost everyone, to be heading for some sort of leading role in the world. He decided in childhood that, despite his uneven academic performance, he was definitely going to college. In his own words, he "never doubted it." It was a momentous decision, and decades later he could still name the place and moment when this certainty occurred to him. Even in those "dark years," he found within himself a basic optimism. Throughout his future life, he remained rock-solid confident that, whenever he said he was going to do something, "it was as good as done."

He knew of family background in military service, for Dilworth ancestors had served in both the American Revolution and the Civil War. In light of the war news of the early 1940s and Dilworth tradition, it is not surprising that he viewed a military career as one serious postcollege option for him, or that he strategized toward that end by signing up for and R.O.T.C. at the University of Florida at Gainesville. He was, at the time of college entry, already enrolled in the Air Force Reserve – though he had, in his words, "side-stepped" basic training to finish high school.

At the university, he served as Commissary Manager of his Christian Cooperative residence hall, played harmonica in a band, and used an unreliable 1951 Nash bought for US$300 to get around. He dated rarely and ran a dry-cleaning pickup and delivery service on the side to make ends meet. Yet, he had time for practical jokes and much camaraderie. He noted that he did not spend much time studying, and concentrated largely on the opportunities for social learning that he had lacked in a strict upbringing. He was especially proud that he qualified as a member of the R.O.T.C. precision drill team, and did so three years in succession. In his final year, he carried a 40-hour course load successfully, graduating in June 1959 with a degree in Advertising and Public Relations and a commission as Second Lieutenant, U.S. Army Reserves. In August of the same year, he married Marcella Aldridge, an English major at the university. After a short honeymoon, he left for Indiana for active duty and the 10-week Basic Officer Course, while Marcella worked on her teaching internship and certification.

Lex was next posted to the U.S. Army Reception Center at Fort Jackson, South Carolina, where, first, he served in records and then was placed in charge of the Personal Affairs Branch. There, troops were interviewed and personal information recorded for emergency use. This seems to have been the first firm step in the direction of the high office he attained toward the end of his Army career, an appointment received soon after his promotion to Brigadier General. In 1986, he was named The Adjutant General of the Army (TAG), 54th in succession since the Continental Army of the American Revolution (1775), to take charge of a very wide range of personnel-related functions. One major part was supplying postal services for the entire military establishment of the United States, including Army, Navy and Air Force. He was also given charge for all security clearances for Army personnel, both civilian and military. Further responsibilities were overseeing the offices managing assessment of personnel physical disabilities. Lag time was a serious problem there.

In his memoir, Lex added that "Other core pieces of TAGO included Casualty and Memorial Affairs, Awards and Decorations, a Safety Office, a budget organization, and an organization called the Environmental Support Group" dealing with "legal matters related to the use of Agent Orange in Vietnam." He was expected, as a first priority, to "set up a Transition Management Program for those leaving the service." He accomplished the installation of this pioneer program after a round of briefings inside the government and the military. It soon became clear that he was being asked to restructure the entire organization. This he proceeded to do, introducing expert systems, reducing lag time in processing by as much as 40%. Some functions were justifiably sent off to other organizations and some new functions came to reside in TAGO. One of these was the Central Identification Laboratory in Hawaii, tasked with recovering and identifying remains of U.S. military personnel who died in Vietnam and elsewhere. Another piece involved interface with soldiers' dependents experiencing difficulties such as not receiving spousal payments, or intervening on behalf of those enlisted in the Army to fill high specialty positions in order to make repayment of student loans the enlisted men might have paid easily had they remained in civilian life.

Lex served two years as The Adjutant General before leaving for what would be his last Army assignment, with the Training and Doctrine Command (TRADOC) at Fort Monroe, Virginia. TRADOC is charged with responsibility for the entire Army training base, in all branches and at multiple installations. This includes the National Training Center at Fort Irwin, California, the training and deployment of Army Reserves, Force Modernization, and even law enforcement with its efforts to retrain and rehabilitate service personnel at the military prison at Fort Leavenworth, Kansas. Internal training for his own staff people did not escape Lex's attention. He mandated appropriate computer literacy training and adjusted job descriptions accordingly. Curiously, one of the tasks Lex was called upon to accomplish – and one of the most satisfying ones – was a second round of activism around the Transition Management Program which he had spearheaded successfully while he was Adjutant General but which, in the early days of the George H. Bush administration, had been killed by stripping away its entire budget.

By this time, Lex was already self-started at work on an even more comprehensive transition strategy. He delighted in telling the story thus: "Seeing no Army strategy around how to manage our military personnel resources, I had personally designed a strategic framework to do that." He called his analysis and procedural planning to the attention of Major General Bill Reno, who was serving as the Director of Planning, Analysis, and Evaluation in the Chief of Staff's Office in the Pentagon. Reno's review consisted of examining "Godzilla," a preliminary schema for the new transition plan that covered 22 feet of wall space. But, despite its monstrous size and detail, Lex was assured that "Reno loved it." Then Lex was asked to graph and present the proposed strategy in such a way as to "show *how* what we did to manage and develop our personnel needed to change as we reduced the size of the Army." It took civilian support to override internal officer opposition and see this tasking through to its conclusion. The new Assistant Secretary of the Army for Manpower and Reserve Affairs, G. Kim Wincup, assigned Lex to head the task force to get the program installed. To make that order stick, it was reinforced to the Army Staff by Undersecretary of the Army John Shannon. The program, renamed the "Army Career and Alumni Program" (ACAP), was the first of its kind in the military, and has been a model for other services.

This was a triumph, a far-reaching contribution and likely the apex of positive changes Lex was able to make in the organizations he tackled in his long years of military service. The depth and extent of his distinguished Army career cannot possibly be given full justice in these brief biographical notes, and so these highlights must serve as exemplars of the rest of the Army years that earned him promotion to General Officer standing. His memoir speaks of the outstanding soldiers and their officers that he admired, and frankly also, of some he did not. He covers the events that raised his great interest in world affairs and political science, and reflects upon how he grew personally in each new posting and assignment. One thing he concedes is that he never abandoned his enjoyment of practical jokes, even when they turned on him, since humor served to brighten the routines of the day. One thing he could not bear was a posting that did not challenge and engage his energies. Taking action to make bad situations better or good situations great was always an ethical imperative and a driving force for Lex.

Army stories are augmented early on with interspersed and poignant memories of his personal life with his first wife, Marcella, and their children, Robert and Alexa. Though time spent with them was often far too short, Lex makes it clear that he loved being with them and sharing with them in fun, like throwing Frisbees together in the Shenandoah parklands. Farther on, references to family also include his later marriage (1981) to Doris Smith Connor, and life with her and her children, Suzanne and Eddie, from a previous marriage. The second family was with him during his tour of duty in Germany and thereafter.

For *Fogs of War and Peace*, Lex wrote this succinct summary of his service record, marking notable periods: "He served for over thirty-one years in the Army, including five years in Asia and another three in Europe. Six tours of duty were spent in the Washington area, two in the Army Chief of Staff's Office in the Pentagon. He was appointed as the 54th Adjutant General of the Army (TAG). He served twice with infantry divisions, in Vietnam and Korea, including service as a division chief of staff." His tour as Chief of Staff was with the 2nd Infantry Division during a confrontation with North Korean forces in 1976. Among many other positions of high responsibility, he also served at West Point as Comptroller of the National Guard and Director of Resource Management for the Academy.

Lex was determined to be a ready-to-fight "warrior first," as the Army required of him and as he required of his own subordinates. But it was also obvious to him that organization and communication skills, as well as intuitive and strategic thinking, were among his strong suits. Fortunately, he realized that these added up to major contributions he could make to the service itself. These would extend far beyond the Army into the post-service lives of the men and women he led, as well as reaching out among the civilian employees in his jurisdiction.

He was an inveterate learner, never believing that he knew all he wanted or needed to know. He had convictions and opinions, but they were always subject to revision in the light of new information. His capacity for careful listening was finely tuned and, if he found himself to have "heard" in error, he was the first to admit it. Once, when he was informally introduced as speaker to an audience of academics, he heard himself fondly characterized as "an education junkie." At first he seemed a little taken aback, but he considered and then conceded the point. His three Master's Degrees (Public Administration at the University of Oklahoma, Education at Columbia University, and Military Art and Science at the U.S. Army Command and General Staff College); his Doctoral Degree in Education from Columbia University innumerable Army training schools; and extended training programs at such schools as Harvard University, University of Michigan, and

Northwestern University – added to his professorship at a major university – might well tell tales of a learning "addiction." To further make the case, let it be noted that Lex had served as Adjunct Professor at college level before: at John Jay College for Criminal Justice, teaching public administration courses in 1984–5, at Boston University Overseas Program (Europe), teaching business courses in 1983–4, and at the University of Maryland (Far East) teaching political science in 1975.

Lex could not imagine being an insightful, effective leader without being, simultaneously, a heavy-duty learner. On the Myers-Briggs personality inventory, he scored off the charts as an "intuitive," and this is often a characteristic of high-potential and creative individuals. Certainly, he learned to "read" people, see their latent capability even when it was hidden from them, and either coax or demand (and, sometimes, both) that they live up to it. He asked nothing of anyone that he was not willing to tackle himself, and believed that people respond best to a challenge that will stretch their known capacities and make room for new learning and development.

In 1991, heading for his first civilian job in the Florida Department of Labor and Employment Security after only a few days of Army retirement, Lex was simultaneously beginning his weekend independent study Adult Education and Human Resource Development doctoral program (AEGIS) at Teachers College, Columbia University. The dual undertaking had him commuting between postings on a weekly basis. Stymied by bureaucratic ineptness and a climate of reverse racism that stalled many of the initiatives he proposed, Lex was successful in renaming his organization the Human Resource Development and Management Bureau and in establishing a "Hub of Excellence" lecture series. He engaged three outstanding speakers: Steve Kerr, who was a consultant to Jack Welch at General Electric and who was later titled Chief Learning Officer there; Jerry Harvey, author of the book about crossed expectations called *The Abilene Paradox*; and Henry Cisneros, who became Secretary of Housing and Urban Development (HUD) in the Clinton administration.

His doctoral program advisor, Victoria Marsick, told Lex that Reg Revans was planning a trip to the U.S. and might be available to spend a day with him in Florida. The rest is history, as the saying goes, for Reg and Lex connectedly powerfully from the very beginning of that visit. Their conversations about action learning began as soon as Lex had Reg installed in his hotel room, and, for four or five hours, broken only thinly by a 9 pm dinner, they continued to talk. At breakfast the following day, Reg told the story of his besting the long jump record of Harold Abrahams, an Olympic champion in one of the running events of 1928 and the subject of the movie "Chariots of Fire." Thus began the friendship and mutual respect between these two men, life-long mentors of others, who readily embraced a new relationship and all it promised for learning with and from each other.

They had much in common in their separate crusades against politicized or thoughtless, ill-conceived decisions and the disastrous fallout of such errors, and were clearly of the same mind about investing faith in the ability of ordinary human beings to be problem-solvers of a very high order. Lex was pleased that, on that day, Reg "gave a splendid lecture on action learning to a large gathering" of Department employees. After the lecture, Lex and Reg continued their discussions until Reg caught his plane. Lex called this "an important life event," including an acceptance of Reg's precepts regarding action learning. He saw easily the possibilities in action learning for producing transformations of the sort theorized by another Columbia University mentor, Jack Mezirow, in his books on the transformative learning that is lodged in critical life events.

Not long thereafter, Lex accepted a position on the faculty in the School of Education, Virginia Commonwealth University, where, for the next 12 years, he taught adult education and Human Resource Development (HRD). Steadily working to create curriculum and build the program there – making it more experiential and applied, as well as raising the students' achievement expectations – Lex began also to affiliate with other HRD professors around the country in the recently chartered Academy of Human Resource Development (AHRD). Lex brought Reg Revans to his University to speak to students and faculty, and to work with them on an informal basis. The result was the formation of a small independent unit of the International Foundation for Action Learning, and action learning "sets" (teams) were formed in Lex's classes and sent on their first missions as action learners.

Lex went further, bringing Reg to the 1994 first annual AHRD conference (March 3–6) as a keynote speaker. A series of annual action learning preconference sessions were established, to afford continuity of information and to trade experiences among those who were interested in pursuing the use of Reg Revans' precepts, in order to promote self-understanding and expand capacities to address organization problems.

As an outcome of his efforts and the U.K. contacts he had made, Lex was invited to collaborate with leaders from the Revans Centre for Action Learning at Salford University in England, where the Revans archives were kept (since moved to Manchester University). An early joint project was the convocation of 80 interested leaders from 17 different countries to the First Action Learning and Mutual Collaboration Congress at Heathrow in 1995. Because of illness of the U.K. conference planner, Lex assumed major responsibility for organizing the Congress, recruiting participants, and serving on the advisory board. Lord Butterfield aided financially and supported the Congress by attending personally. Revans was present throughout the two days of action learning set work and reflections. This gathering set the stage for future working relationships with others across a broad spectrum of organizations. Most of these were in commonwealth nations, although some central European countries like Romania and Poland were involved in follow-up conversations and activities. At another point in 1995, Lex returned to England for the formal dedication of the Revans Centre for Action Learning and Research.

The following year, Lex organized a successful two-week program, entirely action learning based, with sets tackling troublesome aspects of the merger and reorganization of two hospitals in Manchester, complicated by mandates for reduction in force. While a few guest speakers were included to help kick off the program, the participants very soon expressed their preference for concentrating on the set work, faced as they were with unraveling serious problems and providing new insights within a short time frame. Thirty-one students from the U.S., Canada, and Australia participated. Only one or two had ever had prior experience with any health care facility. Separate reflection papers required by Lex on process and on personal gains and insights became 62 anonymous data sources for a qualitative research project jointly conducted by Virginia Commonwealth and Georgia State universities.

In 1997, Lex was asked to join the Research-to-Practice Committee of the American Society for Training and Development (ASTD). He succeeded to the chairmanship in 2000, set several new tasks and directions, and mounted a campaign to learn more about challenges facing the HRD field from carefully selected, broad-based HRD and industry professionals in a Future Search Conference. Lex relinquished the chairmanship of the ASTD committee at the end of his term of office and, by May 2002, he and a colleague at Georgia State University had begun experimenting with action learning groups that were composed of both Romanian and American students. There were unexpected challenges, some involving communications technology, but the outcomes were a useful first step toward bridging gaps between university education and business applications in this former Communist economy.

Since 1995, Lex had been actively collaborating with Verna Willis, originator and lead faculty member of the Human Resource Development degree programs at Georgia State University in Atlanta. They teamed up for a variety of projects, articles and presentations intended to advance the understanding and acceptance of action learning as a premier way to develop people and organizations. In 2003, they coauthored *Action Learning: Images and Pathways,* a book for which Reg Revans wrote an extensive foreword verifying that his own views of the process he pioneered had been carefully followed, based on the extensive interactions both authors had had with Reg over a period of years. The book is generally accepted as a basic primer for action learning. Both have contributed additional information and insights to the present volume, and are internationally recognized for their work.

In 2004, as part of his own company, Strategic Learning Scenarios, Lex entered a post-university period of consulting in a variety of corporations and public sector organizations. When he was invited to participate in the annual Global Forum on Executive Development and Business Driven

Action Learning in 2006, his unquenchable interest in international affairs and action learning came together and created a new burst of energy. From this came the agreement with Yury Boshyk to coedit this book and its companion volume.

Many have wondered what defining experiences in Lex's life prepared him so well for conscientious and inspiring leadership. In his words, one answer is: "I really believe that what we become is an assemblage of what we learn and how we are treated along the way." He cannot recall receiving positive feedback from his father, which made him all the more determined to extend encouragement to others. There was an example set for him by a caring mother, who read to him and did many neighborhood and family kindnesses. By third grade, he was reading as many as three books a week, and his passion for reading never ceased. He read widely in his adult life, and one of his favorite sources of information was *The Economist*.

He completed his elementary education in a total of four different schools, and the best years, occasioned by a "failed" third grade in one school and the need to repeat it in another, were spent in a private Lutheran parochial school, where a daily requirement was learning Lutheran Catechism and hymns. His mother scrimped and saved to pay his tuition. This was his first sustained experience with Christian Protestantism and, at such an early age, a few nurturing teachers there may have helped to establish faith and moral bearings in ways of which he was not wholly aware. He was baptized and confirmed in the Lutheran faith in Florida during his freshman year in college. It was not until around the time of his retirement from Virginia Commonwealth University that a new friendship with another determined advocate of action learning led him to membership in the Mormon Church. As a constant learner, Lex was forever open to new ideas. He may have been the best observer of his life experiences when he said that he assembled what he learned and how he was treated, added to these his "inherent optimism" and worked constantly at becoming the person he wanted to be.

Lex Dilworth prophetically wrote: "If I have a gift in life, it has been the ability to focus all my energy and intellect at the point of need." That is what he was doing when he was writing and editing for this book, and that is how he has always approached his work life. In his personal relationships, Lex has also learned and exercised what some call "emotional intelligence" with all the sensitivity, insight, caring and effectiveness that the term implies. Those who have known Lex well are assured that he has been a worthy successor to Reg Revans, faithful to Reg's conceptual frameworks and practices, and believing wholeheartedly in the efficacy of traditional action learning. What Lex has further contributed is his own fine intellect, his enormous capacity for work, and his passionate commitment to the values and causes he believed in.

Glossary

Robert L. Dilworth

Introduction

This glossary contains some of the more commonly used terminology and singular initiatives associated with the evolution of action learning. Rather than refer to "sets" as Revans did, we refer to "teams" in order to be clear. There was no known differentiation between sets and teams by Revans. It was simply his preferred way of referring to teams engaged in action learning.

Action

The centerpiece of action learning is action, in that the experience is to lead to action. As Reg Revans states, there is no learning without action and no action without learning. The action to be taken/project serves as the engine that drives the process, promoting learning and critical reflection.

Action learning

Action learning is a process of reflecting on one's work and beliefs in a supportive/confrontational environment of one's peers for the purpose of gaining new insights, and resolving real business and community problems in real time (Dilworth and Willis, 2003; Willis's definition: 11).

Action learning set or team

A group of four to eight individuals, what Revans called a "set," selected to participate in an action learning experience. There is no assigned leader within the team. All members of the team enjoy equal status. Revans considered five to be the ideal team size (Revans, 1983: 7–8).

Action learning team process questionnaire (ALTPQ)

An instrument developed by John Bing of ITAP International and Robert L. Dilworth of Virginia Commonwealth University to monitor the internal action learning team group dynamics, as seen through the eyes of its members (i.e., their perceptions). It is administered online, with member responses kept anonymous. Both quantitative (Likert scale based) and qualitative responses are involved. Results are reported back to team members as a profile of what is occurring in the team across a field of 32 indicators (e.g., equalization of work load within the team, quality of internal communications and team effectiveness). Positives and negatives related to the action learning experience are also plotted. Dealing with the group dynamics, using the ALTPQ as a reference point, becomes part of the learning experience for the team.

Action reflection learning (ARL)

This is a form of action learning that places special emphasis on critical reflection and transformative learning, with a learning coach to help participants strike a better balance between work on their project and learning from doing that work. The Management Institute of Lund (Sweden) was a pioneer of this approach. "Different from Revans, MIL developed a focus on learning coaches, working with participants in a co-learner relationship, but taking accountability for assertively catalyzing learning in the process" (Yorks et al., 2002: 19–29).

Belgian Experiment

An action learning program conducted in Belgium in the 1960s with governmental sponsorship, involving a consortium of the five leading Belgian universities and major companies. Developed and orchestrated by Reg Revans, action learning's principal pioneer, it involved action learning teams of five senior corporate executives, each dealing with an unfamiliar problem of great complexity that was centered in an industry other than their own, as they shared with their set colleagues concerns and insights on the learning taking place, "learning from and with each other" (Revans, 1980: 39–48).

Business driven action learning

This is a term used to describe a results-focused orientation to individual leadership development and organizational learning and change. It can be summarized as emphasizing both business results and the integration of individual development, team effectiveness and organizational strategy (Boshyk, 2002: 36–52).

Traditional (also called "classic") approach to action learning

It centers on the philosophy and teachings of Reg Revans, principal pioneer of action learning. Some of its most basic precepts are outlined in Dilworth (2010) as part of Explaining Traditional Action Learning: Its Basic Concepts and Beliefs. (See also Weinstein, 2002: 3–18).

Coal Board and collieries

Revans was, for a time, associated with the Coal Board in England and, as part of that involvement, he elected to spend a great deal of time underground with the miners at the coalface. He studied the group dynamics, concluding that "small is dutiful" (similar to the "small is beautiful" terminology coined by E. M. Schumacher). Revans found that when small teams were empowered and allowed to become involved in planning their own work, the teams were significantly more productive than teams managed in an autocratic way. The safety records were also considerably better. He proposed that a "staff college" be created where there could be open discussion of ideas between management and workers. In the end, Revans' proposal was not supported – largely, in his view, because the senior manages did not want to dilute their control over the enterprise. Revans was influenced by the work of Likert regarding the use of small teams – what Revans came to call "action learning sets."

Client

The person or persons who will be relating to the action learning team or individual members (depending on the action learning model being used) in refining the problem statement in the client organization and receiving the results of the action learning effort.

Critical reflection

This involves a purposeful effort to reflect on one's experiences in depth in order to reveal the underlying assumptions that govern our lives and perceptions of the world. This goes beyond mere reflection. As Gregory Bateson has indicated, it is "Level Three Learning." "You look for the why behind the why." Edger Schien has referred to it as "Triple Loop Learning." You end up both exposing and "unfreezing" underlying assumptions, some of them carried with us indiscriminately since early childhood, and testing them against the realities that we now face. In action learning, critical reflection can occur both individually and in collective dialogue within the action learning set.

Everyone bring one (EBO) model

This is an action learning team in which each member brings a different problem to the table, usually from that member's workplace.

Four squares

A model used by Revans to demonstrate that problems we confront in our lives are either familiar or unfamiliar, and they occur in a familiar or unfamiliar setting. He designed a simple display with four quadrants to show the four alternative situations (e.g., familiar problem in an unfamiliar setting). Revans argues that the greatest learning occurs when we find ourselves confronting an unfamiliar problem in an unfamiliar setting. He viewed that as the personification of a learning organization. Revans believed that when we find ourselves confronting the unfamiliar, we are then inclined to ask fresh questions and challenge our long-held assumptions.

Future search conferences

This modality was pioneered by Marvin Weisbord and Sandra Janoff, cofounders and directors of the Future Search Network. It has been used extensively around the world in dealing with difficult problems, with the goal of arriving at common ground as a foundation for action. A Future Search conference usually involves bringing a diverse group of 64 to 72 participants together to address a major issue (Weisbord and Janoff, 2000).

The large group is subdivided into "regular stakeholder groups" of roughly eight members, composed of functional groups (e.g., business people, press, clergy, government officials, people from financial institutions, human resource professionals). During the Future Search conference, which usually lasts about 16 hours over three days, participants will be further assigned to "mixed stakeholder groups," each containing members from the regular stakeholder groups. Each mixed group, in effect becomes a microcosm of the whole.

Weisbord considers this a form of action learning. However, as is true of the GE workouts, which are similarly short in duration, the time for reflection can be limited.

GE workout/change acceleration program (CAP)

This is an organization development (OD) strategy that was inaugurated throughout General Electric (GE), beginning in 1989. It was driven by the belief that the values emphasized at GE's corporate university at Crotonville, New York, were being lost when managers returned to their workplace (Ashkenas et al. (2002); Ulrich et al. (2002)). The workout was an effort, considered highly successful by the company, to embed these values in the everyday work life of GE. It is considered by GE to be a form of action learning. In its typical form, a group (e.g., 32 members) is brought together and then subdivided into teams of eight. Covering as few as three days, both the overall group and the teams are a part of the process as it unfolds. Teams are empowered to present recommendations to top management in face-to-face meetings, with an expectation of immediate decisions.

Hospital Internal Communications (HIC) Project

In the 1960s, Revans became involved with what came to be called the Hospital Internal Communication (HIC) Project/Study. It involved the ten largest hospitals in London. The impetus for the initiative was the fact that the hospitals were experiencing staff morale problems, patient morbidity rates that were considered excessive, hospital stays that were too long, and attrition rates that were exceptionally high (as much as 67% for nurses). Small groups were sent from one hospital to another, where they observed familiar problems but in an unfamiliar setting. The groups did not operate as action learning teams. Nonetheless, each small group (it might only be three) would discuss their findings, and then the overall group would meet to discuss what needed to be done across the hospitals. It led to a number of initiatives. Results showed, when compared with nonparticipating hospitals (a quasi control group), that patient morbidity rates had gone down, staff turnover reduced, hospital stays shortened, and staff morale improved. The overall conclusion drawn was that lack of effective intercommunication between doctors and patients, nurses and doctors, and between all parties, had been counter-productive and that, when intercommunication improved, positive results began to become evident (Revans, 1980: 29–38).

Hybrid set

This is a term used when members of multiple teams are mixed together to form hybrid sets for the purpose of broadening the exchange of views on learning that is taking place. By bringing a cross-section of teams together, the intense project orientation tends to be temporarily diffused, elevating the likelihood that reflection on learning can occur.

Joint project model

This is an action learning team where all members are dealing with a common problem, usually one of great complexity. Revans would refer to such an experience as "partners in adversity," since all team members were confronting a common and vexing challenge.

Learning coach

Also referred to as an advisor, facilitator, or mentor. The role varies in relation to the application of action learning involved, but the learning coach usually helps guide the action learning process, to include assistance in determining the appropriate project and arriving at team composition. The learning coach role can range from omnipresence in team meetings (e.g., action reflection learning) to interruptive involvement based on need and invitation of the team membership. Reg Revans believed in minimal facilitation and intervention of the learning coach, convinced that the team members themselves were the best facilitators, and that managing the team dynamics was part of the learning yield.

Learning equation

Revans suggests that learning equals programmed knowledge, what he refers to as "P," plus questioning insight, or the "Q" factor: $L = P + Q$. He espouses the belief that, while both the P and the Q are necessary for learning to occur, the P (formal and accrued learning) needs to be preceded by the Q and its free-ranging address of what is happening and needs to occur. In other words, the Q drives the P (Revans, 1983: 28).

Nile Project

This was a project, spawned by the Belgian Experiment, described elsewhere in the glossary. It involved 13 Egyptian companies and used a very similar methodology (Revans, 1982: 372–425).

Programmed knowledge

This encompasses all the forms of formal/instrumental learning to which we are commonly exposed, including lectures, textbooks, case studies, simulations and puzzles. Revans states that all forms of programmed knowledge travel out of what has occurred in the past, and therefore represent imperfect formulations in dealing with problems that we either are facing now or might expect to face in the future.

Questioning Insight (Q)

The Q factor hinges on asking the right questions. Revans indicates that we need an added infusion of the Q factor in dealing with the fast paced times in which we live, since our capacity to learn is now often outstripped by the velocity of the change forces around us. Through Questioning Insight we are able to test the adequacy of the available P and determine whether it is flawed or a bad match with what we need. In some cases, we will find it necessary to discount existing P and create new P. If we had started with the existing P rather than Q, we might have been inclined to accept P that would have led us in the wrong direction.

Structure *d'acceuil*

A term used by Revans to describe an internal "client group" inside a company or organization that either assists an outside action learner or action learning team (set) to help examine an issue and then implement recommendations for change, and/or to take on the responsibility themselves for implementing the recommended changes (Revans, 1980: 45).

System Alpha

This is the first of three interlinked systems of thought and action in Revan's concept of action learning. It features iterative, evolving analysis of a real problem situation in an organizational context. During the process, unexpected roots and ramifications are discovered. Novel attacks on problems can be mounted when action learners continually ask themselves the questions: "What is happening?", "What ought to be happening?", "How can it be made to happen?" The same questions will apply at different points throughout the inquiry. These questions are pivotal in arriving at an initial problem statement and tracking the migration of the problem over time as new insights are gained (Revans, 1982: 333–48).

System Beta

This system resembles the use of the scientific method in the physical and life sciences. Revans calls it "intelligent trial and error." Beta elaborates on what is derived from System Alpha, applying fact-finding and assumption-testing procedures to check what is being learned. System Beta includes research, data collection and interpretation, and other discovery methods. Survey and/or observation, trial hypothesis or theory, experiment (test), audit (evaluation), and review, ratification, or rejection of results are all necessary Beta processes. System Beta uses whatever is revealed to pursue new avenues of inquiry that might yield a better solution (Revans, 1982: 336–45).

System Gamma

This system, grounded in critical reflection, is embedded in all the action learning processes. Revans called it "symbiotic" with Alpha and Beta. It demands an honest search for understanding of the realities and value systems of self and others, since it is these realities and values that guide what people say and do. Revans insists that greater self-knowledge leads to greater interpersonal competence and more sensitive organizational skills. System Gamma, with the transformational change opportunities it offers, is at the very core of action learning and the energy source for its powerful effects (Revans, 1982: 345–8).

Transformative learning

We are transformed, to the extent we are able to either modify or jettison assumptions that are revealed as no longer having meaning, replacing them with new and more fully differentiated points of view and frames of reference (Mezirow and Associates, 2000). Learning in and of itself contains the seeds of transformation. When we learn, we are transformed.

Virtual organization/virtuality

Action learning in a virtual mode involves doing most, if not all, of the set business/interaction by teleconference, email or other electronic means, as opposed to face-to-face interaction. This provides special challenges to a modality predicated on intimate, direct, and regular face-to-face contact where all the senses are engaged. The challenge is further magnified when dealing cross-culturally with global teams. This is relatively unexplored ground with respect to action learning.

References

Ashkenas, R., Ulrich, D., Jick, T., and Kerr, S. (2002) *The Boundaryless Organization: Breaking the China of Organizational Structure* (San Francisco: Jossey-Bass).

Boshyk, Y. (2002) "Why Business Driven Action Learning?", in Y. Boshyk (ed.), *Action Learning Worldwide* (Basingstoke, U.K./New York: Palgrave Macmillan).

Dilworth, R. and Willis, V. (2003) *Action Learning: Images and Pathways* (Malabar, FL: Krieger).

Dilworth R. L. (2010) "Explaining Traditional Action Learning: Concepts and Beliefs", in Y. Boshyk and R. L. Dilworth(eds), *Action Learning: History and Evolution* (Basingstoke, U.K./New York: Palgrave Macmillan), P. 3.

Mezirow, J. and Associates (2000) *Learning as Transformation* (San Fransisco: Jossey-Bass).

Revans, R. (1980) *Action Learning* (London: Blond & Briggs).

Revans, R. (1982) *The Origins and Growth of Action Learning* (Bromley, Kent: Chartwell-Bratt).

Revans, R. (1983) *The ABC of Action Learning* (Bromley, Kent: Chartwell-Bratt).

Ulrich, D., Kerr, S. and Ashkenas, R. *The GE Workout: How to Implement GE'S Revolutionary Method for Busting Bureaucracy and Attacking organizational Problems – Fast!* (New York: McGrraw-Hill).

Weinstein, K (2002) "Action Learning: The Classic Approach", in Y. Boshyk (ed.), *Action Learning Worldwide* (NewYork: Palgrave Macmillan).

Weisbord, M. and Janoff, S. (2000) *Future Search: An Action Guide to Finding Common Ground in Organizations and Communities*, 2nd edition (San Francisco: Berrett-Koehler).

Yorks, L., O'Neil, J., and Marsick (eds.) (2002) "Action Reflection Learning and Critical Reflection Approaches", in Y. Boshyk (ed.), *Action Learning Worldwide* (Basingstoke, U.K./New York: Palgrave Macmillan).

Index